The economic nature of the firm

A reader

Edited by

Louis Putterman

BROWN UNIVERSITY

and

Randall S. Kroszner

UNIVERSITY OF CHICAGO

Cambridge University Press

Cambridge
London   New York   New Rochelle
Melbourne   Sydney

Published by the Press Syndicate of the University of Cambridge
The Pitt Building, Trumpington Street, Cambridge CB2 1RP
40 West 20th Street, New York, NY 10011–4211, USA
10 Stamford Road, Oakleigh, Melbourne 3166, Australia

© Cambridge University Press 1996

First published 1996

Printed in the United States of America

Library of Congress Cataloging-in-Publication Data

The economic nature of the firm : a reader / edited by Louis
Putterman, Randall S. Kroszner.
p.   cm.
ISBN 0-521-47092-7 (hc). — ISBN 0-521-55628-7 (pbk.)
1. Managerial economics.   2. Business enterprises.   3. Industrial
organization.   4. Microeconomics.   I. Putterman, Louis G.
II. Kroszner, Randy.
HD30.22.E25   1996   95-43915
338.5—dc20   CIP

A catalog record for this book is available from the British Library

ISBN 0–521–47092–7 Hardback
0–521–55628–7 Paperback✓

The economic nature of the firm

Contents

Contents

Editors' preface

With the exception of this Preface and the Introduction, the present volume consists of selections from material previously published in books or professional journals. With each piece is included a source note that gives the full bibliographic reference of the original work and acknowledges those who granted permission to use the material. In the case of articles, the degree of completeness versus abridgement is indicated by the phrases "reprinted from," "reprinted with minor abridgements," "reprinted with abridgements," and "excerpted from," in increasing order of abridgement. Book excerpts are understood to constitute only small selections from the originals. The chapter or section from which each portion is taken has been indicated in section headings within such selections. Ellipses within both book and journal selections are used to indicate omitted portions. However, where footnotes have been deleted, no notation has been made, and the remaining notes have been renumbered consecutively.

Minor alterations in style have been made for purposes of consistency. The references have been gathered into a single listing at the end of the book, and bibliographic particulars have been added, when necessary and feasible, to make the references as complete as possible and to have them accord with the standard format of major professional journals. Reference data, except for citations of authors' names and the dates of publication, have been moved to this list from the text and notes. Authors' notes of acknowledgment, which often appear at the beginning of the original journal papers, have been removed on grounds that they are frequently dated or unimportant to the purposes of this volume, and in order to conserve space. In their place, a very brief biographical note on the authors has been added to each selection.

We have found inspiration and help from many sources. Putterman's introduction to the literature collected here came from both the graduate microeconomics course and further reading and discussion with Sidney Winter, then at Yale University. Kroszner encountered many of the included items as an undergraduate working with Putterman at Brown University on the first edition of this book. Kroszner went on to receive his Ph.D. in economics from Harvard University in 1990 and is currently Associate Professor of Business Economics at the Graduate School of Business of the University of Chicago.

The idea for the initial volume was encouraged by Lee Alston, Wesley Cohen, Gregory Dow, Michael McPherson, Oliver Williamson, Gordon Winston, and especially Victor Goldberg, who helped shape its contents. For our subsequent reading of the literature, we are especially indebted to Tyler Cowen Dow, Joseph Kalt, Bentley MacLeod, Gil Skillman, and Luigi Zingales. We thank the authors who have given permission to reprint their work, and especially Bengt Holmstrom, Paul Milgrom, and Oliver Williamson, who also contributed suggestions and encouragement. Finally, our thanks to Donna Lau and My Do for help in assembling biographical information, copyrights, and bibliography, and to Scott Parris and others at Cambridge University Press for their support and assistance with this project.

The economic nature of the firm: a new introduction

LOUIS PUTTERMAN and
RANDALL S. KROSZNER

A decade ago, noticing the increasing attention being paid to questions of economic organization and the nature of firms, we put together the initial version of this reader. At that time, we noted the growing frequency of references to writings such as Ronald Coase's 1937 classic and work published in the 1970s by Armen Alchian and Harold Demsetz, by Michael Jensen and William Meckling, and by Oliver Williamson. The years that followed have seen those and related works serve as the core of a literature that has deepened in institutional detail, branched out into empirical studies, and inspired progress in formal analysis. Coase's pioneering role was recognized with the awarding of a Nobel Memorial Prize in Economic Science in 1991.[1] Williamson's ideas, which build on those of Coase and incorporate a number of new elements, have occupied a prominent place in the study of organizations by economists and students of related disciplines.[2] What can be called the "new institutional economics" has had increasing influence, as shown by its treatment in a growing formal analytical literature by such writers as Oliver Hart, Bengt Holmstrom, and Paul Milgrom,[3] a marked departure from a time when the "mathematical formalist" and nonmathematical literatures included few citations by the one of the other.[4] With hindsight suggesting that our original selection of "classic writings" had indeed brought together core sources in the emerging literature, and with the fruits of more recent research providing the basis for further steps forward, we now introduce an updated reader on the economic nature of the firm.

How production and related activities are organized, and the relations be-

---

[1] On the centrality of "The Nature of the Firm" to his overall contribution, see Coase's Nobel Lecture (1992). Also see Williamson and Winter, eds. (1991), a volume honoring the fiftieth anniversary of that paper's publication, and Williamson (1994).

[2] Papers using these ideas appear regularly in *Journal of Economic Behavior and Organization, Journal of Law, Economics and Organization,* and the *Journal of Institutional and Theoretical Economics* (JITE). See, for example, the March 1993 JITE "Symposium on the New Institutional Economics: Recent Progress and Expanding Frontiers." Critical assessments of this approach appear in Pitelis, ed. (1993), in Dietrich, ed. (1994), and in Groenewegen, ed. (1995).

[3] Some examples are Grossman and Hart (1986), Hart and Moore (1990), and Holmstrom and Milgrom (1991 [and this reader]). Hart and Holmstrom (1987) and Holmstrom and Tirole (1989) provide surveys of the technical literature developing "new institutional economics" themes. See also the text by Milgrom and Roberts (1992).

[4] See Jensen (1983) and Putterman (1986), footnote 29.

tween actors involved in these activities, is a subject interest in which crosses several disciplinary boundaries. As before, students of law, organizational behavior, management, finance, and related fields should find this compilation of economics sources on the organization problem quite useful to their own endeavors. Indeed, some of these fields were concerned with issues raised in our literature at a time when economists seemed resistant to such a discussion. The debates of the 1950s and 1960s, when some neoclassical economists defended "black box" theories of the firm against "behavioralist" and "managerialist" challenges,[5] now seem happily behind us, as the attempt to better understand what accounts for the contractual and organizational structure of business enterprises has gained legitimacy and benefitted from the development of new analytical tools and concepts.[6] As economists' newly honed methods and newly directed lines of inquiry make further contributions to the understanding of these matters, controversy over the appropriate scope for inquiry has given way to the debate of views in organizational economics itself; and the discussion of why there are firms, what determines firm–market boundaries, and why firms are organized as they are has become a topic of broad interest. The pieces collected in this volume include the most influential contributions to this evolving body of work.

Although we see the gap between formal theory and discursive approaches as having narrowed in recent years, this volume will continue to emphasize works of the latter kind. Verbal presentations are accessible to a wider audience, including both scholars in some of the disciplines mentioned above and advanced undergraduate students of those disciplines and economics. Just as the better ideas in the discursive literature tend eventually to be taken up in formal models, so the better ideas in the formal literature are soon, if not simultaneously, given nonmathematical exposition. We excerpt mostly verbal portions of some technical papers representing such ideas and favor discursive treatments where possible. The equations and graphs we include are either unusually accessible and illuminating or are retained for a hint of the flavor of the original.[7]

We also concentrate on the theoretical literature rather than on empirical

---

[5] See Machlup (1967). Coase (1991b, p. 52) draws attention to related issues and notes the omission of a relevant passage of his 1937 paper in the first edition of this reader. In recognition of that paper's importance and in deference to Professor Coase, we reprint it in its entirety in the present volume.

[6] For a discussion of the disappearance and rediscovery of the theory of the firm in the history of economic thought, see McNulty (1984).

[7] We select, for example, Hart (1989) rather than Grossman and Hart (1986) or Hart and Moore (1990); Weitzman and Kruze's verbal discussion gives the gist of the repeated game literature on incentives; and we include Bowles and Gintis (1990) rather than Bowles (1985) or Shapiro and Stiglitz (1984).

work. This is the realm in which new interpretive ideas are born, though the ideas developed here should ultimately prove their power in analyzing cases and data. Empirical literature related to the ideas represented in this volume has expanded rapidly in recent years – primarily since the earlier edition of this reader was published – but doing justice to that literature would require another volume, not a few additions to the present one.[8]

The papers and edited texts collected here fall into four overlapping groups. The first of these consists of selections from some of the older, classic writings on our topic, plus some more recent pieces, all helping to introduce the general theme of the economic nature of the firm and its place in the market system. (The term "division of labor" appears in the section title in its broadest meaning, that of the specialization of activities and roles, on the parts of both individuals and institutions, in complex economies.) The section begins with Adam Smith's classic discussion of the division of labor in the manufacturing establishment and in society as a whole and its relationship to the development of markets. Next included is Karl Marx's discussion of the productivity effects of "cooperation" in the workshop, of the capitalist character of the factory system, and of the relations between firm and market, production and exchange. There follow excerpts from writings by Frank Knight, who emphasized the role of risk bearing in determining economic arrangements, and Friedrich Hayek, who gave the classic discussion of the relationship between information, the level of economic decision making, and the price system. Victor Goldberg's piece on "relational exchange" introduces the importance of idiosyncratic investment not only for the vertical integration question, discussed similarly by Klein, Crawford, and Alchian and Williamson, but also for repeated interfirm transactions of the type considered by G. B. Richardson. Finally, having begun the section with Adam Smith's "invisible hand" view of the market, we conclude it with a selection of Alfred Chandler's "visible hand" perspective on corporate resource allocation in the modern business enterprise.

Part II of our reader contains papers dealing with the scope of the firm. Coase's famous paper, which simultaneously presents a theory of the differences between internal and market resource allocation, initiates this literature with the argument that a firm will expand until the cost of undertaking additional transactions through market exchange falls below the cost of undertaking those transactions within a common hierarchical structure. In the pieces

[8] Examples of this burgeoning empirical literature include Crocker and Masten (1991), Goldberg and Erickson (1987), Joskow (1985, 1987, 1988a, 1988b), Hubbard and Weiner (1991), Kenney and Klein (1983), Klein (1988), Kroszner and Rajan (1995), Leffler and Rucker (1991), Masten and Crocker (1988), and Mulherin (1986). Klein and Shelanski (1994) provide an exhaustive survey of this empirical research.

that follow, by Klein, Crawford, and Alchian and by Williamson, Coase's focus on costs of using the price mechanism and on limited entrepreneurial attention gives way to a theory of integrated ownership in the presence of idiosyncratic investment. While using much the same explanatory framework as Klein et al. to account for full vertical integration,[9] Williamson's piece adds the dimension of transaction frequency and attempts to account for intermediate modes, which he labels relational (or "bilateral") and neoclassical (or "trilateral") contracting. The classic reference to these forms bridging the gap between arms length exchange and internal organization, which is due to G. B. Richardson, serves as the fourth piece in this section.

Whereas Klein et al. and our initial selection by Williamson offer explanations for vertical integration, they have less to say about what limits the growth of firms. The fifth piece in this section, from Williamson's 1985 book, attempts to address that issue and go beyond the managerial attention approach of Coase and the control loss counterpart to that approach that was used earlier by Williamson himself. Williamson asks why the head office of a decentralized conglomerate could not give its divisions effective autonomy, thus replicating the "high powered incentives" of the market, while outdoing the market by the selective imposition of rationalizing and coordinating measures. His answer is that selective intervention is impossible, and that it follows from this that the incentives facing agents in firms are typically "lower powered" than those of independent entrepreneurs or the self-employed. Milgrom and Roberts' paper, which appears next, offers another reason why hierarchy becomes costly: Because subordinates can pursue private ends by distorting the information they supply to their superiors, decision makers are forced to discount the information provided them and may even find it optimal to restrict information flows. A more synthetic treatment of the scope question is provided by David Teece in the last piece in the section, which, while drawing on the work of authors including Coase and Williamson, gives equal emphasis to questions of learning and competence that are emphasized by writers such as Edith Penrose and Richard Nelson and Sidney Winter.[10]

Part III deals with internal organization and the human factor, which in most instances contracts with the firm under what economists term "the em-

---

[9] Earlier thinking along similar lines to that of Klein, Crawford, and Alchian is found in Williamson (1971, 1975).

[10] The latter emphasis places Teece's work partly into the position that Winter (1991) assigns to evolutionary economics rather than the transaction cost economics that is better represented in the present reader. While both approaches differ from prior orthodoxy in assuming that agents are "boundedly rational," evolutionary economics differs from transaction cost economics, according to Winter, in that the former is primarily concerned with production, whereas the latter is principally concerned with exchange.

ployment relation." Several of the papers here give centrality to the question of how effort is elicited when the contribution of the individual is costly to observe, and hence to reward appropriately, in a team setting. Alchian and Demsetz's provocative and influential discussion, which explains the hiring of employees by a residual-claiming employer through its analysis of this problem, is the first selection here. Karl Marx had anticipated the modern agency approach to the employment relationship with his discussion of the "extraction" of "labor" from "labor-power" (see Part I), and radical economists have made important contributions to the internal organization literature by expanding upon Marx's insights.[11] In their now-classic "efficiency wage" model, Shapiro and Stiglitz (1984) rediscovered the role of Marx's "reserve army of the unemployed" in parallel with radical writers like Samuel Bowles (1985). Whereas this approach has a more macroeconomic aim in the hands of Shapiro and Stiglitz, the focus of Bowles and coauthor Herbert Gintis, in the piece included here, is on other issues, including doubts about whether the capitalist employment relation is in fact the most efficient solution to the team-effort problem.[12]

In the third article of this section, by Williamson, Michael Wachter, and Jeffrey Harris, the monitoring problem takes second place to the previously noted problem of idiosyncratic investment. These authors argue that firms attempt to prevent haggling over, and possible extraction of, the rents from firm-specific human capital. They do this by designing internal job ladders that orient employees toward the long run while permitting some relaxation of current period monitoring, with resulting benefits for "atmosphere" and hence employee effort. We present an excerpt from Holmstrom and Milgrom's recent article, which provides new formal results on the design of incentives by principals, as the fourth piece in this section. In it, the authors corroborate an old intuition that offers an explanation for the "lower powered incentives" referred to by Williamson.

With the partial exception of Williamson et al., the papers considered thus far in this section adopt a standard motivational model in which agents are strictly rational and are concerned with their private incomes and leisure only. The next two papers depart from those assumptions. Harvey Leibenstein analyzes the effort-elicitation problem as a game played between employer and employees. He departs from the rationality assumption by assigning

---

[11] Their emphasis on the "effort extraction" problem contrasts with an increasing tendency to ignore Marx's labor-based value (i.e., price) theory, or to treat the latter as of normative or sociological importance only. See, in addition to other works cited, Goldberg (1980a), Stephen Marglin (1974), and Richard Edwards (1979).

[12] For a parallel exposition and interesting comments by Stiglitz and Williamson, see the exchange in the Winter 1993 issue of the *Journal of Economic Perspectives,* pp. 83–114.

important roles to history, organizational culture, and inertia. George Akerlof presents an unconventional efficiency wage model in which failure to pay workers in proportion to their individual contributions stems not from a difficulty in monitoring – a problem that does *not* apply in the example offered by him – but instead from a relationship between workers' effort levels and their moral assessments of the employer.

In addition to principal–agent approaches of the kinds featured in Holmstrom and Milgrom's work or the simpler setup of Shapiro and Stiglitz, the formal literature has modelled effort "tournaments," and effort choice as a repeated game.[13] This last approach is discussed by Martin Weitzman and Douglas Kruse in the last piece in Part III, which attempts to explain why profit sharing has been associated with higher productivity in the modern workplace, confounding predictions of free-rider type behavior.

The final section, Part IV, concerns questions of firm organization and behavior related to financing and ownership. The first three papers present different approaches to the problem of "separation of ownership and control" in the modern corporation, brought to prominence by a 1932 book by legal and economic scholars Adolf Berle and Gardiner Means.[14] These papers begin with a brief excerpt from Henry Manne's frequently cited argument regarding the monitoring function of the market for corporate takeovers. Next comes a contribution by Eugene Fama, which develops a second view of markets as monitors of internal discretionary behavior, this one focusing on managerial compensation as an ultimate source of managerial accountability. The third piece in this group is a major portion of the article by Jensen and Meckling that has helped to spawn a large literature in the field of corporate finance, and that – similar to Manne but both more broadly and more subtly – answers questions about the financier–manager relationship with reference to the monitoring properties of capital markets.

The fourth piece of this section teams Fama and Jensen. Taking the idea that corporations incur greater agency costs than closely held firms as a given, they ask why the corporate form is ever chosen and answer with a formal argument about capital requirements, and with less formalized discussions about comparative advantage in managing versus financing and about the risk-reducing benefits of limited liability and diversification. The Fama–Jensen paper is followed by a stimulating dissent from the conventional view by Demsetz. That author provides reasons why a nonowner manager may engage

---

[13] On "tournaments," see Lazear and Rosen (1981) and Malcomson (1984). For examples of the repeated game approach, see MacLeod (1987) and MacLeod and Malcomson (1988).

[14] The enormous impact of Berle and Means' *The Modern Corporation and Private Property* is demonstrated in the special issue of the *Journal of Law and Economics* (June 1983) on the fiftieth anniversary of its publication. See especially the article by Stigler and Friedland (1983).

6

in *less,* not more, discretionary behavior than a proprietor, and he raises doubts about characterizing most large corporations as "diffusely owned."

The final two papers go beyond questions of financing to treat the institution of firm ownership more broadly. Hart, in a discursive treatment of ideas developed in more formal, coauthored papers, argues that the essence of ownership is not the right to residual income or the responsibility for monitoring, but rather the right to make decisions that have not otherwise been determined in prior negotiations between parties to an enterprise. Building partly on the ideas of Klein et al. and Williamson, he argues that the efficient assignment of this residual control right is to the owner of the more idiosyncratic investments that the activity requires, a position that implies that *inter*specialized assets should be commonly owned. Finally, Putterman, in a paper integrating financial agency and control right concerns, suggests that the supply of risk-bearing and financing services, substantially determined by the distribution of wealth, has implications not only for the financial but also for the internal incentive structure of firms. He argues that the factors that lead to the nonidentity of owners and labor suppliers can also be viewed as being responsible for the characteristic incentive problems of the workplace. And he notes that the unbundling of the control, revenue, and alienation aspects of ownership, while problematic, shows signs of alleviating the trade-offs between efficient risk bearing and provision of incentives.

We organize our discussion of the literature from which our readings are drawn around a set of themes that feature prominently in it. Viewing firms as distinctive modes of organizing economic activity, the literature attempts to explain the related questions: Why do they exist? and What determines their sizes and scopes? Two still more fundamental questions which are bound up with, and in some respects prior to these first two, however, are: Just what is the thing we call a firm? and How distinctive are firms as organizing modes? Or relatedly, how sharp are the boundaries between them and the environments in which they operate? Since the answers to all of these questions are closely intertwined, the order in which we take them up is to some degree arbitrary. As a matter of convenience, we choose to begin with a provisional discussion of what firms are, then move to the explanation of their existence and the determinants of their sizes and scopes, and deal last with the extensive literature on the sharpness of firm/market distinctions. We will inevitability have begun to touch upon that literature under the earlier topics, and it will also bring us back full circle to the question of the firm's nature.

After considering the questions just raised, the remainder of our introduction moves into a more detailed discussion of how firms are organized, with a focus on two types of relationships: those involving ownership of assets and those involving contracting with labor providers. Contributors to the literature can be roughly classified into three groups: those who view the employment contract as the essence of the firm, those who view asset ownership as its essence, and those who see both sets of relations as equally important or as manifestations of a common principle. We will then survey the parallel literatures on agency and incentive issues in the relations between managers and workers, on the one hand, and between owners and managers, on the other. Finally, we will discuss the question of why firms might be organized as they are (for example, with respect to the distributions of control rights and risk bearing and the concentration of ownership) and how this might matter to our view of their economic nature or essence.

What is a firm?

In standard microeconomics, as mentioned earlier, firms are the economy's basic units of production, just as households are its units of consumption. Firms purchase inputs such as labor services and materials from households and from other firms, transform these inputs into goods and services, and sell the latter to households and firms with the objective of maximizing the difference between their revenue and their outlay. Firms differ from households in that they maximize profit rather than utility and in the different activities (consumption versus production) in which each engages.

In the literature exemplified by this reader, however, most authors conceptualize firms as something more than simply profit-seeking transformers of inputs into outputs. A set of factor owners could hypothetically agree today to contribute their inputs at the going rate so as to produce something for which an unmet demand is perceived, divide any surplus earnings, and go their separate ways tomorrow according to newly observed opportunities. But hypothetical producers' coalitions of this type would differ from the literature's *firms* because the latter usually entail (a) long-term contracts between at least some input providers and (b) an assignment of control rights in which some agents hire others and direct them in the activities of production. Rather than being momentary assemblages of cooperating factor suppliers, then, firms are ongoing organizations that manage and coordinate the activities of participating actors.

Asking where the boundaries of the firm lie raises some difficult theoretical issues. But most authors have relatively simple notions of control and of ownership in mind when deciding where one firm ends and another begins. Few if any question that a company having multiple plants producing the same or even different products should be treated as a single firm so long as the right to the residual earnings and to hire and fire the managers of subunits belongs to a central managing organ that either itself "owns" or is responsible to the owner or owners of the overall entity. We return to the centrality of ownership to both the nature and the definition of the firm later in this essay.

Why are there firms?

That the discussion above is but a first pass at the question of what firms are becomes clearer when we encounter the literature on *why* there are firms. If by firm one meant simply an entity that engages in the transformation of inputs into outputs, then the "why are there firms?" question could be answered trivially by noting that there is a demand for the products in question at prices at least equal to the combined cost of the required inputs. But while product demand may explain production, it hardly explains the need for an organization of production, much less a production organization with such characteristic features as long-term contracts, risk bearing by owners, and hierarchical or centralized coordination of those engaged in the production process. "Why are there firms?" is a question to Coase, Williamson, and others, because with most of microeconomic theory assuming that the price system coordinates the allocation of resources to their most valued uses, such organizations might appear to have no economic *raison d'etre*.

If standard theory offered any explanation for the existence of firms, it would seem to have been a technological one. Factors of production are needed in certain combinations, and some scales of production are more efficient than others. That the assembly of automobiles in large factory buildings in which hundreds of workers are arrayed along assembly lines should be coordinated by some sort of organizing entity, rather than by independently contracting workers each owning particular subsets of the tools and machines making up the factory as a whole, could seem obvious enough to those who failed to inquire more deeply. But on further inspection, this obviousness gives way to a mystery. For, as Williamson in particular has forcefully argued, there is no technological reason why the participants in this production process could not each operate their own firms, buying and selling their semiassembled components as they move along the production line. Even an accepted "technological" requirement of coordination or management fails to explain the firm as organization, for the contributors of varying specialized inputs could simply contract for managerial services from other specialized agents, just as independent farmers contract for storage and other services with specialized entities in their industry. It is the puzzle of what *organizational* factors give rise to the existence of an overarching framework of ownership, management, and coordination that motivates the prominent hypotheses of Coase, Williamson, Alchian and Demsetz, and others.

Coase initiated the contemporary literature by pointing out that when economic agents interact with one another, they incur "transaction costs" that vary with the mode of interaction. In the market, he argued, agents interact by negotiating exchanges, with prices serving as signals of the opportunities facing each supplier of a service or demander of a product. In a firm, on the other hand, a central coordinator or entrepreneur manages the allocation of resources such as the machinery owned by him and the personnel that he employs. Were the production process to be undertaken through market interactions alone, writes Coase, the interacting parties would have to negotiate new actions and new terms of exchange each time a change in market or technological conditions made profitable a change in the activity being undertaken. Owners of the substations of the hypothetical production line discussed above would have to determine the prices at which to exchange their semi-finished products – a difficult task in the absence of external markets for such goods – and these prices would be subject to change in response to changes in factor supply, technical conditions, and so on. Such trivial matters as a breakdown in a piece of equipment, a stoppage of electricity, or a small change in the most profitable product mix would give rise to costly renegotiation of the full set of bilateral exchanges. The costs of such renegotiation, and of what Coase referred to as the "price discovery process," could be economized by agreement to a framework of ongoing relations under which a central coordinator would be granted the authority to reassign tasks and to offer altered payments as new contingencies arose.

While Coase's ideas attracted enough attention to be cited and even reprinted occasionally in the early postwar decades following their initial publication, the "transaction cost" approach was largely ignored by the modernizers of economic theory who gained increasing dominance in those years. Parsimony and mathematical rigor were the order of the day, and theories that appeared capable of predicting economic phenomena using simple axioms held sway. In such an environment, the concept of "transaction costs" tended to be viewed as a vague and plastic one, inviting suspicions that it might be casually molded to explain whatever anomalies the analyst felt unable to explain by more "rigorous" methods.

By the 1970s, however, an increasing number of economists had come to view existing theory as failing to explain the organizational dimensions of the economy at the microlevel. As theorists began attacking this flaw by treating problems of information and agency with formal tools, Williamson developed a variant of transaction cost economics that would dominate the organizational literature, quite broadly, and inspire a good deal of subsequent formal analysis as well. In Williamson's approach, as in Coase's, the market and firms were treated as discrete modes of organizing economic activity, and the choice among these modes was hypothesized to be dictated by economizing with respect to the cost of transactions among the different parties involved. Whereas Coase emphasized the costs of price discovery and negotiation, however, Williamson put his emphasis on the problem of investment in assets specific to a given venture. In an argument made in parallel by Klein, Crawford, and Alchian, and later partially echoed by theorists Sanford Grossman and Oliver Hart, he suggested that when agents contemplated investing in assets that would have far lower returns outside of the activities to which they were initially dedicated, they would become subject to the possibility that owners of complementary assets would attempt to extract opportunistically their "quasi rents" (the difference in returns between the dedicated and next-best uses) by threatening to withdraw their own inputs. The threat of quasi rent appropriation (or in Williamson's terminology "hold up") would prevent such investments from being made without organizational safeguards, of which common ownership or vertical integration was the simplest example. Thus, the stations on our hypothetical assembly line would be owned and managed by an integrated entity rather than by firms transacting across market interfaces, because separate firms would risk "hold up," whence any who dared own one would face unacceptable danger.

Rather than transaction costs, Alchian and Demsetz's theory of the firm focused on costs of monitoring. Alchian and Demsetz assumed a technological condition for the existence of firms – it is economical for many hands to produce jointly – and wedded to this a behavioral or motivational problem. When production is joint and there are no individual products from which to infer input contributions, they argued, workers have incentives to withhold promised effort unless monitored so that acts of shirking can be punished by payment adjustments or by firing. But the classical free-rider problem afflicting effort discretion will equally afflict the provision of monitoring unless the monitor is herself monitored or is motivated by some other means. Because one cannot posit a monitor of each monitor ad infinitem, Alchian and Demsetz posited a final (and central) monitor who is motivated by claim to the activity's residual income and who can maximize the value of that claim (and of the right to sell the firm) by exercising discretion over the team's composition and matching resources to uses in production. Thus, firms come into being when technological conditions (increasing returns and costly measurement of input contributions) make centralized ownership and monitoring a superior alternative to either unmonitored revenue sharing or lower-productivity small scale production.[15]

[15] Although Alchian and Demsetz do not rule out the possibility that revenue-sharing teams will generate some mutual monitoring, they argue that the level of such monitoring would be suboptimal since the incentive to monitor would itself be subject to a free-rider problem. By contrast, the literature on profit sharing (surveyed by Weitzman and Kruse, 1990 [and this reader] and other papers in Blinder, ed., 1990) often argues that mutual monitoring and the reduction of specialized monitoring costs is a key to the positive productivity effects of that practice. See also the theoretical and empirical analysis of Dong and Dow (1993) and the discussion of technological and other dimensions of the issue by Putterman (1984).

Although Williamson rejects the "technical nonseparabilities" element of Alchian and Demsetz's theory as being insufficiently general, he does not reject the idea that monitoring costs may be a determinant of organizational form. In *The Economic Institutions of Capitalism,* he labels the monitoring approach a "branch" of transaction cost economics, with Yoram Barzel (1982) as its key developer (see also Kenney and Klein, 1983). Economizing on the costs of measuring intermediate outputs at each stage of the production process is at the core of Barzel's theory of the firm. Assume that it is difficult to assess the value of the output at each stage so that monitoring the inputs may provide useful information about the value of the intermediate good. Workers along a production line could be organized as separate one-worker firms or integrated into a single firm. If the workers are separate firms, then each worker/firm will have to monitor the inputs of the worker/firm directly preceding it as well as those of all of the worker/firms in the prior stages of the production process whose products are intermediate inputs. The firm, then, emerges as a means of centralizing monitoring and, thereby, avoiding costly redundancy in that function.

Before leaving this discussion, it is interesting to ask whether an approach that predates Coase's, namely Frank Knight's theory of entrepreneurship, does not constitute a reasonable theory of why firms exist, in its own right. Knight emphasized the riskiness of the production enterprise: Inputs will be exhausted before the quality and quantity of output, the price at which the product can be sold, or whether it can be sold at all are known with certainty.[16] Someone will have to bear risk if production is to be undertaken, but differences in willingness to do this, partly conditioned on wealth and partly on confidence in one's ability to make appropriate judgments, suggest that this function might not be shared equally by participants in the production process. On the other hand, once some agents accept these risks and guarantee the payments of others, the problem of moral hazard dictates that the risk bearers must also be given the right to supervise their insurees, lest the latter take their economic security as an invitation to shirk responsibility. Thus, the firm is born as an organization of individuals engaging in a common production process with an internal division of labor where some insure and supervise, others are insured and accept supervision.

One could ask, of course, why the workers involved do not form separate firms, each with its own insurer-supervisor? If economies of supervision suffice to address that problem, then Knight's approach does indeed seem to offer a theory of the firm on a par with those discussed above. Just why it has been more influential in the fields of labor and macroeconomics than in the

---

[16] Israel Kirzner (1973, 1979) instead emphasizes the discovery of potentially profitable opportunities as the key element of entrepreneurship. Firms may arise to aid entrepreneurs in exploiting these discoveries.

literature presently under discussion is something of a mystery, but one to which Coase's very directed criticism might offer a clue. When he wrote his own seminal paper, Coase considered Knight's approach to be "the most interesting . . . and probably the most widely accepted" explanation for the existence of firms. In arguing against it, he says that "the fact that certain people have better judgment or better knowledge does not mean that they can only get an income from it by themselves actively taking part in production"; and he contends that the guarantee of income to a worker does not necessitate the assuming of supervisory powers since "[a] large proportion of jobs are done to contract" where "the contractor is guaranteed a certain sum providing [only that] he performs certain acts." Coase's main reason for rejecting Knight, however, seems to be found in his statement that "nowhere does Professor Knight give a reason why the price mechanism should be superseded." This suggests that Knight's lack of commonality with the "discrete contracting modes"/"market and hierarchy" orientation of both Coase and Williamson, along with a certain antipathy to risk-centered approaches by those and related writers, caused the Knightian approach to be discounted in the post-1970 flowering of both transaction cost and, more generally, "new institutional" economics.[17] On the other hand, the absence of a trenchant analysis of monitoring problems, and the informality of Knight's treatment of what have since come to be known as agency problems, have reduced his influence on both the "monitoring branch" of the new institutional economics and on more mathematical theorizing. The influence of Knightian reasoning on the financial contracting area of firm theory will nonetheless be shown (in a later section) to have been strong, if not always explicitly recognized.[18]

What determines a firm's size and scope?

A prominent aspect of the Coasian approach to the firm is its argument that firms are spheres of planning and that by virtue of the importance of intrafirm planning to the overall coordination of economic activity, so-called market economies (as contrasted with "planned" economies of the now-defunct Sovi-

[17] To be sure, Williamson suggests (1985, p. 3, footnote 3) that Coase's criticism was misplaced, lauds Knight as a precursor in the analysis of opportunism (op. cit., p. 6) and bounded rationality (p. 133) problems, and laments that "Knight's keen behavioral insights never gained prominence" (p. 3). He goes on to say that "[a]ttention has focused instead on the technical distinction between risk and uncertainty that he had introduced" and that "[h]ad Knight used a nontechnical term, such as 'opportunism,' . . . that result might have been avoided" (op. cit., p. 3). This seems significant in view of the fact that Williamson (pp. 388–90) lists risk neutrality as a maintained assumption of transaction cost economics.

[18] A formalization of Knight's ideas on entrepreneurship and the assumption of risk is given by Kihlstrom and Laffont (1979). Similar reasoning is used by Montias (1970), Meade (1972), Neuberger and James (1973), and Putterman (1993a), and formalized by Bowles and Gintis (1995), to explain why most firms are controlled by capital suppliers.

et type) are in fact composites of planning and market coordination, with the scope of each coordinating mechanism being determined by competition. As we have seen, transactions come to be organized within firms rather than "in the market," according to Coase, when the supersession of the price mechanism by the authority of the entrepreneur-coordinator is more economical than a series of exchanges negotiated between the relevant parties. With regard to the question of why this does not continue to be the case as firms grow ever larger, Coase suggests that there must be diminishing returns to the coordinator's attention, including an increasing possibility of mistakes that would be more cataclysmic in nature for an extremely large firm.

Without a theory of multitier hierarchy, however, Coase's argument is incomplete. A given manager's attention may indeed be inevitably limited, but a manager might employ other managers to look after aspects or divisions of his firm, so one must posit costs of agency, or some type of control loss, to complete this line of reasoning. An Alchian–Demsetz-like argument about the incentive effect of concentrated residual claims, plus some agency costs of the type implicit in their theory and expounded more explicitly by Jensen and Meckling (1976b), might do the job. Williamson, in earlier work (1967b), Beckmann (1983), Calvo and Wellisz (1978), and McAfee and McMillan (1991) have likewise modelled tendencies for management cost per unit of output to rise as the number of managers (or of personnel managed) increases, and an argument by Milgrom and Roberts that we review shortly supplies another way of supporting Coase's presumption. Williamson, on the other hand, has questioned his own earlier argument about control loss and offered an alternative explanation of the limits to firm size that focuses on the incentives more than on the costs of management.

In his 1985 book (and Chapter 11 of this reader) Williamson asks why a "superfirm," wherein what were previously independent firms are run as "autonomous" subdivisions, cannot do everything that the once independent firms could do but at least sometimes improve upon their performance by imposing coordination or rationalizing moves from the corporate center. His basic answer is that one cannot simultaneously posit real divisional autonomy *and* central powers of intervention. Indeed, if the center has the right to intervene when it sees (or claims) rationalizing opportunities, then the division heads cannot be put on "high powered incentive" contracts mimicking those they would enjoy as independent entrepreneurs. With such contracts, the center's right to intervene would cause managers to bear all the risks of residual claimants without the full responsibilities.[19] For this reason, the granting of intervention rights would in fact tend to be accompanied by a

---

[19] Note here the commonality with the Knightian idea that he who bears the risk holds the control.

degree of income insurance that would inevitably dilute or "lower the power" of division managers' incentives, and thus the level of their managerial attentiveness and energies. In other words, the firm's Williamsonian advantages – providing safeguards to investors in complementary specific assets – are at some point offset by its inability to replicate the "high powered incentives" of agents directly exposed to market forces by way of a residual claim.

In contrast to Williamson, Paul Milgrom and John Roberts explain the cost of expanded bureaucratic or hierarchical control with an argument that is applicable even when there is only one layer of management. The key to their argument is that information pertinent to optimal managerial decision making is dispersed among agents employed by the enterprise. To make fully informed decisions, a manager must elicit such information from subordinates; but attempting to do so makes him subject to their self-interested provision of selective or distorted information. Drawing on the literature on rent seeking that arose to analyze costs of government intervention in such areas as trade policy, Milgrom and Roberts point out that subordinates stand to gain personally from providing managers with suggestions and information that may advance their own careers. Because it is costly for managers to filter out good from bad information, it becomes optimal simply to restrict the information flow, although managers then act on less than full information. Moreover, the larger the organization, the larger the information filtering costs and the larger the losses in efficiency because of decisions made with more incomplete information at the level of management. In supplying a countervailing cost likely to eventually offset any initial benefits from administering resource allocation within an organization, Milgrom and Roberts' version of the rent-seeking story thus bolsters the logic of Hayek's seminal argument that beyond some point, at least, bureaucratic centralization cannot dominate the price system as a method for using dispersed information in the management of a society's resources.

Of course, whatever factors make coordination within a firm desirable in the first place must also be taken into account in determining its optimal scale; that scale is reached, presumably, when the marginal gains of internalization (whether due to lessened negotiation and price discovery costs, to the amelioration of asset specificity problems, or to other factors) equal the marginal costs of integrated management, such as those discussed in the preceding paragraphs. Both Coase's and Williamson's explanations of the existence of firms, for example, suggest that firms will be larger in those industries in which products pass through more stages as intermediate goods without outside markets, or where the ability to flexibly redeploy resources is of greater importance. The asset-specificity approach of Williamson and of Klein, Crawford, and Alchian, as well as Hart's asset-complementarity variant, suggest that firms will be larger, as measured by capital stocks, when production

15

processes call for using larger sets of interspecialized assets or for more expensive individual assets within those sets. Ordinary economies of scale may be relevant here, insofar as they dictate the optimal size of capital goods or the fineness (and specificity) of the internal division of labor. David Teece (1980, 1982 [and this reader]) examines the sources of scope economies to provide a theory of the multiproduct firm. If economies of scope are due to the common use of a specialized and indivisible asset, Teece argues, the multi-product firm arises as the efficient form for organizing the production of the goods requiring that specialized asset.

How sharp the firm/market distinction?

We noted that one reason for the initially limited impact of Coase's explanation for the existence of firms is that his appeal to the phenomenon of transactions costs was viewed by some economists as being vague and open to arbitrary application. Another cause of reservations regarding the Coasian theory of the firm has been its depiction of intrafirm organization as a discretely different mode of economic coordination in which managerial control supersedes (his term) the price mechanism.[20] Although perhaps not intended to do so by Coase himself,[21] this approach linked itself to the debate over the virtues of planning versus the market, with Coase's argument that planning is one of the normal modes of coordination in a *market* economy being potentially provocative to the anti-socialist camp.[22] Moreover, Coase's view of the firm seemed to challenge the belief that economic life could be explained in terms of rational, individual responses to market constraints and opportunities. Whether firm and market are distinct modes of organization, whether one form shades into the other, or whether the firm is nothing other than a congeries of market interactions has become a topic of intense debate in the literature with which we are concerned.

Coase identified the planned coordination within firms with the intended planning under socialism, suggesting that the main difference between the two was that the scope of the one was determined by competition, that of the other

[20] For example, "'vertical' integration, involving as it does the *supersession* of the price mechanism" (Coase, 1937, pp. 388–9); "It was not until machinery drew workers into one locality that it paid to *supersede* the price mechanism and the firm emerged" (op. cit., p. 397, note 4); "nowhere does Professor Knight give a reason why the price mechanism should be *superseded*" (op. cit., p. 401). Italics added.

[21] See Coase (1991a, 1991b).

[22] During the 1920s and 1930s, Ludwig von Mises and Hayek engaged in a lively debate with Oskar Lange, Fred Taylor, and Maurice Dobb about the possibility of rational economic calculation in a centrally planned economy, that is, one in which market forces do not determine prices. However, philosophically inspired resistance to Coase's firm/market distinction surfaced mainly in the 1970s and 1980s, without much reference to this debate. On the Socialist Calculation Debate, see Bardhan and Roemer, eds. (1993) and Hayek (1972).

by political authority.[23] In viewing planning and the authority of the employment relationship as the essence of the firm, and the absence of authority and
governance by independent contracting as the essence of the market, Coase
revisited a distinction made much earlier by an author of whose work on the
topic he appeared unaware. "Division of labor within the workshop" wrote
Marx "implies the undisputed authority of the capitalist over men" whereas
"division of labor within the society brings into contact independent
commodity-producers, who acknowledge no other authority but that of competition." Although sharing none of Marx's antipathy for the market and
showing no inclination to call the employer's authority "undisputed," Coase,
too, placed emphasis on authority in the employment relation as a hallmark of
the firm. "We can best approach the question of what constitutes a firm by
considering the legal relationship normally called that of 'master and servant'
or 'employer and employee,'" writes Coase, who then proceeds to quote from
Batt's *Law of Master and Servant:* "It is [the] right of control or interference . . . which is the dominant characteristic in this relation and marks
off the servant from an independent contractor."[24]

Much of the ensuing discussion has concerned itself with Coase's proposal
that the line between firm and market could be drawn where the employment
relationship is distinguished from the hiring of an independent contractor.
Masten (1988) follows Coase in citing Batt and other legal sources, suggesting that the obligation of the employee towards the employer is central to what
we call a firm. By contrast, Alchian and Demsetz reject the concept of an
authority relation, arguing that because both worker and employer can terminate their relationship when they find it in their interest to do so, an employee's response to managerial directions reflects only a mutually beneficial
exchange of the most conventional sort. And Steven Cheung (1983) argues
that it is unimportant to determine exactly what constitutes a firm and when a
transaction takes place between independent agents as opposed to within
firms.

Ultimately, whether the firm constitutes a domain of bureaucratic direction
that is shielded from market forces or simply "a nexus for a set of contracting
relationships among individuals" (as Jensen and Meckling put it) is a function
of the completeness of markets and the ability of market forces to penetrate
intrafirm relationships. For example, authority as such is not modelled in the
principal–agent literature, except perhaps insofar as the principal designs the
contract; for in these models, the principal takes the worker's market-given
reservation utility as a datum, and there is no exercise of managerial control

---

[23] Coase (1937) p. 389, note 3, which appears as footnote 14 of Chapter 7 in this reader.
[24] Coase (1937) pp. 403–4. For an extended discussion of the plan/market distinction in Marx
and in modern economic theory, see Pagano (1985). On the firms/markets distinction, also see
Hayek (1972) and Khalil (1994).

17

once the contract is in place. If market forces determine rewards and each agent selects the application of her endowments that brings the highest return (or utility), then there is no scope for the operation of firms as a separate allocation mechanism, over and above the market. On the other hand, factors that render markets incomplete may open up just such a possibility.

Alchian and Demsetz, for example, concede that competition for either working or monitoring positions by external market agents is insufficient to deter internal shirking. In their view, a central agent must have the power to reward effort and to penalize shirking, including possibly by firing. While such powers do not distinguish the central agent from any other competitive actor, for Alchian and Demsetz, they may indeed do so in a nonmarket clearing environment of the type that arises in efficiency wage models, as argued by Bowles and Gintis. Moreover, Alchian and Demsetz's view of the firm as "an alternative kind of market," while rhetorically suggestive of a more market-oriented view, is in fact not very different from that of Coase or Williamson, because what is distinctive about the firm, by their account, is that the manager's superior knowledge of internal resources permits more efficient resource allocation than can be accomplished by less informed external agents. The firm does appear to be an alternative or supplementary allocative mechanism to the market, in their view.

Standing shoulder to shoulder with the "nexus of contracts" school, Benjamin Klein (1983, p. 373) asserts that "Coase mistakenly made a sharp distinction between intrafirm and interfirm transactions, claiming that while the latter represented market contracts, the former represented planned direction. Economists now recognize that such a sharp distinction does not exist and that it is useful to consider also transactions occurring within the firm as representing market (contractual) relationships." Our discussion in this section suggests, though, that such a consensus has yet to be reached.[25]

On another level, however, there has been much less disagreement between the contending approaches. Insofar as the debate over the firm/market distinction is about whether firms and markets are *discrete* alternatives or whether there are intermediate forms, with the one effectively shading into the other, most authors evince openness to the second approach. In his recently reprinted classic,[26] George Richardson (1972 [and this reader]) emphasizes the ubiquity of intermediate forms of organization and coordination. Richardson argues that it is inappropriate conceptually and empirically to think of firms as "islands of planned coordination in a sea of market relations. . . . Firms are not islands but are linked together in patterns of cooperation and affiliation."

[25] For another position similar to Klein's, see Cheung (1983). On the opposite end of the spectrum, see Williamson's methodological discussion on "comparative institutional assessment of discrete institutional alternatives" (1985, p. 42) and Simon (1991).
[26] See Richardson (1990) and the foreword by David Teece.

He concludes that the "dichotomy between firms and market, between directed and spontaneous coordination . . . ignores the institutional fact of interfirm cooperation and assumes away the distinct method of cooperation that this can provide."[27] That differences over the nature of the firm/market distinction do not extend to the question of forms intermediate between firm and market is demonstrated by Williamson's choice of subtitle for his 1985 book – *Firms, Markets, Relational Contracting* – to recognize just such forms. Interfirm relations bearing such firmlike qualities as a long-term character, incompleteness of terms, and explicit governance remedies are likewise emphasized by Victor Goldberg in his work on "relational exchange."

Ownership relations and employment relations

As a "nexus of contracts," firms entail relations between suppliers of specific and generic inputs, sellers of managerial, technical, and other labor services, providers of equity and debt finance, and customers. But the literature on firms as governance or control structures singles out two kinds of relationships for special attention. The centrality of employment relationships in approaches such as that of Coase has been discussed. Centrality of an alternative relationship, that of the ownership of physical assets, has been the focus of other writers, epitomized by Grossman and Hart.

Grossman and Hart (see also Hart, 1989 [and this reader]) take issue with the notion that employers exert any special degree of control over employees by virtue of the employment relation.[28] As an alternative, Grossman and Hart suggest that it is the ability to determine how physical assets will be used, and thus which human agents will have access to them, that is the essence of control of the firm. As Hart puts it, the asymmetry between employer and employee that has been glossed over by Alchian and Demsetz is that while the employee can sever his relationship with the employer, thus depriving the firm of his particular talents, when the employer separates the employee from the firm, he also deprives him of his tools, which stay with the employer. Even the right to residual income is secondary, in Hart's view, to the ability to make such decisions over the disposition of assets as have not been settled by prior agreement.

Most of the writers surveyed here would appear to place themselves somewhere between Coase's transaction cost and Hart's "property rights" ap-

[27] For a discussion of Richardson's work, see Loasby (1986).
[28] Grossman and Hart (1986, p. 165) question Arrow's assumption (1975) that integration improves communication among units. Williamson (1985, p. 155), by contrast, asserts that managers have better access to company information than do external auditors because of employee allegiance. Williamson, Wachter, and Harris also refer to superior intrafirm communication of employee ratings. See, also, the discussions in Masten (1988), Riordan (1990), and Putterman (1995).

19

proaches. Williamson, and Klein, Crawford, and Alchian, emphasize specificity of physical assets as a cause of internal control, but Williamson's belief in the presumptive superiority of internal audits[29] puts him closer to Coase, and Alchian (1984) views the firm as a coalition, with some emphasis on human assets. Alchian and Demsetz, in an approach more recently favored by Holmstrom and Milgrom also (discussed in a later section), place the monitor/worker relationship at the center of their explanation of the firm; but those writers also make ownership of physical assets part of the bundle of core rights held by the central agent (for reasons that again pertain to monitoring). Even Masten, whose position appears closest to Coase, states that "the distinction between ownership and governance roles of the firm is a spurious one" (1988, p. 195).

Ownership and employment relations are distinguished by the fact that the employer can at most control the current services of the employee, not the stock of labor capacity itself. This distinction is important, for example, to the implications of the asset-specificity paradigm. When two physical assets are highly specialized to one another, advocates of this paradigm argue, it is efficient that they be under common ownership and control. While the same might otherwise have been said where human capital is concerned, prohibition of owning persons means that full integration of human capital (except, perhaps, that of a proprietor) into the firm is not an option. Williamson treats this problem by arguing that human assets are usually not as specific to the firm as are physical ones, and by suggesting that the risk of investing in specialized assets can be mitigated, in labor's case, by safeguards embedded in the employment contract.[30] But collective ownership by workers, or joint participation in management, might logically follow from the analysis where specific human inputs are more important than nonhuman ones.

The relationships between firm, capital goods, and employees demands further attention, also, when defining the firm. As Putterman (1988) argues, viewing the firm as a coalition of agents that includes its employees is inconsistent with the legal notion of the firm as economic agent (and, hence, the "legal fiction" with which Jensen and Meckling associate the firm as a "nexus of contracts"). The firm enters employment contracts on one side of the contracting process, the employees on the other. Although not an actual person, the legal agent called the firm is ultimately controlled by another group of agents, its owners, who may delegate managerial tasks to a subset of employees. The firm may own certain capital goods, and intangible capital, such as reputation, may also adhere to it; but the prohibition on owning the human capital of others means that its employees are not *within* the firm, seen

---

[29] See the previous note.

[30] See Williamson, Wachter, and Harris (1975 [and this reader]) and Williamson (1985, ch. 12).

20

this way, even if their independence is attenuated while the employment relation is in effect. The distinction between the firm as legal entity and the firm as a coalition, organization, or association of agents becomes clear when the ownership of firm changes hands: The firm in the first sense is a tradable commodity, which the firm as an organization cannot possibly be.[31]

Workers and incentives

By concentrating on the discussion regarding the element of authority in the management of the firm's personnel, thus far, we have left aside the larger issue of incentives. Even if the manager could count on the complete obedience of the worker to her commands, as might be suggested by a simple reading of Coase or, say, of Simon's similar treatment (1951), motivating employees would remain a problem insofar as there are situations in which the employee has better information than the manager regarding situations to be responded to.[32] In simpler settings in which the only difficulty lies in the elicitation of effort, imperfect or costly observability and worker self-interest may render the problem equally severe.

Assuming that the firm's profits are increasing in the worker's effort and decreasing in her pay, while the worker's utility bears the opposite relationship to these variables, employer and employee interests are diametrically opposed. The resulting conflict can be resolved by contractual stipulation, but only if enforcement costs are trivial. When effort is not observable without cost, and when the cost of monitoring makes it rational that it be imperfectly observed on the margin, workers may have incentives to shirk. Alchian and Demsetz suggest solving the problem through profit-motivated monitoring, but their solution is one in which rewards are still imperfectly correlated with effort, so a degree of shirking remains. Holmstrom (1982) provided an alternative theoretical solution, in which the central agent observes output and does not need to monitor labor inputs. If aggregate output falls below that associated with each worker providing the stipulated effort level, all workers are punished, though only one may have shirked. Although sufficient in principle to deter shirking without monitoring, the approach would appear to be impractical, whether due to incentive incompatibility, uncertain production functions, or considerations of fairness and enforceability.[33] Thus, a growing

---

[31] Hart makes a similar point. "[I]dentify the firm with all the nonhuman assets that belong to it. . . . . Human assets, however, are not included. Since human assets cannot be bought or sold, management and workers presumably own their human capital both before and after any merger." (Hart, 1989, p. 1766 [and this reader]).

[32] See the discussion of the distinction between consummate and perfunctory cooperation in Williamson, Wachter, and Harris (op. cit.). A similar idea is developed by Clague (1993) under the term "EIR behavior" (for effort, initiative, and responsibility).

[33] On the relevant incentive compatability problem, see Eswaran and Kotwal (1984) and MacLeod (1987).

formal literature, including Calvo and Wellicz (1978), Shapiro and Stiglitz (1984), and Bowles (1985), continues to attach importance to monitoring.

Simple efficiency wage models like that of Shapiro and Stiglitz differ from the intuition of Alchian and Demsetz in that monitoring leads to a zero-shirking outcome. The employer pays an above-market-clearing wage to give the employee reason to prefer keeping the job, then selects a probability of detecting shirking by hiring or undertaking a particular amount of monitoring. As emphasized by Bowles, monitoring and wage rents are substitutes in the elicitation of effort in such a model. The employer's problem, then, is to select a profit-maximizing combination of the two that, when workers are homogeneous and there is a credible threat of firing, fully deters shirking.

Williamson's approach to the incentive problem, in his joint paper with Wachter and Harris (1975 [and this reader]), is one that is simultaneously a treatment of the problem of firm-specific human capital, which these authors view as at least equally salient. Workers can "hold up" their employers for higher remuneration not only by threatening to quit – a threat that is the less credible as the specific component of skill becomes larger – but also by working in a merely "perfunctory" manner. To tie workers' interests to the firm and to reduce opportunistic haggling, workers are exposed to the possibility of advancing up firms' internal job ladders if they exhibit "consummate" performance over time. The approach is also said to cut down on the frequency of monitoring, which carries not only direct but also indirect costs, in the form of harm to worker morale. This informal depiction of an incentive mechanism later formalized in the "tournaments" literature thus also encompasses a somewhat broader view of the motivation problem. Rather than providing an alternative explanation of the phenomenon modelled by authors like Shapiro and Stiglitz, of course, Williamson et al. may be seen to be analyzing a different type of employment situation (for example, that of skilled, white collar workers as opposed to participants in the "primary labor market").[34]

A different reason for not monitoring more intensively, and indeed for not offering "higher powered" rewards in organizations, is provided by Holmstrom and Milgrom (1991a [and this reader]). A worker's job may have both relatively measurable and relatively unmeasurable dimensions. If pay is made contingent on the measurable part of effort or productivity, the unmeasured aspect may be neglected. Holmstrom and Milgrom's formalization of a point frequently made in discussions of the quantity–quality trade-off inherent in piece-rate systems[35] is one of a number of contributions of an

---

[34] See also the depiction of alternative types of effort control environments by Edwards (1979).

[35] See Lawler (1971), Stiglitz (1975), Nalbantian, ed. (1987). Holmstom and Milgrom's idea also closely parallels the classical literature on the "problem of success indicators" in Soviet-type economies; see Nove (1958).

analysis that considers the implications of potentially multitask jobs for reward schemes, job design, and the choice between self-employment and employment by a firm (see next section).

In a different spirit, Leibenstein, who earlier (1966) marshalled evidence that firms' external environments often permit their continued operation with enormous differences in technical efficiency, argues that variations in managerial and worker effort largely account for these differences. In Leibenstein (1982 [and this reader]), he views effort choice by workers and treatment of workers by the firm as a prisoners' dilemma, in which more than one equilibrium is possible. He departs from the neoclassical depiction of such a situation by arguing that outcomes are determined by norms or conventions rather than rationality. Both relatively high and relatively low effort conventions may persist over time, depending on the history of management initiatives, labor relations, and other factors. Neither the invisible hand of the market nor the visible hand of management necessarily drives firms towards an efficient outcome.

The "efficiency wage" family of models, in which effort choice responds positively to the wage paid, has its origin in work by Leibenstein (1963, ch. 6) on the physiological link between effort and earnings in poor countries. A recent variant that incorporates considerations reminiscent of Williamson et al.'s "atmosphere" and Leibenstein's "norms" is the "gift exchange" model of George Akerlof (1982 [and this reader]). Akerlof considers the case of a firm that has perfect information on the output of its employees, yet pays wages that are both unrelated to variations in output and above the going level. As an explanation, he suggests that by working side by side, the workers in the company in question had developed concern for one another's welfare and did not wish to see those who find it more difficult to work at a fast pace being penalized. In exchange for humane treatment of their co-workers, the more able workers provided effort in excess of the minimum required to keep their jobs, without extra compensation. Work in excess of their required effort minima was also in part offered in reciprocity for the firm's payment of wages greater than required to keep workers on the job. Akerlof calls the employer–employee relationship here a *gift* exchange because each side offers the other something beyond what market forces require and does so without explicit negotiation, and voluntarily, although in expectation of reciprocity. While introducing these "sociological" elements, Akerlof emphasizes that each side behaves rationally, in view of its objectives, which in the firm's case are simply those of maximizing profits. The model has the same macroeconomic implication as do those of Shapiro–Stiglitz, Bowles, and others: Namely, some workers seek employment at or below the wage that firms offer, but wages fail to fall so as to clear the labor market.

The sort of egalitarianism that Akerlof seeks to explain is one of a number of common compensation phenomena that George Baker, Michael Jensen, and Kevin Murphy (1988) find puzzling, from a neoclassical standpoint. Another such practice is profit sharing, which appears to have become increasingly common in large American firms during the 1980s. As Baker et al. see it, economic theory suggests that the direct effect of a profit share on effort will be negligible if the firm is large enough that the effort of an individual worker makes little difference to per worker output; applying the logic of Alchian and Demsetz, moreover, there may be important indirect effects, because the incentives of core agents, including those governing monitoring, must be diluted if profit is shared with rank-and-file workers. In their article excerpted in this reader, Martin Weitzman and Douglas Kruse explain the possible efficacy of profit sharing using a repeated game approach. They note that the problem of effort choice under a sharing scheme has the characteristic of a prisoners' dilemma, that the problem is typically played out repeatedly over time, and that the literature on such games shows that both efficient and inefficient equilibria are possible.[36] Like Leibenstein, they suggest that non-economic factors – their own examples include societal or company culture – may determine which equilibrium in fact obtains. They also note that profit sharing may induce mutual monitoring and moral pressure on fellow workers and that, even if the incentives to engage in such monitoring or pressuring are small, the effects could be substantial under appropriate configurations of workplace technology and preferences.[37]

Ownership, control, and finance

Many of the theories discussed so far (for example, those of Coase or of Alchian and Demsetz) assume that the manager of the firm is herself the owner and residual claimant. Such an assumption may be an appropriate simplification for some purposes, and it may more or less reflect the realities of many smaller firms, but since managers and owners are different individuals in many larger firms, it leaves a considerable area in need of further theoretical analysis. To be sure, the owner–manager relationship is amenable to some of the same agency-theoretic treatment as is that between managers and workers, and one might therefore expect to find here mostly variations on themes already explored. In point of fact, however, the problem involves some rather different considerations, partly because it is bound up with questions of financial contracting in which institutions having no exact parallels in the sphere of labor play an important role.

[36] MacLeod (1987) models this explicitly for a workers' cooperative.

[37] A discussion of the relative importance of incentives to monitor versus technology of monitoring is provided by Putterman (1984) in a critical appraisal of Alchian and Demsetz's approach. Mutual monitoring and peer pressure are discussed by Bradley and Gelb (1981) and by Kandel and Lazear (1992), among others.

The Economic Nature of the Firm: A New Introduction

The literature on financial agency owes much to the provocative assertion of Adolf Berle and Gardiner Means (1932) that because dispersed shareholders have little incentive to monitor closely the managers of a corporation, nonowner managers are able to direct firms toward ends other than profit seeking. Authors such as Henry Manne, Eugene Fama, and Jensen and Meckling respond to Berle and Means by identifying ways in which financial institutions might make managers responsive to the interests of outside owners despite diffuse ownership and small managerial ownership stakes. Although disagreeing about the degree to which such institutions align managers' and shareholders' interests, all find reason for scepticism of Berle and Means' view.

Manne's article (1965 [and this reader]) is a seminal contribution to the literature on the market for corporate control. Manne argues that the potential of a corporate takeover, that is, a controlling equity interest being bought by outside investors who believe that the firm can be more profitable under alternative management, keeps the incumbent managers on their toes, even if the frequency of actual takeovers is relatively low. The effectiveness of takeovers as a disciplinary device has been the subject of much debate and research.[38] Authors such as Grossman and Hart (1980) have argued that in theory, free-rider problems may reduce the effectiveness of the takeover market. Various defense strategies employed by incumbent management also may reduce the discipline takeovers provide. The evidence on takeovers, however, indicates that on average actual takeovers are effective means for improving corporate performance, in terms of both returns to stockholders and operating efficiency.[39]

Fama's basic argument (in his 1980 paper, reprinted in this reader) is that, in the long run, managers can expect to be rewarded in direct proportion to their contributions to shareholder wealth and that they accordingly have essentially perfect incentives to maximize firm value (or, equivalently, the present discounted value of the firm's future profit stream). He presents a formal model in which managers earn current wages equal to weighted averages of estimated past marginal productivity (contribution to firm value). Although current pay fails to reflect current performance, the assumption that estimates of past performance are unbiased means that lifetime compensation is expected to change in exact proportion to changes in current effectiveness. In arguing that compensation accurately tracks past performance, Fama relies heavily on the assertion that competition among managers causes the information needed for such tracking to reach those who set or approve compensation in an effective fashion.

[38] See the Symposium in the *Journal of Economic Perspectives*, Winter 1988.

[39] Jarrell, Brickley, and Netter (1988), Kaplan (1989), and Healy, Palepu, and Ruback (1992) document the consequences of takeovers and buyouts.

Jensen and Meckling model an owner-manager who, for portfolio diversification or other reasons, seeks to reduce his ownership stake.[40] In this model, the manager's choice between maximizing the value of his firm and enjoying consumption on the job is determined by preferences and relative prices, with the price of consumption on the job being an increasing function of the manager's ownership stake. Because a reduction in the size of the manager's stake leads to a lower price and thus a larger amount of consumption, it also produces a decline in the firm's value. Potential outside owners rationally anticipate this effect, so a manager cannot sell shares at the value they would have had were he full owner but has to accept an appropriately reduced price. The upshot is that the manager personally bears the cost of his value-reducing actions, which gives him an incentive to bond himself or to invite monitoring so as to be able to enjoy a reduced ownership stake with less personal wealth reduction. While Jensen and Meckling differ from Fama because "managerial shirking" or nonwealth maximizing behavior is not fully eliminated, in their model, their argument has the similar implication that rational capital markets make managers pay for their personal consumption, creating a pressure towards verifiable wealth maximizing by managers with even small ownership stakes.[41]

Since the costliness of determining when behavior is wealth maximizing means that managers are never perfect agents of owners, in their model, Jensen and Meckling's analysis suggests that resources invested in a firm will always have their highest return when the manager is full owner. Why, then, do we in practice observe many firms whose managers hold small or zero shares? Just as Alchian and Demsetz argue that production takes place in teams despite the fact that it is not rational to eliminate all shirking given team production – in that case, due to the countervailing benefits of economies of scale – so it can be argued that delegating management is sometimes efficient, despite persistent agency costs that could in principle be eliminated by full owner management. The countervailing benefits in the case of management and ownership, according to Fama and Jensen (1985 [and this reader]), come from two basic sources.

In the first place, those authors argue, there is not always a perfect coincidence between the possession of managerial talent and the possession of wealth with which to finance a firm. Because an owner-run firm will return less value in the hands of an owner who is an incompetent manager, there may be gains from trade between wealthy financiers and nonwealthy talented

---

[40] A formalization of Jensen and Meckling in which the demand for a limited stake is endogenous is given by Kihlstrom and Matthews (1990).

[41] Indeed, the argument may hold even for managers with no stakes, provided that they at least occasionally have reason to raise outside equity, because it implies that the cost of such equity – or the value at which shares can be sold – is proportional to the level of anticipated "shirking."

managers, despite agency costs. Second, even if all wealthy persons were talented managers, there might not be enough persons sufficiently wealthy to individually own all of the potentially profitable firms. Moreover, risk-averse individuals have a preference for holding diversified portfolios of assets and are willing to sacrifice some wealth in order to do so. Although a given project could in theory be better managed by a solo owner-manager, Fama and Jensen suggest in their diagrammatic argument that it may be better to have it be slightly inefficiently managed by professional managers at an optimal level of capitalization than to have it be efficiently managed by an owner-manager at a suboptimal level of capitalization. Thus, larger or riskier projects will tend to have outside financing, whereas smaller or less risky projects will tend to be owned and financed by the persons who manage them.

Harold Demsetz (1983 [and this reader]) takes issue with the Jensen–Meckling–Fama approach in at least one respect. He resists the idea that managers who are partial or nonowners will enjoy more consumption on the job than will full owner-managers. The crux of Demsetz's argument is that consumption on the job is not necessarily a bad to the full owner-manager, since there is nothing irrational about doing some of one's consumption at work if it is valued at least as much as the cost in reduced profits. Since an outside owner places no direct value on a hired manager's consumption on the job, on the other hand, and since in addition she has difficulty in monitoring it, she may forbid some forms of consumption that she would engage in were she herself managing the firm. Demsetz also departs from some of the literature by resisting the characterization of corporations as "diffusely held," providing evidence of significant ownership concentration in many large firms, of substantial shareholding by upper level managers, and of a large share of the compensation of upper level managers which derives from shareholding.[42]

Beyond questions of agency such as those addressed by the authors discussed thus far, one can ask broader questions about the nature of the ownership both of firms' assets and of firms as such. Alchian and Demsetz argue that firms will own many of the capital goods with which they work because the cost of having their rate of usage and resulting deterioration monitored by outside owners can thus be avoided. Holmstrom and Milgrom point out that when the direct user of the machine is an employee and when the rate of utilization and maintenance is difficult for even the employer to observe, it

---

[42] Because the emphasis in this reader is on the theoretical rather than empirical literature, and because the material presented in Demsetz (1983) is no more than an "opening shot" in a widening and still contentious literature, we have not reprinted most of the portion of the paper dealing with this part of Demestz's argument. The interested reader may wish to see pp. 387–90 in Demsetz (1983), along with Demsetz and Lehn (1985). Holderness, Kroszner, and Sheehan (1995) examine how ownership structure has evolved since the 1930s. Jensen and Warner (1988) present a thorough survey of the empirical literature on ownership and corporate governance.

may be better for the worker to own the machine (and perhaps to be self-employed). This is particularly likely to be the case when the existence of a maintenance observability problem makes it optimal for the employer to desist from offering "high powered" incentives for the measurable tasks that the employee performs with the machine, for reasons discussed earlier. Whether or not the worker will become self-employed depends, in their model, on her degree of risk aversion. However, Williamson's point about trade between owners of interspecialized assets, Barzel's point about the cost of monitoring stages of a sequential production process, or the general point of the asset-specificity approach (shared by Klein, Crawford, and Alchian and by Grossman and Hart) that assets specialized to each other may be best owned in common also may rule out the hiving off of the worker and machine as a separate firm.

Some reservations regarding the asset specificity arguments of Williamson and of Klein, Crawford, and Alchian are also worth mentioning here. First, Monteverde and Teece (1982b) argue that the logic of those authors' positions implies that interspecialized assets should be co-owned but not that they need to be managed by the same firm. For example, if a railroad exists only to serve a particular mine, the mine owner should also own the railroad's capital stock, but he could hire a separate firm to operate it.

Milgrom and Roberts provide another criticism. The appropriation of rents from one party to a specialized exchange by another party to that same exchange, they point out, is a redistribution of the returns from the joint project but need not affect the aggregate level of those returns. Because the appropriation hazard does not affect efficiency, risk-neutral parties should simply proceed to contract for the exchange, deducting any estimated anticipation of appropriation from their reservation prices. Their argument is said to hold even for some specifications of risk aversion. A possible answer to it, however, is that efficiency would be affected if the parties invested real resources in efforts at appropriation (for example, temporarily shutting down the railroad to add credibility to a threat to do so permanently unless better compensated). Such a response, indeed, is very much in the rent-seeking tradition from which Milgrom and Roberts' own theory of bureaucracy derives.[43] The presence of asymmetric information, which might, for example, lead to the adoption of such bargaining strategies, is also precluded in Milgrom and Roberts' critique.

As noted previously, Hart argues that Williamson is unclear about what disciplinary advantages a manager has relative to an independent contractor and, hence, why production should take place in a firm rather than through

---

[43] This seems to be the idea behind Milgrom and Roberts' informal treatment of the issue in their textbook; see Milgrom and Roberts (1992), pp. 307–8.

market contracts. Hart's approach instead emphasizes the importance of residual control rights over assets that are complementary to the labor input, so that discipline over labor is exercised only indirectly. The theory implies that interspecialized assets should be owned in common and that the owner of a resource that is critical to a project should hold the residual rights of control.

Hart's "property rights" approach might thus be thought to constitute a theory of why the capital owner must run the firm, but it does not do so without additional assumptions or restrictions. This is because if all of the interspecialized or critical resources are capital goods, then transfer of ownership to a different party has no consequence for efficiency.[44] Only when the owner of a specialized or critical capital good also has specialized human capital, such as unique knowledge of how to employ that good, can the theory dictate the identity of the owner. Specialized human capital dictates ownership, whereas specialized physical capital does not, because only the former is not in principle transferable.

Williamson (1985, ch. 12) and Putterman (1993a) inquire into why it is the providers of capital who own and control most firms. Williamson argues that while credit can be provided to firms where redeployable assets are available as collateral, specialized and intangible assets must be financed by equity holders, who provide funds without guaranteed return of even the invested principal. He compares equity holders to managers and other investors in firm-specific assets, arguing that only the former lack contractual safeguards of the sort that managers can obtain through their terms of employment. The unprotected status of equity holders thus calls for the grant of control over the firm.

Putterman (1993a) suggests that this argument by Williamson, although couched in terms of asset specificity, is essentially a variant of the Knightian argument about moral hazard and risk bearing. According to that argument (as discussed earlier), the bearer of risk, who guarantees a return to other agents in the firm, demands control rights as a way of assuring that the insured agents do not abuse their security. Putterman further points out that, despite the alleged separation of ownership and control in corporations, ultimate control rights remain in the hands of the shareholders and indeed *must* remain there if the mechanisms discussed by Manne, Fama, and others are to be of any effect.[45] Thus Knight's intuition about moral hazard appears to have enormous explanatory power even in the world of the large corporation. Putterman

---

[44] That is, while the theory implies that *some* capital owners should own the firm, it does not imply that *any particular* capital owner must do so.

[45] That the market for corporate control could not exist without the attachment of control rights to shareholding is obvious. Fama's argument that managerial compensation will track how well managers' perform from the shareholders' standpoint also makes no sense without "the market for outside takeovers providing discipline of last resort." Fama and Jensen (1983b) assign a similar role to shareholders' control rights.

also argues that the primary determinant of who holds that bundle of control, residual, and alienation rights that we call ownership is probably the ability and willingness to provide financial resources and bear risk, a Knightian approach shorn of the emphasis on nonfinancial aspects of entrepreneurship.[46] He points out that identification of the boundaries of the firm with the boundaries of common ownership is perhaps underappreciated (for example, in Williamson's transaction cost economics), and suggests that the disassociation of ownership from labor should be seen as the fundamental source of the incentive problems that preoccupy so much of the internal organization literature. While worker ownership can in some cases address those problems and may also give workers direct utility, workers' limited wealth and consequent high risk aversion and demand for portfolio diversification make that option quite costly to them.[47]

Conclusion

In this introduction we have considered some of the major issues addressed by the literature sampled in our reader. These included: What is a firm? Why are there firms? What determines firms' sizes and scopes? And, how sharp is the distinction between intrafirm transactions and transactions in the market? We found most authors treating firms as somewhat distinctive devices for coordinating production activities, marked by long-term contracts and by an assignment of residual control rights to a subset of agents who supply equity finance. But we found considerable controversy regarding the strength of the firm/market distinction, paralleling controversy over the meaning of authority within the organization.

We found a variety of explanations for organization of activity in firms, ranging from Coase's economizing on the costs of pricing transactions to Williamson's safeguards against appropriation of quasi rents to Barzel's economizing on and Alchian and Demsetz's motivation of monitoring effort and to Knight's provision of insurance in exchange for control. Determinants of firm size similarly varied, including the domain of interspecialized assets consideration implicit in the asset-specificity approach and corresponding technologi-

[46] For an alternative viewpoint emphasizing the importance of existing wealth as a means of attracting finance, rather than the ability to bear risk, see Newman (1995).

[47] The attractiveness of the employee-ownership option also depends on whether the virtuous effects of profit sharing discussed by Weitzman and Kruse, or the harmful consequences posited by Alchian and Demsetz, win out in practice and on whether worker ownership means losses in the gains from specialization in management (on which see the exchange between Williamson, 1980, and Putterman, 1984) or increasing decision-making costs due to heterogeneity of preferences (as argued by Hansmann, 1988). The tradeability of enterprise control rights serves efficiency, among other reasons being the informational advantages of publicly quoted share prices, but by rendering firms less social organizations and more commodities, it might imply some social costs (see Putterman, 1993a).

cal considerations in the monitoring approaches, with arguments about "high" and "low powered" incentives, about costs of bureaucracy, and about limited managerial attention called upon to provide limits to indefinite expansion.

Finally, we discussed two key relations observed in firms – those of ownership and those of employment – beginning by pointing to a difference among authors regarding the relative importance of each to the nature of the firm. The rest of our discussion reviewed the models of the employment relationship and incentives that constitute Part III and the analyses of financial agency and ownership issues that constitute Part IV of this reader.

The literature on the economic nature – and in particular the internal and contractual structure – of firms has progressed considerably from the days when neoclassical economists ignored institutions, and institutionalists were ill prepared to discourse with formal theorists. Where once an interest in what goes on inside "the black box" of the firm had a faint scent of disloyalty to the enterprise of economics, such an interest is now part of the frontier of economic research. Not all "neo-institutional" insights have been absorbed by formal theory, so theorists seeking better answers to the still-perplexing questions of the field would do well to explore the literature sampled here. That firm theorists disagree among themselves about firm–market boundaries, the nature of the employment relation, and other issues may be a reflection of a field that is still relatively youthful, but it also holds out the promise of more lively discussion yet to come. We are pleased to present this sourcebook for that discussion to another generation of participants.

PART I

Within and among firms: the division of labor

CHAPTER 1

From *The Wealth of Nations*

ADAM SMITH

Adam Smith (1723–90) was born in Kirkcaldy, Scotland. He received a Master of Arts degree from the University of Glasgow in 1740 and subsequently was Professor of Moral Philosophy at that university from 1752 to 1763 and commissioner of customs for Scotland from 1778 to 1790. *The Wealth of Nations* established Smith as the founding figure in classical political economy.

Of the division of labour

(From book I, chapter 1)

The greatest improvement in the productive powers of labour, and the greater part of the skill, dexterity, and judgment with which it is any where directed, or applied, seem to have been the effects of the division of labour.

The effects of the division of labour, in the general business of society, will be more easily understood by considering in what manner it operates in some particular manufactures. It is commonly supposed to be carried furthest in some very trifling ones; not perhaps that it really is carried further in them than in others of more importance: but in those trifling manufactures which are destined to supply the small wants of but a small number of people, the whole number of workmen must necessarily be small; and those employed in every different branch of the work can often be collected into the same workhouse and placed at once under the view of the spectator. In those great manufactures, on the contrary, which are destined to supply the great wants of the great body of the people, every different branch of the work employs so great a number of workmen that it is impossible to collect them all into the same workhouse. We can seldom see more, at one time, than those employed in one single branch. Though in such manufactures, therefore, the work may really be divided into a much greater number of parts, than in those of a more

From Adam Smith, *An Inquiry into the Nature and Causes of The Wealth of Nations,* originally published 1776. Excerpted from the Modern Library Edition, edited by Edwin Cannan. New York, 1937.

trifling nature, the division is not near so obvious and has accordingly been much less observed.

To take an example, therefore,[1] from a very trifling manufacture, but one in which the division of labour has been very often taken notice of, the trade of the pin maker; a workman not educated to this business (which the division of labour has rendered a distinct trade) nor acquainted with the use of the machinery employed in it (to the invention of which the same division of labour has probably given occasion) could scarce, perhaps, with his utmost industry, make one pin in a day and certainly could not make twenty. But in the way in which this business is now carried on, not only the whole work is a peculiar trade, but it is divided into a number of branches, of which the greater part are likewise peculiar trades. One man draws out the wire, another straights it, a third cuts it, a fourth points it, a fifth grinds it at the top for receiving the head; to make the head requires two or three distinct operations; to put it on, is a peculiar business, to whiten the pins is another; it is even a trade by itself to put them into the paper; and the important business of making a pin is, in this manner, divided into about eighteen distinct operations, which, in some manufactories, are all performed by distinct hands, though in others the same man will sometimes perform two or three of them. I have seen a small manufactory of this kind where ten men only were employed, and where some of them consequently performed two or three distinct operations. But though they were very poor, and therefore but indifferently accommodated with the necessary machinery, they could, when they exerted themselves, make among them about twelve pounds of pins in a day. There are in a pound upwards of four thousand pins of a middling size. Those ten persons, therefore, could make among them upwards of forty-eight thousand pins in a day. Each person, therefore, making a tenth part of forty-eight thousand pins, might be considered as making four thousand eight hundred pins in a day. But if they had all wrought separately and independently, and without any of them having been educated to this particular business, they certainly could not each of them have made twenty, perhaps not one pin in a day; that is, certainly, not the two hundred and fortieth, perhaps not the four thousand eight hundredth part of what they are at present capable of performing, in consequence of a proper division and combination of their different operations.

In every other art and manufacture, the effects of the division of labour are similar to what they are in this very trifling one; though, in many of them, the labour can neither be so much subdivided nor reduced to so great a simplicity of operation. The division of labour, however, so far as it can be introduced, occasions, in every art, a proportionable increase of the productive powers of

[1] Another and perhaps more important reason for taking an example like that which follows is the possibility of exhibiting the advantages of division of labour in statistical form.

labour. The separation of different trades and employments from one another seems to have taken place, in consequence of this advantage. This separation too is generally carried furthest in those countries which enjoy the highest degree of industry and improvement; what is the work of one man in a rude state of society, being generally that of several in an improved one.

. . .

This great increase of the quantity of work, which, in consequence of the division of labour, the same number of people are capable of performing, is owing to three different circumstances; first, to the increase of dexterity in every particular workman; secondly, to the saving of the time which is commonly lost in passing from one species of work to another; and lastly, to the invention of a great number of machines which facilitate and abridge labour and enable one man to do the work of many.

First, the improvement of the dexterity of the workman necessarily increases the quantity of the work he can perform; and the division of labour, by reducing every man's business to some one simple operation, and by making this operation the sole employment of his life, necessarily increases very much the dexterity of the workman. A common smith, who, though accustomed to handle the hammer, has never been used to make nails, if upon some particular occasion he is obliged to attempt it, will scarce, I am assured, be able to make above two or three hundred nails in a day, and those too very bad ones. A smith who has been accustomed to make nails, but whose sole or principal business has not been that of a nailer, can seldom with his utmost diligence make more than eight hundred or a thousand nails in a day. I have seen several boys under twenty years of age who had never exercised any other trade but that of making nails, and who, when they exerted themselves, could make, each of them, upwards of two thousand three hundred nails in a day. The making of a nail, however, is by no means one of the simplest operations. The same person blows the bellows, stirs or mends the fire as there is occasion, heats the iron, and forges every part of the nail: In forging the head too he is obliged to change his tools. The different operations into which the making of a pin, or of a metal button, is subdivided, are all of them much more simple, and the dexterity of the person, of whose life it has been the sole business to perform them, is usually much greater. The rapidity with which some of the operations of those manufacturers are performed, exceeds what the human hand could, by those who had never seen them, be supposed capable of acquiring.

Secondly, the advantage which is gained by saving the time commonly lost in passing from one sort of work to another is much greater than we should at first view be apt to imagine it. It is impossible to pass very quickly from one kind of work to another that is carried on in a different place and with quite different tools. A country weaver, who cultivates a small farm, must lose a good deal of time in passing from his loom to the field and from the field to his loom. When the two trades can be carried on in the same workhouse, the loss of time is no doubt much less. It is even in this case, however, very considerable. A man commonly saunters a little in turning his hand from one sort of employment to another. When he first begins the new work he is seldom very keen and hearty; his mind, as they say, does not go to it, and for some time he rather trifles than applies to good purpose. The habit of sauntering and of indolent careless application, which is naturally, or rather necessarily, acquired by every country workman who is obliged to change his work and his tools every half hour, and to apply his hand in twenty different ways almost every day of his life, renders him almost always slothful and lazy and incapable of any vigorous application even on the most pressing occasions. Independent, therefore, of his deficiency in point of dexterity, this cause alone must always reduce considerable the quantity of work which he is capable of performing.

Thirdly, and lastly, every body must be sensible how much labour is facilitated and abridged by the application of proper machinery. It is unnecessary to give any example. I shall only observe, therefore, that the invention of all those machines by which labour is so much facilitated and abridged seems to have been originally owing to the division of labour. Men are much more likely to discover easier and readier methods of attaining any object, when the whole attention of their minds is directed towards that single object, than when it is dissipated among a great variety of things. But in consequence of the division of labour, the whole of every man's attention comes naturally to be directed towards some one very simple object. It is naturally to be expected, therefore, that some one or other of those who are employed in each particular branch of labour should soon find out easier and readier methods of performing their own particular work, wherever the nature of it admits of such improvement. A great part of the machines made use of in those manufactures in which labour is most subdivided were originally the inventions of common workmen, who, being each of them employed in some very simple operation, naturally turned their thoughts towards finding out easier and readier methods of performing it. Whoever has been much accustomed to visit such manufactures must frequently have been shewn very pretty machines, which were the inventions of such workmen, in order to facilitate and quicken their own particular part of the work. In the first fire engines, a boy was constantly employed to open and shut alternately the communication between the boiler and the cylinder, according as the piston either ascended or descended. One of those boys, who loved to play with his companions, observed that, by tying a string from the handle of the valve which opened this communication to another part of the machine, the valve would open and shut without his assistance and leave him at liberty to divert himself with his play fellows. One of the greatest improvements that has been made upon this machine, since it was first invented, was in this manner the discovery of a boy who wanted to save his own labour.

All the improvements in machinery, however, have by no means been the inventions of those who had occasion to use the machines. Many improvements have been made by the ingenuity of the makers of the machines, when to make them became the business of a peculiar trade; and some by that of those who are called philosophers or men of speculation, whose trade it is not to do any thing but to observe every thing and who, upon that account, are often capable of combining together the powers of the most distant and dissimilar objects. In the progress of society, philosophy or speculation becomes, like every other employment, the principal or sole trade and occupation of a particular class of citizens. Like every other employment too, it is subdivided into a great number of different branches, each of which affords occupation to a peculiar tribe or class of philosophers; and this subdivision of employment in philosophy, as well as in every other business, improves dexterity and saves time. Each individual becomes more expert in his own peculiar branch, more work is done upon the whole, and the quantity of science is considerably increased by it.

It is the great multiplication of the productions of all the different arts, in consequence of the division of labour, which occasions, in a well-governed society, that universal opulence which extends itself to the lowest ranks of the people. Every workman has a great quantity of his own work to dispose of beyond what he himself has occasion for; and every other workman being exactly in the same situation, he is enabled to exchange a great quantity of his own goods for a great quantity, or, what comes to the same thing, for the price of a great quantity of theirs. He supplies them abundantly with what they have occasion for, and they accommodate him as amply with what he has occasion for, and a general plenty diffuses itself through all the different ranks of the society.

Observe the accommodation of the most common artificer or day labourer in a civilized and thriving country, and you will perceive that the number of people of whose industry a part, though but a small part, has been employed in procuring him this accommodation, exceeds all computation. The woollen coat, for example, which covers the day labourer, as coarse and rough as it may appear, is the produce of the joint labour of a great multitude of workmen. The shepherd, the sorter of wool, the wool comber or carder, the dyer, the scribbler, the spinner, the weaver, the fuller, the dresser, with many others, must all join their different arts in order to complete even this homely production. How many merchants and carriers, besides, must have been employed in transporting the materials from some of those workmen to others who often live in a very distant part of the country! How much commerce and navigation in particular, how many shipbuilders, sailors, sail makers, rope makers must have been employed in order to bring together the different drugs made use of by the dyer, which often come from the remotest corners of the world! What a variety of labour too is necessary in order to produce the tools of the meanest of those workmen! To say nothing of such complicated machines as the ship of the sailor, the mill of the fuller, or even the loom of the weaver, let us consider only what a variety of labour is requisite in order to form that very simple machine, the shears with which the shepherd clips the wool. The miner, the builder of the furnace for smelting the ore, the feller of the timber, the burner of the charcoal to be made use of in the smelting house, the brick maker, the bricklayer, the workmen who attend the furnace, the millwright, the forger, the smith must all of them join their different arts in order to produce them. Were we to examine, in the same manner, all the different parts of his dress and household furniture; the coarse linen shirt which he wears next his skin; the shoes which cover his feet; the bed which he lies on and all the different parts which compose it; the kitchengrate at which he prepares his victuals; the coals which he makes use of for that purpose, dug from the bowels of the earth and brought to him perhaps by a long sea and a long land carriage; all the other utensils of his kitchen; all the furniture of his table; the knives and forks; the earthen or pewter plates upon which he serves up and divides his victuals; the different hands employed in preparing his bread and his beer; the glass window which lets in the heat and the light and keeps out the wind and the rain, with all the knowledge and art requisite for preparing that beautiful and happy invention, without which these northern parts of the world could scarce have afforded a very comfortable habitation; together with the tools of all the different workmen employed in producing those different conveniences; if we examine, I say, all these things, and consider what a variety of labour is employed about each of them, we shall be sensible that without the assistance and cooperation of many thousands, the very meanest person in a civilized country could not be provided, even according to, what we very falsely imagine, the easy and simple manner in which he is commonly accommodated. Compared, indeed, with the more extravagant luxury of the great, his accommodation must no doubt appear extremely simple and easy; and yet it may be true, perhaps that the accommodation of an European prince does not always so much exceed that of an industrious and frugal peasant, as the accommodation of the latter exceeds that of many an African king, the absolute master of the lives and liberties of ten thousand naked savages.

. . .

That the division of labour is limited by the extent of the market

(From book I, chapter 3)

As it is the power of exchanging that gives occasion to the division of labour, so the extent of this division must always be limited by the extent of that power, or in other words, by the extent of the market. When the market is very small, no person can have any encouragement to dedicate himself entirely to one employment, for want of the power to exchange all that surplus part of the produce of his own labour, which is over and above his own consumption, for such parts of the produce of other men's labour as he has occasion for.

There are some sorts of industry, even of the lowest kind, which can be carried on no where but in a great town. A porter, for example, can find employment and subsistence in no other place. A village is by much too narrow a sphere for him; even an ordinary market town is scarce large enough to afford him constant occupation. In the lone houses and very small villages which are scattered about in so desert a country as the Highlands of Scotland, every farmer must be butcher, baker, and brewer for his own family. In such situations we can scarce expect to find even a smith, a carpenter, or a mason within less than twenty miles of another of the same trade. The scattered families that live at eight or ten miles distance from the nearest of them must learn to perform themselves a great number of little pieces of work, for which, in more populous countries, they would call in the assistance of those workmen. Country workmen are almost every where obliged to apply themselves to all the different branches of industry that have so much affinity to one another as to be employed about the same sort of materials. A country carpenter deals in every sort of work that is made of wood; a country smith in every sort of work that is made of iron. The former is not only a carpenter, but a joiner, a cabinet maker, and even a carver in wood, as well as a wheelwright, a ploughwright, a cart and wagon maker. The employments of the latter are still more various. It is impossible there should be such a trade as even that of the nailer in the remote and inland parts of the Highlands of Scotland. Such a workman at the rate of a thousand nails a day, and three hundred working days in the year, will make three hundred thousand nails in the year. But in such a situation it would be impossible to dispose of one thousand, that is, of one day's work in the year.

As by means of water carriage a more extensive market is opened to every sort of industry than what land carriage alone can afford it, so it is upon the seacoast, and along the banks of navigable rivers, that industry of every kind naturally begins to subdivide and improve itself, and it is frequently not till a long time after that those improvements extend themselves to the inland parts of the country.

. . .

On joint stock companies

(From book V, chapter 1)

Joint stock companies, established either by royal charter or by act of parliament differ in several respects, not only from regulated companies but from private copartneries.

First, in a private copartnery, no partner, without the consent of the company, can transfer his share to another person or introduce a new member into the company. Each member, however, may, upon proper warning, withdraw from the copartnery and demand payment from them of his share of the common stock. In a joint stock company, on the contrary, no member can demand payment of his share from the company; but each member can, without their consent, transfer his share to another person and thereby introduce a new member. The value of a share in a joint stock is always the price which it will bring in the market; and this may be either greater or less, in any proportion, than the sum which its owner stands credited for in the stock of the company.

Secondly, in a private copartnery, each partner is bound for the debts contracted by the company to the whole extent of his fortune. In a joint stock company, on the contrary, each partner is bound only to the extent of his share.

The trade of a joint stock company is always managed by a court of directors. This court, indeed, is frequently subject, in many respects, to the controul of a general court of proprietors. But the greater part of those proprietors seldom pretend to understand any thing of the business of the company, and when the spirit of faction happens not to prevail among them, give themselves no trouble about it, but receive contentedly such half yearly or yearly dividend as the directors think proper to make to them. This total exemption from trouble and from risk, beyond a limited sum, encouraged many people to become adventurers in joint stock companies, who would, upon no account, hazard their fortunes in any private copartnery. Such companies, therefore, commonly draw to themselves much greater stocks than any private copartnery can boast of. The trading stock of the South Sea Company, at one time, amounted to upwards of thirty-three millions eight hundred thousand pounds. The dividend capital of the Bank of England amounts, at present, to ten millions seven hundred and eighty thousand pounds. The directors of such companies, however, being the managers rather of other people's money than of their own, it cannot well be expected, that they should watch over it with the same anxious vigilance with which the partners in a private copartnery frequently watch over their own. Like the stewards of a rich man, they are apt to consider attention to small matters as not for their master's honour and very easily give themselves a dispensation from having it. Negligence and profusion, therefore, must always prevail, more or less, in the management of the affairs of such a company. It is upon this account that joint stock companies for foreign trade have seldom been able to maintain the competition against private adventurers. They have, accordingly, very seldom succeeded without an exclusive privilege, and frequently have not succeeded with one. Without an exclusive privilege they have commonly mismanaged the trade. With an exclusive privilege they have both mismanaged and confined it.

. . .

But a joint stock company, consisting of a small number of proprietors, with a moderate capital, approaches very nearly to the nature of the private copartnery and may be capable of nearly the same degree of vigilance and attention.

. . .

On education

(From book V, chapter 1)

In the progress of the division of labour, the employment of the far greater part of those who live by labour, that is, of the great body of the people, comes to be confined to a few very simple operations, frequently to one or two. But the understandings of the greater part of men are necessarily formed by their ordinary employments. The man whose whole life is spent in performing a few simple operations, of which the effects too are, perhaps, always the same, or very nearly the same, has no occasion to exert his understanding or to exercise his invention in finding out expedients for removing difficulties which never occur. He naturally loses, therefore, the habit of such exertion and generally becomes as stupid and ignorant as it is possible for a human creature to become. The torpor of his mind renders him, not only incapable of relishing or bearing a part in any rational conversation, but of conceiving any generous, noble, or tender sentiment, and consequently of forming any just judgment concerning many even of the ordinary duties of private life. Of the great and extensive interests of his country he is altogether incapable of judging; and unless very particular pains have been taken to render him otherwise, he is equally incapable of defending his country in war. The uniformity of his stationary life naturally corrupts the courage of his mind and makes him regard with abhorrence the irregular, uncertain, and adventurous life of a soldier. It corrupts even the activity of his body, and renders him incapable of exerting his strength with vigour and perseverance, in any other employment than that to which he has been bred. His dexterity at his own particular trade seems, in this manner, to be acquired at the expense of his intellectual, social, and marital virtues. But in every improved and civilized society this is the state into which the labouring poor, that is, the great body of the people, must necessarily fall, unless government takes some pains to prevent it.

It is otherwise in the barbarous societies, as they are commonly called, of hunters, of shepherds, and even of husbandmen in that rude state of husbandry which precedes the improvement of manufactures and the extension of foreign commerce. In such societies the varied occupations of every man oblige every man to exert his capacity and to invent expedients for removing difficulties which are continually occurring. Invention is kept alive, and the mind is not suffered to fall into that drowsy stupidity, which, in a civilized society, seems to benumb the understanding of almost all the inferior ranks of people. In those barbarous societies, as they are called, every man, it has already been observed, is a warrior. Every man too is in some measure a statesman and can form a tolerable judgment concerning the interest of the society and the conduct of those who govern it. How far their chiefs are good judges in peace, or good leaders in war, is obvious to the observation of almost every single man among them. In such a society indeed, no man can well acquire that improved and refined understanding, which a few men sometimes possess in a more civilized state. Though in a rude society there is a good deal of variety in the occupations of every individual, there is not a good deal in those of the whole society. Every man does, or is capable of doing, almost every thing which any other man does, or is capable of doing. Every man has a considerable degree of knowledge, ingenuity, and invention; but scarce any man has a great degree. The degree, however, which is commonly possessed, is generally sufficient for conducting the whole simple business of the society. In a civilized state, on the contrary, though there is

44

From The Wealth of Nations

little variety in the occupations of the greater part of individuals, there is an almost infinite variety in those of the whole society. These varied occupations present an almost infinite variety of objects to the contemplation of those few, who, being attached to no particular occupation themselves, have leisure and inclination to examine the occupations of other people. The contemplation of so great a variety of objects necessarily exercises their minds in endless comparisons and combinations, and renders their understandings, in an extraordinary degree, both acute and comprehensive. Unless those few, however, happen to be placed in some very particular situations, their great abilities, though honourable to themselves, may contribute very little to the good government or happiness of their society. Notwithstanding the great abilities of those few, all the nobler parts of the human character may be, in a great measure, obliterated and extinguished in the great body of the people.

The education of the common people requires, perhaps, in a civilized and commercial society, the attention of the public more than that of people of some rank and fortune. People of some rank and fortune are generally eighteen or nineteen years of age before they enter upon that particular business, profession, or trade by which they propose to distinguish themselves in the world. They have before that full time to acquire, or at least to fit themselves for afterwards acquiring, every accomplishment which can recommend them to the public esteem, or render them worthy of it.

. . .

It is otherwise with the common people. They have little time to spare for education. Their parents can scarce afford to maintain them even in infancy. As soon as they are able to work, they must apply to some trade by which they can earn their subsistence. That trade too is generally so simple and uniform as to give little exercise to the understanding; while, at the same time, their labour is both so constant and so severe that it leaves them little leisure and less inclination to apply to, or even to think of, any thing else.

But though the common people cannot, in any civilized society, be so well instructed as people of some rank and fortune, the most essential parts of education, however, to read, write, and account, can be acquired at so early a period of life that the greater part even of those who are to be bred to the lowest occupations have time to acquire them before they can be employed in those occupations. For a very small expense the public can facilitate, can encourage, and can even impose upon almost the whole body of the people, the necessity of acquiring those most essential parts of education.

. . .

45

CHAPTER 2

From *Capital*

KARL MARX

Karl Marx (1818–83) was born in Trier, Germany. He earned a Ph.D. degree at the University of Jena in 1841. Beginning in 1849, he resided in London where he took up economic studies in the British Museum. His three volume work, *Capital,* is the cornerstone of what has come to be known as Marxian political economy.

The buying and selling of labour-power

(From chapters 5 and 6)

. . .

We have shown that surplus-value cannot be created by circulation, and, therefore, that in its formation, something must take place in the background, which is not apparent in the circulation itself.

. . .

The consumption of labour-power is completed, as in the case of every other commodity, outside the limits of the market or of the sphere of circulation. Accompanied by Mr. Moneybags and by the possessor of labour-power, we therefore take leave for a time of this noisy sphere, where everything takes place on the surface and in view of all men, and follow them both into the hidden abode of production, on whose threshold there stares us in the face "No admittance except on business." Here we shall see, not only how capital produces, but how capital is produced. We shall at last force the secret of profit making.

This sphere that we are deserting, within whose boundaries the sale and purchase of labor-power goes on, is in fact a very Eden of the innate rights of

From Karl Marx, *Capital: A Critique of Political Economy, Volume I: The Process of Capitalist Production,* edited by Frederick Engels, originally published 1867. Excerpted from the translation of the Third German Edition by Samuel Moore and Edward Aveling. New York: International Publishers, 1967.

man. There alone rule Freedom, Equality, Property, and Bentham. Freedom, because both buyer and seller of a commodity, say of labour-power, are constrained only by their own free will. They contract as free agents, and the agreement they come to is but the form in which they give legal expression to their common will. Equality, because each enters into relation with the other, as with a simple owner of commodities, and they exchange equivalent for equivalent. Property, because each disposes only of what is his own. And Bentham, because each looks only to himself. The only force that brings them together and puts them in relation with each other is the selfishness, the gain and the private interests of each. Each looks to himself only, and no one troubles himself about the rest, and just because they do so, do they all, in accordance with the preestablished harmony of things, or under the auspices of an all-shrewd providence, work together to their mutual advantage, for the common weal and in the interest of all.

On leaving this sphere of simple circulation or of exchange of commodities, which furnishes the "Free-trade Vulgaris" with his views and ideas, and with the standard by which he judges a society based on capital and wages, we think we can perceive a change in the physiognomy of our dramatis personae. He, who before was the money owner, now strides in front as capitalist; the possessor of labour-power follows as his labourer. The one with an air of importance, smirking, intent on business; the other, timid and holding back, like one who is bringing his own hide to market and has nothing to expect but – a hiding.

Cooperation

(From chapter 13)

. . .

Capitalist production only then really begins, as we have already seen, when each individual capital employs simultaneously a comparatively large number of labourers; when consequently the labour process is carried on on an extensive scale and yields, relatively, large quantities of products. A greater number of labourers working together, at the same time, in one place (or, if you will, in the same field of labour), in order to produce the same sort of commodity under the mastership of one capitalist, constitutes, both historically and logically, the starting point of capitalist production. With regard to the mode of production itself, manufacture, in its strict meaning, is hardly to be distinguished, in its earliest stages, from the handicraft trades of the guilds otherwise than by the greater number of workmen simultaneously employed by one and the same individual capital. The workshop of the mediaeval master handicraftsman is simply enlarged.

. . .

Even without an alteration in the system of working, the simultaneous employment of a large number of labourers effects a revolution in the material conditions of the labour process. The buildings in which they work, the storehouses for the raw material, the implements and utensils used simultaneously or in turns by the workmen, in short, a portion of the means of production, are now consumed in common. On the one hand, the exchange value of these means of production is not increased; for the exchange value of a commodity is not raised by its use value being consumed more thoroughly and to greater advantage. On the other hand, they are used in common and therefore on a larger scale than before. A room where twenty weavers work at twenty looms must be larger than the room of a single weaver with two assistants. But it costs less labour to build one workshop for twenty persons than to build ten to accommodate two weavers each; thus the value of the means of production that are concentrated for use in common on a large scale does not increase in direct proportion to the expansion and to the increased useful effect of those means. When consumed in common, they give up a smaller part of their value to each single product; partly because the total value they part with is spread over a greater quantity of products and partly because their value, though absolutely greater, is, having regard to their sphere of action in the process, relatively less than the value of isolated means of production. Owing to this, the value of a part of the constant capital falls, and in proportion to the magnitude of the fall, the total value of the commodity also falls. The effect is the same as if the means of production had cost less. The economy in their application is entirely owing to their being consumed in common by a large number of workmen. Moreover, this character of being necessary conditions of social labour, a character that distinguishes them from the dispersed and relatively more costly means of production of isolated, independent labourers, or small masters, is acquired even when the numerous workmen assembled together do not assist one another, but merely work side by side. A portion of the instruments of labour acquires this social character before the labour process itself does so.

. . .

When numerous labourers work together side by side, whether in one and the same process or in different but connected processes, they are said to cooperate, or to work in cooperation.

From Capital

Just as the offensive power of a squadron of cavalry, or the defensive power of a regiment of infantry, is essentially different from the sum of the offensive or defensive powers of the individual cavalry or infantry soldiers taken separately, so the sum total of the mechanical forces exerted by isolated workmen differs from the social force that is developed when many hands take part simultaneously in one and the same undivided operation, such as raising a heavy weight, turning a winch, or removing an obstacle. In such cases the effect of the combined labour could either not be produced at all by isolated individual labour, or it could only be produced by a great expenditure of time or on a very dwarfed scale. Not only have we here an increase in the productive power of the individual, by means of cooperation, but the creation of a new power, namely, the collective power of masses.

Apart from the new power that arises from the fusion of many forces into one single force, mere social contact begets in most industries an emulation and a stimulation of the animal spirits that heighten the efficiency of each individual workman. Hence it is that a dozen persons working together will, in their collective working day of 144 hours, produce far more than twelve isolated men each working 12 hours, or than one man who works twelve days in succession. The reason of this is that man is, if not as Aristotle contends, a political, at all events a social animal.

. . .

As general rule, labourers cannot cooperate without being brought together: their assemblage in one place is a necessary condition of their cooperation. Hence wage labourers cannot cooperate, unless they are employed simultaneously by the same capital, the same capitalist, and unless therefore their labour-powers are bought simultaneously by him. The total value of these labour-powers, or the amount of the wages of these labourers for a day, or a week, as the case may be, must be ready in the pocket of the capitalist, before the workmen are assembled for the process of production. The payment of 300 workmen at once, though only for one day, requires a greater outlay of capital than does the payment of a smaller number of men, week by week, during a whole year. Hence the number of the labourers that cooperate, or the scale of cooperation, depends, in the first instance, on the amount of capital that the individual capitalist can spare for the purchase of labour-power; in other words, on the extent to which a single capitalist has command over the means of subsistence of a number of labourers.

And as with the variable, so it is with the constant capital. For example, the outlay on raw material is 30 times as great, for the capitalist who employs 300 men, as it is for each of the 30 capitalists who employ 10 men. The value and quantity of the instruments of labour used in common do not, it is true, increase at the same rate as the number of workmen, but they do increase very considerably. Hence, concentration of large masses of the means of production in the hands of individual capitalists is a material condition for the cooperation of wage labourers, and the extent of the cooperation, or the scale of production, depends on the extent of this concentration.

We saw in a former chapter that a certain minimum amount of capital was necessary in order that the number of labourers simultaneously employed, and, consequently, the amount of surplus value produced, might suffice to liberate the employer himself from manual labour, to convert him from a small master into a capitalist, and thus formally to establish capitalist production. We now see that a certain minimum amount is a necessary condition for the conversion of numerous isolated and independent processes into one combined social process.

We also saw that at first, the subjection of labour to capital was only a formal result of the fact that the labourer, instead of working for himself, works for and consequently under the capitalist. By the cooperation of numerous wage labourers, the sway of capital develops into a requisite for carrying on the labour process itself, into a real requisite of production. That a capitalist should command on the field of production is now as indispensable as that a general should command on the field of battle.

All combined labour on a large scale requires, more or less, a directing authority, in order to secure the harmonious working of the individual activities and to perform the general functions that have their origin in the action of the combined organism, as distinguished from the action of its separate organs. A single violin player is his own conductor; an orchestra requires a separate one. The work of directing, superintending, and adjusting becomes one of the functions of capital from the moment that the labour under the control of capital becomes cooperative. Once a function of capital, it acquires special characteristics.

The directing motive, the end and aim of capitalist production, is to extract the greatest possible amount of surplus value and consequently to exploit labour-power to the greatest possible extent. As the number of the cooperating labourers increases, so too does their resistance to the domination of capital and, with it, the necessity for capital to overcome this resistance by counterpressure. The control exercised by the capitalist is not only a special function, due to the nature of the social labour process, and peculiar to that process, but it is, at the same time, a function of the exploitation of a social labour process and is consequently rooted in the unavoidable antagonism between the exploiter and the living and labouring raw material he exploits.

Again, in proportion to the increasing mass of the means of production, now no longer the property of the labourer but of the capitalist, the necessity increases for some effective control over the proper application of those means.[1] Moreover, the cooperation of wage labourers is entirely brought about by the capital that employs them. Their union into one single productive body and the establishment of a connexion between their individual functions are matters foreign and external to them, are not their own act, but the act of the capital that brings and keeps them together. Hence the connexion existing between their various labours appears to them, ideally, in the shape of a preconceived plan of the capitalist and, practically, in the shape of the authority of the same capitalist, in the shape of the powerful will of another, who subjects their activity to his aims. If, then, the control of the capitalist is in substance twofold by reason of the twofold nature of the process of production itself – which, on the one hand, is a social process for producing use values, on the other, a process for creating surplus value – in form that control is despotic. As cooperation extends its scale, this despotism takes forms peculiar to itself. Just as at first the capitalist is relieved from actual labour so soon as his capital has reached that minimum amount with which capitalist production, as such, begins, so now, he hands over the work of direct and constant supervision of the individual workmen, and groups of workmen, to a special kind of wage labourer. An industrial army of workmen, under the command of a capitalist, requires, like a real army, officers (managers), and sergeants (foremen, overlookers), who, while the work is being done, command in the name of the capitalist. The work of supervision becomes their established and exclusive function. When comparing the mode of production of isolated peasants and artisans with production by slave labour, the political economist counts this labour of superintendence among the *faux frais* of production.[2] But, when considering the capitalist mode of production, he, on the contrary, treats the work of control made necessary by the cooperative character of the labour process as identical with the different work of control necessitated by the capitalist character of that process and the antagonism of interests between capitalist and labourer. It is not because he is a leader of industry that a man is a capitalist; on the contrary, he is a leader of industry because he is a capitalist. The leadership of industry is an attribute of capital, just as in feudal times the functions of general and judge were attributes of landed property.

[1] That Philistine paper, the *Spectator,* states that after the introduction of a sort of partnership between capitalist and workmen in the "Wirework Company of Manchester," "the first result was a sudden decrease in waste, the men not seeing why they should waste their own property any more than any other master's, and waste is, perhaps, next to bad debts, the greatest source of manufacturing loss." The same paper finds that the main defect in the Rochdale cooperative experiments is this: "They showed that associations of workmen could manage shops, mills, and almost all forms of industry with success, and they immediately improved the condition of the men but then they did not leave a clear place for masters." Quelle horreur!

[2] Professor Cairnes, after stating that the superintendence of labour is a leading feature of production by slaves in the Southern States of North America, continues: "The peasant proprietor (of the North), appropriating the whole produce of his toil, needs no other stimulus to exertion. Superintendence is here completely dispensed with." (Cairnes, 1862, pp. 48, 49).

The labourer is the owner of his labour-power until he has done bargaining for its sale with the capitalist; and he can sell no more than what he has – i.e., his individual, isolated labour-power. This state of things is in no way altered by the fact that the capitalist, instead of buying the labour-power of one man, buys that of 100 and enters into separate contracts with 100 unconnected men instead of with one. He is at liberty to set the 100 men to work, without letting them cooperate. He pays them the value of 100 independent labour-powers, but he does not pay for the combined labour-power of the hundred. Being independent of each other, the labourers are isolated persons, who enter into relations with the capitalist but not with one another. This cooperation begins only with the labour process, but they have then ceased to belong to themselves. On entering that process, they become incorporated with capital. As cooperators, as members of a working organism, they are but special modes of existence of capital. Hence, the productive power developed by the labourer when working in cooperation is the productive power of capital. This power is developed gratuitously, whenever the workmen are placed under given conditions, and it is capital that places them under such conditions. Because this power costs capital nothing, and because, on the other hand, the labourer himself does not develop it before his labour belongs to capital, it appears as a power with which capital is endowed by Nature – a productive power that is immanent in capital.

. . .

Division of labour and manufacture

(From chapter 14)

. . .

Section 2. – the detail labourer and his implements

If we now go more into detail, it is, in the first place, clear that a labourer who all his life performs one and the same simple operation converts his whole body into the automatic, specialised implement of that operation. Consequently, he takes less time in doing it than the artificer who performs a whole series of operations in succession. But the collective labourer, who constitutes the living mechanism of manufacture, is made up solely of such specialised detail labourers. Hence, in comparison with the independent handicraft, more is produced in a given time, or the productive power of labour is increased. Moreover, when once this fractional work is established as the exclusive function of one person, the methods it employs become perfected. The workman's continued repetition of the same simple act, and the concentration of his attention on it, teach him by experience how to attain the desired effect with the minimum of exertion. But since there are always several generations of labourers living at one time, and working together at the manufacture of a given article, the technical skill, the tricks of the trade thus acquired, become established and are accumulated and handed down. Manufacture, in fact, produces the skill of the detail labourer by reproducing, and systematically driving to an extreme within the workshop, the naturally developed differentiation of trades, which it found ready to hand in society at large. . . .

. . .

An artificer, who performs one after another the various fractional operations in the production of a finished article, must at one time change his place, at another his tools. The transition from one operation to another interrupts the flow of his labour and creates, so to say, gaps in his working day. These gaps close up so soon as he is tied to one and the same operation all day long; they vanish in proportion as the changes in his work diminish. The resulting increased productive power is owing either to an increased expenditure of labour-power in a given time – i.e., to increased intensity of labour – or to a decrease in the amount of labour-power unproductively consumed. The extra expenditure of power, demanded by every transition from rest to motion, is made up for by prolonging the duration of the normal velocity when once acquired. On the other hand, constant labour of one uniform kind disturbs the intensity and flow of a man's animal spirits, which find recreation and delight in mere change of activity.

. . .

Section 4. – division of labour in manufacture, and division of labour in society

We first considered the origin of Manufacture, then its simple elements, then the detail labourer and his implements, and finally, the totality of the mechanism. We shall now lightly touch upon the relation between the division of labour in manufacture and the social division of labour, which forms the foundation of all production of commodities.

. . .

Since the production and the circulation of commodities are the general prerequisites of the capitalist mode of production, division of labour in manufacture demands that division of labour in society at large should previously have attained a certain degree of development. Inversely, the former division reacts upon and develops and multiplies the latter.

. . .

But, in spite of the numerous analogies and links connecting them, division of labour in the interior of a society, and that in the interior of a workshop, differ not only in degree but also in kind. The analogy appears most indisputable where there is an invisible bond uniting the various branches of trade. For instance the cattle breeder produces hides, the tanner makes the hides into leather, and the shoemaker, the leather into boots. Here the thing produced by each of them is but a step towards the final form, which is the product of all their labours combined. There are, besides, all the various industries that supply the cattle breeder, the tanner, and the shoemaker with the means of production. Now it is quite possible to imagine, with Adam Smith, that the difference between the above social division of labour and the division in manufacture is merely subjective, exists merely for the observer, who, in a manufacture, can see with one glance all the numerous operations being performed on one spot, while in the instance given above, the spreading out of the work over great areas, and the great number of people employed in each branch of labour, obscure the connexion. But what is it that forms the bond between the independent labours of the cattle breeder, the tanner, and the shoemaker? It is the fact that their respective products are commodities. What, on the other hand, characterises division of labour in manufactures? The fact that the detail labourer produces no commodities.[3] It is only the common product of all the detail labourers that becomes a commodity. Division of labour in society is brought about by the purchase and sale of the products of different branches of industry, while the connexion between the detail operations in a workshop is due to the sale of the labour-power of several workmen to one capitalist, who applies it as combined labour-power. The division of labour in the workshop implies concentration of the means of production in the hands of one capitalist; the division of labour in society implies their dispersion among many independent producers of commodities. While within the workshop, the iron law of proportionality subjects definite numbers of workmen to definite functions, in the society outside the work-

---

[3] "There is no longer anything which we can call the natural reward of individual labour. Each labourer produces only some part of a whole, and each part, having no value or utility in itself, there is nothing on which the labourer can seize, and say: It is my product; this I will keep to myself." (Th. Hodgeskin, 1825, p. 25.)

From Capital

shop, chance and caprice have full play in distributing the producers and their means of production among the various branches of industry. The different spheres of production, it is true, constantly tend to an equilibrium: for, on the one hand, while each producer of a commodity is bound to produce a use value, to satisfy a particular social want, and while the extent of these wants differs quantitatively, still there exists an inner relation which settles their proportions into a regular system, and that system one of spontaneous growth; and, on the other hand, the law of the value of commodities ultimately determines how much of its disposable working time society can expend on each particular class of commodities. But this constant tendency to equilibrium, of the various spheres of production, is exercised only in the shape of a reaction against the constant upsetting of this equilibrium. The a priori system on which the division of labour, within the workshop, is regularly carried out becomes in the division of labour within the society an a posteriori, nature-imposed necessity, controlling the lawless caprice of the producers, and perceptible in the barometrical fluctuations of the market prices. Division of labour within the workshop implies the undisputed authority of the capitalist over men, that are but parts of a mechanism that belongs to him. The division of labour within the society brings into contact independent commodity producers, who acknowledge no other authority but that of competition, of the coercion exerted by the pressure of their mutual interests; just as in the animal kingdom, the *bellum omnium contra omnes* more or less preserves the conditions of existence of every species. The same bourgeois mind which praises division of labour in the workshop, life-long annexation of the labourer to a partial operation, and his complete subjection to capital as being an organisation of labour that increases its productiveness – that same bourgeois mind denounces with equal vigour every conscious attempt to socially control and regulate the process of production as an inroad upon such sacred things as the rights of property, freedom, and unrestricted play for the bent of the individual capitalist. It is very characteristic that the enthusiastic apologists of the factory system have nothing more damning to urge against a general organisation of the labour of society than that it would turn all society into one immense factory.

In a society with capitalist production, anarchy in the social division of labour and despotism in that of the workshop are mutual conditions the one of the other. . . .

. . .

While division of labour in society at large, whether such division be brought about or not by exchange of commodities, is common to economic formations of society the most diverse, division of labour in the workshop, as practised

55

by manufacture, is a special creation of the capitalist mode of production alone.

. . .

In manufacture, as well as in simple cooperation, the collective working organism is a form of existence of capital. The mechanism that is made up of numerous individual detail labourers belongs to the capitalist. Hence, the productive power resulting from a combination of labours appears to be the productive power of capital. Manufacture proper not only subjects the previously independent workman to the discipline and command of capital, but, in addition, creates a hierarchic gradation of the workmen themselves. While simple cooperation leaves the mode of working by the individual for the most part unchanged, manufacture thoroughly revolutionises it and seizes labour-power by its very roots. It converts the labourer into a crippled monstrosity by forcing his detail dexterity at the expense of a world of productive capabilities and instincts; just as in the States of La Plata they butcher a whole beast for the sake of his hide or his tallow. Not only is the detail work distributed to the different individuals, but the individual himself is made the automatic motor of a fractional operation, and the absurd fable of Menenius Agrippa, which makes man a mere fragment of his own body, becomes realised. If, at first, the workman sells his labour-power to capital, because the material means of producing a commodity fail him, now his very labour-power refuses its services unless it has been sold to capital. Its functions can be exercised only in an environment that exists in the workshop of the capitalist after the sale. By nature unfitted to make anything independently, the manufacturing labourer develops productive activity as a mere appendage of the capitalist's workshop. As the chosen people bore in their features the sign manual of Jehovah, so division of labour brands the manufacturing workman as the property of capital.

The knowledge, the judgment, and the will, which, though in ever so small a degree, are practised by the independent peasant or handicraftsman, in the same way as the savage makes the whole art of war consist in the exercise of his personal cunning – these faculties are now required only for the workshop as a whole. Intelligence in production expands in one direction, because it vanishes in many others. What is lost by the detail labourers is concentrated in the capital that employs them. It is a result of the division of labour in manufactures that the labourer is brought face to face with the intellectual potencies of the material process of production, as the property of another and as a ruling power. This separation begins in simple cooperation, where the capitalist represents the single workman, the oneness and the will of the associated labour. It is developed in manufacture which cuts down the labourer into a detail labourer. It is completed in modern industry, which makes science a productive force distinct from labour and presses it into the service of capital.

. . .

"The understandings of the greater part of men," says Adam Smith, "are necessarily formed by their ordinary employments. The man whose whole life is spent in performing a few simple operations . . . has no occasion to exert his understanding. . . . He generally becomes as stupid and ignorant as it is possible for a human creature to become." After describing the stupidity of the detail labourer he goes on: "The uniformity of his stationary life naturally corrupts the courage of his mind. . . . It corrupts even the activity of his body and renders him incapable of exerting his strength with vigour and perseverance in any other employments than that to which he has been bred. His dexterity at his own particular trade seems in this manner to be acquired at the expense of his intellectual, social, and martial virtues. But in every improved and civilised society, this is the state into which the labouring poor, that is, the great body of the people, must necessarily fall."[4] For preventing the complete deterioration of the great mass of the people by division of labour, A. Smith recommends education of the people by the State, but prudently, and in homoeopathic doses. G. Garnier, his French translator and commentator, who, under the first French Empire, quite naturally developed into a senator, quite as naturally opposes him on this point. Education of the masses, he urges, violates the first law of the division of labour, and with it "our whole social system would be proscribed." "Like all other divisions of labour," he says, "that between hand labour and head labour is more pronounced and decided in proportion as society (he rightly uses this word, for capital, landed property, and their State) becomes richer. This division of labour, like every other, is an effect of past, and a cause of future progress . . . ought the government then to work in opposition to this division of labour, and to hinder its natural course? Ought it to expend a part of the public money in the attempt to confound and blend together two classes of labour, which are striving after division and separation?"[5]

Some crippling of body and mind is inseparable even from division of labour in society as a whole. Since, however, manufacture carries this social separation of branches of labour much further, and also, by its peculiar division, attacks the individual at the very roots of his life, it is the first to afford the materials for, and to give a start to, industrial pathology.

[4] A. Smith (1937 [1776]), Bk. v., ch. i, art. ii.
[5] G. Garnier (1796), vol. V. of his translation of A. Smith, pp. 4–5.

"To subdivide a man is to execute him, if he deserves the sentence, to assassinate him if he does not. . . . The subdivision of labour is the assassination of a people."[6]

. . .

The factory

(From chapter 15, section 4)

. . . Every kind of capitalist production, in so far as it is not only a labour process but also a process of creating surplus value, has this in common, that it is not the workman that employs the instruments of labour, but the instruments of labour that employ the workman. But it is only in the factory system that this inversion for the first time acquires technical and palpable reality. By means of its conversion into an automaton, the instrument of labour confronts the labourer, during the labour process, in the shape of capital, of dead labour, that dominates, and pumps dry, living labour-power. The separation of the intellectual powers of production from the manual labour, and the conversion of those powers into the might of capital over labour, is, as we have already shown, finally completed by modern industry erected on the foundation of machinery. The special skill of each individual insignificant factory operative vanishes as an infinitesimal quantity before the science, the gigantic physical forces, and the mass of labour that are embodied in the factory mechanism and, together with that mechanism, constitute the power of the "master." This "master," therefore, in whose brain the machinery and his monopoly of it are inseparably united, whenever he falls out with his "hands," contemptuously tells them: "The factory operatives should keep in wholesome remembrance the fact that theirs is really a low species of skilled labour; and that there is none which is more easily acquired, or of its quality more amply remunerated, or which by a short training of the least expert can be more quickly, as well as abundantly, acquired. . . . The master's machinery really plays a far more important part in the business of production than the labour and the skill of the operative, which six months' education can teach, and a common labourer can learn."[7] The technical subordination of the workman to the uniform motion of the instruments of labour, and the peculiar composition of the body of workpeople, consisting as it does of individuals of both sexes and of all ages, give rise to a barrack discipline, which is elaborated into a complete system in the

[6] D. Urquhart (1855), p. 119.
[7] "The Master Spinners' and Manufacturers' Defence Fund. Report of the Committee" (1854), p. 17.

From Capital

factory, and which fully develops the before mentioned labour of overlooking, thereby dividing the workpeople into operatives and overlookers, into private soldiers and sergeants of an industrial army. "The main difficulty [in the automatic factory] . . . lay . . . above all in training human beings to renounce their desultory habits of work, and to identify themselves with the unvarying regularity of the complex automaton. To devise and administer a successful code of factory discipline, suited to the necessities of factory diligence, was the Herculean enterprise, the noble achievement of Arkwright! Even at the present day, when the system is perfectly organised and its labour lightened to the utmost, it is found nearly impossible to convert persons past the age of puberty, into useful factory hands."[8] The factory code in which capital formulates, like a private legislator, and at his own good will, his autocracy over his workpeople, unaccompanied by that division of responsibility, in other matters so much approved of by the bourgeoisie, and unaccompanied by the still more approved representative system, this code is but the capitalistic caricature of that social regulation of the labour process which becomes requisite in cooperation on a great scale, and in the employment in common, of instruments of labour and especially of machinery. The place of the slave driver's lash is taken by the overlooker's book of penalties. All punishments naturally resolve themselves into fines and deductions from wages, and the law-giving talent of the factory Lycurgus so arranges matters that a violation of his laws is, if possible, more profitable to him than the keeping of them.

. . .

[8] Ure (1835), p. 15.

CHAPTER 3

From *Risk, Uncertainty, and Profit*

FRANK KNIGHT

Frank Knight (1885–1972) was born in McLean County, Illinois. He received a Ph.D. degree from Cornell University in 1916. When *Risk, Uncertainty and Profit* was published in 1921, he was Associate Professor of Economics at the State University of Iowa. He later became Morton D. Hall Distinguished Service Professor of Social Science and Philosophy at the University of Chicago.

Structures and methods for meeting uncertainty

(From chapter 8)

. . .

It is therefore seen that the insurance principle can be applied even in the almost complete absence of scientific data for the computation of rates. . . .

. . . The fact which limits the application of the insurance principle to business risks generally is not therefore their inherent uniqueness alone, and the subject calls for further examination. This task will be undertaken in detail in the next chapter, which deals with entrepreneurship. At this point we may anticipate to the extent of making two observations: first, the typical uninsurable (because unmeasurable and this because unclassifiable) business risk relates to the exercise of judgment in the making of decisions by the business man; second, although such estimates do tend to fall into groups within which fluctuations cancel out and hence to approach constancy and measurability, this happens only *after the fact* and, especially in view of the brevity of a

Excerpted from Frank Knight, *Risk, Uncertainty and Profit*. New York: Houghton Mifflin Co., 1921; eighth impression published by Kelley and Millman, New York, 1957.

man's active life, can only to a limited extent be made the basis of prediction. Furthermore, the classification or grouping can only to a limited extent be carried out by any agency outside the person himself who makes the decisions because of the peculiarly obstinate connection of a *moral hazard* with this sort of risks. The decisive factors in the case are so largely on the inside of the person making the decisions that the "instances" are not amenable to objective description and external control.

Manifestly these difficulties, insuperable when the "consolidation" is to be carried out by an external agency such as an insurance company or association, fall away in so far as consolidation can be effected within the scale of operations of a single individual; and the same will be true of an organization if responsibility can be adequately centralized and unity of interest secured. The possibility of thus reducing uncertainty by transforming it into a measurable risk through grouping constitutes a strong incentive to extend the scale of operations of a business establishment. This fact must constitute one of the important causes of the phenomenal growth in the average size of industrial establishments which is a familiar characteristic of modern economic life. In so far as a single business man, by borrowing capital or otherwise, can extend the scope of his exercise of judgment over a greater number of decisions or estimates, there is a greater probability that bad guesses will be offset by good ones and that a degree of constancy and dependability in the total results will be achieved. In so far uncertainty is eliminated and the desideratum of rational activity realized.

Not less important is the incentive to substitute more effective and intimate forms of association for insurance, so as to eliminate or reduce the moral hazard and make possible the application of the insurance principle of consolidation to groups of ventures too broad in scope to be "swung" by a single enterpriser. Since it is capital which is especially at risk in operations based on opinions and estimates, the form of organization centers around the provisions relating to capital. It is undoubtedly true that the reduction of risk to borrowed capital is the principal desideratum leading to the displacement of individual enterprise by the partnership and the same fact with reference to both owned and borrowed capital explains the substitution of corporate organization for the partnership. The superiority of the higher form of organization over the lower from this point of view consists both in the extension of the scope of operations to include a larger number of individual decisions, ventures, or "instances," and in the more effective unification of interest which reduces the moral hazard connected with the assumption by one person of the consequences of another person's decisions.

The close connection between these two considerations is manifest. It is the special "risk" to which large amounts of capital loaned to a single enterpriser are subject which limits the scope of operations of this form of business unit by making it impossible to secure the necessary property resources. On the other hand, it is the inefficiency of organization, the failure to secure effective unity of interest, and the consequent large risk due to moral hazard when a partnership grows to considerable size, which in turn limit its extension to still larger magnitudes and bring about the substitution of the corporate form of organization. With the growth of large fortunes it becomes possible for a limited number of persons to carry on enterprises of greater and greater magnitude, and today we find many very large businesses organized as partnerships. Modifications of partnership law giving this form more of the flexibility of the corporation with reference to the distribution of rights of control, of participation in income, and of title to assets in case of dissolution have also contributed to this change.

With reference to the first of our two points above mentioned, the extension of the scope of operations, the corporation may be said to have solved the organization problem. There appears to be hardly any limit to the magnitude of enterprise which it is possible to organize in this form, so far as mere ability to get the public to buy the securities is concerned. On the second score, however, the effective unification of interests, though the corporation has accomplished much in comparison with other forms of organization, there is still much to be desired. Doubtless the task is impossible, in any absolute sense; nothing but a revolutionary transformation in human nature itself can apparently solve this problem finally, and such a change would, of course, obliterate all moral hazards at once, without organization. In the meanwhile the internal problems of the corporation, the protection of its various types of members and adherents against each other's predatory propensities, are quite as vital as the external problem of safeguarding the public interests against exploitation by the corporation as a unit.

Another important aspect of the relations of corporate organization to risk involves what we have called "diffusion" as well as consolidation. The minute divisibility of ownership and ease of transfer of shares enables an investor to distribute his holdings over a large number of enterprises in addition to increasing the size of a single enterprise. The effect of this distribution on risk is evidently twofold. In the first place, there is to the investor a further offsetting through consolidation; the losses and gains in different corporations in which he owns stock must tend to cancel out in large measure and provide a higher degree of regularity and predictability in his total returns. And again, the chance of loss of a small fraction of his total resources is of less moment even proportionally than a chance of losing a larger part.

. . .

Enterprise and profit

(From chapter 9)   ·

. . .

When uncertainty is present and the task of deciding what to do and how to do it takes the ascendancy over that of execution, the internal organization of the productive groups is no longer a matter of indifference or a mechanical detail.[1] Centralization of this deciding and controlling function is imperative; a process of "cephalization," such as has taken place in the evolution of organic life, is inevitable, and for the same reasons as in the case of biological evolution. Let us consider this process and the circumstances which condition it. The order of attack on the problem is suggested by the classification worked out in Chapter VII of the elements in uncertainty in regard to which men may in large measure differ independently.

In the first place, occupations differ in respect to the kind and amount of knowledge and judgment required for their successful direction as well as in the kind of abilities and tastes adapted to the routine operation. Productive groups or establishments now compete for managerial capacity as well as skill, and a considerable rearrangement of personnel is the natural result. The final adjustment will place each producer in the place where his particular combination of the two kinds of attributes seems to be most effective.

But a more important change is the tendency of the groups themselves to specialize, finding the individuals with the greatest managerial capacity of the requisite kinds and placing them in charge of the work of the group, submitting the activities of the other members to their direction and control. It need hardly be mentioned explicitly that the organization of industry depends on the fundamental fact that the intelligence of one person can be made to direct in a general way the routine manual and mental operations of others. It will also be taken into account that men differ in their powers of effective control over other men as well as in intellectual capacity to decide what should be done. In addition, there must come into play the diversity among men in degree of confidence in their judgment and powers and in disposition to act on their opinions, to "venture." This fact is responsible for the most fundamental change of all in the form of organization, the system under which the confident and venturesome "assume the risk" or "insure" the doubtful and timid by guaranteeing to the latter a specified income in return for an assignment of the actual results.

[1] See above, Chapter IV, p. 106, note. [ed: in the book from which this excerpt is taken]

Uncertainty thus exerts a fourfold tendency to select men and specialize functions: (1) an adaptation of men to occupations on the basis of kind of knowledge and judgment; (2) a similar selection on the basis of degree of foresight, for some lines of activity call for this endowment in a very different degree from others; (3) a specialization within productive groups, the individuals with superior managerial ability (foresight and capacity of ruling others) being placed in control of the group and the others working under their direction; and (4) those with confidence in their judgment and disposition to "back it up" in action specialize in risk taking. The close relations obtaining among these tendencies will be manifest. We have not separated confidence and venturesomeness at all, since they act along parallel lines and are little more than phases of the same faculty – just as courage and the tendency to minimize danger are proverbially commingled in all fields, though they are separable in thought. In addition the tendencies number (3) and (4) operate together. With human nature as we know it, it would be impracticable or very unusual for one man to guarantee to another a definite result of the latter's actions without being given power to direct his work. And on the other hand the second party would not place himself under the direction of the first without such a guaranty. The result is a "double contract" of the type famous in the history of the evasion of usury laws. It seems evident also that the system would not work at all if good judgment were not in fact generally associated with confidence in one's judgment on the part both of himself and others. That is, men's judgment of their own judgment and of others' judgment as to both kind and grade must in the large be much more right than wrong.[2]

The result of this manifold specialization of function is *enterprise and the wage system of industry.* Its existence in the world is a direct result of the fact of uncertainty; our task in the remainder of this study is to examine this phenomenon in detail in its various phases and divers relations with the economic activities of man and the structure of society. It is not necessary or inevitable, not the only conceivable form or organization, but under certain conditions has certain advantages, and is capable of development in different degrees. The essence of enterprise is the specialization of the function of *responsible direction* of economic life, the neglected feature of which is the inseparability of these *two* elements, *responsibility* and *control.* Under the enterprise system, a special social class, the business men, direct economic activity; they are in the strict sense the producers, while the great mass of the population merely furnish them with productive services, placing their persons and their property at the disposal of this class; the entrepreneurs *also*

---

[2] The statement implies that a man's judgment has in an effective sense a true or objective value. This assumption will be justified by the further course of the argument.

guarantee to those who furnish productive services a fixed remuneration. Accurately to define these functions and trace them through the social structure will be a long task, for the specialization is never complete; but at the end of it we shall find that in a free society the two are essentially inseparable. Any degree of effective exercise of judgment, or making decisions, is in a free society coupled with a corresponding degree of uncertainty bearing, of taking the responsibility for those decisions.

. . .

CHAPTER 4

The use of knowledge in society

FRIEDRICH HAYEK

Friedrich Hayek (1899–1992) was born in Vienna, Austria. He earned degrees in law and politics at the University of Vienna in 1921 and 1923, and in 1940, he received a Doctor of Science degree in economics from the University of London. At the time of publication of this paper, he was Tooke Professor of Political Economy and Statistics at the London School of Economics. He later served as professor at the University of Chicago and the University of Frieburg. In 1974, he was awarded the Nobel Memorial Prize in Economic Science.

I

What is the problem we wish to solve when we try to construct a rational economic order?

On certain familiar assumptions the answer is simple enough. *If* we possess all the relevant information, *if* we can start out from a given system of preferences, and *if* we command complete knowledge of available means, the problem which remains is purely one of logic. That is, the answer to the question of what is the best use of the available means is implicit in our assumptions. The conditions which the solution of this optimum problem must satisfy have been fully worked out and can be stated best in mathematical form: put at their briefest, they are that the marginal rates of substitution between any two commodities or factors must be the same in all their different uses.

This, however, is emphatically *not* the economic problem which society faces. And the economic calculus which we have developed to solve this logical problem, though an important step toward the solution of the economic problem of society, does not yet provide an answer to it. The reason for this is that the "data" from which the economic calculus starts are never for the whole society "given" to a single mind which could work out the implications, and can never be so given.

Reprinted in abridged form from Friedrich Hayek, "The Use of Knowledge in Society," *The American Economic Review*, 35 (1945): 519–30, by permission of the editors.

The peculiar character of the problem of a rational economic order is determined precisely by the fact that the knowledge of the circumstances of which we must make use never exists in concentrated or integrated form but solely as the dispersed bits of incomplete and frequently contradictory knowledge which all the separate individuals possess. The economic problem of society is thus not merely a problem of how to allocate "given" resources – if "given" is taken to mean given to a single mind which deliberately solves the problem set by these "data." It is rather a problem of how to secure the best use of resources known to any of the members of society for ends whose relative importance only these individuals know. Or, to put it briefly, it is a problem of the utilization of knowledge not given to anyone in its totality.

This character of the fundamental problem has, I am afraid, been rather obscured than illuminated by many of the recent refinements of economic theory, particularly by many of the uses made of mathematics. Though the problem with which I want primarily to deal in this paper is the problem of a rational economic organization, I shall in its course be led again and again to point to its close connections with certain methodological questions. Many of the points I wish to make are indeed conclusions toward which diverse paths of reasoning have unexpectedly converged. But as I now see these problems, this is no accident. It seems to me that many of the current disputes with regard to both economic theory and economic policy have their common origin in a misconception about the nature of the economic problem of society. This misconception in turn is due to an erroneous transfer to social phenomena of the habits of thought we have developed in dealing with the phenomena of nature.

II

In ordinary language we describe by the word "planning" the complex of interrelated decisions about the allocation of our available resources. All economic activity is in this sense planning; and in any society in which many people collaborate, this planning, whoever does it, will in some measure have to be based on knowledge which, in the first instance, is not given to the planner but to somebody else, which somehow will have to be conveyed to the planner. The various ways in which the knowledge on which people base their plans is communicated to them is the crucial problem for any theory explaining the economic process. And the problem of what is the best way of utilizing knowledge initially dispersed among all the people is at least one of the main problems of economic policy – or of designing an efficient economic system.

The answer to this question is closely connected with that other question which arises here, that of *who* is to do the planning. It is about this question that all the dispute about "economic planning" centers. This is not a dispute about whether planning is to be done or not. It is a dispute as to whether planning is to be done centrally, by one authority for the whole economic system, or is to be divided among many individuals. Planning in the specific sense in which the term is used in contemporary controversy necessarily means central planning – direction of the whole economic system according to one unified plan. Competition, on the other hand, means decentralized planning by many separate persons. The halfway house between the two, about which many people talk but which few like when they see it, is the delegation of planning to organized industries, or, in other words, monopoly.

Which of these systems is likely to be more efficient depends mainly on the question, under which of them we can expect that fuller use will be made of the existing knowledge. And this, in turn, depends on whether we are more likely to succeed in putting at the disposal of a single central authority all the knowledge which ought to be used but which is initially dispersed among many different individuals, or in conveying to the individuals such additional knowledge as they need in order to enable them to fit their plans in with those of others.

. . .

IV

If it is fashionable today to minimize the importance of the knowledge of the particular circumstances of time and place, this is closely connected with the smaller importance which is now attached to change as such. Indeed, there are few points on which the assumptions made (usually only implicitly) by the "planners" differ from those of their opponents as much as with regard to the significance and frequency of changes which will make substantial alterations of production plans necessary. Of course, if detailed economic plans could be laid down for fairly long periods in advance and then closely adhered to, so that no further economic decisions of importance would be required, the task of drawing up a comprehensive plan governing all economic activity would appear much less formidable.

It is, perhaps, worth stressing that economic problems arise always and only in consequence of change. So long as things continue as before, or at least as they were expected to, there arise no new problems requiring a decision, no need to form a new plan. The belief that changes, or at least day-to-day adjustments, have become less important in modern times implies the contention that economic problems also have become less important. This belief in the decreasing importance of change is, for that reason, usually held by the same people who argue that the importance of economic considerations has been driven into the background by the growing importance of technological knowledge.

Is it true that, with the elaborate apparatus of modern production, economic decisions are required only at long intervals, as when a new factory is to be erected or a new process to be introduced? Is it true that, once a plant has been built, the rest is all more or less mechanical, determined by the character of the plant, and leaving little to be changed in adapting to the ever-changing circumstances of the moment?

The fairly widespread belief in the affirmative is not, so far as I can ascertain, borne out by the practical experience of the business man. In a competitive industry at any rate – and such an industry alone can serve as a test – the task of keeping cost from rising requires constant struggle, absorbing a great part of the energy of the manager. How easy it is for an inefficient manager to dissipate the differentials on which profitability rests, and that it is possible, with the same technical facilities to produce with a great variety of costs, are among the commonplaces of business experience which do not seem to be equally familiar in the study of the economist. The very strength of the desire, constantly voiced by producers and engineers, to be able to proceed untrammeled by considerations of money costs, is eloquent testimony to the extent to which these factors enter into their daily work.

. . .

V

If we can agree that the economic problem of society is mainly one of rapid adaptation to changes in the particular circumstances of time and place, it would seem to follow that the ultimate decisions must be left to the people who are familiar with these circumstances, who know directly of the relevant changes and of the resources immediately available to meet them. We cannot expect that this problem will be solved by first communicating all this knowledge to a central board which, after integrating *all* knowledge, issues its orders. We must solve it by some form of decentralization. But this answers only part of our problem. We need decentralization because only thus can we ensure that the knowledge of the particular circumstances of time and place will be promptly used. But the "man on the spot" cannot decide solely on the basis of his limited but intimate knowledge of the facts of his immediate surroundings. There still remains the problem of communicating to him such further information as he needs to fit his decisions into the whole pattern of changes of the larger economic system.

How much knowledge does he need to do so successfully? Which of the events which happen beyond the horizon of his immediate knowledge are of relevance to his immediate decision, and how much of them need he know?

There is hardly anything that happens anywhere in the world that *might* not have an effect on the decision he ought to make. But he need not know of these events as such, nor of *all* their effects. It does not matter for him *why* at the particular moment more screws of one size than of another are wanted, *why* paper bags are more readily available than canvas bags, or *why* skilled labor, or particular machine tools, have for the moment become more difficult to acquire. All that is significant for him is *how much more or less* difficult to procure they have become compared with other things with which he is also concerned, or how much more or less urgently wanted are the alternative things he produces or uses. It is always a question of the relative importance of the particular things with which he is concerned, and the causes which alter their relative importance are of no interest to him beyond the effect on those concrete things of his own environment.

It is in this connection that what I have called the economic calculus proper helps us, at least by analogy, to see how this problem can be solved, and in fact is being solved, by the price system. Even the single controlling mind, in possession of all the data for some small, self-contained economic system, would not – every time some small adjustment in the allocation of resources had to be made – go explicitly through all the relations between ends and means which might possibly be affected. It is indeed the great contribution of the pure logic of choice that it has demonstrated conclusively that even such a single mind could solve this kind of problem only by constructing and constantly using rates of equivalence (or "values," or "marginal rates of substitution"), i.e., by attaching to each kind of scarce resource a numerical index which cannot be derived from any property possessed by that particular thing, but which reflects, or in which is condensed, its significance in view of the whole means–end structure. In any small change he will have to consider only these quantitative indices (or "values") in which all the relevant information is concentrated; and by adjusting the quantities one by one, he can appropriately rearrange his dispositions without having to solve the whole puzzle *ab initio,* or without needing at any stage to survey it at once in all its ramifications.

Fundamentally, in a system where the knowledge of the relevant facts is dispersed among many people, prices can act to coordinate the separate actions of different people in the same way as subjective values help the individual to coordinate the parts of his plan. It is worth contemplating for a moment a very simple and commonplace instance of the action of the price system to see what precisely it accomplishes. Assume that somewhere in the world a new opportunity for the use of some raw material, say tin, has arisen or that one of the sources of supply of tin has been eliminated. It does not matter for our purpose – and it is very significant that it does not matter – which of these two causes has made tin more scarce. All that the users of tin need to know is that some of the tin they used to consume is now more profitably employed elsewhere, and that in consequence they must economize tin. There is no need for the great majority of them even to know where the more urgent need has arisen or in favor of what other needs they ought to husband the supply. If only some of them know directly of the new demand, and switch resources over to it, and if the people who are aware of the new gap thus created in turn fill it from still other sources, the effect will rapidly spread throughout the whole economic system and influence not only all the uses of tin but also those of its substitutes and the substitutes of these substitutes, the supply of all the things made of tin, and their substitutes, and so on; and all this without the great majority of those instrumental in bringing about these substitutions knowing anything at all about the original cause of these changes. The whole acts as one market, not because any of its members survey the whole field, but because their limited individual fields of vision sufficiently overlap so that through many intermediaries the relevant information is communicated to all. The mere fact that there is one price for any commodity – or rather that local prices are connected in a manner determined by the cost of transport, etc. – brings about the solution which (it is just conceptually possible) might have been arrived at by one single mind possessing all the information which is in fact dispersed among all the people involved in the process.

. . .

CHAPTER 5

Relational exchange: economics and complex contracts

VICTOR GOLDBERG

Victor Goldberg was born in 1941 in Washington, D.C. He received a
Ph.D. in economics at Yale University in 1970. At the time of publication of this paper, he was Professor of Economics at the University of
California, Davis. He is currently Thomas J. Maciore Professor of Law
at Columbia University.

For the past few decades the primary thrust of microeconomic theory has been
to abstract from real-world complexity and to focus on the workings of impersonal markets. While that line of analysis has been highly productive, the
great emphasis on impersonal markets has not been without cost. The standard paradigm influences the direction of research, suggesting certain questions and ignoring others. It does not, for example, help us discover why
certain activities are carried on within firms rather than in the impersonal
markets. Moreover, it provides wrong or misleading answers to other questions. Why do we observe sharing contracts, cost-plus pricing, or sticky
wages? In recent years a countermovement has developed emphasizing the
costs of the current focus and the virtues of explicitly confronting those issues
that have been abstracted from. This new literature has not, in general, entailed a rejection of standard microeconomics. Rather it has complemented it.

This new literature is still in its infancy and its jargon, not surprisingly, is in
disarray. The contributors have labeled their work the new institutionalism,
markets and hierarchies, the transactions cost–, property rights–, obligational
markets–, administered contracts–, or relational exchange–approach. I will
try to sweep aside terminological quibbles and force on the various approaches a common language. Taking an author's prerogative, I will use my
own – relational exchange.[1]

In the following section I will present the essential elements of the relational exchange framework. The following sections will consider some of the

Reprinted in abridged form from Victor Goldberg, "Relational Exchange: Economics and
Complex Contracts," *American Behavioral Scientist,* 23, no. 3 (January/February 1980): 337–
52. Copyright© 1980 by Sage Publications. Reprinted by permission of Sage Publications, Inc.

[1] In fact, it is borrowed from Ian Macneil (1974). In earlier papers I used the administered
contracts nomenclature (see Goldberg, 1976, 1977, 1979). See also Williamson (1975), Wachter
and Williamson (1978); Klein, Crawford, and Alchian (1978); Alchian and Demsetz (1972);
Cheung (1969); and Jensen and Meckling (1976b).

implications of this approach for regulation, macroeconomics, and antitrust. Concluding remarks follow.

Relational exchange

We begin with an obvious empirical fact. Much economic activity takes place within long-term, complex, perhaps multiparty contractual (or contractlike) relationships; behavior is, in varying degrees, sheltered from market forces. The implicit contract of utility regulation, the contractual network that constitutes a firm, franchise agreements, pensions, and collective bargaining agreements are examples. Granted this, we can then proceed along two different lines. First, we can attempt to explain why relationships take the form that they do; why does a particular firm own its retail outlets rather than selling through franchised outlets or discount stores? Second, what impact does the relationship's structure have beyond the relationship? Do the price adjustment rules used in employment contracts or in regulated industries give the wrong short-run signals thereby exacerbating unemployment? Since economists attempt both to explain and prescribe, these questions can also be recast in normative terms: How should parties structure their relationships (from the point of view of the parties or other groups – perhaps society as a whole)?

To make headway in understanding the essential features of relational exchange it is convenient to set up a stylized problem. Consider two parties contemplating entering into a contract who must establish rules to structure their future relationship. The parties can have competing alternatives both at the formation stage and within the relationship. The choice of rules will depend upon the anticipated outcomes. The choice will also reflect three significant facts about the world that are so obvious that only an economist would feel compelled to recognize them explicitly. First, people are not omniscient; their information is imperfect and improvable only at a cost. Second, not all people are saints all of the time; as the relationship unfolds there will be opportunities for one party to take advantage of the other's vulnerability, to engage in strategic behavior, or to follow his own interests at the expense of the other party. The actors will, on occasion, behave opportunistically. Third, the parties cannot necessarily rely on outsiders to enforce the agreement cheaply and accurately.

If we assume that the agreement reflects the balancing of the parties' interests given the tools available, the efficacy of those tools in different contexts, and the constraints facing the decision makers, then we have the framework for a predictive model. Under conditions M we should expect to observe structure N; or if we observe structure N, then we should expect to find conditions M. This is, of course, an overly mechanical representation. A

73

more modest formulation is that the agreements reflect the purposive behavior of the parties.

The relational exchange framework directs attention to a number of concerns often overlooked in standard microeconomics. It also suggests that in many contexts the significance of the static optimality sort of questions, with which economists typically deal, has been overrated. The parties will be willing to absorb a lot of apparent static inefficiency in pursuit of their relational goals.

Within the contract, each party makes expenditures, receives benefits, and confers benefits on the other party at various times. The timing of the streams of benefits and costs need not coincide. For example, X might have planted crops and contracted with Y for harvesting them. Or X might agree to paint Y's house with Y paying upon completion. If X had cheap, effective legal remedies available (or if he could rely on Y's need to maintain his reputation)[2] then the noncoincidence of the streams of costs and benefits to the parties would be immaterial. But if external enforcement is imperfect, X is vulnerable to being held up by Y.

If as the relationship unfolds the costs incurred by X are much greater than the benefits he has received (as in the harvesting example), Y can convincingly threaten to breach the contract even though at this point Y has incurred no costs and received no benefits. Y could conceivably force X to revise the contract price down (or wage up) to the point at which X is indifferent between completing the agreement or terminating it. In the other case, X's vulnerability is even greater. Not only does he incur a cost before receiving payment, but Y also receives benefits before paying.

The vulnerability can, of course, be reduced by deliberately structuring the relationship to make the stream of benefits and costs for each party more nearly coincident. Progress payments (for custom-made capital goods or defense contracts) and instalment sales contracts are examples of such phased performance in which one party's performance consists of making payment. The parties' options are not restricted to adjusting the payment stream to a fixed production schedule. The timing of production as well as the techniques used in production (e.g., less fixed, specialized capital), and the characteristics of the output (e.g., greater standardization) can all be altered to enhance the contract's enforceability.

Suppose that one party has to make a considerable initial investment and that the value of the investment depends on continuation of the relationship. An employee investing in firm-specific capital is one example[3]; a second

---

[2] The discipline of future dealings, either with a particular party or with the market, is in many instances a more effective constraint on a party's behavior than is the formal law.

[3] Learning how to use an information-processing system that is unique to a single firm would

would be an electric utility building a plant to serve a particular area. Both will be reluctant to incur the high initial costs without some assurance of subsequent rewards. Other things equal, the firmer that assurance the more attractive the investment. So, for example, if the utility customers agree to give it the exclusive right to serve them for twenty years, then the utility would find construction of a long-lived plant more attractive than if it did not have such assurance. Of course, if a new, superior technology were likely to appear within three years, the customers would not want the long-lived plant built. Nevertheless, there will be lots of instances in which the parties will find it efficacious to protect one party's reliance on the continuation of the relationship.

Since circumstances will change in ways not anticipated at the formation stage, the parties will desire some means for adjusting the relationship to take those new circumstances into account. As an example, consider a contract in which X agrees to build a custom-made machine for Y who will use it to produce a new product. Before the machine's construction is completed, Y decides that marketing the new product will be unprofitable and wants to cancel its order. Ideally, X would want some mechanism in the contract which would require that Y take his reliance into account when weighing the merits of continuation versus breach. (Likewise, Y would want X to take into account his costs of continuing if X had the legal right to enforce the initial agreement.) If the parties acted totally in good faith – if we assume no opportunistic behavior – then this does not present a problem. They can simply inform each other of the costs of continuation versus breach (accurately, by assumption), choose the optimal strategy, and divide in some manner the benefits or costs arising from this optimal solution. But, of course, both X and Y will have incentives to be less than completely honest. The spectre of opportunistic behavior hangs over the relationship. If the parties cannot draw upon a reservoir of trust or rely on the discipline of future dealings, they will require some mechanisms for balancing the reliance and flexibility interests.

The parties must establish some sort of governance mechanism for the relationship. The initial agreement will, in general, be neither self-enforcing nor self-adjusting. Prices (deductibles and co-payments in insurance contracts for example) and simple adjustment rules (like indexing) can, of course, be used to influence the parties' behavior. These passive devices can be supplemented by – or supplanted by – more activist forms of governance. These activist forms include extensive monitoring or policing of behavior to detect

---

be an example. The skill is valuable so long as the worker remains with the firm; if he were fired that skill would be worthless and the time spent acquiring it goes for nought.

and punish violations of the agreement. In addition, it will often be advantageous to postpone decisions until more facts are known and to assign to someone the task of making that future decision. If that someone is one of the parties, this arrangement can be characterized as establishing an authority relationship – the decider has authority over the future behavior of the other party (see Simon, 1951). X agrees that Y can tell him what to do. The question of the scope of Y's authority can be a source of great friction as those familiar with labor history can attest.

Because standard microeconomics emphasizes market exchange and suppresses consideration of behavior that occurs within relationships sheltered from market forces, economists have tended to view elements that facilitate such sheltering with hostility and suspicion. The spirit of the relational exchange approach is quite different. It recognizes that the sheltering is inevitable and, moreover, that it can be functional. Contracting parties will often find it in their mutual interest to increase the isolation of at least one of them from alternatives – to make it more difficult (costly) to leave this particular relationship. To protect X's reliance, for example, the parties would want to make exit expensive for Y. Or, as a second example, A's ability to exercise authority over B can be enhanced if he can threaten to impose costs on a recalcitrant B; that threat can be made credible by making termination costly for B. The relational exchange approach focuses our attention on the reasons why parties might want to erect exit barriers and on the rich array of institutional devices which might be utilized for that purpose.

The organizing theme of much of the new literature is "efficiency." People will adopt certain arrangements because these are more efficient than alternatives, given the opportunities and difficulties confronting them. The analysis need not, however, be an apology for existing institutions: Whatever is, is right. Efficiency is contextual. Given the social context, the parties will attempt to arrange their affairs as best they can. If the context were different, then the efficient structure would also differ. So, to take an extreme example, one might argue that in the best of all possible worlds collective bargaining agreements would be inefficient; but they might be an intelligent (efficient) response in a world characterized by the threat of labor violence.[4] At a different level of analysis, we can take the existence of collective bargaining as given – it is part of the social context. We need not worry about whether it is good, bad, efficient, stupid, or immoral. It simply is. Granted that, we can then ask such questions as: Will increased job security for union members result in predictable changes in the organization of work? For example, will employers now invest more heavily in giving workers firm-specific skills and

---

[4] I develop this point at some length in Goldberg (1980b). This approach runs the risk of becoming an empty tautology. It should be viewed as a plausible research strategy rather than as a more grandiose statement about social institutions.

76

redesign the production process to take advantage of these skilled workers? Or we might investigate the techniques employed to govern the relationship (less authority, more "due process" or "voice"). Likewise, on the prescriptive level, we will be led to search for mechanisms for adjusting ongoing relationships to changing conditions, and other problems foreign to the world of conventional economic theory.

. . .

CHAPTER 6

From *The Visible Hand*

ALFRED CHANDLER

Alfred Chandler was born in 1918 in Guyencourt, Delaware. He received a Ph.D. degree from Harvard University in 1952. He is Strauss Professor of Business History, Emeritus, at Harvard Business School. *The Visible Hand* was awarded the Bancroft and Pulitzer prizes.

Introduction: the visible hand

The title of this book indicates its theme but not its focus or purpose. Its purpose is to examine the changing processes of production and distribution in the United States and the ways in which they have been managed. To achieve this end it focuses on the business enterprise that carried out these processes. Because the large enterprise administered by salaried managers replaced the small traditional family firm as the primary instrument for managing production and distribution, the book concentrates specifically on the rise of modern business enterprise and its managers. It is a history of a business institution and a business class.

The theme propounded here is that modern business enterprise took the place of market mechanisms in coordinating the activities of the economy and allocating its resources. In many sectors of the economy the visible hand of management replaced what Adam Smith referred to as the invisible hand of market forces. The market remained the generator of demand for goods and services, but modern business enterprise took over the functions of coordinating flows of goods through existing processes of production and distribution, and of allocating funds and personnel for future production and distribution. As modern business enterprise acquired functions hitherto carried out by the market, it became the most powerful institution in the American economy and its managers the most influential group of economic decision makers. The rise of modern business enterprise in the United States, therefore, brought with it managerial capitalism.

From The Visible Hand

Modern business enterprise defined

Modern business enterprise is easily defined. . . . It has two specific characteristics: it contains many distinct operating units and it is managed by a
hierarchy of salaried executives.

Each unit within the modern multiunit enterprise has its own administrative
office. Each is administered by a full-time salaried manager. Each has its own
set of books and accounts which can be audited separately from those of the
large enterprise. Each could theoretically operate as an independent business
enterprise.

In contrast, the traditional American business firm was a single-unit business enterprise. In such an enterprise an individual or a small number of
owners operated a shop, factory, bank, or transportation line out of a single
office. Normally this type of firm handled only a single economic function,
dealt in a single product line, and operated in one geographic area. Before the
rise of the modern firm, the activities of one of these small, personally owned
and managed enterprises were coordinated and monitored by market and price
mechanisms.

Modern enterprise, by bringing many units under its control, began to
operate in different locations, often carrying on different types of economic
activities and handling different lines of goods and services. The activities of
these units and the transactions between them thus became internalized. They
became monitored and coordinated by salaried employees rather than market
mechanisms.

Modern business enterprise, therefore, employs a hierarchy of middle and
top salaried managers to monitor and coordinate the work of the units under
its control. Such middle and top managers form an entirely new class of
businessmen. Some traditional single-unit enterprises employed managers
whose activities were similar to those of the lowest level managers in a
modern business enterprise. Owners of plantations, mills, shops, and banks
hired salaried employees to administer or assist them in administering the
unit. As the work within single operating units increased, these managers
employed subordinates – foremen, drivers, and mates – to supervise the
workforce. But as late as 1840 there were no middle managers in the United
States – that is, there were no managers who supervised the work of other
managers. At that time nearly all top managers were owners; they were either
partners or major stockholders in the enterprise they managed.

The multiunit enterprise administered by a set of salaried middle and top
managers can then properly be termed modern. Such enterprises did not exist
in the United States in 1840. By World War I this type of firm had become the
dominant business institution in many sectors of the American economy. By
the middle of the twentieth century, these enterprises employed hundreds and

79

even thousands of middle and top managers who supervised the work of dozens and often hundreds of operating units employing tens and often hundreds of thousands of workers. These enterprises were owned by tens or hundreds of thousands of shareholders and carried out billions of dollars of business annually. Even a relatively small business enterprise operating in local or regional markets had its top and middle managers. Rarely in the history of the world has an institution grown to be so important and so pervasive in so short a period of time.

. . .

Before I enter the complexities of the historical experience, it seems wise to outline a list of general propositions to make more precise the primary concerns of the study. They give some indication at the outset of the nature of modern business enterprise and suggest why the visible hand of management replaced the invisible hand of market mechanisms. I set these forth as a guide through the intricate history of interrelated institutional changes that follows.

The first proposition is that modern multiunit business enterprise replaced small traditional enterprise when administrative coordination permitted greater productivity, lower costs, and higher profits than coordination by market mechanisms.

This proposition is derived directly from the definition of a modern business enterprise. Such an enterprise came into being and continued to grow by setting up or purchasing business units that were theoretically able to operate as independent enterprises – in other words, by internalizing the activities that had been or could be carried on by several business units and the transactions that had been or could be carried on between them.

Such an internalization gave the enlarged enterprise many advantages.[1] By routinizing the transactions between units, the costs of these transactions were lowered. By linking the administration of producing units with buying and distributing units, costs for information on markets and sources of supply were reduced. Of much greater significance, the internalization of many units permitted the flow of goods from one unit to another to be administratively coordinated. More effective scheduling of flows achieved a more intensive use of facilities and personnel employed in the processes of production and distribution and so increased productivity and reduced costs. In addition,

---

[1] Ronald Coase (1937) provides a pioneering analysis of the reasons for internalizing of operating units. His work is expanded upon by Oliver Williamson, particularly in Williamson (1970), p. 7. Useful articles on coordination and allocation within the enterprise are Kenneth J. Arrow (1964), H. Leibenstein (1966), A. A. Alchian and H. Demsetz (1972), and G. B. Richardson (1972).

administrative coordination provided a more certain cash flow and more rapid payment for services rendered. The savings resulting from such coordination were much greater than those resulting from lower information and transactions costs.

The second proposition is simply that the advantages of internalizing the activities of many business units within a single enterprise could not be realized until a managerial hierarchy had been created.

Such advantages could be achieved only when a group of managers had been assembled to carry out the functions formerly handled by price and market mechanisms. Whereas the activities of single-unit traditional enterprises were monitored and coordinated by market mechanisms, the producing and distributing units within a modern business enterprise are monitored and coordinated by middle managers. Top managers, in addition to evaluating and coordinating the work of middle managers, took the place of the market in allocating resources for future production and distribution. In order to carry out these functions, the managers had to invent new practices and procedures which in time became standard operating methods in managing American production and distribution.

Thus the existence of a managerial hierarchy is a defining characteristic of the modern business enterprise. A multiunit enterprise without such managers remains little more than a federation of autonomous offices. Such federations were formed to control competition between units or to assure enterprises of sources of raw materials or outlets for finished goods and services. The owners and managers of the autonomous units agreed on common buying, pricing, production, and marketing policies. If there were no managers, these policies were determined and enforced by legislative and judicial rather than administrative means. Such federations were often able to bring small reductions in information and transactions costs, but they could not lower costs through increased productivity. They could not provide the administrative coordination that became the central function of modern business enterprise.

The third proposition is that modern business enterprise appeared for the first time in history when the volume of economic activities reached a level that made administrative coordination more efficient and more profitable than market coordination.

Such an increase in volume of activity came with new technology and expanding markets. New technology made possible an unprecedented output and movement of goods. Enlarged markets were essential to absorb such output. Therefore modern business enterprise first appeared, grew, and continued to flourish in those sectors and industries characterized by new and advancing technology and by expanding markets. Conversely in those sectors and industries where technology did not bring a sharp increase in output and where markets remained small and specialized, administrative coordination was rarely more profitable than market coordination. In those areas modern business enterprise was late in appearing and slow in spreading.

The fourth proposition is that once a managerial hierarchy had been formed and had successfully carried out its function of administrative coordination, the hierarchy itself became a source of permanence, power, and continued growth.

In Werner Sombart's phrase, the modern business enterprise took on "a life of its own."[2] Traditional enterprises were normally short lived. They were almost always partnerships which were reconstituted or disbanded at the death or retirement of a partner. If a son carried on the father's business, he found new partners. Often the partnership was disbanded when one partner decided he wanted to work with another businessman. On the other hand, the hierarchies that came to manage the new multiunit enterprises had a permanence beyond that of any individual or group of individuals who worked in them. When a manager died, retired, was promoted, or left an office, another was ready and trained to take his place. Men came and went. The institution and its offices remained.

The fifth proposition is that the careers of the salaried managers who directed these hierarchies became increasingly technical and professional.

In these new business bureaucracies, as in other administrative hierarchies requiring specialized skills, selection and promotion became increasingly based on training, experience, and performance rather than on family relationship or money. With the coming of modern business enterprise, the businessman, for the first time, could conceive of a lifetime career involving a climb up the hierarchical ladder. In such enterprises, managerial training became increasingly longer and more formalized. Managers carrying out similar activities in different enterprises often had the same type of training and attended the same types of schools. They read the same journals and joined the same associations. They had an approach to their work that was closer to that of lawyers, doctors, and ministers than that of the owners and managers of small traditional business enterprises.

---

[2] Werner Sombart (1930), vol. III, p. 200. Though there is very little written on the nature of coordination and allocation of resources and activities within the firm, there is a vast literature on the bureaucratic nature of modern business enterprise and on the goals and motives of business managers. Almost none of this literature, however, looks at the historical development of managerial hierarchies or the role and functions of managers over a period of time.

The sixth proposition is that as the multiunit business enterprise grew in size and diversity and as its managers became more professional, the management of the enterprise became separated from its ownership.

The rise of modern business enterprise brought a new definition of the relationship between ownership and management and therefore a new type of capitalism to the American economy. Before the appearance of the multiunit firm, owners managed and managers owned. Even when partnerships began to incorporate, their capital stock stayed in the hands of a few individuals or families. These corporations remained single-unit enterprises which rarely hired more than two or three managers. The traditional capitalist firm can, therefore, be properly termed a personal enterprise.

From its very beginning, however, modern business enterprise required more managers than a family or its associates could provide. In some firms the entrepreneur and his close associates (and their families) who built the enterprise continued to hold the majority of stock. They maintained a close personal relationship with their managers, and they retained a major say in top management decisions, particularly those concerning financial policies, allocation of resources, and the selection of senior managers. Such a modern business enterprise may be termed an entrepreneurial or family one, and an economy or sectors of an economy dominated by such firms may be considered a system of entrepreneurial or family capitalism.

Where the creation and growth of an enterprise required large sums of outside capital, the relationship between ownership and management differed. The financial institutions providing the funds normally placed part-time representatives on the firm's board. In such enterprises, salaried managers had to share top management decisions, particularly those involving the raising and spending of large sums of capital, with representatives of banks and other financial institutions. An economy or sector controlled by such firms has often been termed one of financial capitalism.

In many modern business enterprises neither bankers nor families were in control. Ownership became widely scattered. The stockholders did not have the influence, knowledge, experience, or commitment to take part in the high command. Salaried managers determined long-term policy as well as managing short-term operating activities. They dominated top as well as lower and middle management. Such an enterprise controlled by its managers can properly be identified as managerial, and a system dominated by such firms is called managerial capitalism.

As family- and financier-controlled enterprises grew in size and age they became managerial. Unless the owners or representatives of financial houses became full-time career managers within the enterprise itself, they did not have the information, the time, or the experience to play a dominant role in top-level decisions. As members of the boards of directors they did hold veto power. They could say no, and they could replace the senior managers with other career managers; but they were rarely in a position to propose positive alternative solutions. In time, the part-time owners and financiers on the board normally looked on the enterprise in the same way as did ordinary stockholders. It became a source of income and not a business to be managed. Of necessity, they left current operations and future plans to the career administrators. In many industries and sectors of the American economy, managerial capitalism soon replaced family or financial capitalism.

The seventh proposition is that in making administrative decisions, career managers preferred policies that favored the long-term stability and growth of their enterprises to those that maximized current profits.

For salaried managers the continuing existence of their enterprises was essential to their lifetime careers. Their primary goal was to assure continuing use of and therefore continuing flow of material to their facilities. They were far more willing than were the owners (the stockholders) to reduce or even forego current dividends in order to maintain the long-term viability of their organizations. They sought to protect their sources of supplies and their outlets. They took on new products and services in order to make more complete use of existing facilities and personnel. Such expansion, in turn, led to the addition of still more workers and equipment. If profits were high, they preferred to reinvest them in the enterprise rather than pay them out in dividends. In this way the desire of the managers to keep the organization fully employed became a continuing force for its further growth.

The eighth and final proposition is that as the large enterprises grew and dominated major sectors of the economy, they altered the basic structure of these sectors and of the economy as a whole.

The new bureaucratic enterprises did not, it must be emphasized, replace the market as the primary force in generating goods and services. The current decisions as to flows and the long-term ones as to allocating resources were based on estimates of current and long-term market demand. What the new enterprises did do was to take over from the market the coordination and integration of the flow of goods and services from the production of raw materials through the several processes of production to the sale to the ultimate consumer. Where they did so, production and distribution came to be concentrated in the hands of a few large enterprises. At first this occurred in only a few sectors or industries where technological innovation and market growth created high-speed and high-volume throughput. As technology became more sophisticated and as markets expanded, administrative coordination replaced market coordination in an increasingly larger portion of the economy. By the middle of the twentieth century the salaried managers of a relatively small number of large mass-producing, large mass-retailing, and large mass-transporting enterprises coordinated current flows of goods through the processes of production and distribution and allocated the resources to be used for future production and distribution in major sectors of the American economy. By then, the managerial revolution in American business had been carried out.[3]

These basic propositions fall into two parts. The first three help to explain the initial appearance of modern business enterprise: why it began when it did, where it did, and in the way it did. The remaining five concern its continuing growth: where, how, and why an enterprise once started continued to grow and to maintain its position of dominance. This institution appeared when managerial hierarchies were able to monitor and coordinate the activities of a number of business units more efficiently than did market mechanisms. It continued to grow so that these hierarchies of increasingly professional managers might remain fully employed. It emerged and spread, however, only in those industries and sectors whose technology and markets permitted administrative coordination to be more profitable than market coordination. Because these areas were at the center of the American economy and because professional managers replaced families, financiers, or their representatives as decision makers in these areas, modern American capitalism became managerial capitalism.

Historical realities are, of course, far more complicated than these general propositions suggest. Modern business enterprise and the new business class that managed it appeared, grew, and flourished in different ways even in the different sectors and in the different industries they came to dominate. Varying needs and opportunities meant that the specific substance of managerial tasks differed from one sector to another and from one industry to another. So too did the specific relationships between managers and owners. And once a managerial hierarchy was fully established, the sequence of its development varied from industry to industry and from sector to sector.

Nevertheless, these differences can be viewed as variations on a single theme. The visible hand of management replaced the invisible hand of market forces where and when new technology and expanded markets permitted a historically unprecedented high volume and speed of materials through the processes of production and distribution. Modern business enterprise was thus the institutional response to the rapid pace of technological innovation and increasing consumer demand in the United States during the second half of the nineteenth century.

---

[3] James Burnham (1941) who was the first to describe and analyze that phenomenon, gives in Chapter 7 a definition of the managerial class in American business but makes no attempt to describe the history of that class or the institution that brought it to power.

PART II

The scope of the firm

CHAPTER 7

The nature of the firm

RONALD COASE

Ronald Coase was born in Middlesex, England, in 1910. He received a
Bachelor's (B. Com.) degree from the University of London in 1932
and a Doctor of Science degree in economics from the same school in
1951. When this article was published, he was Assistant Lecturer at the
London School of Economics. He is currently Professor Emeritus of
Economics and Senior Fellow in Law and Economics at the University
of Chicago Law School. In 1991, he was awarded the Nobel Memorial
Prize in Economic Science.

Economic theory has suffered in the past from a failure to state clearly its
assumptions. Economists in building up a theory have often omitted to examine the foundations on which it was erected. This examination is, however,
essential not only to prevent the misunderstanding and needless controversy
which arise from a lack of knowledge of the assumptions on which a theory is
based, but also because of the extreme importance for economics of good
judgment in choosing between rival sets of assumptions. For instance, it is
suggested that the use of the word "firm" in economics may be different from
the use of the term by the "plain man."[1] Since there is apparently a trend in
economic theory towards starting analysis with the individual firm and not
with the industry,[2] it is all the more necessary not only that a clear definition
of the word "firm" should be given but that its difference from a firm in the
"real world," if it exists, should be made clear. Mrs. Robinson has said that
"the two questions to be asked of a set of assumptions in economics are: Are
they tractable? and: Do they correspond with the real world?"[3] Though, as
Mrs. Robinson points out, "more often one set will be manageable and the
other realistic," yet there may well be branches of theory where assumptions
may be both manageable and realistic. It is hoped to show in the following
paper that a definition of a firm may be obtained which is not only realistic in
that it corresponds to what is meant by a firm in the real world, but is tractable
by two of the most powerful instruments of economic analysis developed by
Marshall, the idea of the margin and that of substitution, together giving the

Reprinted from Ronald Coase, "The Nature of the Firm," *Economica*, 4 (1937): 386–405, by
permission of the publisher.
[1]Joan Robinson (1932), p. 12.   [2]See N. Kaldor (1934).   [3]Kaldor (op. cit.), p. 6.

idea of substitution at the margin.[4] Our definition must, of course, "relate to formal relations which are capable of being *conceived* exactly."[5]

I

It is convenient if, in searching for a definition of a firm, we first consider the economic system as it is normally treated by the economist. Let us consider the description of the economic system given by Sir Arthur Salter.[6] "The normal economic system works itself. For its current operation it is under no central control; it needs no central survey. Over the whole range of human activity and human need, supply is adjusted to demand, and production to consumption, by a process that is automatic, elastic and responsive." An economist thinks of the economic system as being coordinated by the price mechanism and society becomes not an organization but an organism.[7] The economic system "works itself." This does not mean that there is no planning by individuals. These exercise foresight and choose between alternatives. This is necessarily so if there is to be order in the system. But this theory assumes that the direction of resources is dependent directly on the price mechanism. Indeed, it is often considered to be an objection to economic planning that it merely tries to do what is already done by the price mechanism.[8] Sir Arthur Salter's description, however, gives a very incomplete picture of our economic system. Within a firm, the description does not fit at all. For instance, in economic theory we find that the allocation of factors of production between different uses is determined by the price mechanism. The price of factor A becomes higher in X than in Y. As a result, A moves from Y to X until the difference between the prices in X and Y, except in so far as it compensates for other differential advantages, disappears. Yet in the real world, we find that there are many areas where this does not apply. If a workman moves from department Y to department X, he does not go because of a change in relative prices, but because he is ordered to do so. Those who object to economic planning on the grounds that the problem is solved by price movements can be answered by pointing out that there is planning within our economic system which is quite different from the individual planning mentioned above and which is akin to what is normally called economic planning. The example given above is typical of a large sphere in our modern economic system. Of course, this fact has not been ignored by economists. Marshall introduces organization as a fourth factor of production; J. B. Clark gives the coordinating function to the entrepreneur; Professor Knight introduces managers who coordinate. As D. H. Robertson points out, we find "islands of conscious power in this ocean of unconscious

[4]J. M. Keynes (1933), pp. 223–4.   [5]L. Robbins (1935), p. 63.
[6]This description is quoted with approval by D. H. Robertson (1930), p. 85, and by Arnold Plant (1932). It appears in *Allied Shipping Control*, pp. 16–17.
[7]See F. A. Hayek (1933).   [8]See F. A. Hayek (1933).

cooperation like lumps of butter coagulating in a pail of buttermilk."[9] But in view of the fact that it is usually argued that coordination will be done by the price mechanism, why is such organization necessary? Why are there these "island of conscious power"? Outside the firm, price movements direct production, which is coordinated through a series of exchange transactions on the market. Within a firm, these market transactions are eliminated and in place of the complicated market structure with exchange transactions is substituted the entrepreneur-coordinator, who directs production.[10] It is clear that these are alternative methods of coordinating production. Yet having regard to the fact that if production is regulated by price movements, production could be carried on without any organization at all, well might we ask, why is there any organization?

Of course, the degree to which the price mechanism is superseded varies greatly. In a department store, the allocation of the different sections to the various locations in the building may be done by the controlling authority or it may be the result of competitive price bidding for space. In the Lancashire cotton industry, a weaver can rent power and shop room and can obtain looms and yarn on credit.[11] This coordination of the various factors of production is, however, normally carried out without the intervention of the price mechanism. As is evident, the amount of "vertical" integration, involving as it does the supersession of the price mechanism, varies greatly from industry to industry and from firm to firm.

It can, I think, be assumed that the distinguishing mark of the firm is the supersession of the price mechanism. It is, of course, as Professor Robbins points out, "related to an outside network of relative prices and costs,"[12] but it is important to discover the exact nature of this relationship. This distinction between the allocation of resources in a firm and the allocation in the economic system has been very vividly described by Mr. Maurice Dobb when discussing Adam Smith's conception of the capitalist:

. . . It began to be seen that there was something more important than the relations inside each factory or unit captained by an undertaker; there were the relations of the undertaker with the rest of the economic world outside his immediate sphere . . . the undertaker busies himself with the division of labour inside each firm and he plans and organises consciously,

but

. . . he is related to the much larger economic specialisation of which he himself is merely one specialised unit. Here, he plays his part as a single cell in a larger organism, mainly unconscious of the wider role he fills.[13]

[9]D. H. Robertson (1930), p. 85.
[10]In the rest of this paper I shall use the term entrepreneur to refer to the person or persons who, in a competitive system, take the place of the price mechanism in the direction of resources.
[11]*Survey of Textile Industries*, p. 26.   [12]L. Robbins (1932), p. 71.
[13]Maurice Dobb (1925), p. 20 Cf.; also, Henderson, (1922), pp. 3–5.

⌐In view of the fact that while economists treat the price mechanism as a
coordinating instrument, they also admit the coordinating function of the
"entrepreneur," it is surely important to inquire why coordination is the work
of the price mechanism in one case and of the entrepreneur in another.⌐ The
purpose of this paper is to bridge what appears to be a gap in economic theory
between the assumption (made for some purposes) that resources are allocated
by means of the price mechanism and the assumption (made for other purposes) that this allocation is dependent on the entrepreneur-coordinator. We
have to explain the basis on which, in practice, this choice between alternatives is effected.[14]

II

Our task is to attempt to discover why a firm emerges at all in a specialized
exchange economy. The price mechanism (considered purely from the side of
the direction of resources) might be superseded if the relationship which
replaced it was desired for its own sake. This would be the case, for example,
if some people preferred to work under the direction of some other person.
Such individuals would accept less in order to work under someone, and firms
would arise naturally from this. But it would appear that this cannot be a very
important reason, for it would rather seem that the opposite tendency is
operating if one judges from the stress normally laid on the advantage of
"being one's own master."[15] Of course, if the desire was not to be controlled
but to control, to exercise power over others, then people might be willing to
give up something in order to direct others; that is, they would be willing to
pay others more than they could get under the price mechanism in order to be
able to direct them. But this implies that those who direct pay in order to be
able to do this and are not paid to direct, which is clearly not true in the
majority of cases.[16] Firms might also exist if purchasers preferred commodities which are produced by firms to those not so produced; but even in spheres
where one would expect such preferences (if they exist) to be of negligible

[14]It is easy to see when the State takes over the direction of an industry that, in planning it, it is
doing something which was previously done by the price mechanism. What is usually not realized
is that any business man in organizing the relations between his departments is also doing
something which could be organized through the price mechanism. There is therefore point in
Mr. Durbin's answer to those who emphasize the problems involved in economic planning that
the same problems have to be solved by business men in the competitive system. (See Durbin,
1936.) The important difference between these two cases is that economic planning is imposed on
industry while firms arise voluntarily because they represent a more efficient method of organizing production. In a competitive system, there is an "optimum" amount of planning!

[15]See Harry Dawes (1934), who instances "the trek to retail shopkeeping and insurance work
by the better paid of skilled men due to the desire (often the main aim in life of a worker) to be
independent" (p. 86).

[16]Nonetheless, this is not altogether fanciful. Some small shopkeepers are said to earn less than
their assistants.

importance, firms are to be found in the real world.[17] Therefore there must be other elements involved.

The main reason why it is profitable to establish a firm would seem to be that there is a cost of using the price mechanism. The most obvious cost of "organizing" production through the price mechanism is that of discovering what the relevant prices are.[18] This cost may be reduced, but it will not be eliminated, by the emergence of specialists who will sell this information. The costs of negotiating and concluding a separate contract for each exchange transaction which takes place on a market must also be taken into account.[19] Again, in certain markets, e.g., produce exchanges, a technique is devised for minimizing these contract costs; but they are not eliminated. It is true that contracts are not eliminated when there is a firm but they are greatly reduced. A factor of production (or the owner thereof) does not have to make a series of contracts with the factors with whom he is cooperating within the firm, as would be necessary, of course, if this cooperation were as a direct result of the working of the price mechanism. For this series of contracts is substituted one. At this stage, it is important to note the character of the contract into which a factor enters that is employed within a firm. The contract is one whereby the factor, for a certain remuneration (which may be fixed or fluctuating), agrees to obey the directions of an entrepreneur *within certain limits*.[20] The essence of the contract is that it should only state the limits to the powers of the entrepreneur. Within these limits, he can therefore direct the other factors of production.

There are, however, other disadvantages – or costs – of using the price mechanism. It may be desired to make a long-term contract for the supply of some article or service. This may be due to the fact that if one contract is made for a longer period, instead of several shorter ones, then certain costs of making each contract will be avoided. Or, owing to the risk attitude of the people concerned, they may prefer to make a long rather than a short-term contract. Now, owing to the difficulty of forecasting, the longer the period of the contract is for the supply of the commodity or service, the less possible, and indeed, the less desirable it is for the person purchasing to specify what the other contracting party is expected to do. It may well be a matter of indifference to the person supplying the service or commodity which of several courses of action is taken,

[17]G. F. Shove (1933), p. 116, note I, points out that such preferences may exist, although the example he gives is almost the reverse of the instance given in the text.

[18]According to N. Kaldor (1934), it is one of the assumptions of static theory that: "All the relevant prices are known to all individuals." But this is clearly not true of the real world.

[19]This influence was noted by Professor Usher when discussing the development of capitalism. He says: "The successive buying and selling of partly finished products were sheer waste of energy" (1921, p. 13). But he does not develop the idea nor consider why it is that buying and selling operations still exist.

[20]It would be possible for no limits to the powers of the entrepreneur to be fixed. This would be voluntary slavery. According to Professor Batt (1929), p. 18, such a contract would be void and unenforceable.

but not to the purchaser of that service or commodity. But the purchaser will not know which of these several courses he will want the supplier to take. Therefore, the service which is being provided is expressed in general terms, the exact details being left until a later date. All that is stated in the contract is the limits to what the persons supplying the commodity or service are expected to do. The details of what the supplier is expected to do are not stated in the contract but are decided later by the purchaser. When the direction of resources (within the limits of the contract) becomes dependent on the buyer in this way, that relationship which I term a "firm" may be obtained.[21] A firm is likely therefore to emerge in those cases where a very short-term contract would be unsatisfactory. It is obviously of more importance in the case of services – labor – than it is in the case of the buying of commodities. In the case of commodities, the main items can be stated in advance and the details which will be decided later will be of minor significance.

We may sum up this section of the argument by saying that the operation of a market costs something and by forming an organization and allowing some authority (an "entrepreneur") to direct the resources, certain marketing costs are saved. The entrepreneur has to carry out his function at less cost, taking into account the fact that he may get factors of production at a lower price than the market transactions which he supersedes, because it is always possible to revert to the open market if he fails to do this.

The question of uncertainty is one which is often considered to be very relevant to the study of the equilibrium of the firm. It seems improbable that a firm would emerge without the existence of uncertainty. But those, for instance, Professor Knight, who make the *mode of payment* the distinguishing mark of the firm – fixed incomes being guaranteed to some of those engaged in production by a person who takes the residual, and fluctuating, income – would appear to be introducing a point which is irrelevant to the problem we are considering. One entrepreneur may sell his services to another for a certain sum of money, while the payment to his employees may be mainly or wholly a share in profits.[22] The significant question would appear to be why the allocation of resources is not done directly by the price mechanism.

Another factor that should be noted is that exchange transactions on a market and the same transactions organized within a firm are often treated differently by governments or other bodies with regulatory powers. If we consider the operation of a sales tax, it is clear that it is a tax on market transactions and not on the same transactions organized within the firm. Now

[21]Of course, it is not possible to draw a hard and fast line which determines whether there is a firm or not. There may be more or less direction. It is similar to the legal question of whether there is the relationship of master and servant or principal and agent. See the discussion of this problem presented later.

[22]The views of Professor Knight are examined later in more detail.

since these are alternative methods of "organization" – by the price mechanism or by the entrepreneur – such a regulation would bring into existence firms which otherwise would have no raison d'être. It would furnish a reason for the emergence of a firm in a specialized exchange economy. Of course, to the extent that firms already exist, such a measure as a sales tax would merely tend to make them larger than they would otherwise be. Similarly, quota schemes, and methods of price control which imply that there is rationing, and which do not apply to firms producing such products for themselves, by allowing advantages to those who organize within the firm and not through the market, necessarily encourage the growth of firms. But it is difficult to believe that it is measures such as have been mentioned in this paragraph which have brought firms into existence. Such measures would, however, tend to have this result if they did not exist for other reasons.

These, then, are the reasons why organizations such as firms exist in a specialized exchange economy in which it is generally assumed that the distribution of resources is "organized" by the price mechanism. A firm, therefore, consists of the system of relationships which comes into existence when the direction of resources is dependent on an entrepreneur.

The approach which has just been sketched would appear to offer an advantage in that it is possible to give a scientific meaning to what is meant by saying that a firm gets larger or smaller. A firm becomes larger as additional transactions (which could be exchange transactions coordinated through the price mechanism) are organized by the entrepreneur and becomes smaller as he abandons the organization of such transactions. The question which arises is whether it is possible to study the forces which determine the size of the firm. Why does the entrepreneur not organize one less transaction or one more? It is interesting to note that Professor Knight considers that:

> . . . the relation between efficiency and size is one of the most serious problems of theory, being, in contrast with the relation for a plant, largely a matter of personality and historical accident rather than of intelligible general principles. But the question is peculiarly vital because the possibility of monopoly gain offers a powerful incentive to *continuous and unlimited* expansion of the firm, which force must be offset by some equally powerful one making for decreased efficiency (in the production of money income) with growth in size, if even boundary competition is to exist.[23]

Professor Knight would appear to consider that it is impossible to treat scientifically the determinants of the size of the firm. On the basis of the concept of the firm developed above, this task will now be attempted.

It was suggested that the introduction of the firm was due primarily to the existence of marketing costs. A pertinent question to ask would appear to be (quite apart from the monopoly considerations raised by Professor Knight),

[23]Frank Knight (1933).

why, if by organizing one can eliminate certain costs and in fact reduce the cost of production, are there any market transactions at all?[24] Why is not all production carried on by one big firm? There would appear to be certain possible explanations.

First, as a firm gets larger, there may be decreasing returns to the entrepreneur function, that is, the costs of organizing additional transactions within the firm may rise.[25] Naturally a point must be reached where the costs of organizing an extra transaction within the firm are equal to the costs involved in carrying out the transaction in the open market, or to the costs of organizing by another entrepreneur. Secondly, it may be that as the transactions which are organized increase, the entrepreneur fails to place the factors of production in the uses where their value is greatest, that is, fails to make the best use of the factors of production. Again, a point must be reached where the loss through the waste of resources is equal to the marketing costs of the exchange transaction in the open market or to the loss if the transaction was organized by another entrepreneur. Finally, the supply price of one or more of the factors of production may rise, because the "other advantages" of a small firm are greater than those of a large firm.[26] Of course, the actual point where the expansion of the firm ceases might be determined by a combination of the factors mentioned above. The first two reasons given most probably correspond to the economists' phrase of "diminishing returns to management."[27]

The point has been made in the previous paragraph that a firm will tend to expand until the costs of organizing an extra transaction within the firm become equal to the costs of carrying out the same transaction by means of an exchange on the open market or the costs of organizing in another firm. But if the firm stops its expansion at a point below the costs of marketing in the open market and at a point equal to the costs of organizing in another firm, in most cases (excluding the case of "combination"[28]), this will imply that there is a

---

[24]There are certain marketing costs which could only be eliminated by the abolition of "consumers' choice" and these are the costs of retailing. It is conceivable that these costs might be so high that people would be willing to accept rations because the extra product obtained was worth the loss of their choice.

[25]This argument assumes that exchange transactions on a market can be considered as homogeneous; which is clearly untrue in fact. This complication is taken into account later.

[26]For a discussion of the variation of the supply price of factors of production to firms of varying size, see E. A. G. Robinson (1931). It is sometimes said that the supply price of organizing ability increases as the size of the firm increases because men prefer to be the heads of small independent businesses rather than the heads of departments in a large business. See Jones (1927), p. 531, and Macgregor (1906), p. 63. This is a common argument of those who advocate rationalization. It is said that larger units would be more efficient, but owing to the individualistic spirit of the smaller entrepreneurs, they prefer to remain independent, apparently in spite of the higher income which their increased efficiency under rationalization makes possible.

[27]This discussion is, of course, brief and incomplete. For a more thorough discussion of this particular problem, see N. Kaldor (1934) and E. A. G. Robinson (1934).

[28]A definition of this term is given later.

market transaction between these two producers, each of whom could organize it at less than the actual marketing costs. How is the paradox to be resolved? If we consider an example the reason for this will become clear. Suppose A is buying a product from B and that both A and B could organize this marketing transaction at less than its present cost. B, we can assume, is not organizing one process or stage of production, but several. If A therefore wishes to avoid a market transaction, he will have to take over all the processes of production controlled by B. Unless A takes over all the processes of production, a market transaction will still remain, although it is a different product that is bought. But we have previously assumed that as each producer expands he becomes less efficient; the additional costs of organizing extra transactions increase. It is probable that A's cost of organizing the transactions previously organized by B will be greater than B's cost of doing the same thing. A therefore will take over the whole of B's organization only if his cost of organizing B's work is not greater than B's cost by an amount equal to the costs of carrying out an exchange transaction on the open market. But once it becomes economical to have a market transaction, it also pays to divide production in such a way that the cost of organizing an extra transaction in each firm is the same.

Up to now it has been assumed that the exchange transactions which take place through the price mechanism are homogeneous. In fact, nothing could be more diverse than the actual transactions which take place in our modern world. This would seem to imply that the costs of carrying out exchange transactions through the price mechanism will vary considerably as will also the costs of organizing these transactions within the firm. It seems therefore possible that, quite apart from the question of diminishing returns, the costs of organizing these transactions within the firm may be greater than the costs of carrying out the exchange transactions in the open market. This would necessarily imply that there were exchange transactions carried out through the price mechanism, but would it mean that there would have to be more than one firm? Clearly not, for all those areas in the economic system where the direction of resources was not dependent directly on the price mechanism could be organized within one firm. The factors which were discussed earlier would seem to be the important ones, though it is difficult to say whether "diminishing returns to management" or the rising supply price of factors is likely to be the more important.

Other things being equal, therefore, a firm will tend to be larger:

(a) the less the costs of organizing and the slower these costs rise with an increase in the transactions organized;

(b) the less likely the entrepreneur is to make mistakes and the smaller the increase in mistakes with an increase in the transactions organized;

(c) the greater the lowering (or the less the rise) in the supply price of factors of production to firms of larger size.

Apart from variations in the supply price of factors of production to firms of different sizes, it would appear that the costs of organizing and the losses through mistakes will increase with an increase in the spatial distribution of the transactions organized, in the dissimilarity of the transactions, and in the probability of changes in the relevant prices.[29] As more transactions are organized by an entrepreneur, it would appear that the transactions would tend to be either different in kind or in different places. This furnishes an additional reason why efficiency will tend to decrease as the firm gets larger. Inventions which tend to bring factors of production nearer together, by lessening spatial distribution, tend to increase the size of the firm.[30] Changes like the telephone and the telegraph which tend to reduce the cost of organizing spatially will tend to increase the size of the firm. All changes which improve managerial technique will tend to increase the size of the firm.[31] [32]

It should be noted that the definition of a firm which was given above can be used to give more precise meanings to the terms "combination" and "integration."[33] There is a combination when transactions which were previously organized by two or more entrepreneurs become organized by one. This becomes integration when it involves the organization of transactions which were previously carried out between the entrepreneurs on a market. A firm can expand in

[29]This aspect of the problem is emphasized by N. Kaldor (1934). Its importance in this connection had been previously noted by E. A. G. Robinson (1931), pp. 83–106. This assumes that an increase in the probability of price movements increases the costs of organizing within a firm more than it increases the cost of carrying out an exchange transaction on the market – which is probable.

[30]This would appear to be the importance of the treatment of the technical unit by E. A. G. Robinson (1931), pp. 27–33. The larger the technical unit, the greater the concentration of factors and therefore the firm is likely to be larger.

[31]It should be noted that most inventions will change both the costs of organizing and the costs of using the price mechanism. In such cases, whether the invention tends to make firms larger or smaller will depend on the relative effect on these two sets of costs. For instance, if the telephone reduces the costs of using the price mechanism more than it reduces the costs of organizing, then it will have the effect of reducing the size of the firm.

[32]An illustration of these dynamic forces is furnished by Maurice Dobb (1928), p. 68. "With the passing of bonded labour the factory, as an establishment where work was organised under the whip of the overseer, lost its raison d'être until this was restored to it with the introduction of power machinery after 1846." It seems important to realize that the passage from the domestic system to the factory system is not a mere historical accident but is conditioned by economic forces. This is shown by the fact that it is possible to move from the factory system to the domestic system, as in the Russian example, as well as vice versa. It is the essence of serfdom that the price mechanism is not allowed to operate. Therefore, there has to be direction from some organizer. When, however, serfdom passed, the price mechanism was allowed to operate. It was not until machinery drew workers into one locality that it paid to supersede the price mechanism and the firm again emerged.

[33]This is often called "vertical integration," combination being termed "lateral integration."

either or both of these two ways. The whole of the "structure of competitive industry" becomes tractable by the ordinary technique of economic analysis.

III

The problem which has been investigated in the previous section has not been entirely neglected by economists, and it is now necessary to consider why the reasons given above for the emergence of a firm in a specialized exchange economy are to be preferred to the other explanations which have been offered.

It is sometimes said that the reason for the existence of a firm is to be found in the division of labor. This is the view of Professor Usher, a view which has been adopted and expanded by Mr. Maurice Dobb. The firm becomes

. . . the result of an increasing complexity of the division of labour. . . . The growth of this economic differentiation creates the need for some integrating force without which differentiation would collapse into chaos; and it is as the integrating force in a differentiated economy that industrial forms are chiefly significant.[34]

The answer to this argument is an obvious one. The "integrating force in a differentiated economy" already exists in the form of the price mechanism. It is perhaps the main achievement of economic science that it has shown that there is no reason to suppose that specialization must lead to chaos.[35] The reason given by Mr. Maurice Dobb is therefore inadmissible. What has to be explained is why one integrating force (the entrepreneur) should be substituted for another integrating force (the price mechanism).

The most interesting reasons (and probably the most widely accepted) which have been given to explain this fact are those to be found in Professor Knight's *Risk, Uncertainty and Profit.* His views will be examined in some detail.

Professor Knight starts with a system in which there is no uncertainty:

. . . acting as individuals under absolute freedom but without collusion men are supposed to have organised economic life with the primary and secondary division of labour, the use of capital, etc., developed to the point familiar in present-day America. The principal fact which calls for the exercise of the imagination is the internal organisation of the productive groups or establishments. With uncertainty entirely absent, every individual being in possession of perfect knowledge of the situation, there would be no occasion for anything of the nature of responsible management or control of productive activity. Even marketing transactions in any realistic sense would not be found. The flow of raw materials and productive services to the consumer would be entirely automatic.[36]

[34]Maurice Dobb (1928), p. 10. Professor Usher's views are to be found in Usher (1921), pp. 1–18.
[35]Cf. J. B. Clark (1900), p. 19, who speaks of the theory of exchange as being the "theory of the organisation of industrial society."
[36]Frank Knight (1921), p. 267.

Professor Knight says that we can imagine this adjustment as being "the result of a long process of experimentation worked out by trial-and-error methods alone," while it is not necessary "to imagine every worker doing exactly the right thing at the right time in a sort of 'pre-established harmony' with the work of others. There might be managers, superintendents, etc., for the purpose of coordinating the activities of individuals," though these managers would be performing a purely routine function, "without responsibility of any sort."[37]

Professor Knight then continues:

With the introduction of uncertainty – the fact of ignorance and the necessity of acting upon opinion rather than knowledge – into this Eden-like situation, its character is entirely changed. . . . With uncertainty present, doing things, the actual execution of activity, becomes in a real sense a secondary part of life; the primary problem or function is deciding what to do and how to do it.[38]

This fact of uncertainty brings about the two most important characteristics of social organization.

In the first place, goods are produced for a market on the basis of entirely impersonal prediction of wants, not for the satisfaction of the wants of the producers themselves. The producer takes the responsibility of forecasting the consumers' wants. In the second place, the work of forecasting and at the same time a large part of the technological direction and control of production are still further concentrated upon a very narrow class of producers, and we meet with a new economic functionary, the entrepreneur. . . . When uncertainty is present and the task of deciding what to do and how to do it takes the ascendancy over that of execution the internal organisation of the productive groups is no longer a matter of indifference or a mechanical detail. Centralisation of this deciding and controlling function is imperative, a process of "cephalisation" is inevitable.[39]

The most fundamental change is:

. . . the system under which the confident and venturesome assume the risk or insure the doubtful and timid by guaranteeing to the latter a specified income in return for an assignment of the actual results. . . . With human nature as we know it, it would be impracticable or very unusual for one man to guarantee to another a definite result of the latter's actions without being given power to direct his work. And on the other hand the second party would not place himself under the direction of the first without such a guarantee. . . . The result of this manifold specialisation of function is the enterprise and wage system of industry. Its existence in the world is the direct result of the fact of uncertainty.[40]

These quotations give the essence of Professor Knight's theory. The fact of uncertainty means that people have to forecast future wants. Therefore, you get a special class springing up who direct the activities of others to whom

[37]Knight (1921), pp. 267–8.   [38]Knight (1921), p. 268.
[39]Knight (1921), pp. 268–95.   [40]Knight (1921), pp. 269–70.

they give guaranteed wages. It acts because good judgment is generally associated with confidence in one's judgment.[41]

Professor Knight would appear to leave himself open to criticism on several grounds. First of all, as he himself points out, the fact that certain people have better judgment or better knowledge does not mean that they can only get an income from it by themselves actively taking part in production. They can sell advice or knowledge. Every business buys the services of a host of advisers. We can imagine a system where all advice or knowledge was bought as required. Again, it is possible to get a reward from better knowledge or judgment not by actively taking part in production but by making contracts with people who are producing. A merchant buying for future delivery represents an example of this. But this merely illustrates the point that it is quite possible to give a guaranteed reward providing that certain acts are performed without directing the performance of those acts. Professor Knight says that "with human nature as we know it it would be impracticable or very unusual for one man to guarantee to another a definite result of the latter's actions without being given power to direct his work." This is surely incorrect. A large proportion of jobs are done to contract, that is, the contractor is guaranteed a certain sum providing he performs certain acts. But this does not involve any direction. It does mean, however, that the system of relative prices has been changed and that there will be a new arrangement of the factors of production.[42] The fact that Professor Knight mentions that the "second party would not place himself under the direction of the first without such a guarantee" is irrelevant to the problem we are considering. Finally, it seems important to notice that even in the case of an economic system where there is no uncertainty Professor Knight considers that there would be coordinators, though they would perform only a routine function. He immediately adds that they would be "without responsibility of any sort," which raises the question by whom are they paid and why? It seems that nowhere does Professor Knight give a reason why the price mechanism should be superseded.

IV

It would seem important to examine one further point and that is to consider the relevance of this discussion to the general question of the "cost curve of the firm."

It has sometimes been assumed that a firm is limited in size under perfect

---

[41]Knight (1921), p. 270.

[42]This shows that it is possible to have a private enterprise system without the existence of firms. Though, in practice, the two functions of enterprise, which actually influences the system of relative prices by forecasting wants and acting in accordance with such forecasts, and management, which accepts the system of relative prices as being given, are normally carried out by the same persons, yet it seems important to keep them separate in theory. This point is further discussed later.

competition if its cost curve slopes upward,[43] while under imperfect competition, it is limited in size because it will not pay to produce more than the output at which marginal cost is equal to marginal revenue.[44] But it is clear that a firm may produce more than one product and, therefore, there appears to be no prima facie reason why this upward slope of the cost curve in the case of perfect competition or the fact that marginal cost will not always be below marginal revenue in the case of imperfect competition should limit the size of the firm.[45] Mrs. Robinson[46] makes the simplifying assumption that only one product is being produced. But it is clearly important to investigate how the number of products produced by a firm is determined, while no theory which assumes that only one product is in fact produced can have very great practical significance.

It might be replied that under perfect competition, since everything that is produced can be sold at the prevailing price, then there is no need for any other product to be produced. But this argument ignores the fact that there may be a point where it is less costly to organise the exchange transactions of a new product than to organise further exchange transactions of the old product. This point can be illustrated in the following way. Imagine, following von Thunen, that there is a town, the consuming centre, and that industries are located around this central point in rings. These conditions are illustrated in the following diagram in which A, B, and C represent different industries.

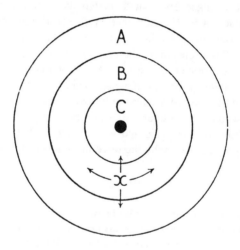

[43]See Kaldor (op. cit.) and Robinson (1934).
[44]Mr. Robinson calls this the imperfect competition solution for the survival of the small firm.
[45]Mr. Robinson's conclusion, (op cit.) p. 249, note 1, would appear to be definitely wrong. He is followed by Horace J. White, Jr. (1936), p. 645, note 27. Mr. White states: "It is obvious that the size of the firm is limited in conditions of monopolistic competition."
[46]Robinson (1934).

Imagine an entrepreneur who starts controlling exchange transactions from *x*. Now as he extends his activities in the same product (*B*), the cost of organising increases until at some point it becomes equal to that of a dissimilar product which is nearer. As the firm expands, it will therefore from this point include more than one product (*A* and *C*). This treatment of the problem is obviously incomplete,[47] but it is necessary to show that merely proving that the cost curve turns upwards does not give a limitation to the size of the firm. So far we have only considered the case of perfect competition; the case of imperfect competition would appear to be obvious.

To determine the size of the firm, we have to consider the marketing costs (that is, the costs of using the price mechanism), and the costs of organising of different entrepreneurs, and then we can determine how many products will be produced by each firm and how much of each it will produce. It would, therefore, appear that Mr. Shove[48] in his article on "imperfect competition" was asking questions which Mrs. Robinson's cost curve apparatus cannot answer. The factors mentioned above would seem to be the relevant ones.

V

Only one task now remains, and that is to see whether the concept of a firm which has been developed fits in with that existing in the real world. We can best approach the question of what constitutes a firm in practice by considering the legal relationship normally called that of "master and servant" or "employer and employee."[49] The essentials of this relationship have been given as follows:

(1) The servant must be under the duty of rendering personal services to the master or to others on behalf of the master, otherwise the contract is a contract for sale of goods or the like.

(2) The master must have the right to control the servant's work, either personally or by another servant or agent. It is this right of control or interference, of being entitled to tell the servant when to work (within the hours of service) and when not to work, and what work to do and how to do it (within the terms of such service) which is the dominant characteristic in this relation and marks off the servant from an independent contractor, or from one employed merely to give to his employer the fruits of his

[47]As has been shown above, location is only one of the factors influencing the cost of organising.

[48]G. F. Shove, "The Imperfection of the Market," *Economic Journal,* March, 1933, p. 115. In connection with an increase in demand in the suburbs and the effect on the price charged by suppliers, Mr. Shove asks, ". . . why do not the old firms open branches in the suburbs?" If the argument in the text is correct, this is a question which Mrs. Robinson's apparatus cannot answer.

[49]The legal concept of "employer and employee" and the economic concept of a firm are not identical, in that the firm may imply control over another person's property as well as over their labor. But the identity of these two concepts is sufficiently close for an examination of the legal concept to be of value in appraising the worth of the economic concept.

labour. In the latter case, the contractor or performer is not under the employer's control in doing the work or effecting the service; he has to shape and manage his work so as to give the result he has contracted to effect.[50]

We thus see that it is the fact of direction which is the essence of the legal concept of "employer and employee," just as it was in the economic concept which was developed above. It is interesting to note that Professor Batt says further:

> That which distinguishes an agent from a servant is not the absence or presence of a fixed wage or the payment only of commission on business done, but rather the freedom with which an agent may carry out his employment.[51]

We can, therefore, conclude that the definition we have given is one which approximates closely to the firm as it is considered in the real world.

Our definition is, therefore, realistic. Is it manageable? This ought to be clear. When we are considering how large a firm will be the principle of marginalism works smoothly. The question always is, will it pay to bring an extra exchange transaction under the organizing authority? At the margin, the costs of organizing within the firm will be equal either to the costs of organizing in another firm or to the costs involved in leaving the transaction to be "organized" by the price mechanism. Business men will be constantly experimenting, controlling more or less, and in this way, equilibrium will be maintained. This gives the position of equilibrium for static analysis. But it is clear that the dynamic factors are also of considerable importance, and an investigation of the effect changes have on the cost of organizing within the firm and on marketing costs generally will enable one to explain why firms get larger and smaller. We thus have a theory of moving equilibrium. The above analysis would also appear to have clarified the relationship between initiative or enterprise and management. Initiative means forecasting and operates through the price mechanism by the making of new contracts. Management proper merely reacts to price changes, rearranging the factors of production under its control. That the business man normally combines both functions is an obvious result of the marketing costs which were discussed above. Finally, this analysis enables us to state more exactly what is meant by the "marginal product" of the entrepreneur. But an elaboration of this point would take us far from our comparatively simple task of definition and clarification.

[50]Batt (1929), p. 6.   [51]Batt (1929), p. 7.

CHAPTER 8

Vertical integration, appropriable rents, and the competitive contracting process

BENJAMIN KLEIN, ROBERT CRAWFORD, AND ARMEN ALCHIAN

Benjamin Klein was born in 1943 in New York City. He received a Ph.D. in economics at the University of Chicago in 1970. Since 1978, he has been Professor of Economics at the University of California, Los Angeles.

Robert Crawford was born in 1943 in Medicine Hat, Alberta, Canada. He received a Ph.D. in economics from Carnegie–Mellon University in 1976. Since 1978, he has been Associate Professor of Economics at Brigham Young University.

Armen Alchian was born in 1914 in Fresno, California. He received a Ph.D. in economics at Stanford University in 1943. When this article was published, he was Professor of Economics at the University of California, Los Angeles, where he is currently Professor Emeritus.

More than forty years have passed since Coase's fundamental insight that transaction, coordination, and contracting costs must be considered explicitly in explaining the extent of vertical integration.[1] Starting from the truism that profit-maximizing firms will undertake those activities that they find cheaper to administer internally than to purchase in the market, Coase forced economists to begin looking for previously neglected constraints on the trading process that might efficiently lead to an intrafirm rather than an interfirm transaction. This paper attempts to add to this literature by exploring one particular cost of using the market system – the possibility of postcontractual opportunistic behavior.

Opportunistic behavior has been identified and discussed in the modern analysis of the organization of economic activity. Williamson, for example,

Reprinted with abridgements from Benjamin Klein, Robert Crawford, and Armen Alchian, "Vertical Integration, Appropriable Rents, and the Competitive Contracting Process," *Journal of Law and Economics*, 21 (1978): 297–326. Copyright © 1978. Reprinted with the permission of the University of Chicago Press.
[1]R. H. Coase (1937).

has referred to effects on the contracting process of *"ex post* small numbers opportunism,"[2] and Teece has elaborated:

Even when all of the relevant contingencies can be specified in a contract, contracts are still open to serious risks since they are not always honored. The 1970's are replete with examples of the risks associated with relying on contracts . . . [O]pen displays of opportunism are not infrequent and very often litigation turns out to be costly and ineffectual.[3]

The particular circumstance we emphasize as likely to produce a serious threat of this type of reneging on contracts is the presence of appropriable specialized quasi rents. After a specific investment is made and such quasi rents are created, the possibility of opportunistic behavior is very real. Following Coase's framework, this problem can be solved in two possible ways: vertical integration or contracts. The crucial assumption underlying the analysis of this paper is that, as assets become more specific and more appropriable quasi rents are created (and therefore the possible gains from opportunistic behavior increase), the costs of contracting will generally increase more than the costs of vertical integration. Hence, *ceteris paribus,* we are more likely to observe vertical integration.

I. Appropriable quasi rents of specialized assets

Assume an asset is owned by one individual and rented to another individual. The quasi-rent value of the asset is the excess of its value over its salvage value, that is, its value in its next best *use* to another renter. The potentially appropriable specialized portion of the quasi rent is that portion, if any, in excess of its value to the second highest-valuing *user.* If this seems like a distinction without a difference, consider the following example.

Imagine a printing press owned and operated by party A. Publisher B buys printing services from party A by leasing his press at a contracted rate of $5,500 per day. The amortized fixed cost of the printing press is $4,000 per day and it has a current salvageable value if moved elsewhere of $1,000 (daily rental equivalent). Operating costs are $1,500 and are paid by the printing-press owner, who prints final printed pages for the publisher. Assume also that a second publisher C is willing to offer at most $3,500 for daily service. The current quasi rent on the installed machine is $3,000 (= $5,500 − $1,500 − $1,000), the revenue minus operating costs minus salvageable value. However, the daily quasi rent from publisher B relative to use of the machine for publisher C is only $2,000 (= $5,500 − $3,500). At $5,500 revenue daily from publisher B the press owner would break even on his investment. If the publisher were then able to cut his offer for the press from $5,500 down to

---

[2]Oliver E. Williamson (1975).   [3]David J. Teece (1976).

almost $3,500, he would still have the press service available to him. He would be appropriating $2,000 of the quasi rent from the press owner. The $2,000 difference between his prior agreed-to daily rental of $5,500 and the next best revenue available to the press once the machine is purchased and installed is less than the quasi rent and therefore is potentially appropriable. If no second party were available at the present site, the entire quasi rent would be subject to threat of appropriation by an unscrupulous or opportunistic publisher.

Our primary interest concerns the means whereby this risk can be reduced or avoided. In particular, vertical integration is examined as a means of economizing on the costs of avoiding risks of appropriation of quasi rents in specialized assets by opportunistic individuals. This advantage of joint ownership of such specialized assets, namely, economizing on contracting costs necessary to insure nonopportunistic behavior, must of course be weighed against the costs of administering a broader range of assets within the firm.[4]

An appropriable quasi rent is not a monopoly rent in the usual sense, that is, the increased value of an asset protected from market entry over the value it would have had in an open market. An appropriable quasi rent can occur with no market closure or restrictions placed on rival assets. Once installed, an asset may be so expensive to remove or so specialized to a particular user that if the price paid to the owner were somehow reduced, the asset's services to that user would not be reduced. Thus, even if there were free and open competition for entry to the market, the specialization of the installed asset to a particular user (or more accurately the high costs of making it available to others) creates a quasi rent but no "monopoly" rent. At the other extreme, an asset may be costlessly transferable to some other user at no reduction in value, while at the same time, entry of similar assets is restricted. In this case, monopoly rent would exist, but no quasi rent.

We can use monopoly terminology to refer to the phenomenon we are discussing as long as we recognize that we are not referring to the usual monopoly created by government restrictions on entry or referring to a single supplier or even highly concentrated supply. One of the fundamental premises of this paper is that monopoly power, better labeled "market power," is pervasive. Because of transaction and mobility costs, "market power" will exist in many situations not commonly called monopolies. There may be many potential suppliers of a particular asset to a particular user but once the

---

[4]Vertical integration does not completely avoid contracting problems. The firm could usefully be thought of as a complex nonmarket contractual network where very similar forces are present. Frank Knight stressed the importance of this more than 50 years ago when he stated: "[T]he internal problems of the corporation, the protection of its various types of members and adherents against each other's predatory propensities, are quite as vital as the external problem of safe-guarding the public interest against exploitation by the corporation as a unit." Frank H. Knight (1964).

investment in the asset is made, the asset may be so specialized to a particular user that monopoly or monopsony market power, or both, is created.

A related motive for vertical integration that should not be confused with our main interest is the optimal output and pricing between two successive monopolists or bilateral monopolists (in the sense of marginal revenue less than price). A distortion arises because each sees a distorted marginal revenue or marginal cost.[5] While it is true that this successive monopoly distortion can be avoided by vertical integration, the results of the integration could, for that purpose alone, be achieved by a long term or a more detailed contract based on the true marginal revenue and marginal costs. Integrated ownership will sometimes be utilized to economize on such precontractual bargaining costs. However, we investigate a different reason for joint ownership of vertically related assets – the avoidance of postcontractual opportunistic behavior when specialized assets and appropriable quasi rents are present. One must clearly distinguish the transaction and information costs of reaching an agreement (discovering and heeding true costs and revenues and agreeing upon the division of profits) and the enforcement costs involved in assuring compliance with an agreement, especially one in which specialized assets are involved. It is this latter situation which we here explore as a motivation for intrafirm rather than interfirm transactions.

We maintain that if an asset has a substantial portion of quasi rent which is strongly dependent upon some other particular asset, both assets will tend to be owned by one party. For example, reconsider our printing press example. Knowing that the press would exist and be operated even if its owner got as little as $1,500, publisher B could seek excuses to renege on his initial contract to get the weekly rental down from $5,500 to close to $3,500 (the potential offer from publisher C, the next highest-valuing user at its present site). If publisher B could effectively announce he was not going to pay more than, say, $4,000 per week, the press owner would seem to be stuck. This unanticipated action would be opportunistic behavior (which by definition refers to unanticipated nonfulfillment of the contract) if the press owner had installed the press at a competitive rental price of $5,500 anticipating (possibly naively) good faith by the publisher. The publisher, for example, might plead that his newspaper business is depressed and he will be unable to continue unless rental terms are revised.

Alternatively, and maybe more realistically, because the press owner may have bargaining power due to the large losses that he can easily impose on the publisher (if he has no other source of press services quickly available), the press owner might suddenly seek to get a higher rental price than $5,500 to

---

[5]This matter of successive and bilateral monopoly has long been known and exposited in many places. See, for example, Robert Bork (1954); Fritz Machlup and Martha Taber (1960), where the problem is dated back to Cournot's statement in 1838.

capture some newly perceived increase in the publisher's profits. He could do this by alleging breakdowns or unusually high maintenance costs. This type of opportunistic behavior is difficult to prove and therefore litigate.

As we shall see, the costs of contractually specifying all important elements of quality varies considerably by type of asset. For some assets it may be essentially impossible to effectively specify all elements of quality and therefore, vertical integration is more likely. But even for those assets used in situations where all relevant quality dimensions can be unambiguously specified in a contract, the threat of production delay during litigation may be an effective bargaining device. A contract therefore may be clearly enforceable but still subject to postcontractual opportunistic behavior. For example, the threat by the press owner to break its contract by pulling out its press is credible even though illegal and possibly subject to injunctive action. This is because such an action, even in the very short run, can impose substantial costs on the newspaper publisher.[6]

This more subtle form of opportunistic behavior is likely to result in a loss of efficiency and not just a wealth-distribution effect. For example, the publisher may decide, given this possibility, to hold or seek standby facilities otherwise not worthwhile. Even if transactors are risk neutral, the presence of possible opportunistic behavior will entail costs as real resources are devoted to the attempt to improve posttransaction bargaining positions in the event such opportunism occurs. In particular, less specific investments will be made to avoid being "locked in."[7] In addition, the increased uncertainty of quality and quantity leads to larger optimum inventories and other increased real costs of production.

This attention to appropriable specialized quasi rents is not novel. In addi-

---

[6]While newspaper publishers generally own their own presses, book publishers generally do not. One possible reason book publishers may be less integrated may be because a book is planned further ahead in time and can economically be released with less haste. Presses located in any area of the United States can be used. No press is specialized to one publisher, in part because speed in publication and distribution to readers are generally far less important for books than newspapers, and therefore appropriable quasi rents are not created. Magazines and other periodicals can be considered somewhere between books and newspapers in terms of the importance of the time factor in distribution. In addition, because magazines are distributed nationally from at most a few plants, printing presses located in many different alternative areas are possible competitors for an existing press used at a particular location. Hence, a press owner has significantly less market power over the publisher of a magazine compared to a newspaper and we find magazines generally printed in nonpublisher-owned plants. (See W. Eric Gustafson, 1959). But while a magazine printing press may be a relatively less specific asset compared to a newspaper printing press, appropriable quasi rents may not be trivial (as possibly they are in the case of book printing). The magazine printing contract is therefore unlikely to be of a short-term one-transaction form but will be a long-term arrangement.

[7]The relevance for private investments in underdeveloped, politically unstable, that is, "opportunistic," countries is painfully obvious. The importance for economic growth of predictable government behavior regarding the definition and enforcement of property rights has frequently been noted.

tion to Williamson's[8] pathbreaking work in the area, Goldberg's[9] perceptive analysis of what he calls the "hold up" problem in the context of government regulation is what we are discussing in a somewhat different context. Goldberg indicates how some government regulation can usefully be considered a means of avoiding or reducing the threat of loss of quasi rent. (Goldberg treats this as the problem of providing protection for the "right to be served.") He also recognizes that this force underlies a host of other contractual and institutional arrangements such as stockpiling, insurance contracts, and vertical integration. Our analysis will similarly suggest a rationale for the existence of particular institutions and the form of governmental intervention or contractual provisions as alternatives to vertical integration in a wide variety of cases.

II. Contractual Solutions

The primary alternative to vertical integration as a solution to the general problem of opportunistic behavior is some form of economically enforceable long-term contract. Clearly a short-term (for example, one transaction, non-repeat sale) contract will not solve the problem. The relevant question then becomes when will vertical integration be observed as a solution and when will the use of the market-contracting process occur. Some economists and lawyers have defined this extremely difficult question away by calling a long-term contract a form of vertical integration.[10] Although there is clearly a continuum here, we will attempt not to blur the distinction between a long-term rental agreement and ownership. We assume the opportunistic behavior we are concentrating on can occur only with the former.[11]

For example, if opportunism occurs by the owner-lessor of an asset failing to maintain it properly for the user-lessee and hence unexpectedly increasing the effective rental price, legal remedies (proving contract violation) may be very costly. On the other hand, if the user owned the asset, then the employee who failed to maintain the asset properly could merely be fired.[12] If the

[8]Oliver E. Williamson (1971) and Williamson (1975).   [9]Victor P. Goldberg (1976).
[10]See, for example, Friedrich Kessler and Richard H. Stern (1959).
[11]It is commonly held that users of assets that can be damaged by careless use and for which the damage is not easy to detect immediately are more likely to own rather than rent the assets. However, these efficient maintenance considerations apply to short-term contracts and are irrelevant if the length of the long-term rental contract coincides with the economic life of the asset. Abstracting from tax considerations, the long-term contract remains less than completely equivalent to vertical integration only because of the possibility of postcontractual opportunistic reneging. These opportunistic possibilities, however, may also exist within the firm; see note 4 *supra*.
[12]We are abstracting from any considerations of a firm's detection costs of determining proper maintenance. Ease of termination also analytically distinguishes between a franchiser–franchisee arrangement and a vertically integrated arrangement with a profit-sharing manager. If cheating occurs, it is generally cheaper to terminate an employee rather than a franchisee. (The law has been changing recently to make it more difficult to terminate either type of laborer.) But the more

110

employee could still effectively cheat the owner-user of the asset because of his specific ability to maintain the asset, then the problem is that vertical integration of a relevant asset, the employee's human capital, has not occurred. For the moment, however, we will concentrate solely on the question of long-term rental versus ownership of durable physical assets.[13]

Long-term contracts used as alternatives to vertical integration can be assumed to take two forms: (1) an explicitly stated contractual guarantee legally enforced by the government or some other outside institution or (2) an implicit contractual guarantee enforced by the market mechanism of withdrawing future business if opportunistic behavior occurs. Explicit long-term contracts can, in principle, solve opportunistic problems, but, as suggested already, they are often very costly solutions. They entail costs of specifying possible contingencies and the policing and litigation costs of detecting violations and enforcing the contract in the courts.[14] Contractual provisions specifying compulsory arbitration or more directly imposing costs on the opportunistic party (for example, via bonding) are alternatives often employed to economize on litigation costs and to create flexibility without specifying every possible contingency and quality dimension of the transaction.

Since every contingency cannot be cheaply specified in a contract or even known and because legal redress is expensive, transactors will generally also rely on an implicit type of long-term contract that employs a market rather than legal enforcement mechanism, namely, the imposition of a capital loss by the withdrawal of expected future business. This goodwill market-enforcement mechanism undoubtedly is a major element of the contractual alternative to vertical integration. Macaulay provides evidence that relatively informal, legally unenforceable contractual practices predominate in business relations and that reliance on explicit legal sanctions is extremely rare.[15] Instead, business firms are said to generally rely on effective extralegal market sanc-

---

limited job-tenure rights of an employee compared to a franchisee reduce his incentive to invest in building up future business, and the firm must trade off the benefits and costs of the alternative arrangements. A profit-sharing manager with an explicit long-term employment contract would essentially be identical to a franchisee.

[13]The problems involved with renting specific human capital are discussed below.

[14]The recent Westinghouse case dealing with failure to fulfill uranium-supply contracts on grounds of "commercial impossibility" vividly illustrates these enforcement costs. Nearly three years after outright cancellation by Westinghouse of their contractual commitment, the lawsuits have not been adjudicated and those firms that have settled with Westinghouse have accepted substantially less than the original contracts would have entitled them to. A recent article by Paul L. Joskow (1977) analyzes the Westinghouse decision to renege on the contract as anticipated risk sharing and therefore, using our definition, would not be opportunistic behavior. However, the publicity surrounding this case and the judicial progress to date are likely to make explicit long-term contracts a less feasible alternative to vertical integration in the situations we are analyzing.

[15]Stewart Macaulay (1963).

BENJAMIN KLEIN, ROBERT CRAWFORD, AND ARMEN ALCHIAN

tions, such as the depreciation of an opportunistic firm's general goodwill because of the anticipated loss of future business, as a means of preventing nonfulfillment of contracts.

One way in which this market mechanism of contract enforcement may operate is by offering to the potential cheater a future "premium," more precisely, a price sufficiently greater than average variable (that is, avoidable) cost to assure a quasi-rent stream that will exceed the potential gain from cheating.[16] The present-discounted value of this future premium stream must be greater than any increase in wealth that could be obtained by the potential cheater if he, in fact, cheated and were terminated. The offer of such a long-term relationship with the potential cheater will eliminate systematic opportunistic behavior.[17]

The larger the potential one-time "theft" by cheating (the longer and more costly to detect a violation, enforce the contract, switch suppliers, and so forth) and the shorter the expected continuing business relationship, the higher this premium will be in a nondeceiving equilibrium. This may therefore partially explain both the reliance by firms on long-term implicit contracts with particular suppliers and the existence of reciprocity agreements among firms. The premium can be paid in seemingly unrelated profitable reciprocal business. The threat of termination of this relationship mutually suppresses opportunistic behavior.[18]

[16]The following discussion of the market enforcement mechanism is based upon the analysis of competitive equilibrium under costly quality information developed in Benjamin Klein and Keith Leffler (1979), which formally extends and more completely applies the analysis in Benjamin Klein (1974). It is similar to the analysis presented in Gary S. Becker and George J. Stigler (1974), of insuring against malfeasance by an employer. This market-enforcement mechanism is used in Benjamin Klein and Andrew McLaughlin (1978) (unpublished manuscript), to explain franchising arrangements and particular contractual provisions such as resale price maintenance, exclusive territories, initial specific investments, and termination clauses.

[17]Formally, this arrangement to guarantee nonopportunistic behavior unravels if there is a last period in the relationship. No matter how high the premium, cheating would occur at the start of the last period. If transactors are aware of this, no transaction relying on trust (that is, the expectation of another subsequent trial) will be made in the penultimate period, because it becomes the last period, and so on. If some large lump-sum, final-period payment such as a pension as part of the market-enforcement scheme, as outlined by Gary S. Becker and George J. Stigler (1974), this last-period problem is obvious. One solution to this unrecognized last-period problem is the acceptance of some continuing third party (for example, escrow agents or government enforcers) to prevent reneging on the implicit contracts against reneging we are outlining. Alternatively, the potential loss of value of indefinitely long-lived salable brand-name assets can serve as deterrents to cheating even where the contract between two parties has a last period. If one party's reputation for nonopportunistic dealings can be sold and used in later transactions in an infinite-time-horizon economy, the firm that cheats in the "last" period to any one buyer from the firm experiences a capital loss. This may partially explain the existence of conglomerates and their use of identifying (not product-descriptive) brand names.

[18]Although it may not always be in one's narrow self-interest to punish the other party in such a reciprocal relationship since termination may impose a cost on both, it may be rational for one to adopt convincingly such a reaction function to optimally prevent cheating. R. L. Trivers (1971)

112

The premium stream can be usefully thought of as insurance payments made by the firm to prevent cheating.[19] As long as both parties to the transaction make the same estimate of the potential short-run gain from cheating, the quantity of this assurance that will be demanded and supplied will be such that no opportunistic behavior will be expected to occur.[20] If postcontractual reneging is anticipated to occur, either the correct premium will be paid to optimally prevent it or, if the premium necessary to eliminate reneging is too costly, the particular transaction will not be made.

We are not implicitly assuming here that contracts are enforced costlessly and cannot be broken, but rather that given our information-cost assumptions, parties to a contract know exactly when and how much a contract will be broken. An unanticipated broken contract, that is, opportunistic behavior, is therefore not possible in this particular equilibrium. In the context of this model, expected wealth maximization will yield some opportunistic behavior only if we introduce a stochastic element. This will alter the informational equilibrium state such that the potential cheater's estimate of the short-run gain from opportunistic behavior may be at times greater than the other firm's estimate. Hence, less than an optimal premium will be paid and opportunistic behavior will occur.

The firms collecting the premium payments necessary to assure fulfillment of contractual agreements in a costly information world may appear to be earning equilibrium "profits" although they are in a competitive market. That is, there may be many, possibly identical, firms available to supply the services of nonopportunistic performance of contractual obligations yet the premium will not be competed away if transactors cannot costlessly guarantee contractual performance. The assurance services, by definition, will not be supplied unless the premium is paid and the mere payment of this premium produces the required services.

discusses similar mechanisms such as "moralistic aggression" which he claims have been genetically selected to protect reciprocating altruists against cheaters. Similarly, throughout the discussion we implicitly assume that cheating individuals can only cheat once and thereafter earn the "competitive" rate of return. They may, however, be forced to earn less than the competitive wage if they are caught cheating, that is, take an extra capital loss (collusively, but rationally) imposed by other members of the group. This may explain why individuals may prefer to deal in business relations with their own group (for example, members of the same church or the same country club) where effective social sanctions can be imposed against opportunistic behavior. Reliance on such reciprocal business relationships and group enforcement mechanisms is more likely where governmental enforcement of contracts is weaker. Nathaniel H. Leff (1978), for example, documents the importance of such groups in less-developed countries. Industries supplying illegal products and services would likely be another example.

[19]It is, of course, an insurance scheme that not only pools risks but also alters them.

[20]As opposed to the analysis of Michael R. Darby and Edi Karni (1973), the equilibrium quantity of opportunistic behavior or "fraud" will be zero under our assumptions of symmetrical information.

Any profits are competed away in equilibrium by competitive expenditures on fixed (sunk) assets, such as initial specific investments (for example, a sign) with low or zero salvage value if the firm cheats, necessary to enter and obtain this preferred position of collecting the premium stream.[21] These fixed (sunk) costs of supplying credibility of future performance are repaid or covered by future sales on which a premium is earned. In equilibrium, the premium stream is then merely a normal rate of return on the "reputation," or "brand-name" capital created by the firm by these initial expenditures. This brand-name capital, the value of which is highly specific to contract fulfillment by the firm, is analytically equivalent to a forfeitable collateral bond put up by the firm which is anticipated to face an opportunity to take advantage of appropriable quasi rents in specialized assets.

While these initial specific investments or collateral bonds are sometimes made as part of the normal (minimum-cost) production process and therefore at small additional cost, transaction costs and risk considerations do make them costly. We can generally say that the larger the appropriable specialized quasi rents (and therefore the larger the potential short-run gain from opportunistic behavior) and the larger the premium payments necessary to prevent contractual reneging, the more costly this implicit contractual solution will be. We can also expect the explicit contract costs to be positively related to the level of appropriable quasi rents since it will pay to use more resources (including legal services) to specify precisely more contingencies when potential opportunities for lucrative contractual reneging exist.

Although implicit and explicit contracting and policing costs are positively related to the extent of appropriable specialized quasi rents, it is reasonable to assume, on the other hand, that any internal coordination or other ownership costs are not systematically related to the extent of the appropriable specialized quasi rent of the physical asset owned. Hence we can reasonably expect the following general empirical regularity to be true: the lower the appropriable specialized quasi rents, the more likely that transactors will rely on a contractual relationship rather than common ownership. And conversely, integration by common or joint ownership is more likely, the higher the appropriable specialized quasi rents of the assets involved.

III. Example of appropriable specialized quasi rent

This section presents examples of quasi rents where the potential for their appropriation serves as an important determinant of economic organization. A series of varied illustrations, some quite obvious and others rather subtle, will

[21]A more complete analysis of market equilibrium by the use of specific capital in guaranteeing contract enforcement is developed in Benjamin Klein and Keith Leffler (1979).

make the analysis more transparent and provide suggestive evidence for the relevance of the protection of appropriable quasi rents as an incentive to vertically integrate. It also suggests the direction of more systematic empirical work that obviously is required to assess the significance of this factor relative to other factors in particular cases. Where this force towards integration (that is, the economizing on contracting costs necessary to assure nonopportunistic behavior in the presence of appropriable quasi rents) does not appear to dominate, important insights regarding the determinants of particular contracting costs and contract provisions are thereby provided.[22]

. . .

B. Petroleum industry

Appropriable quasi rents exist in specialized assets of oil refineries, pipelines, and oil fields. This leads to common ownership to remove the incentive for individuals to attempt to capture the rents of assets owned by someone else.

Suppose several oil wells are located along a separately owned pipeline that leads to a cluster of independently owned refineries with no alternative crude supply at comparable cost. Once all the assets are in place (the wells drilled and the pipeline and refineries constructed) the oil-producing properties and the refineries are specialized to the pipeline. The portion of their value above the value to the best alternative user is an appropriable specialized quasi rent. The extent of the appropriable quasi rent is limited, in part, by the costs of entry to a potential parallel pipeline developer. Since pipelines between particular oil-producing properties and particular refineries are essentially natural monopolies, the existing pipeline owner may have a significant degree of market power.

These specialized producing and refining assets are therefore "hostage" to the pipeline owner. At the "gathering end" of the pipeline, the monopsonist pipeline could and would purchase all its oil at the same well-head price regardless of the distance of the well from the refinery. This price could be as low as the marginal cost of getting oil out of the ground (or its reservation value for future use, if higher) and might not generate a return to the oil-well owner sufficient to recoup the initial investment of exploration and drilling.

----

[22]It is important to recognize that not only will contracting and enforcement costs of constraining opportunistic behavior determine the form of the final economic arrangement adopted by the transacting parties, but they will also influence the firm's production function. That is, the level of specific investment and therefore the size of the potentially appropriable quasi rent is not an independent "technological" datum in each of these following cases, but is economically determined in part by transaction costs.

At the delivery-to-refinery end of the pipeline, the pipeline owner would be able to appropriate the "specialized-to-the-pipeline quasi rents" of the refineries. The pipeline owner could simply raise the price of crude oil at least to the price of alternative sources of supply to each refinery that are specialized to the pipeline. Given the prospects of such action, if the pipeline owner were an independent monopsonist facing the oil explorers and a monopolist to the refinery owners, everyone (explorers and refiners) would know in advance their vulnerability to rent extraction. Therefore oil-field owners and refinery owners would, through shared ownership in the pipeline, remove the possibility of subsequent rent extraction.

The problem would not be completely solved if just the oil field or the refineries (but not both) were commonly owned with the pipeline, since the local monopoly (or monopsony) would persist vis-à-vis the other. Prospectively, one would expect the common ownership to extend to all three stages. If several refineries (or oil fields) were to be served by one pipeline, all the refinery (or oil field) owners would want to jointly own the pipeline. A common practice is a jointly owned company which "owns" the pipeline with the shares by producers and refiners in the pipeline company corresponding roughly to the respective shares of oil to be transported.[23]

Consider other inputs in the production process. The oil tanker, for example, is specialized to crude oil transportation. But since it is essentially equi-valued by many alternative users, the appropriable quasi rent is near zero. So we would expect oil tankers not to be extensively owned by refiners or producers. Similarly, the assets used for refinery construction are not specialized to any single refiner or refinery and they should also not be commonly owned with the refinery.

. . .

[23]Jane Atwood and Paul Kobrin (1977) find an extremely high positive correlation between a firm's crude production and its share of ownership in the pipeline. On the other hand, natural gas pipelines, although apparently economically similar in terms of potentially appropriable quasi rents, do not appear to be vertically integrated. Rather than joint-ownership arrangements with the gas producers, these pipelines are often independently owned. The difference may be due to more effective FPC (and now the Federal Energy Regulatory Commission) regulation (of the wellhead and citygate gas prices and the implied pipeline tariff) compared to the direct Interstate Commerce Commission regulation of oil pipelines as common carriers. Regulation of oil pipeline tariffs could, for example, be easily evaded by opportunistic decreases in the wellhead prices paid for oil. More complete government regulation of gas prices may effectively prevent opportunistic behavior by the natural gas pipeline owners, and thereby serve as an alternative to vertical integration (see Victor P. Goldberg, 1976). Edmund Kitch informs us that the evidence does indicate a much greater degree of vertical integration of natural gas pipelines in the period before FPC regulation.

C. Specific human capital

The previous analysis has dealt with examples of physical capital. When specific human capital is involved, the opportunism problem is often more complex and, because of laws prohibiting slavery, the solution is generally some form of explicit or implicit contract rather than vertical integration.

For example, consider the following concrete illustration from the agricultural industry. Suppose someone owns a peach orchard. The ripened peaches, ready for harvest, have a market value of about $400,000. So far costs of $300,000 have been paid and the remaining harvesting and shipping costs will be $50,000 ($5,000 transport and $45,000 labor), leaving $50,000 as the competitive return on the owner's capital. Assume the laborers become a union (one party to whom the crop is now specialized) and refuse to pick unless paid $390,000. That would leave $5,000 for transport and only $5,000 for the owner of the peach orchard, instead of the $350,000 necessary to cover incurred costs and the cost of capital. If the union had power to exclude other pickers, it could extract all the appropriable quasi rent of that year's crop specialized to that particular labor union's service. The union would be extracting not just the usual monopoly rents involved in raising wages, but also the short-run appropriable quasi rents of the farmer's specific assets represented by the ripened peaches. This gain to the union is a one-period return because obviously the farmer will not make any additional specific investments in the future if he knows it will be appropriated by the union.

To reduce this risk of appropriation, the farmer may have a large clan family (or neighbors of similar farms) do his picking. Because of diseconomies of scale, however, this "cooperative" solution is not generally the lowest-cost arrangement and some reliance on market contracting will be necessary. The individual farmer, for example, may want the labor union to put up a forfeitable bond to compensate him in the event the union under threat of strike asks for more wages at harvest time. Alternatively, but equivalently, the collateral put up by the union could be the value of the brand-name capital of the union, a value which will depreciate if its leaders engage in opportunistic behavior. The farmer would then make a continuing brand-name payment to the union (similar to the premium payment noted above) for this collateral.[24]

The market value of the union's reputation for reliability of contract observance is the present-discounted value of these brand-name payments which

---

[24]If the premium is a payment of the union per unit time, then the arrangement is identical to a collateral-bond arrangement where the union collects the interest on the bond as long as no opportunistic behavior occurs. Because of possible legal difficulties of enforcing such an arrangement, however, the premium may be reflected in the price (that is, a higher wage).

BENJAMIN KLEIN, ROBERT CRAWFORD, AND ARMEN ALCHIAN

will be greater than any short-run opportunistic gain to the union leaders that could be obtained by threats at harvest time. These payments which increase the cost to the union of opportunistic behavior would be substantial for a perishable product with a large appropriable quasi rent. It is therefore obvious why producers of highly perishable crops are so antagonistic to unionization of field labor. They would be especially hostile to unions without established reputations regarding fulfillment of contract and with politically motivated (and possibly myopic) leaders.[25]

In addition to implicit (brand-name) contracts, opportunistic union behavior may be prevented by use of explicit contracts, often with some outside arbitration as an element of the contract-enforcement mechanism. Although it is difficult for an outsider to distinguish between opportunistic behavior and good-faith modifications of contract, impartial arbitration procedures may reduce the necessity of explicitly specifying possible contingencies and thereby reduce the rigidity of the explicit long-term contract.[26]

When the problem is reversed and quasi rents of firm-specific human capital of employees may be opportunistically appropriated by the firm, implicit and explicit long-term contracts are also used to prevent such behavior. Because of economies of scale in monitoring and enforcing such contracts, unions may arise as a contract cost-reducing institution for employees with investments in specific human capital.[27]

[25]It is interesting to note in this context that California grape farmers preferred the established Teamsters Union to the new, untried, and apparently more politically motivated field-workers union organized by Cesar Chavez.

Since unions are not "owned," union leaders will not have the proper incentive to maximize the union's value; they will tend more to maximize returns during their tenure. If, however, union leadership (ownership) were salable, the leaders would have the optimal incentive to invest in and conserve the union's brand-name capital. They therefore would not engage in opportunistic actions that may increase current revenue while decreasing the market value of the union. "Idealistic" union leaders that do not behave as if they own the union may, in fact, produce less wealth-maximizing action than would "corrupt" leaders, who act as if they personally own the union. Alternatively, the current members of the union may have control, not in the sense of having directly salable shares, but in the sense that the valuable union asset can be transferred to their children or relatives. If government regulations force union members to give away these rights to future rents (for example, by forcing them to admit minorities and eliminate nepotism), we can expect them to intentionally depreciate or not create the reputation capital of the union by opportunistic strikes. See Benjamin Klein (1974) where similar problems with regard to the supply of money by nonprivately owned, nonwealth-maximizing firms are discussed.

[26]An interesting legal case in this area is *Publishers' Ass'n v. Newspaper & Mail Del. Union,* 114 N.Y.S. 2d, 401 (1952). The union authorized and sanctioned a strike against the New York Daily News although the collective bargaining agreement had "no-strike" and arbitration clauses. The Daily News took the union to arbitration, and the arbitrator found actual damages of $2,000 and punitive damages of $5,000 if the union again violated the contract. (The court, however, overturned the punitive damages for technical reasons.) See David E. Feller (1973) for a discussion of the flexibility obtained with arbitration provisions in labor contracts.

[27]We should explicitly note that we are not considering unions as cartelizing devices, the usually analyzed motivation for their existence. This force is obviously present in many cases (for example, interstate trucking) but is distinct from our analysis.

In addition to narrow contract-monitoring economies of scale, a union creates a continuing long-term employment relationship that eliminates the last-period (or transient employee) contract-enforcement problem and also creates bargaining power (a credible strike threat) to more cheaply punish a firm that violates the contract. Even when the specific human-capital investment is made by the firm, a union of employees may similarly reduce the contract-enforcement costs of preventing individual-worker opportunism. There are likely to be economies of scale in supply credibility of contract fulfillment, including the long-term continuing relationship aspect of a union. The existence of a union not only makes it more costly for a firm to cheat an individual worker in his last period but also makes it more costly for an individual worker in his last period to cheat the firm, because the union has the incentive (for example, withholding pension rights) to prevent such an externality on the continuing workers. Therefore unions are more likely to exist when the opportunistic cheating problem is greater, namely, when there is more specific human capital present.[28]

. . .

D. Leasing inputs and ownership of the firm

Examination of leasing companies should reveal that leases are less common (or too expensive) for assets with specialized quasi rents that could be appropriated by the lessee or lessor. Leasing does not occur in the obvious cases of elevators or the glass of windows in an office building where postinvestment bilaterally appropriable quasi rents are enormous, while the furniture in the building is often rented. In banks, the safe is owned by the bank, but computers (though not the memory discs) are sometimes rented.[29] Though this may seem like resorting to trivialities, the fact that such leasing arrangements are taken for granted merely corroborates the prior analysis.

The standard example of leasing arrangements occurs with transportation capital, such as the planes, trucks, or cars used by a firm. This capital is generally easily movable and not very specific. But leasing arrangements are

[28]When allowing for this "reverse" effect of employee-specific capital, and therefore higher wages, on the formation of unions, the usual positive effect of unions on wages appears to vanish. See, for example, O. Ashenfelter and G. Johnson (1972) and Peter Schmidt and Robert P. Strauss (1976).

[29]In addition to computers being less specific and hence possessing smaller appropriable quasi rents than elevators, firms (for example, IBM) that supply computers generally possess extremely valuable brand names per unit of current sales due to a large anticipated growth in demand. Since there are some quasi rents associated with the use of a computer by a bank that could possibly be appropriated by threat of immediate removal, we would expect that if rental contracts existed, they would be more likely be with highly credible firms with high anticipated demand growth.

far from universal because some of this capital can be quite specific and quasi rents appropriated. For example, early American steam locomotives were specialized to operating conditions such as high speed, hill climbing, short hauls, heavy loads, sharp corners, as well as types of coal for fuel. Slight differences in engines created significant differences in operating costs. High specialization made it desirable for the rail companies to own locomotives (as well as the land on which water was available for steam). The advent of the more versatile, less specialized, diesel locomotive enabled more leasing and equipment trust financing. Similarly, Swift, the meat packer and innovator of the refrigerator car for transporting slaughtered beef, owned the specialized refrigerator cars it used.[30]

On the other hand, some capital may be quite specific to other assets in a firm's productive process and yet leased rather than owned. These cases provide useful insights into the nature of the contracting costs underlying our analysis. For example, consider the fact that agricultural land, a highly specific asset, is not always owned but often is rented. Land rented for farming purposes is typically for annual crops, like vegetables, sugar beets, cotton, or wheat, while land used for tree crops, like nuts, dates, oranges, peaches, apricots, or grape vines – assets that are highly specialized to the land – is usually owned by the party who plants the trees or vines.[31] However, long-term rental arrangements even for these "specialized asset" crops are not entirely unknown.

It is instructive to recognize why land-rental contracts, rather than vertical integration, can often be used without leading to opportunistic behavior. The primary reason is because it is rather cheap to specify and monitor the relevant contract terms (the quality of the good being purchased) and to enforce this particular rental contract. In addition, the landowner generally cannot impose a cost on the farmer by pulling the asset out or reducing the quality of the asset during the litigation process. Note the contrast with labor rental where it is essentially impossible to effectively specify and enforce quality elements (for example, all working conditions and the effort expended by workers) and where the possibility of withdrawal by strike or lockout is real and costly. Therefore, we do observe firms making highly specific investments in, for

---

[30]The great bulk of all refrigerator cars are not owned by the railroads, but rather by shipper-users such as packers and dairy companies. See Robert S. Henry (1942).

[31]While 25% of vegetable and melon farms in California in 1974 were fully owned by the farm operator, 82% of fruit and nut tree farms were fully owned, a significantly different ownership proportion at the 99% confidence interval. Similarly, the ownership proportions of cash grain and cotton farms were 40% and 39%, respectively, both also significantly different at the 99% confidence interval from the proportions of fruit and nut tree farm ownership. See 1 U.S. Dep't of Commerce, Bureau of the Census, 1974 Census of Agriculture, State and County Data, pt. 5, at tab. 28. Summary by Tenure of Farm Operator and Type of Organization, *id.*, 1974, California, pp. 1-29 to 1-30.

example, trees or buildings on land they do not own but only rent long term.[32] This is because credible postcontractual opportunistic threats by the land-owner are not possible. However, if the landowner can vary the quality of the land, for example, by controlling the irrigation system to the crops or the electricity supply to a building, then a significant possibility of postinvestment opportunistic behavior exists and we would therefore expect vertical integration.[33]

One specific asset that is almost always owned by the firm is its trade-name or brand-name capital and, in particular, the logo it uses to communicate to consumers. If this asset were rented from a leasing company, the problems would be obvious. The firm would be extremely hesitant to make any investments to build up its goodwill, for example, by advertising or by successful performance, because such investments are highly specific to that "name." The quasi rents could be appropriated by the leasing company through increases in the rental fee for the trade name. Not only would the firm not invest in this specific asset, but there would be an incentive for the firm to depreciate a valuable rented brand name. Although these problems seem insurmountable, rental of the capital input of a firm's brand name is not entirely unknown. In fact, franchisors can be thought of as brand-name leasing companies. A franchisee is fundamentally a renter of the brand-name capital (and logo) owned by the franchisor. Because of the specific capital problems noted above, direct controls are placed on franchisee behavior. The rental payment is usually some form of profit-sharing arrangement and, although the franchisee is legally considered to be an independent firm, the situation is in reality much closer to vertical integration than to the standard contractual relationship of the independent market.

Finally, the analysis throws light on the important question of why the owners of a firm (the residual claimants) are generally also the major capitalists of the firm.[34] As we have seen, owners may rent the more generalized capital but will own the firm's specific capital. This observation has implications for recent discussions of "industrial democracy," which fail to recognize that although employees may own and manage a firm (say, through their

---

[32]Rental terms may be related to sales of the firm using the land in order to share the risk of real-value changes and to reduce the risk of nominal land-value changes involved with a long-term contract.

[33]Coase's example of a monopolist selling more of a durable good, say land, after initially selling a monopoly quantity at the monopoly price is analytically identical to the problem of postcontractual opportunistic behavior. Existing contractual relationships indicate, however, that the land case may be relatively easy to solve because it may not be expensive to make a credible contract regarding the remaining land. But, one of Coase's indicated solutions, the short-term rental rather than sale of the land is unlikely because it would discourage specific (to land) investments by the renter (such as building a house, developing a farm, and so forth) for fear of appropriation. See R. H. Coase (1972).

[34]We are grateful to Earl Thompson for discerning this implication.

union), they will also have to be capitalists and own the specific capital. It will generally be too costly, for example, for the worker-owners to rent a plant because such a specific investment could be rather easily appropriated from its owners after it is constructed. Therefore it is unlikely to be built. A highly detailed contractual arrangement together with very large brand-name premium payments by the laborers would be necessary to assure nonopportunistic behavior. This is generally too expensive an alternative and explains why capitalists are usually the owners of a firm.[35]

E. Social institutions

Much of the previous analysis has dealt with tangible capital. Contractual arrangements involving such assets are often cheaper than complete vertical integration, even when the assets are highly specific (for example, the land-rental case). As the discussion on human capital suggests, however, when the specific assets involved are intangible personal assets, the problems of contract enforcement become severe. In addition, when the number of individuals involved (or the extent of the specific capital) becomes very large, ownership arrangements often become extremely complex.

For example, consider country clubs. Golf country clubs are social, in addition to being golfing, organizations. Sociability of a country club involves substantial activities away from the golf course: dinners, dances, parties, cards, games, and general social activities with friends who are members of the club. However, some golf courses are operated with very few social activities for the set of members and their families. The social clubs (usually called "country clubs") are mutually owned by the members, whereas golf courses with virtually no off-course social activity often are privately owned with members paying daily golf fees without owning the golf course.

Mutual ownership is characteristic of the social country club because the specialized quasi rent of friendship is collected by each member whose friendship is specialized to the other members. The members' behavior toward one

[35] Armen A. Alchian and Harold Demsetz, "Production, Information Costs, and Economic Organization," 62 *Am. Econ. Rev.* 777 (1972), claim that if the owner of the firm also owns the firm's capital, it supplies evidence that he can pay for rented inputs, including labor. This appears to be incorrect since the owner could supply credibility by using some of his assets completely unrelated to the production process, such as treasury bonds, for collateral. Michael C. Jensen and William H. Meckling (unpublished manuscript, Feb. 1977) emphasize the costs of monitoring managerial performance and the maintenance of rented capital, and the problems of efficiently allocating risks in a pure-rental firm. They also note that it is "impossible" for a firm to rent all the productive capital assets because many of them are intangible and therefore "it is impossible to repossess the asset if the firm refused to pay the rental fee" (1977, p. 20). This argument is similar to our analysis of opportunistic behavior. However, rather than asserting that such rentals are impossible, we would merely recognize the extremely high contracting costs generally present in such situations. More importantly, we claim that such an argument also extends to the rental of tangible specific capital.

another constitutes an investment in forming valuable friendships, a congenial milieu, and rapport among the members. Each member has invested in creating that congenial milieu and atmosphere specialized to the other members. And its value could be stolen or destroyed by opportunistic behavior of a party authorized to admit new members.

To see how, suppose the club were owned by someone other than the members. Once the membership value is created by the interpersonal activities of the members, the owner of the club could then start to raise the fees for continuing members. Assuming some costs of the members moving away en masse and forming a new club, the owner could expropriate by higher fees some of the specialized quasi-rent value of the sociability created by the members' specialization to each other in their own group. Alternatively, the owner could threaten to break the implicit contract and destroy some of the sociability capital by selling admission to "undesirable" people who want to consort with the existing members.

Similarly, if the social country club were owned by the members as a corporation with each member owning a share of stock salable without prior approval of existing members (as is the case for the business corporation), a single member could, by threatening to sell to an "undesirable" potential member, extract some value of congeniality from the current members, as a payment for not selling.[36]

An extreme case of this general problem is a marriage. If each mate had a transferable share salable to a third party, there would be far fewer marriages with highly specific investments in affection and children. If a relationship is not one of specialized interest (specialized to a particular other party) or if it required no investment by any member, then the marriage relationship would be more like a corporation. As it is one of highly specific investments, marriages have historically been mutually owned entities, with permission of both parties generally required for alteration of membership. Government arbitration of this relationship to prevent postinvestment opportunistic behavior by either party can contribute toward lower bargaining costs and investments of resources (recoverable dowries) by both parties to improve their respective postinvestment bargaining positions, and, most importantly, create confidence that opportunistic behavior will not be successful. The legislative movement to "no-fault" divorce suggests that modern marriages may have less specific assets than formerly.[37]

. . .

---

[36]The "free-rider" problems of bribing an opportunistic member to prevent sale to an "undesirable" member are obvious. This analysis could be applied to social clubs such as Elks, Masonic Order, and so forth.

[37]Similarly, people whose work is highly specialized to each other will be partners (common

IV. Concluding comment

We should emphasize in conclusion that most business relationships are neither likely to be as simple as the standard textbook polar cases of vertical integration or market contract nor as easily explained as some of the above examples. When particular examples are examined in detail, business relationships are often structured in highly complex ways not represented by either a simple rental contract or by simple vertical integration. . . .

. . .

. . . Once we attempt to add empirical detail to Coase's fundamental insight that a systematic study of transaction costs is necessary to explain particular forms of economic organization, we find that his primary distinction between transactions made within a firm and transactions made in the marketplace may often be too simplistic. Many long-term contractual relationships (such as franchising) blur the line between the market and the firm. It may be more useful to merely examine the economic rationale for different types of particular contractual relationships in particular situations and consider the firm as a particular kind or set of interrelated contracts.[38] Firms are therefore, by definition, formed and revised in markets and the conventional sharp distinction between markets and firms may have little general analytical importance. The pertinent economic question we are faced with is, "what kinds of contracts are used for what kinds of activities, and why?"

ownership). For example, attorneys that have become highly specialized to their coattorneys will become partners, whereas new associates will at first be employees. A small team of performers (Laurel and Hardy, Sonny and Cher) who were highly specialized to each other would be "partners" (co-owners) rather than employee and employer. While it is still difficult to enforce such contracts and prevent postcontractual opportunistic behavior by either party, joint ownership creates an incentive for performance and specific investment not present in an easily terminable employer–employee contract that must rely solely on the personal brand-name reputation of contracting parties. Trust, including the reputation of certifying institutions such as theatrical agents, law schools, and so on, and the presence of social sanctions against opportunistic partners remain important.

[38]If we think of firms as collections of interrelated contracts rather than the collection of goods operative in the contracts, the question of who "owns" the firm (the set of contacts) appears somewhat nonsensical. It may be useful to think solely of a set of claimants to various portions of the value consequences of the contractual coalition, with no "owner" of the firm.

CHAPTER 9

The governance of contractual relations

OLIVER WILLIAMSON

Oliver Williamson was born in Superior, Wisconsin, in 1932. He received a Ph.D. in economics at Carnegie-Mellon University in 1963. When this chapter was published, he was Gordon B. Tweedy Professor of Economics of Law and Organization at Yale University. Since 1988, he has taught at the University of California, Berkeley, where he is currently Edgar F. Kaiser Professor of Business Administration, Professor of Economics, and Professor of Law.

. . .

Contractual variety is the source of numerous puzzles with which the study of the economic institutions of capitalism is appropriately concerned. Transaction cost economics maintains that such variety is mainly explained by underlying differences in the attributes of transactions. Efficiency purposes are served by matching governance structures to the attributes of transactions in a discriminating way.

. . .

1. Contracting traditions

There is widespread agreement that the discrete transaction paradigm – "sharp in by clear agreement; sharp out by clear performance" (Macneil, 1974, p. 738) – has served both law and economics well. But there is also increasing awareness that many contractual relations are not of this well-defined kind. A deeper understanding of the nature of contract has emerged as the legal-rule emphasis associated with the study of discrete contracting has given way to a more general concern with the contractual purposes to be served. Macneil's distinctions among classical, neoclassical, and relational law are instructive.

1.1 Classical contract law

As Macneil observes, any system of contract law has the purpose of facilitating exchange. What is distinctive about classical contract law is that it attempts to do so by enhancing discreteness and intensifying "presentiation" (1978, p. 862), where presentiation has reference to efforts to "make or render present in place or time; to cause to be perceived or realized at present" (1978, p. 863, n. 25). The economic counterpart to complete presentiation is contingent claims contracting, which entails comprehensive contracting whereby all relevant future contingencies pertaining to the supply of a good or service are described and discounted with respect to both likelihood and futurity.

Classical contract law endeavors to implement discreteness and presentiation in several ways. For one thing, the identity of the parties to a transaction is treated as irrelevant. In that respect it corresponds exactly with the "ideal" market transaction in economics. Second, the nature of the agreement is carefully delimited, and the more formal features govern when formal (for example, written) and informal (for example, oral) terms are contested. Third, remedies are narrowly prescribed so that, "should the initial presentiation fail to materialize because of nonperformance, the consequences are relatively predictable from the beginning and are not open-ended" (Macneil, 1978, p. 864). Additionally, third-party participation is discouraged (p. 864). The emphasis is thus on legal rules, formal documents, and self-liquidating transactions.

1.2 Neoclassical contract law

Not every transaction fits comfortably into the classical contracting scheme. In particular, for long-term contracts executed under conditions of uncertainty complete presentiation is apt to be prohibitively costly if not impossible. Problems of several kinds arise. First, not all future contingencies for which adaptations are required can be anticipated at the outset. Second, the appropriate adaptations will not be evident for many contingencies until the circumstances materialize. Third, except as changes in states of the world are unambiguous, hard contracting between autonomous parties may well give rise to veridical disputes when state-contingent claims are made. In a world where (at least some) parties are inclined to be opportunistic, whose representations are to be believed?

Faced with the prospective breakdown of classical contracting in such circumstances, three alternatives are available. One would be to forgo such transactions altogether. A second would be to remove those transactions from the market and organize them internally instead. Adaptive, sequential decision making would then be implemented under unified ownership and with the assistance of hierarchial incentive and control systems. Third, a different contracting relation that preserves trading but provides for additional governance structure might be devised. This last brings us to what Macneil refers to as neoclassical contracting.

As Macneil observes, "Two common characteristics of long-term contracts are the existence of gaps in their planning and the presence of a range of processes and techniques used by contract planners to create flexibility in lieu of either leaving gaps or trying to plan rigidly" (1978, p. 865). Third-party assistance in resolving disputes and evaluating performance often has advantages over litigation in serving these functions of flexibility and gap filling. . . .

A recognition that the world is complex, that agreements are incomplete, and that some contracts will never be reached unless both parties have confidence in the settlement machinery thus characterizes neoclassical contract law. . . .

. . .

1.3 Relational contracting

The pressures to sustain ongoing relations "have led to the spinoff of many subject areas from the classical, and later the neoclassical, contract law system, e.g., much of corporate law and collective bargaining" (Macneil, 1978, p. 885). Progressively increasing the "duration and complexity" of contracts has thus resulted in the displacement of even neoclassical adjustment processes by adjustment processes of a more thoroughly transaction-specific, ongoing-administrative kind. The fiction of discreteness is fully displaced as the relation takes on the properties of a "minisociety with a vast array of norms beyond those centered on the exchange and its immediate processes" (Macneil, 1978, p. 901). By contrast with the neoclassical system, where the reference point for effecting adaptations remains the original agreement, the reference point under a truly relational approach is the "entire relation as it has developed [through] time. This may or may not include an 'original agreement'; and if it does, may or may not result in great deference being given it" (Macneil, 1978, p. 890).

The spinoff to which Macneil refers notwithstanding, commercial law, labor law, and corporate law all possess striking commonalities.

2. Efficient governance

As discussed above, the principal dimensions for describing transactions are asset specificity, uncertainty, and frequency. It will facilitate the argument in

127

this section to assume that uncertainty is present in sufficient degree to pose an adaptive, sequential decision requirement, and to focus on asset specificity and frequency. Three frequency classes – one-time, occasional, and recurrent – and three asset specificity classes – nonspecific, mixed, and highly specific – will be considered. To simplify the argument further, the following assumptions are made: (1) Suppliers and buyers intend to be in business on a continuing basis; thus the special hazards posed by fly-by-night firms can be disregarded. (2) Potential suppliers for any given requirement are numerous – which is to say that *ex ante* monopoly in ownership of specialized resources is assumed away. (3) The frequency dimension refers strictly to buyer activity in the market. (4) The investment dimension refers to the characteristics of investments made by suppliers.

Although discrete transactions are intriguing – for example, purchasing local spirits from a shopkeeper in a remote area of a foreign country one expects never again to visit or refer his friends – few transactions have such a totally isolated character. For those that do not, the difference between one-time and occasional transactions is not apparent. Accordingly, only occasional and recurrent frequency distinctions will be maintained. The two-by-three matrix shown in Figure 9.1 thus describes the six types of transactions to which governance structures must be matched. Illustrative transactions appear in the cells.

The question now is how Macneil's contracting classifications correspond

		Investment Characteristics		
		Nonspecific	Mixed	Idiosyncratic
Frequency	Occasional	Purchasing standard equipment	Purchasing customized equipment	Constructing a plant
	Recurrent	Purchasing standard material	Purchasing customized material	Site-specific transfer of intermediate product across successive stages

Figure 9.1. Illustrative Transactions

to the description of transactions in Figure 9.1. Several propositions are suggested immediately: (1) Highly standardized transactions are not apt to require specialized governance structure. (2) Only recurrent transactions will support a highly specialized governance structure. (3) Although occasional transactions of a nonstandardized kind will not support a transaction-specific governance structure, they require special attention nonetheless. In terms of Macneil's three-way classification of contract, classical contracting presumably applies to all standardized transactions (whatever the frequency), relational contracting develops for transactions of a recurring and non-standardized kind, and neoclassical contracting is needed for occasional nonstandardized transactions.

Specifically, classical contracting is approximated by what is described below as market governance, neoclassical contracting involves trilateral governance, and the relational contracts that Macneil describes are organized in bilateral or unified governance structures. Consider these seriatim.

2.1 Market governance

Market governance is the main governance structure for nonspecific transactions of both occasional and recurrent contracting. Markets are especially efficacious when recurrent transactions are contemplated, since both parties need only consult their own experience in deciding to continue a trading relationship or, at little transitional expense, turn elsewhere. Being standardized, alternative purchase and supply arrangements are presumably easy to work out.

Nonspecific but occasional transactions are ones for which buyers (and sellers) are less able to rely on direct experience to safeguard transactions against opportunism. Often, however, rating services or the experience of other buyers of the same good can be consulted. Given that the good or service is of a standardized kind, such experience rating, by formal and informal means, will provide incentives for parties to behave responsibly.

To be sure, such transactions take place within and benefit from a legal framework. But such dependence is not great. As S. Todd Lowry puts it, "the traditional economic analysis of exchange in a market setting properly corresponds to the legal concept of *sale* (rather than contract), since sale presumes arrangements in a market context and requires legal support primarily in enforcing transfers of title" (1976, p. 12). He would thus reserve the concept of contract for exchanges where, in the absence of standardized market alternatives, the parties have designed "patterns of future relations on which they could rely" (1976, p. 13).

The assumptions of the discrete contracting paradigm are rather well satisfied for transactions where markets serve as a main governance mode. Thus the specific identity of the parties is of negligible importance; substantive content is determined by reference to formal terms of the contract; and legal rules apply. Market alternatives are mainly what protect each party against opportunism by his opposite. Litigation is strictly for settling claims; concentrated efforts to sustain the relation are not made, because the relation is not independently valued.

2.2 Trilateral governance

The two types of transactions for which trilateral governance is needed are occasional transactions of the mixed and highly specific kinds. Once the principals to such transactions have entered into a contract, there are strong incentives to see the contract through to completion. Not only have specialized investments been put in place, the opportunity cost of which is much lower in alternative uses, but the transfer of those assets to a successor supplier would pose inordinate difficulties in asset valuation. The interests of the principals in sustaining the relation are especially great for highly idiosyncratic transactions.

Market relief is thus unsatisfactory. Often the setup costs of a transaction-specific governance structure cannot be recovered for occasional transactions. Given the limits of classical contract law for sustaining such transactions, on the one hand, and the prohibitive cost of transaction-specific (bilateral) governance, on the other, an intermediate institutional form is evidently needed. Neoclassical contract law has many of the sought-after qualities. Thus rather than resorting immediately to court-ordered litigation – with its transaction-rupturing features – third-party *assistance* (arbitration) in resolving disputes and evaluating performance is employed instead. (The use of the architect as a relatively independent expert to determine the content of form construction contracts is an example [Macneil, 1978, p. 566].) Also, the expansion of the specific performance remedy in past decades is consistent with continuity purposes – though Macneil declines to characterize specific performance as the "primary neoclassical contract remedy" (1978, p. 879). The section of the Uniform Commercial Code that permits the "seller aggrieved by a buyer's breach . . . unilaterally to maintain the relation" is yet another example.

2.3 Bilateral governance

The two types of transactions for which specialized governance structure are commonly devised are recurring transactions supported by investments of the mixed and highly specific kinds. The fundamental transformation applies because of the nonstandardized nature of the transactions. Continuity of the trading relation is thus valued. The transactions' recurrent nature potentially permits the cost of specialized governance structures to be recovered.

Two types of transaction-specific governance structures for intermediate product market transactions can be distinguished: bilateral structures, where the autonomy of the parties is maintained, and unified structures, where the transaction is removed from the market and organized within the firm subject to an authority relation (vertical integration). Bilateral structures have only recently received the attention they deserve, and their operation is least well understood. . . .

Highly idiosyncratic transactions are ones where the human and physical assets required for production are extensively specialized, so there are no obvious scale economies to be realized through interfirm trading that the buyer (or seller) is unable to realize himself (through vertical integration). In the case, however, of mixed transactions, the degree of asset specialization is less complete. Accordingly, outside procurement for those components may be favored by scale economy considerations.

As compared with vertical integration, outside procurement also maintains high-powered incentives and limits bureaucratic distortions. . . . Problems with market procurement arise, however, when adaptability and contractual expense are considered. Whereas internal adaptations can be effected by fiat, outside procurement involves effecting adaptations across a market interface. Unless the need for adaptations has been contemplated from the outset and expressly provided for by the contract, which often is impossible or prohibitively expensive, adaptations across a market interface can be accomplished only by mutual, follow-on agreements. Inasmuch as the interests of the parties will commonly be at variance when adaptation proposals (originated by either party) are made, a dilemma is evidently posed.

On the one hand, both parties have an incentive to sustain the relationship rather than to permit it to unravel, the object being to avoid the sacrifice of valued transaction-specific economies. On the other hand, each party appropriates a separate profit stream and cannot be expected to accede readily to any proposal to adapt the contract. What is needed, evidently, is some way for declaring admissible dimensions for adjustment such that flexibility is provided under terms in which both parties have confidence. This can be accomplished partly by (1) recognizing that the hazards of opportunism vary with the type of adaptation proposed and (2) restricting adjustments to those where the hazards are least. But the spirit within which adaptations are effected is equally important (Macaulay, 1963, p. 61).

. . .

2.4 Unified governance

Incentives for trading weaken as transactions become progressively more idiosyncratic. The reason is that as human and physical assets become more specialized to a single use, and hence less transferable to other uses, economies of scale can be as fully realized by the buyer as by an outside supplier. The choice of organizing mode then turns entirely on which mode has superior adaptive properties. As discussed in Chapter 4 of Williamson (1985), vertical integration will ordinarily appear in such circumstances.

The advantage of vertical integration is that adaptations can be made in a sequential way without the need to consult, complete, or revise interfirm agreements. Where a single ownership entity spans both sides of the transaction, a presumption of joint profit maximization is warranted. Thus price adjustments in vertically integrated enterprises will be more complete than in interfirm trading. And, assuming that internal incentives are not misaligned, quantity adjustments will be implemented at whatever frequency serves to maximize the joint gain to the transaction.

Unchanging identity at the interface coupled with extensive adaptability in both price and quantity is thus characteristic of highly idiosyncratic transactions. Market contracting gives way to bilateral contracting, which in turn is supplanted by unified contracting (internal organization) as asset specificity progressively deepens.[1]

The efficient match of governance structures with transactions that results from the foregoing is shown in Figure 9.2.

3. Uncertainty

The proposed match of governance structures with transactions considers only two of the three dimensions for describing transactions: asset specificity and

---

[1]Note that this transaction cost rationale for internal organization is very different from that originally advanced by Coase. He argued that there are two factors that favor organizing production in the firm as compared with the market: the cost of "discovering what the relevant prices are" is purportedly lower, and the "costs of negotiating and concluding a separate contract for each exchange transaction which takes place on a market" are reduced (Coase, 1952, p. 336). His 1972 treatment of the main differences between firms and markets invokes precisely these same two factors (Coase, 1972, p. 63). Expressed in terms of the behavioral assumptions on which I rely, Coase (implicitly) acknowledges bounded rationality but makes no reference to opportunism. Indeed, to contend, as he does, that Knight offers no reason for superseding the price system, since "[w]e can imagine a system where all advice or knowledge was bought as required" (Coase, 1952, p. 346), is essentially to deny that markets for information are beset by opportunism. Coase is not only silent on the contracting hazards and maladaptations on which I rely to explain nonstandard contracting, but he makes no mention of the need to dimensionalize transactions, which is the key to the discriminating approach. Those differences notwithstanding, the debts of transaction cost economics to Coase's early work are beyond adequate acknowledgment.

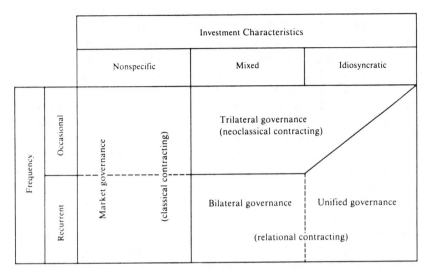

Figure 9.2. Efficient Governance

frequency. The third dimension, uncertainty, is assumed to be present in sufficient degree to pose an adaptive, sequential decision problem. The occasion to make successive adaptations arises because of the impossibility (or costliness) of enumerating all possible contingencies and/or stipulating appropriate adaptations to them in advance. The effects on economic organization of increases in uncertainty above that threshold level have not, however, been considered.

As indicated earlier, nonspecific transactions are ones for which continuity has little value, since new trading relations can be easily arranged by both parties. Increasing the degree of uncertainty does not alter this. Market governance (classical contracting) thus holds across standardized transactions of all kinds, whatever the degree of uncertainty.

Matters change when asset specificity is introduced. Since continuity now matters, increasing the degree of parametric uncertainty makes it more imperative to organize transactions within governance structures that have the capacity to "work things out." Failure to support transaction-specific assets with protective governance structures predictably results in costly haggling and maladaptiveness. Efforts to restore a position on the shifting contract curve may be forgone for this reason. The intrusion of behavioral uncertainty, which is associated with unique events, compounds the difficulties.

. . .

133

Transactions with mixed investment attributes pose especially interesting organizational problems. Unless an appropriate market-assisted governance structure can be devised, such transactions may "flee" to one of the polar extremes as the degree of uncertainty increases. One possibility would be to sacrifice valued design features in favor of a more standardized good or service. Market governance would then apply. Alternatively, the valued design features could be preserved (perhaps even enhanced) and the transaction assigned to internal organization instead. Sometimes, however, it will be feasible to devise nonstandard contracts. . . . Where that is done (and is not prohibited by public policy), bilateral contracting relations between nominally autonomous contracting agents can often survive the stresses of greater uncertainty.

Reductions in uncertainty, of course, warrant shifting transactions in the opposite direction – although such shifts may be delayed if the assets in question are long-lived. To the extent that uncertainty decreases as an industry matures, which is the usual case, the benefits that accrue to internal organization (vertical integration) presumably decline. Accordingly, greater reliance on market procurement is commonly feasible for transactions of recurrent trading in mature industries.

. . .

5. The distribution of transactions

The study of contractual relations plainly involves more than an examination of discrete markets on the one hand and hierarchical organization on the other. As Llewellyn observed in 1931, the exchange spectrum runs the full gamut from pure market to hierarchy and includes complex "future deals" located between market and hierarchy extremes (1931, p. 727). Similarly, George Richardson remarks that "what confronts us is a continuum passing from transactions, such as those on organized commodity markets, where the cooperation element is minimal, through intermediate areas in which there are linkages of traditional connection and good will, and finally to those complex and interlocking clusters, groups and alliances which represent cooperation fully and formally developed" (1972, p. 887). Both Richardson's examples and those more recently developed and discussed by Arthur Stinchcombe (1983) demonstrate that activity in the middle range is extensive. Stewart Macaulay's empirical examination of commercial contracting practices (1963) confirms this.

Suppose that transactions were to be arrayed in terms of the degree to which parties to the trade maintained autonomy. Discrete transactions would thus be

134

located at the one extreme; highly centralized, hierarchical transactions would be at the other; and hybrid transactions (franchising, joint ventures, other forms of nonstandard contracting) would be located in between. What would the resulting distribution of transactions look like?

The three leading candidates are (1) the bimodal distribution, where most transactions cluster at one or the other extreme, (2) the normal distribution, whence the extremes are rare and most transactions display an intermediate degree of interdependence, and (3) the uniform transaction. Whereas I was earlier of the view that transactions of the middle kind were very difficult to organize and hence were unstable, on which account the bimodal distribution was more accurately descriptive (Williamson, 1975), I am now persuaded that transactions in the middle range are much more common. (Such transactions have, moreover, been the object of increasing attention in the economic,[2] legal,[3] and organizations[4] literatures.) But inasmuch as standardized commodity transactions are numerous and as administrative organization is similarly widespread, the tails of the distribution are thick. By a process of elimination, the uniform distribution appears most nearly to correspond with the world of contract as it is. Whatever the empirical realities, greater attention to transactions of the middle range will help to illuminate an understanding of complex economic organization. If such transactions flee to the extremes, what are the reasons? If such transactions can be stabilized, what are the governance processes?

[2]See especially Chapters 7, 8, 10, and 13 [of Williamson (1985)] and the numerous references to the recent economic literature therein.

[3]Macaulay (1963); Macneil (1974); Clarkson, Miller and Muris (1978); Atiyah (1979); Goetz and Scott (1983); Palay (1984); Masten (1984); and Kronman (1985) are examples.

[4]Stinchcombe (1983), Harrison White (1981), Robert Eccles (1981), and Granovetter (1983) are examples.

CHAPTER 10

The organization of industry

G. B. RICHARDSON

George Richardson was born in 1924 in London, England. He received a Master of Arts degree in philosophy, politics, and economics at the University of Oxford. When the present article was published, he was University Reader in Economics at Oxford. After a period of service as Pro-Vice-Chancellor of the University and Warden of Keble College, Oxford, he retired in 1994.

I

I was once in the habit of telling pupils that firms might be envisaged as islands of planned coordination in a sea of market relations. This now seems to me a highly misleading account of the way in which industry is in fact organized. The underlying idea, of course, was of the existence of two ways in which economic activity could be coordinated: the one, conscious planning, holding sway within firms; the other, the price mechanism, operating spontaneously on the relations between firms and between firms and their customers. The theory of the firm, I argued, had as its central core an elaboration of the logic of this conscious planning; the theory of markets analyzed the working of the price mechanism under a variety of alternative structural arrangements.

. . .

Let me now turn to the species of industrial activity that our simple story, based as it is on a dichotomy between firm and market, leaves out of account. What I have in mind is the dense network of cooperation and affiliation by which firms are interrelated. Our theoretical firms are indeed islands, being characteristically well-defined autonomous units buying and selling at arms'

Reprinted with abridgments from G. B. Richardson, "The Organization of Industry," *Economic Journal,* 82 (1972): 883–96, by permission of the publisher.

length in markets. Such cooperation as takes place between them is normally studied as a manifestation of the desire to restrict competition and features in chapters about price agreements and market sharing. But if the student closes his textbook and takes up a business history, or the financial pages of a newspaper, or a report of the Monopolies Commission, he will be presented with a very different picture. Firm A, he may find, is a joint subsidiary of firms B and C, has technical agreements with D and E, subcontracts work to F, is in marketing association with G – and so on. So complex and ramified are these arrangements, indeed, that the skills of a genealogist rather than an economist might often seem appropriate for their disentanglement. But does all this matter? Theories necessarily abstract and it is always easy to point to things they leave out of account. I hope to show that the excluded phenomena in this case are of importance and that by looking at industrial reality in terms of a sharp dichotomy between firm and market we obtain a distorted view of how the system works. Before doing so, however, I wish to dwell a little longer on the several forms that cooperation and affiliation may take; although the arrangements to be described are no doubt well known to the reader, explicit mention may nevertheless help to draw attention to their variety and extent.

II

Perhaps the simplest form of interfirm cooperation is that of a trading relationship between two or more parties which is stable enough to make demand expectations more reliable and thereby to facilitate production planning. The relationship may acquire its stability merely from goodwill or from more formal arrangements such as long-term contracts or shareholding. . . .

Cooperation may frequently take place within the framework provided by subcontracting. An indication of the importance of this arrangement is provided by the fact that about a quarter of the output of the Swedish engineering industry is made up of subcontracted components, while for Japan the corresponding figure is about a third and in that country's automobile industry almost a half. Subcontracting on an international basis, moreover, is said to be becoming more widespread and now a dense network of arrangements links the industries of different countries. . . .

Cooperation also takes place between firms that rely on each other for manufacture or marketing and its fullest manifestation is perhaps to be found in the operations of companies such as Marks and Spencer and British Home Stores. Nominally, these firms would be classified as retail chains, but in reality they are the engineers or architects of complex and extended patterns of coordinated activity. Not only do Marks and Spencer tell their suppliers how

137

much they wish to buy from them, and thus promote a quantitative adjustment of supply to demand, they concern themselves equally with the specification and development of both processes and products.

Mention should be made, finally, of cooperative arrangements specifically contrived to pool or to transfer technology. Surely the field of technical agreements between enterprises is one of the underdeveloped areas of economics. These agreements are commonly based on the licensing or pooling of patents but they provide in a quite general manner for the provision or exchange of know-how through the transfer of information, drawings, tools, and personnel. At the same time they are often associated with the acceptance by the parties to them of a variety of restrictions on their commercial freedom – that is to say with price agreements, market sharing, and the like.

This brief description of the varieties of interfirm cooperation purports to do no more than exemplify the phenomenon. But how is such cooperation to be defined? And how in particular are we to distinguish between cooperation on the one hand and market transactions on the other? The essence of cooperative arrangements such as those we have reviewed would seem to be the fact that the parties to them accept some degree of obligation – and therefore give some degree of assurance – with respect to their future conduct. But there is certainly room for infinite variation in the scope of such assurances and in the degree of formality with which they are expressed. The blanket manufacturer who takes a large order from Marks and Spencer commits himself by taking the appropriate investment and organizational decisions; and he does so in the expectation that this company will continue to put business in his way. In this instance, the purchasing company gives no formal assurance but its past behavior provides suppliers with reason to expect that they can normally rely on getting further orders on acceptable terms. The qualification "normally" is, of course, important, and the supplier is aware that the continuation of orders is conditional on a sustained demand for blankets, satisfaction with the quality of his manufacture, and so on. In a case such as this, any formal specification of the terms and conditions of the assurance given by the supplier would scarcely be practicable and the function of goodwill and reputation is to render it unnecessary.

Where buyer and seller accept no obligation with respect to their future conduct, however loose and implicit the obligation might be, then cooperation does not take place and we can refer to a pure market transaction. Here there is no continuing association, no give and take, but an isolated act of purchase and sale such, for example, as takes place on an organized market for financial securities. The pure market transaction is therefore a limiting case, the ingredient of cooperation being very commonly present, in some degree, in the relationship between buyer and seller. Thus although I shall have occasion to refer to cooperation and market transactions as distinct and alternative modes of coordinating economic activity, we must not imagine that reality exhibits a sharp line of distinction; what confronts us is a continuum passing from transactions, such as those on organized commodity markets, where the cooperative element is minimal, through intermediate areas in which there are linkages of traditional connection and goodwill, and finally to those complex and interlocking clusters, groups, and alliances which represent cooperation fully and formally developed. And just as the presence of cooperation is a matter of degree, so also is the sovereignty that any nominally independent firm is able to exercise on a de facto basis, for the substance of autonomy may often have been given up to a customer or a licensor. A good alliance, Bismarck affirmed, should have a horse and a rider, and, whether or not one agrees with him, there is little doubt that in the relations between firms as well as nation-states, the condition is often met.

III

. . .

It is convenient to think of industry as carrying out an indefinitely large number of *activities,* activities related to the discovery and estimation of future wants; to research, development, and design; to the execution and coordination of processes of physical transformation, the marketing of goods, and so on. And we have to recognise that these activities have to be carried out by organizations with appropriate *capabilities,* or, in other words, with appropriate knowledge, experience, and skills. The capability of an organization may depend upon command of some particular material technology, such as cellulose chemistry, electronics, or civil engineering, or may derive from skills in marketing or knowledge of and reputation in a particular market. Activities which require the same capability for their undertaking I shall call *similar activities.* The notion of capability is no doubt somewhat vague, but no more so perhaps than that of, say, liquidity and, I believe, no less useful. What concerns us here is the fact that organizations will tend to specialize in activities for which their capabilities offer some comparative advantage; these activities will, in other words, generally be similar in the sense in which I have defined the term although they may nevertheless lead the firm into a variety of markets and a variety of product lines. Under capitalism, this degree of specialization will come about through competition but it seems to

139

me likely to be adopted under any alternative system for reasons of manifest convenience.

. . .

IV

I have argued that organizations tend to specialize in activities which, in our special sense of the term, are similar. But the organization of industry has also to adapt itself to the fact that activities may be *complementary*. I shall say that activities are complementary when they represent different phases of a process of production and require in some way or another to be coordinated. But it is important that this notion of complementarity be understood to describe, for instance, not only the relationship between the manufacture of cars and their components, but also the relationship of each of these to the corresponding activities of research and development and of marketing. Now it is clear that similarity and complementarity, as I have defined them, are quite distinct; clutch linings are complementary to clutches and to cars but, in that they are best made by firms with a capability in asbestos fabrication, they are similar to drainpipes and heat-proof suits. Similarly, the production of porcelain insulators is complementary to that of electrical switchgear but similar to other ceramic manufacture. And while the activity of retailing toothbrushes is complementary to their manufacture, it is similar to the activity of retailing soap. This notion of complementarity will require closer definition at a later stage, but it will be convenient first to introduce one further (and final) set of conceptual distinctions.

It is clear that complementary activities have to be coordinated both quantitatively and qualitatively. Polymer production has to be matched, for example, with spinning capacity, both in terms of output volume and product characteristics, and investment in heavy electrical equipment has likewise to be appropriate, in scale and type, to the planned construction of power stations. Now this coordination can be effected in three ways; by *direction,* by *cooperation,* or through *market transactions*. Direction is employed when the activities are subject to a single control and fitted into one coherent plan. Thus where activities are subject to be coordinated by direction it is appropriate that they be *consolidated* in the sense of being undertaken jointly by one organization. Coordination is achieved through cooperation when two or more independent organizations agree to match their related plans in advance. The institutional counterparts to this form of coordination are the complex patterns of cooperation and affiliation which theoretical formulations too often tend to ignore. And, finally, coordination may come about spontaneously through market transactions, without benefit of either direction or cooperation or indeed any purposeful intent, as an indirect consequence of successive interacting decisions taken in response to changing profit opportunities. Let us now make use of this somewhat crude categorization to reinterpret the questions with which we started.

V

What is the appropriate division of labor, we should now ask, between consolidation, cooperation, and market transactions?

If we were able to assume that the scale on which an activity was undertaken did not affect its efficiency, and further that no special capabilities were ever required by the firm undertaking it, then there would be no limit to the extent to which coordination could be affected by direction within one organization. If production could be set up according to "given" production functions with constant returns, no firm need ever buy from, or sell to, or cooperate with any other. Each of them would merely buy inputs, such as land and labor, and sell directly to consumers – which, indeed, is what in our model building they are very often assumed to do. But, of course, activities do exhibit scale economies and do require specialized organizational capabilities for their undertaking, the result being that self-sufficiency of this kind is unattainable. The scope for coordination by direction within firms is narrowly circumscribed, in other words, by the existence of scale economies and the fact that complementary activities need not be similar. The larger the organization the greater the number of capabilities with which one may conceive it to be endowed and the greater the number of complementary activities that can, in principle, be made subject to coordination through direction; but even if a national economy were to be run as a single business, it would prove expedient to trade with the rest of the world. Some coordination, that is to say, must be left either to cooperation or to market transactions and it is to the respective roles of each of these that our attention must now turn.

Building and brick making are dissimilar activities and each is undertaken by large numbers of enterprises. Ideally, the output of bricks ought to be matched to the volume of complementary construction that makes use of them and it is through market transactions that we expect this to come about. Brick makers, in taking investment and output decisions, estimate future market trends; and errors in these estimates are registered in stock movements and price changes which can lead to corrective actions. As we all know, these adjustments may work imperfectly and I have myself argued elsewhere[1] that the model which we

---

[1] In Richardson (1961).

often use to represent this type of market is unsatisfactory. But this is a matter with which we cannot now concern ourselves. What is important, for our present purposes, is to note that impersonal coordination through market forces is relied upon where there is reason to expect aggregate demands to be more stable (and hence predictable) than their component elements. If coordination were to be sought through cooperation, then individual brick makers would seek to match their investment and output plans *ex ante* with individual builders. Broadly speaking, this does not happen, although traditional links between buyers and sellers, such as are found in most markets, do introduce an element of this kind. Individual brick manufacturers rely, for the most part, on having enough customers to ensure some canceling out of random fluctuations in their several demands. And where sales to final consumers are concerned, this reliance on the law of large numbers becomes all but universal. Thus we rely on markets when there is no attempt to match complementary activities *ex ante* by deliberately coordinating the corresponding plans; salvation is then sought, not through reciprocal undertakings, but on that stability with which aggregates, by the law of large numbers, are providentially endowed.

Let us now consider the need to coordinate the production of cans with tin plate or lacquers, of a particular car with a particular brake and a particular brake lining, of a type of glucose with the particular beer in which it is to be used, or a cigarette with the appropriate filter tip. Here we require to match not the aggregate output of a general-purpose input with the aggregate output for which it is needed, but of particular activities which, for want of a better word, we might call *closely complementary*. The coordination, both quantitative and qualitative, needed in these cases requires the cooperation of those concerned; and it is for this reason that the motor car companies are in intimate association with component makers, that Metal Box interests itself in its lacquer suppliers, Imperial Tobacco with Bunzl, and so on. Coordination in these cases has to be promoted either through the consolidation of the activities within organizations with the necessary spread of capabilities, or though close cooperation, or by means of institutional arrangements which, by virtue of limited shareholdings and other forms of affiliation, come somewhere in between.

Here then we have the prime reason for the existence of the complex networks of cooperation and association the existence of which we noted earlier. They exist because of the need to coordinate closely complementary but dissimilar activities. This coordination cannot be left entirely to direction within firms because the activities are dissimilar, and cannot be left to market forces in that it requires not the balancing of the aggregate supply of something with the aggregate demand for it but rather the matching, both qualitative and quantitative, of individual enterprise plans.

142

VI

. . .

It is indeed appropriate to observe that the organization of industry has to adapt itself to the need for coordination of a rather special kind, for coordination, that is to say, between the development of technology and its exploitation. . . .

The indirect exploitation of new technology could be sought, in terms of our nomenclature, either through market transactions or through cooperation with other firms. But technology is a very special commodity and the market for it a very special market. It is not always easy, in the first place, to stop knowledge becoming a free good. The required scarcity may have to be created artificially through a legal device, the patent system, which establishes exclusive rights in the use or the disposal of new knowledge. Markets may then develop in licenses of right. But these are very special markets in that the commercial freedom of those operating within them is necessarily restricted. For suppose that A were to sell to B for a fixed sum a license to make a new product, but at the same time retained the unfettered right to continue to produce and sell the product himself. In this case the long- and short-run marginal costs of production of the good would, for both parties, be below unit costs (because of the fixed cost incurred by A in the development work and by B as a lump sum paid for the license) so that unrestrained competition would drive prices to unremunerative levels. It might at first seem that this danger could be avoided if licenses were charged for as a royalty on sales, which, unlike a fixed sum, would enter into variable costs. But the licensee might still require assurance that the licensor, unburdened by this cost element, would not subsequently set a price disadvantageous to him or even license to others on more favorable terms. These dangers could be avoided if the parties were to bind themselves by price or market-sharing agreements or simply by the prudent adoption of the policy of live and let live. But, in one way or another, it seems likely that competition would in some degree have been diminished.

It would appear, therefore, on the basis of these considerations, that where the creation and exploitation of technology is coordinated through market transactions – transactions in licenses – there will already be some measure of cooperation between the parties. The cooperation may, of course, amount to little more than is required not to rock, or at any rate not to sink, the boat. But there are reasons why it will generally go beyond this. Technology cannot always be transferred simply by selling the right to use a process. It is rarely

G . B . RICHARDSON

reducible to mere information to be passed on but consists also of experience and skills. In terms of Professor Ryle's celebrated distinction, much of it is "knowledge how" rather than "knowledge that." Thus when one firm agrees to provide technology to another it will, in the general case, supply not only licenses but also continuing technical assistance, drawings, designs, and tools. At this stage the relation between the firms becomes clearly cooperative and although, at its inception, there may be a giver and a receiver, subsequent development may lead to a more equal exchange of assistance and the pooling of patents. Arrangements of this kind form an important part of the networks of cooperation and affiliation to which I have made such frequent reference.

VII

This article began by referring to a vision of the economy in which firms featured as islands of planned coordination in a sea of market relations. The deficiencies of this representation of things will by now be clear. Firms are not islands but are linked together in patterns of cooperation and affiliation. Planned coordination does not stop at the frontiers of the individual firm but can be effected through cooperation between firms. The dichotomy between firm and market, between directed and spontaneous coordination, is misleading; it ignores the institutional fact of interfirm cooperation and assumes away the distinct method of coordination that this can provide.

. . .

Let me end with two further observations. I have sought to stress the cooperative element in business relations but by no means take the view that where there is cooperation, competition is no more. Marks and Spencer can drop a supplier; a subcontractor can seek another principal; technical agreements have a stated term and the conditions on which they may be renegotiated will depend on how the strengths of the parties change and develop; the licensee of today may become (as the Americans have found in Japan) the competitor of tomorrow. Firms form partners for the dance but, when the music stops, they can change them. In these circumstances competition is still at work even if it has changed its mode of operation.

Theories of industrial organization, it seems to me, should not try to do too much. Arguments designed to prove the inevitability of this or that particular form of organization are hard to reconcile, not only with the differences between the capitalist and socialist worlds but also with the differences that exist within each of these. . . . It is important, moreover, not to draw too sharp lines of distinction between the techniques of coordination themselves. Cooperation may come close to direction when one of the parties is clearly

144

predominant, and some degree of *ex ante* matching of plans is to be found in all markets in which firms place orders in advance. This points, however, not to the invalidity of our triple distinction but merely to the need to apply it with discretion.[2]

[2]In his article, "The Nature of the Firm" *Economica,* 1937, pp. 386–405, R. H. Coase explains the boundary between firm and market in terms of the relative cost, at the margin, of the kinds of coordination they respectively provide. The explanation that I have provided is not inconsistent with his but might be taken as giving content to the notion of this relative cost by specifying the factors that affect it. My own approach differs also in that I distinguish explicitly between interfirm cooperation and market transactions as modes of coordination.

CHAPTER 11

The limits of firms: incentive and bureaucratic features

OLIVER WILLIAMSON

Oliver Williamson is Professor of Business, Economics, and Law at the University of California, Berkeley. See also the previous paper by Williamson.

Why can't a large firm do everything that a collection of small firms can do and more? That is a variant of a question asked many times before for which an adequate answer has never been devised – to wit, what is responsible for limitations in firm size? Yet another way of putting the same issue is this: Why not organize everything in one large firm?

The trade-off model in Chapter 4 [of Williamson (1985)] offers two reasons why a firm would eschew integration: economies of scale and scope may be sacrificed if the firm attempts to make for itself what it can procure in the market, and the governance costs of internal organization exceed those of market organization where asset specificity is slight. . . . The first is not a thoroughly comparative explanation. If economies of scale are realized by the outside supplier, then the same economies can be preserved upon merger by instructing the supplier to service the market in the future just as it has in the past. The fundamental limitation to firm size thus must turn on the governance cost disabilities of internal organization where asset specificity is insubstantial. But wherein do the firm's comparative disabilities in those governance cost . . . respects reside? . . .

. . .

1. A chronic puzzle

Frank Knight made early reference to the limitations to firm size puzzle when, in 1921, he observed that the "diminishing returns to management is a subject often referred to in economic literature, but in regard to which there is a dearth of scientific discussion" (1965, p. 286, n. 1). And in 1933 he elaborated as follows:

The Limits of Firms: Incentive and Bureaucratic Features

The relation between efficiency and size of firm is one of the most serious problems of theory, being, in contrast with the relation for a plant, largely a matter of personality and historical accident rather than of intelligible general principles. But the question is peculiarly vital, because the possibility of monopoly gain offers a powerful incentive to *continuous and unlimited* expansion of the firm, which force must be offset by some equally powerful one making for decreased efficiency [1965, p. xxiii; emphasis in original].

. . .

A different way of posing the issue is in terms not of horizontal but of vertical integration. Thus Ronald Coase inquired, "Why does the entrepreneur not organize one less transaction or one more?" (1952, p. 339) More generally the issue is, "Why is not all production carried on in one big firm?" (p. 340)

Various answers have been advanced. They all suffer, however, from a failure to adopt and maintain the relevant comparative institutional standard. Thus consider Knight's response: "The question of diminishing returns from entrepreneurship is really a matter of the amount of uncertainty present. To imagine that a man could adequately manage a business enterprise of indefinite size and complexity is to imagine a situation in which effective uncertainty is entirely absent" (1965, pp. 286–87). In effect, Knight attributes limitations upon entrepreneurship to a condition of bounded rationality. As uncertainty increases, problems of organization become increasingly complex, and bounds on cognitive competence are reached. But he does not address the issues in a genuinely comparative manner.

Thus suppose that two firms are competing. In principle, net gains ought always to be available by merging the two. Economies of scale can be more fully exploited. Certain overhead and rivalry expenses can be curtailed. And product prices may improve – at least temporarily. Joining the two does not increase the aggregate uncertainty. Since the gaming moves and replies of rivalry have been removed, uncertainty has arguably been reduced. Moreover – and this is the really critical point – decisions need not be forced to the top but can always be assigned to the level at which the issues are most appropriately resolved. Specifically, by conferring semiautonomous status on what had previously been fully autonomous firms in the premerger period, the best of both worlds can presumably be realized. If, for example, demand or cost interaction effects are such that net gains can be had by moving decisions to the top, it will be done. Those decisions, however, that are most efficiently made at operating levels will remain there. Intervention at the top thus always occurs *selectively,* which is to say only upon a showing of expected net gains. The resulting combined firm can therefore do everything that the two autonomous firms could do previously *and more.* The same argument applies, more-

147

over, not merely to horizontal mergers but also to vertical and conglomerate mergers. The upshot is that, possible public policy restraints (against monopoly, vertical integration, or aggregate size) aside, a compelling reason to explain why all production is not concentrated in one large firm is not reached by Knight's argument.

Although other efforts to explain limitations on firm size have since been made, none addresses the issues in the way I have just posed it. And none really disposes of the puzzle. Thus consider my treatment of limits on firm size in terms of the "control loss" phenomenon (Williamson, 1976b). It involved the application to hierarchical organization of what F. C. Bartlett referred to as the serial reproduction effect in transmitting messages or images between individuals. . . . Bartlett illustrated this graphically with a line drawing of an owl which, when redrawn successively by eighteen individuals, each sketch based on its immediate predecessor, ended up as a recognizable cat; and the farther from the initial drawing one moved, the greater the distortion experienced (1932, pp. 180–81).

I applied the same argument to the firm size dilemma by invoking bounded rationality and noting that limited spans of control are thereby implied. If any one manager can deal directly with only a limited number of subordinates, then increasing firm size necessarily entails adding hierarchical levels. Transmitting information across these levels experiences the losses to which Bartlett referred, which are cumulative and arguably exponential in form. As firm size increases and successive levels of organization are added, therefore, the effects of control loss eventually exceed the gains. A limit upon radial expansion is thus reached in this way.

Plausible though the argument seemed at the time, it does not permit selective intervention of the kind described above. Rather, the entire firm is managed from the top. All information that has a bearing on decisions is transmitted across successive levels from bottom to top; all directives follow the reverse flow down.

The scenario thus contemplates comprehensive (unselective) linkages between stages. Internal organization need not, however, adopt this structure. Suppose instead that the parent firm deals with each of its parts by exercising forbearance with respect to those activities where no net gains are in prospect (in which event the parent directs the operating part to replicate small firm behavior) and intervenes wherever coordination yields net gains. The puzzle to which I referred at the outset is evidently restored – or at least the serial reproduction loss "solution" does not apply – if such selective intervention is admitted.

. . .

148

2. Integration of an owner-managed supply stage

The obvious answer to the puzzle of why firms do not comprehensively integrate is that selective intervention is not feasible. But why should that be? If the reasons were obvious, the puzzle of what is responsible for limitations on firm size would not persist.

I attempt here to identify some of the main reasons why selective intervention breaks down. So as to facilitate the argument, assume that an owner-managed supplier is acquired by the buyer.[1] Assume that this ownership change is accomplished as follows:

1. A price at which the assets are transferred is agreed to.
2. The formula for determining the price at which product is to be transferred from the supply division to the buying division is stipulated.
3. So as to encourage cost economizing, the high-powered incentives that characterize markets are carried over into the firm. Accordingly, the supply division is advised that it will appropriate its net revenues – which are defined as gross revenues less the sum of operating costs, user charges (for asset maintenance and depreciation), and other relevant expenses (e.g. for R & D).
4. Selective intervention will obtain. Accordingly, the supply division is advised to conduct business as usual with the following exception: The supplier will accede to decisions by the buyer to adapt to new circumstances, thereby to realize collective gains, without resistance. Failure to accede is cause for and gives rise to termination.

Unified ownership of the assets of the two stages thus (1) preserves high-powered incentives (rule 3), (2) provides for selective intervention (rule 4), and (3) precludes costly haggling (rule 4). The last two features permit adap-

---

[1]Readers familiar with the recent examination of the costs of vertical integration by Sanford Grossman and Oliver Hart (1984) will recognize that they, like I, trace these costs to incentive impairments that attend unified ownership of successive stages. Their work on these matters and mine were contemporaneous, but I have nevertheless benefited from their treatment and specifically recommend it to those who wish to see these issues developed in a more formal way.

Despite similarities, their work and mine differ in the following significant respects: (1) they ignore the very factors – asset malutilization, accounting contrivances – that I regard as central to incentive distortions in firms; (2) they deny that internal and market organization differ in auditing respects; (3) their "even-handed" insistence that high-powered (transfer pricing) incentives apply in all ownership regimes asymmetrically denies adaptability advantages to integration that weaker (e.g. cost plus) incentives coupled with unified ownership would support; and (4) they disregard the bureaucratic consequences of internal organization. My discussion in this section features asset utilization and accounting effects. Auditing differences are treated in section 4. Salaried management in the preacquisition supply stage is the subject of section 3, and bureaucratic features are addressed in section 5.

tive sequential decision-making economies to be realized by merging what had previously been nonintegrated stages of organization.

Implicit in the argument is the assumption that the two stages are operating in a bilateral exchange relation with each other by reason of investments in transaction-specific assets. Such specificity can take at least four forms: site specificity, physical asset specificity, human asset specificity, and dedicated assets. It will be convenient here to consider only physical asset specificity.

Indeed, given rule 4 above, human asset specificity is effectively ruled out. As developed more fully in Chapter 10 [of Williamson (1985)], it is in the mutual interests of firm and worker to safeguard the employment relation against abrupt termination (by either party) wherever labor develops firm-specific skills and knowledge during the course of its employment. Accordingly, the rule do this/do that or terminate is maladapted to the needs of the parties where firm-specific human assets are considerable. The argument here therefore assumes that the bilateral exchange relation is due entirely to a condition of physical asset specificity. Rule 4 thus applies, whereunder failure to accede to any order to adapt will be cause for termination. Upon realization that successor managements can always be brought in to implement change orders as requested, the incumbent management always acquiesces.

Were this the end of the story, selective intervention with net gains would presumably obtain. In fact, however, numerous measurement difficulties stand in the way of implementing a merger agreement that is attended by high powered incentives. Some of them operate to the disadvantage of the buyer, some work to the disadvantage of the supplier, and others impose losses on both.

2.1 Asset utilization losses

The former owner-manager of the supply stage becomes the manager of the supply division upon sale of the supply stage assets to the buyer. The change of status has immediate and serious incentive effects if the high-powered incentive rules described above are employed. For one thing, the manager who appropriates the net receipts associated with the supply division no longer has the same incentives to utilize equipment with equivalent care and to incur identical preventive maintenance. Since, by assumption, the manager has no firm-specific human assets at stake, the manager behaves myopically with respect to the enterprise. The object being to maximize immediate net receipts, labor costs will be saved by utilizing equipment intensively, and maintenance expense will be deferred to a successor management. Having been paid for his assets upon giving up ownership status, the manager of the supply division proceeds to run them into the ground and leaves the firm to invest his augmented net receipts elsewhere.

150

To be sure, there are checks against asset abuses of both kinds. The new asset owner may insist that certain utilization and maintenance procedures be observed and furthermore monitor the supply division for compliance. Note, however, that added monitoring costs – unneeded in the nonintegrated state – have now been introduced. Additionally, reputation effects can deter managers from behaving irresponsibly. These, however, are imperfect. Some managers may shrug them off if the immediate gains are large enough and if they cannot be required to disgorge their ill-gotten gains. (Swiss bank accounts have attractive features in that respect.)

The upshot is that efficient asset utilization and the use of high-powered incentives experience tensions in an integrated firm – tensions that do not arise when the two production stages are independent. Contrary to the type of selective intervention that I postulated in section 1, the integrated firm *cannot* wholly replicate outside procurement in "business as usual" respects. Instead there are *unavoidable side effects*.

2.2 Accounting contrivances

The price at which a supplier agrees to sell his assets to the buyer will vary with the stream of net receipts that he projects in the postmerger period. Given the high-powered incentives described above, that stream will vary with (1) revenues, (2) costs, and (3) continued employment.

One hazard is that the supplier will be "promised" a favorable net receipt stream, hence accept a low price for transferring asset ownership, only to learn to his dismay that his employment has been terminated. Suppose, out of awareness of such a hazard, the supplier demands and receives a guarantee of continued employment. Such guarantees accomplish little, however, if the net receipts of the supply division can be altered substantially through the exercise of accounting discretion. Expropriation can then be accomplished by indirection.

Net receipts can be squeezed in either or both of two ways. For one, revenues can be reduced by cutting transfer prices. For another, cost imputations can be raised. The supply division is vulnerable in both respects.

Given the impossibility of comprehensive contracting, the transfer pricing rule that is stipulated at the outset will necessarily be incomplete. So as to correct against misalignments, prices will need to be reset periodically to reflect changing circumstances. This can be done by consulting the market if asset specificity is zero. Complications intrude, however, when even a slight degree of asset specificity appears. Thus although the terms under which product is traded between autonomous parties are disciplined by the credible threat that the supplier will retire his specialized assets, rather than use them to support the supplier's specialized procurement needs, if mutually acceptable terms are not reached, the manager of the supply division in the integrated firm does not have the same option. If push comes to shove, the physical assets are no longer his to retire (or, more generally, redeploy). Employment guarantees notwithstanding, the manager of the supply division can, if he refuses to accept the proposed terms, be brushed aside. (He is simply "reassigned.") Upon merger, therefore, the determination of transfer prices has, in effect, become a decision for the purchasing division (which now owns the assets of both parts) to reach unilaterally. The hazard is obvious: Despite assurances to the contrary, prices will be set so as to squeeze the net receipts of the supply stage.

Cost determination is problematic, moreover, whatever the degree of asset specificity. Whereas each stage determines its own accounting practices in the premerger regime, that is no longer permitted – indeed, is wholly implausible – upon merger. Instead, responsibility for the accounting rules will be concentrated on the asset owner. Explicit agreements that limit accounting discretion notwithstanding, the supply stage runs the risk that costs will be reset to its disadvantage.

The upshot is that the supply stage is better advised to discount very heavily any promise that favorable net receipt streams are in prospect and to realize its full bargaining advantage by extracting maximum asset valuation terms at the outset – because a squeeze is in prospect thereafter. But there is more to it. If the use of high-powered incentives in firms is inherently subject to corruption, then the notion that the integrated firm can do everything that the nonintegrated parts could accomplish is a fiction. Instead, the integrated firm does better in some respects and worse in others.

2.3 Incentive ramifications

High-powered incentives in firms give rise to difficulties of two kinds: The assets of the supply stage are not utilized with due care, and the net revenue stream of the supply stage is subject to manipulation. Upon realization that high-powered incentives in firms experience such disabilities, lower-powered incentives are apt to be introduced instead. Were the supply stage management to be compensated mainly by salary and become subject to periodic monitoring (decision review, auditing, and the like), the supply stage would have less need to be concerned with accounting chicanery, and the asset owner's concern with asset dissipation would be lessened.

Low-powered incentives have well-known adaptability advantages. That, after all, is what commends cost plus contracting. But such advantages are not had without cost – which explains why cost plus contracting is embraced reluctantly (Williamson, 1967a). Our first explanation for why firms do not everywhere supplant markets thus is that (1) firms cannot mimic the high-powered incentives of markets without experiencing added costs; (2) although recourse by firms to lower-powered incentives is thereby indicated, that too comes at a cost; and (3) those added costs of internal organization are not offset by comparative adaptability gains under circumstances where [assets are nonspecific], since those are precisely the conditions under which the identity of the parties does not matter, whence classical market contracting works well. The net governance costs of acquiring an owner-operated supply stage are thus positive where asset specificity is slight. . . .

More generally, the argument is this: Incentives and controls are adapted to the attributes of each organizational alternative. To attempt to "hold the rules as nearly constant as possible," on the theory that what works well in one regime ought to apply equally to another, is thus mistaken. The powers and limits of each form of organization must be discovered and respected.

. . .

3. Acquisition of a supply stage in which ownership and management are separated

Suppose, *arguendo,* that vertical integration *of the kind described above* experiences the incentive disabilities that are ascribed to it. It is nevertheless noteworthy that the conditions described above are very special. In particular I have assumed that ownership and management are joined in the preacquisition supply stage. What if that condition does not obtain?

Suppose that an independent supplier undergoes an ownership change before an acquisition of the supplier is even contemplated. Suppose, in particular, that what had been a closely held, owner-managed firm becomes a diffusely held firm in which none of the management has a significant equity interest.

The hazards of using high-powered (net receipt) incentives to compensate the management of this firm will be evident to owners and managers alike. Owners will recognize the asset dissipation hazards, and managers will be concerned that owners will retain influence over accounting, thus posing a risk that net receipt realizations will be manipulated. When those consequences are foreseen, high-powered incentives in this now diffusely owned firm will give way to incentives of a lower-powered kind. Salaried compensation will therefore obtain.

The critical question is whether, in view of the above-described changes that attend the change in ownership of the premerger supply stage, merger incurs any added costs. If it does not, then the acquisition by a purchasing stage of a supply stage in which the ownership has already been sold off

153

would offer the prospect of gain without cost. The gains would presumably take the same form as those ascribed to merger previously: Subgoal pursuit by the supply stage management would be attenuated, so that coordination between the two stages would be accomplished more easily and effectively in the postmerger period when common ownership obtains.

The firm size dilemma to which I referred at the outset would then be restored with only a minor change. The puzzle would now read as follows: Why are not all *diffusely owned* production stages placed under unified ownership, thereby to be organized and operated as one large firm? Unless undisclosed costs of merger are discovered, we are mainly back where we started. Put differently, section 2 is an explication of the Berle and Means problem and does not provide an explanation for limits on vertical integration outside of that special context.

Unremarked merger consequences of three kinds warrant consideration. For one thing, to observe that ownership and management are separated does not establish that ownership is thereafter wholly lacking in control. Differential control effects within merged and nonmerged entities is thus one possibility. Second, the fact that managements in both pre- and postmerger regimes are salaried does not necessarily imply that compensation is disconnected from net receipts. Finally, the possibility that integration affects the internal politics of the corporation with systematic performance consequences warrants scrutiny. The first two consequences are considered here. The third is addressed in section 4.

. . .

4. The costs of bureaucracy

The costs of acquisition discussed in section 2 are mainly ones that will accrue to any separation of ownership from control, merger-related or otherwise. Although the costs of acquisition discussed in section 3 are not confounded in ownership and control respects, they are also more speculative in nature and are probably weaker in effect. The question thus arises as to whether there are other costs of merger that have yet to be identified. In particular, are there undisclosed "costs of bureaucracy" that obtain when successive production stages are joined?

Philip Selznick contends that "the most important thing about [nonmarket] organizations is that, though they are tools, each nevertheless has a life of its own" (1949, p. 10). Instrumental intentions notwithstanding, formal structures can "never succeed in conquering the nonrational dimensions of organizational behavior" (Selznick, 1948, p. 25). Richard Scott summarizes the argument as follows:

[O]rganizational rationality is constrained by "the recalcitrance of the tools of action": persons bring certain characteristics to the organization and develop other commitments as members that restrict their capacity for rational action; organizational procedures become valued ends in themselves; the organization strikes bargains with its environment that compromise present objectives and limit future possibilities [1981, p. 91].

What are the ramifications of such views for economic approaches to the study of organization? One possible economic response is to regard the conditions to which Selznick, Scott, and others refer as noise. Aberrations from rationality are thus treated as error terms. A stronger response is to deny that such behavior even exists. Neither is proposed here. Instead, an informed economic approach to the study of organization will display an interest in and *thereafter make provision for* all regularities of whatever kind. If the behavior in question is systematic, allowance can be made for it in making comparative institutional choices and in organizational design respects. Thus, if some forms of organization are less subject to bureaucratic distortions than others, this will be taken into account in assessing alternative modes. Within modes where distortions are especially severe, moreover, it may be possible to mitigate such conditions by devising checks or organizational reforms.

By comparison with the market failure literature, the literature on bureaucratic failure is relatively underdeveloped. The discussion here merely attempts to identify some of the main life-cycle features that beset internal organization. As compared with market organization, internal organization displays a differential propensity to manage complexity, to forgive error, and to engage in logrolling.

4.1 The propensity to manage

A propensity to manage seems to characterize all forms of bureaucratic organization. To be sure, the public sector is widely thought to be especially culpable in this respect – and probably is. Charles Morris captures the spirit in his reference to "the cost of good intentions." What he characterizes as "the new rationalist style in government" was based on "a confident optimism that the most intractable problems would give way before the resolute assault of intelligent, committed people" (1980, p. 3). But the same attitude also characterizes the private sector (Feldman and March, 1981).

Actually, the propensity to manage has two parts rather than just one. The part to which Morris refers is the *instrumental* propensity: Decision makers project a capacity to manage complexity that is repeatedly refuted by events. Although such a propensity is well-intentioned, problems regularly turn out to be more difficult and/or managerial competence more limited than managers

155

of complexity originally project (Perrow, 1983). Counterexamples to the contrary notwithstanding, this is the main opinion.

The second type of propensity is more reprehensible. It is the *strategic* propensity to use the resources of the organization to pursue subgoals. If, for the reasons given in section 2, pecuniary incentives in firms are weaker than those in markets, then political games and preferences have greater sway. Efforts to tilt the organization, often through greater hands-on management, commonly result.

Odysseus-type solutions are often attractive where *ex ante* resolve is known regularly to break down in the face of recurrent exigencies/temptations. Out of awareness that the call of the Sirens would be well-nigh irresistible, Odysseus instructed that he should be bound to the mast. As Jon Elster points out, "binding oneself is a privileged way of resolving the problem of weakness of will" (1979, p. 37). Such self-denial benefits can be realized within the firm if mergers for which the advocates can identify only limited prospective benefits are refused. The uncounted, but nevertheless predictable, costs attributable to the future propensity to manage will thereby assuredly be avoided.

4.2 Forgiveness

Systems of justice vary systematically with organization. Families are ordinarily presumed to have deep knowledge of the transactions that occur between or impinge on the membership, to employ long time horizons, and to be relatively forgiving.[2] Markets, in contrast, are presumed to have less knowledge of idiosyncratic circumstances, employ shorter time horizons, and are relatively severe (unforgiving).

For the reasons given in section 5, internal organization enjoys comparative auditing advantages. Accordingly, the integrated firm has greater capacity to reach informed decisions on the merits than do nonintegrated trading entities. The confounding of risks and decisions, which complicates market assessments, can thus be unpacked with greater precision and confidence internally. In principal, therefore, internal asset managers can better ascertain whether to continue funding a project than could the capital market.

But there are at least two further consequences. First, the prospect of penalty can and often does elicit inordinate energies. The market is a severe taskmaster, Unless escalator clauses have been expressly agreed to from the outset, unexpected cost increases are absorbed rather than passed through when transactions are mediated by the market. By contrast, unexpected cost increases that occur in trades within the firm are apt to be negotiable. The justification for such increases can be examined more fully within the firm,

---

[2]Of these three aspects, which are all related, forgiveness is the most important and distinctive.

and the hazards of misrepresentation are less severe than in the market. But internal organization is thereby denied access to the supranormal energies that the market is able to mobilize. It is unrealistic to expect that such efforts will be expended if reasoned or plausible explanations can be advanced to support the cost increases in question: Reasoning systems are expected to behave in reasoning ways. (Academics, being the ultimate reasoners, are often unsuited for administrative positions on that account.)

Second, the net benefit calculus employed by firm and market differ. Indeed, a useful definition of forgiveness, at least for purposes of evaluating commercial transactions, is whether "excuses" are evaluated strictly with reference to a pecuniary net benefit calculus or not. As between the two, the market is expected to employ a stricter pecuniary net benefit calculus than is the firm. In this sense, it is less forgiving. A leading reason for this is that the firm maintains greater separability among transactions with the market than it can for transactions that are organized internally.

It is thus easy for a firm to terminate a supplier of a good or service that is supported by nonspecific assets ($k = 0$) at the first indication of failure. Were this same transaction to be organized internally, however, the firm would conduct an inquiry and consider second chances. Partly this is a manifestation of the aforementioned auditing advantage of internal organization. But it is also the case that the firm is unable to treat each internal transaction in a fully separable way. In effect, internal transactions of the $k = 0$ [ed.: nonspecific asset] kind benefit from an association with other internal transactions for which $k > 0$ [ed.: assets are specific].

Thus whereas continuity of transactions of the latter kind is valued from a pecuniary net benefit standpoint, the same is not true for the former. Firms that internalize transactions of both kinds are unable, however, to treat each in a fully discriminating way. A rational decision to "work things out" when things go wrong for $k > 0$ transactions spills over and infects transactions of the $k = 0$ kind. It is unacceptable, both to insiders and to interested observers, for the firm to behave differently. Simple regard for human dignity demands that due process be respected. Barnard's remarks about informal organization are apposite: One of the purposes served by informal organization is that of "maintaining the personality of the individual against certain effects of formal organizations which tend to disintegrate the personality" (Barnard, 1938, p. 122).

Thus whereas extreme market outcomes can be accepted as the luck of the draw, administrative actions are interpreted by all of the affected parties, including interested outsiders (associates, family, friends, and so forth), as merit choices. That places a severe burden of due process on internal organization. A plausible case will not do; a preponderance of evidence is needed if severe penalties are to be meted out. Out of awareness that they operate under the protection of a norm of internal due process, individuals are able to exploit the internal organization in minimum performance respects, and some do.

To be sure, the above described weakening of incentives applies strictly to $k = 0$ activities. The possibility that a merit choice environment intensifies incentives within the firm, as compared with the market, for $k > 0$ activities is not denied. It suffices, however, for the purposes of the argument, that due process spillovers are responsible for incentive attenuation for the $k = 0$ condition.

4.3 Logrolling

Again the issue is not whether internal organization experiences costs but whether differential costs are incurred in moving from nonintegrated to integrated status. I submit that internal operating and investment decisions are more subject to politicization.

a. Operating decisions

Alvin Gouldner contends that the norm of reciprocity is as important and universal as the incest taboo (1961). It finds expression throughout human society – across cultures and degrees of development and over time. Opportunities to give effect to reciprocity, however, vary with the circumstances. In general those opportunities are greater within more highly integrated organizations than in less. Moreover, those opportunities are apt to be given expression – which is a manifestation of the earlier described tendency for internal traders to be more accommodating than autonomous traders. This is not necessarily a bad thing; the prospect of such accommodation is a factor that weighs favorably in evaluating trades that are supported by specific assets. The possibility that it will go beyond the objective merits to include reciprocal managerial back-scratching is, however, a matter for concern and is appropriately taken into account in the decision to internalize incremental transactions.

b. Investment renewal biases

An internal procurement bias is supported by a number of factors. For one thing, the internal supplier that produces mainly for internal uses may be judged to be at a relative disadvantage in the market place. The internal supplier may lack both the large and experienced marketing organization and the established customer connections to which nonintegrated external suppliers have access. In consideration of such conditions, and if fixed costs are nonredeployable, a "preference" for internal procurement might seem appropriate – at least so long as the external price exceeds the variable cost of internal supply.

This may be a specious argument, however, since the nonredeployability of assets may easily be overstated (there may be a secondhand market for the machinery in question) and individual equipment renewal decisions ought eventually to be made with reference to the long-run viability of the internal facility. Managers are notably reluctant, however, to abolish their own jobs, even in the face of employment guarantees. The problems with such guarantees are that while continued employment may be secure, assurances that status will be maintained when a position is eliminated, and that promotion prospects will not be upset upon removal from a known promotion ladder, are unenforceable. A preference for internal supply is thus to be expected and may manifest itself by urging that each equipment replacement decision be made serially, in semi-independent fashion. A fundamentally nonviable internal capability may be uncritically preserved in this way.

4.4 Further remarks

The main benefits of vertical integration, according to the transaction cost economics point of view adopted here, take the form of governance rather than production cost savings. They are discerned by examining the problems that attend autonomous contracting when the parties to a trade are operating in a bilateral exchange relation. The main costs of vertical integration are more difficult to discover, however. They are plainly not of a neoclassical production function kind. Neither are differential governance cost features transparent. Analysis at a more microanalytic level is evidently needed.

. . .

Just as transaction cost reasoning and the examination of microanalytic phenomena has helped to illuminate the factors responsible for market failure, however, I conjecture that similar headway can be made against the subject of bureaucracy if a concerted effort is made here as well.

. . .

5. Low-powered incentives in markets

A symmetrical treatment of economic organization will examine not merely the strains that result when the high-powered incentives associated with markets are introduced into firms, but will also consider whether the low-powered incentives employed by firms can be introduced without strain into markets. The latter question is the matter of concern here.

159

Assume, for the purposes of this section, that the innovative tensions discussed in 2.4 [in Williamson (1985)] are slight. Assume further that the amount of physical asset specificity at the supply stage is great. Integration is thus the indicated form of organization.

Suppose, as a consequence of the factors discussed in subsections 2.1 and 2.2, that the integrated firm decides to transfer product between divisions on the cost plus terms. The supply division thus accedes to requests from the procurement division that it adapt the quantity or quality of the product without resistance. Lest costs be permitted to escalate or economizing opportunities go unnoticed or be forgone, however, the supply division is periodically reviewed in cost and decision respects. Suppose, *arguendo*, that the resulting performance is judged to be satisfactory.

If such low-powered incentives coupled with periodic auditing have advantages in firms, why not replicate the same with markets? That is a different way of putting the question that I posed at the outset – only here the question is, why can't the market replicate the firm? It will be useful to address the question by examining the following more operational statement of the problem: What are the consequences of cost plus contracting between autonomous firms?

Interfirm and intrafirm cost plus contracting differ in at least two significant respects. Both are related to the fact that an autonomous firm has an added degree of freedom that an integrated division does not: It can take its assets and flee. The first difference is that an independent supplier has an incentive to incur costs for strategic purposes that the internal supply division did not. The second is that interfirm auditing cannot be presumed to be as effective as intrafirm auditing.

The strategic difference is this: The independent firm has a stronger incentive to make investments for which reimbursements can plausibly be claimed – in plant and equipment and in human capital – if they give it an added capability to compete for other business. To be sure, both external supplier and the internal supply division can be advised (and may agree) that they are to supply exclusively to the needs of the procurement division. But enforcing such a provision against an independent supplier is apt to be much more difficult. Court ordering is much less effective than administrative fiat in effecting preferences on these matters.

It is sometimes argued that interfirm and intrafirm audits are indistinguishable. Thus Sanford Grossman and Oliver Hart "assume that integration in itself does not make any new variable observable to both parties. Any audits which an employer can have done of her subsidiary are also feasible when the subsidiary is a separate company" (1984, p. 5). I submit that there are reasons to believe otherwise. Specifically, market and internal organization differ in "informal organization" respects. . . . Although Armen Alchian does not make reference to informal organization, he nevertheless acknowledges that "anyone vulnerable to [a] threat of loss (if the coalition is impaired) will seek to preserve not only the coalition but also to reduce the possibility of that threat from the other members of the coalition" (1983, p. 9). If a stronger mutual interest in organizational integrity can be presumed among members of an integrated organization than would exist between independent trading units – because their destinies are more closely tied in the former than in the latter case – then internal auditors can expect to receive greater cooperation, including even hints as to where the "dead bodies lie," than can be presumed when auditing across an autonomous ownership boundary is attempted.

Indeed, the external auditor can ordinarily anticipate only perfunctory co-operation. Since if "our" costs are disallowed then "our" profits will decline and "our" viability may be jeopardized, the employees of the independent supply stage will engage in cost justification and cover-up.

To be sure, divisions also engage in obfuscation and cover-up against internal auditors. Division managements cannot, however, take the physical assets they have accumulated through cost overruns and flee. Termination with and without assets makes a difference. If, therefore, heads must roll in an integrated division where cost excesses have become great, and if guilty and innocent in these circumstances go down together, then it is easy to understand how those who are not implicated in malfeasance will collaborate early and actively with internal auditors.

The upshot is that cost plus contracting in markets cannot be presumed to be identical to cost plus contracting in firms. Transferring a transaction out of the firm and into the market therefore will rarely occur on unchanged cost plus terms but will instead be attended by incentive and governance realignments.

This repeats the argument advanced earlier: Incentives and governance structures that are observed to work well in one organizational milieu do not transfer uncritically to others. To the contrary, organization form, incentive instruments, and governance safeguards must be derived simultaneously.

. . .

CHAPTER 12

Bargaining costs, influence costs, and the organization of economic activity

PAUL MILGROM AND JOHN ROBERTS

Paul Milgrom was born in Detroit, Michigan, in 1948. He received a Ph.D. in business from Stanford University in 1979. When this paper was published, he was Professor of Economics at Stanford University. Since 1993, he has been the Shirley R. and Leonard W. Ely, Jr. Professor of Humanities and Science and Professor of Economics at Stanford University.

John Roberts was born in Winnipeg, Manitoba, in 1945. He received a Ph.D. in economics from the University of Minnesota in 1972. Since 1980, he has been Jonathan B. Lovelace Professor of Economics in the Graduate School of Business, Stanford University.

This chapter is concerned with the economics of organization and management, a relatively new area of study that seeks to analyze the internal structure and workings of economic organizations, the division of activity among these organizations, and the management of relations between them through markets or other higher-level, encompassing organizations.

    The dominant approach to this subject is transaction cost economics, as introduced by Coase (1937, 1960) and developed by several others since, most notably Williamson (1975, 1985). The main tenet of Coase's theory is that economic activities tend to be organized efficiently – that is, so as to maximize the expected total wealth of the parties affected.[1] In this context, two sorts of costs are customarily identified – those of physical production

Reprinted with abridgments from Paul Milgrom and John Roberts, "Bargaining Costs, Influence Costs, and the Organization of Economic Activity," pp. 57–89 in James Alt and Kenneth Shepsle, eds., *Perspectives on Positive Political Economy,* Cambridge: Cambridge University Press. Copyright © Cambridge University Press 1990. Reprinted with the permission of Cambridge University Press.
   [1]Identifying efficiency with expected total wealth maximization requires assumptions that are maintained throughout most of this literature, including risk neutrality (preferences being linear in a freely transferable good, usually money, in terms of which values are expressed), access to a smoothly functioning capital market, and common beliefs about the likelihoods of uncertain events. All of these are clearly restrictive. An important implication of the hypothesis of wealth maximization is that the actions that should (and will) be taken and the way in which benefits of joint action will be shared are determined separately. In particular, such factors as relative bargaining power are irrelevant in determining economic organization. This prediction contrasts sharply with those of Marxian theories, in which power and class interests are prime determinants.

and distribution and those of carrying out necessary exchanges. Because these are typically treated as distinct and separable, the efficiency hypothesis becomes one of transaction cost minimization: The division of activities among firms and between a firm and the market is determined by whether a particular transaction is most efficiently conducted in a market setting or under centralized authority within a firm.

This approach has two conceptual problems. First, the total costs a firm incurs cannot generally be expressed as the sum of production costs – depending only on the technology and the inputs used – and transaction costs – depending only on the way transactions are organized. In general, these two kinds of costs must be considered together; efficient organization is not simply a matter of minimizing transaction costs. Second, the general theory is too vague to be useful. If an existing institution or arrangement appears to be inefficient, one can always claim that it is simply because the observer has not recognized all the relevant transaction costs. To give the theory more power and to generate more specific predictions, recent developments of transaction cost economics have focused on identifying the major components of transaction costs and how they affect the efficient form of organization.

Our principal purpose here is to add two elements to this theory. First, we will argue that the crucial costs associated with using markets to carry out transactions (rather than bringing them within a more complex, formal organization) are the costs of bargaining over short-term arrangements between independent economic agents. This accentuation of short-term bargaining costs contrasts with received theory (as presented by Williamson), which emphasizes asset specificity, uncertainty, and frequency of dealings as the key factors. Second, we identify certain costs attached to the centralized, discretionary decision-making power inherent in formal economic organizations such as firms. Particularly important among these are the costs of essentially political activity within the organization, which we call *influence* costs: the losses that arise from individuals within an organization seeking to influence its decisions for their private benefit (and from their perhaps succeeding in doing so) and from the organization's responding to control this behavior. These costs are an important disability of centralized control and help to explain why integrated internal organization does not always supplant market relations between independent entities.

. . .

Critique and extension of the received theory

Received transaction cost theory emphasizes the implications of the incompleteness of contracts that cover actions to be taken in the uncertain future.

However, we will argue that this emphasis is somewhat misplaced. Instead, we will show that the key to evaluating the efficacy of market transactions is the costs of negotiating suitably detailed short-term contracts. If these costs were always zero, then organizing economic activity through market exchange would always be perfectly efficient. On the other hand, when the costs of negotiating periodic exchange agreements are sufficiently high, then regardless of other factors, such as the presence or absence of specialized assets, potentially important savings are to be realized by placing the activity under a central authority, which can quickly settle potentially costly disputes.

To understand these claims we must first understand what we mean by the terms "short-term" and "bargaining costs." When describing contracts "short-term" refers to a period short enough so that all the information that is relevant for current decisions is already available. Short-term contracts, by definition, do not specify how to act in the longer term as new circumstances arise. We interpret "bargaining costs" expansively, just as we did the term "transaction costs," to include all the costs associated with multilateral bargaining, competitive bidding, and other voluntary mechanisms for determining a mutually acceptable agreement. Bargaining costs include not only the wages paid to the bargainers or the opportunity costs of their time but also the costs of monitoring and enforcing the agreement and any losses from failure to reach the most efficient agreement possible in the most efficient fashion.

With these definitions, having zero short-term bargaining costs means that the bargainers require negligible physical and human resources to reach efficient short-term contracts. (A shot-term contract is *efficient* if there is no other feasible *short-term* contract that both parties would prefer.) However, by definition, bargainers cannot commit themselves through a short-term contract to restrict their long-term behavior in any way, even though they may recognize the long-term impacts of their short-term decisions. For example, the parties to a short-term contract may agree on what investments in specialized assets to make this year and who will pay for these, but they cannot commit themselves to behave benignly next year toward the party who, having paid for the investment, has appropriable quasi rents.

To establish the key role of bargaining costs, suppose that the costs of negotiating short-term contracts were zero. We consider a two-party relationship (such as between a supplier and a customer) for which efficient production demands that the supplier, the customer, or both invest in specialized assets. We assume that the parties meet the standard assumptions of the transaction cost literature in that each is a risk-neutral, financially unconstrained, expected-wealth-maximizing[2] bargainer. The two also share com-

---

[2]This assumption includes the possibilities that the bargainers maximize the expected present value of profits at some fixed discount rates or at discount rates that properly reflect the correla-

mon beliefs about the relative likelihoods of various future contingencies and both are farsighted in the sense that they understand how their current actions and agreements will affect future bargaining opportunities and behavior. They are also opportunistic in the sense that their behavior at any time does not depend on past unbonded promises or on how past costs and benefits have been shared. Finally, we assume that contracts governing prices and behavior in the distant future are prohibitively costly to write because too many contingencies need to be evaluated and described (that is, there is too much uncertainty) but that contracts governing prices, bonus payments, and the actions to be taken in the near term, over which the relevant conditions are already known, are costless to write.

In general Williamsonian terms, the situation involves opportunistic behavior, imperfect long-term contracting, specialized assets, and uncertainty about the future. According to transaction-cost theorists, these conditions are sufficient to prevent a market arrangement based on a series of short-term contracts from yielding an efficient outcome. Nevertheless, we claim that if the costs of bargaining over short-term arrangements were zero – a condition that is apparently consistent with our other specifications – then the market outcome would be efficient. That is, the actions taken by the parties both in the short run *and in the long run* would in *all contingencies* be identical to those that would have been specified in the "ideal contract" – the efficient (possibly long-term and complete) contract the parties would sign if there were no restrictions at all on contracting.

Before proving this proposition and explaining the argument supporting it and the defect in received theory, we should emphasize two points. First, given our assumptions of risk neutrality and common beliefs, the actions taken under an efficient contract do not depend on the bargaining power of the parties involved: Only the distribution of the fruits of the bargain depend on bargaining power. Conversely, because the parties are risk neutral, if the actions they take coincide with those that would be specified in the ideal contract, then the arrangement is efficient, regardless of the payments made between the parties. Second, we do not claim that the inability to write

tion of project returns with other aggregate risks. These objectives for the firm are widely used in the theory of financial economics.

Interestingly, the assumption that the parties are risk-neutral maximizers of expected wealth without financial constraints plays an important role in our analysis. The assumed absence of financial constraints severely limits the applicability of the analysis contained in this section to the problem of investments in human capital, because laws against slavery prohibit the use of human capital as loan collateral. The assumption is also likely to fail in applications to public projects involving health, safety, or environmental quality – projects for which the public's preferences are not easily expressed in terms of risk neutrality and expected pecuniary gains.

When the assumption fails, the efficiency of actions can no longer generally be considered separately from distributional considerations.

complete contracts has no effect on the way the parties' share risks: By their very definition, incomplete contracts imply a limited capacity to make intertemporal or contingent transfers. What *is* unaffected is the set of actions the parties will eventually take and hence the agreement's efficiency.

. . .

To illustrate, consider the relationship between Fisher Body (the supplier) and General Motors (the customer) analyzed by Klein, Crawford, and Alchian. Suppose the relationship lasts for two periods. In the first period, the parties reach an agreement about plant site and design . . . and about the share of the cost of constructing the plant each will bear. Such an agreement specifies only the immediate actions the parties will take and how they will be compensated for these. In the second period, the parties negotiate prices, possibly a fixed transfer payment, quality standards, and a delivery schedule . . . in full knowledge of the circumstances then prevailing (e.g., current model year body designs, demands for various models, the costs and availabilities of steel and substitute materials, and so on, . . . as well as the previously made investments). By our assumption of costless bargaining, regardless of the first-period agreement, the second-period agreement will be efficient given the conditions that prevail then.

Now consider what would happen if the parties were to agree in the initial period to make the efficient plant site and design decisions. Then, the actions taken in the second period would, in all circumstances, agree with those specified under the hypothetical ideal contract. We therefore conclude that the parties could sign a short-term contract in the first period that would lead to them making efficient decisions in both the first and second periods. Actually, by varying who pays for the initial investment in the plant, all distributions of the fruits of these efficient decisions can be attained. Any contract, therefore, that leads to inefficient decision making can be improved upon for both parties by some contract that leads to efficient decision making. Thus, if the costs of short-term bargaining were zero, the agreement reached would indeed lead to efficient actions.

What, then, was wrong with the argument advanced in the first section of this chapter? Why shouldn't the fear of opportunism by General Motors make Fisher Body unwilling to enter into the arrangement? The answer is that Fisher can be compensated for the risk by having General Motors bear part of the plant's cost. Why, then, shouldn't General Motors fear that Fisher will appropriate its quasi rents? Because the agreement can call for General Motors to pay for only as much of the plant's earnings as it expects to appropriate in future negotiations. Threats of appropriation are simply distributional threats; they are not threats to efficient action as long as bargaining costs are zero. Among risk-neutral parties with common beliefs and no private information, distributional threats can be compensated by initial cash payments. The efficiency of market arrangements is limited only by the costs of negotiating efficient short-term contracts. This conclusion points to the central importance of bargaining costs in determining the efficiency of market transactions. We shall study the origins and determinants of bargaining costs in the next section.

The preceding analysis relied on the assumptions that all parties are risk neutral and that they can contract for current actions without restriction. The first of these assumptions is not reasonable when contracting parties are individuals, and the second fails when current actions cannot be precisely monitored. Nevertheless, as Fudenberg, Holmstrom, and Milgrom (1990) have shown, the conclusion that short-term contracts are as good as long-term contracts when no bargaining costs are involved applies equally to situations involving risk-averse bargainers and imperfectly observed actions, provided contractual payments in each period can be made to depend on any information obtained during the period and provided no new information about any period's actions arrives only in later periods.

Our other criticism of early transaction cost theories concerns their relative silence regarding the source, nature, and magnitude of the costs incurred in nonmarket transactions. Indeed, despite the firm beliefs of many economists that markets often hold great advantages over nonmarket forms of organization, *received* transaction cost theory leaves unclear why market transactions are *ever* to be preferred to nonmarket ones.

Identifying the costs of general nonmarket transactions is a task to be approached with great caution. As Chandler (1962) has documented, business organizations have changed substantially and repeatedly over the past century, and the disabilities (transaction costs) suffered by an older form of organization may be overcome by its replacement. Perhaps wisely, then, transaction cost theorists for a long time were largely silent about the source and nature of the costs of centralized organization, although they were certainly aware of the problem. Quite recently, however, Williamson (1985) and Grossman and Hart (1986) have addressed explicitly the disabilities of nonmarket organization.

. . .

[W]e believe that [their] incentive arguments have substantial force. Nevertheless, these theories miss an important class of generally identifiable costs of internal organization that do not depend specifically on control of assets. In the section titled "Costs of Centralized Authority," we argue that the crucial distinguishing characteristic of a firm is not the pattern of asset ownership but the substitution of centralized authority for the relatively unfettered negotiations that characterize market transactions. And, we argue, the very existence of this centralized authority is incompatible with a thoroughgoing policy of efficient selective intervention. The authority to intervene inevitably implies the authority to intervene inefficiently. Yet such interventions, even if they are inefficient overall, can be highly beneficial for particular individuals and groups. Thus, either inefficient interventions will be made and resources will be expended to bring them about or to prevent them, or else the authority to intervene must be restricted. This implies that some efficient interventions must be foregone.

. . .

Costs of centralized authority

. . .

Why can't a centrally planned, consciously coordinated system always do at least as well as an unplanned, decentralized one? For many years scholars, failing to find an answer to this question, have boldly (and we think wrongly) concluded that there is no answer. . . .

Substantially the same puzzle arises in trying to explain why there are any limits to a firm's size and scope. Thus, economists have asked, "Why, if by organizing one can eliminate certain costs and in fact reduce the cost of production, are there any market transactions at all? Why is not all production carried out by one big firm?" And, "Why can't a large firm do everything that a collection of small firms can do, and more?"

The form of these questions assumes that benign, costless, *selective interventions* of the type Williamson considered are possible. This requires a decision maker with the authority to intervene, the interest in doing so only when appropriate, and the ability to consider and reject interventions without distorting the behavior of others in the organization. We argue that these requirements realistically cannot be met.

We take the view that what most distinguishes any centralized organization is the authority and autonomy of its top decision makers or management – that is, their broad rights to intervene in lower-level decisions and the relative immunity of their decisions from intervention by others.[3] Increases in centralized authority carry with them increases in the discretionary power to inter-

---

[3]This contrasts with Coase's view (1937, p. 389) that "the distinguishing mark of the firm is the supersession of the price mechanism" and with the view of Alchian and Demsetz (1972) that a firm is principally a "nexus of contracts."

vene. This increased power necessarily has costs that are avoided in more decentralized contexts. From this perspective, the principles that guide a firm's decision whether to manufacture an input (centralized organization) or to buy it from an independent supplier (decentralized organization) can be applied equally well to evaluate the relative productive efficiency of capitalist and socialist economic systems.

Two kinds of costs generally accompany increases in discretionary centralized authority. Both have the same fundamental cause: The very existence of such authority makes possible its inappropriate use. The first kind arises because those with discretionary authority may misuse it directly, on their own initiative. The second arises because others in the organization may attempt to persuade or manipulate those with authority to use it excessively or inappropriately. Inappropriate interventions, the attempts to induce them, and the organization's efforts to control both – all generate costs of increased centralization.

The first source of the costs of centralized, discretionary authority is inappropriate interventions that occur because individuals with increased authority are unable or unwilling to resist interfering where or in ways that they should not. This may happen simply because the individuals feel an imperative to manage – that is, after all, what managers are paid to do! Business people often cite this imperative to intervene as a characteristic and a cost of government bureaucracies: Bureaucrats look for something to do, whether or not their intervention is likely to be helpful. Private managers are presumably not immune to this failure, let alone to believing that their interventions will be beneficial when they are actually unlikely to be. Another possible reason for inappropriate intervention is that individuals in authority may have personal interests in decisions: Will the empty lot next to the apartment building owned by the park commissioner's cousin be converted into a city park? Will the executive's protégé be appointed to replace a retiring division head? For any of these reasons, authority will be exercised more often and in other ways than efficiency alone dictates.

In a related vein are the costs of outright corruption, which is possible only with discretionary centralized authority: The central authority may seek bribes or other favors and may block efficient decisions when bribes are not paid. . . .

Note that monetary bribes themselves do not necessarily represent an economic inefficiency, because they are but transfers. Rather, the costs of corruption arise first because productive decisions are distorted, either from favoring those who pay bribes or from punishing those who refuse. Secondly, if trust between individuals and faith in the system facilitate economic activity, widespread corruption and bribery may result in further, less direct, but possibly more significant costs.

These costs of discretionary authority depend on flaws in decision makers' incentives, intelligence, or character. Presumably, then, they can be reduced or even eliminated by vesting authority in honest, wise individuals and by giving them incentives to care about organizational performance. However, discretionary authority results in a second kind of cost which is incurred even when the central authority is both incorruptible and intelligent enough not to interfere in operations without good reason. These are what we call *influence costs*.

Influence costs arise first because individuals and groups within the organization expend time, effort, and ingenuity in attempting to affect others' decisions to their benefit and secondly because inefficient decisions result either directly from these influence activities or, less directly, from attempts to prevent or control them.

At first blush, it might seem easy to avoid these costs: Simply have decision makers ignore attempts at influence. If this does not provide a sufficient incentive to deter influence activities, severely punish any such behavior. In some circumstances, this may in fact be possible, and we will assume that organizations follow this policy whenever feasible. However, an essential difficulty exists with such an approach. The policy of ignoring attempts at influence – and, indeed, the policy of selective intervention more generally – is not what macroeconomists call "dynamically consistent" or what game theorists call "subgame perfect." *Ex post,* when relevant information is available and those at lower levels have already taken actions that cannot be reversed, there will be interventions that are now organizationally desirable and that the center will thus want to take. However, recognition of the center's *ex post* incentives will alter the behavior of the organization's members in ways that are organizationally dysfunctional. Thus, the center would like to be able to commit *ex ante* to not making these interventions – that is, to restrict its own discretion. For example, decision makers might want to motivate workers by committing to promote the most productive one. However, after the fact, they would want to renege and promote the worker who, on the basis of training and other credentials, appears best qualified. As long as central decision makers reserve for themselves the right to make selective interventions, commitments are impossible, if only because of the impossibility of complete contracting. Thus, the possibility of attempts at influence will remain and will inevitably exert costs (Milgrom and Roberts, 1988a).

One reason influence is inevitable is that decision makers must rely on others for information that is not easily available to them directly. Central office executives are not islands unto themselves; they commonly rely extensively on others for information, suggestions, and analyses to reach decisions. Moreover, the employees affected by a decision are often the very ones executives must rely on. In such circumstances, employees will have strong reasons to try to influence decisions, and their attempts at influence will impose costs on the organization. For example, employees may distort the information they report or withhold information from the central office and from other employees. Candidates for possible promotions may spend valuable time polishing their credentials, thereby establishing their qualifications for the desired assignment at the expense of current performance (Milgrom and Roberts, 1988a). Managers, worried about how higher authorities will evaluate their performance, may avoid risky but profitable investments because such investments pose career risks if they turn out badly (Holmstrom, 1982). Or, less specifically, employees may simply waste time trying to figure out what issues are on the agenda, how they might be personally affected, and how to shape decisions to their benefit. The loss of productivity from these distortions in the way employees spend their time, report their information, and make their decisions is one category of influence costs. These are costs of discretionary authority because they arise only when an authority exists whose decisions can be influenced.

A second sort of influence cost arises when central authorities make suboptimal decisions because of employees' influence activities, particularly their suppressing or distorting information. In some situations these distortions may be undone by properly accounting for individuals' incentives, and efficient decisions may still be reached (Milgrom and Roberts, 1986). However, when these incentives are unclear or when the underlying information is so complex that unscrambling is impossible, decision makers will have to rely on information that they know is incomplete or inaccurate. Consider, for example, the problems of the U.S. Congress in dealing with military appropriations. Congress must rely on the military for information, and it understands that the military may have incentives to distort the information that it provides. But it is impossible for Congress to disentangle interservice rivalries, individual career ambitions, and genuine concerns with national security, all of which motivate particular spending requests. Even if the incentives of those providing the information to distort or suppress it could be determined, the impossible problem of inferring what information they actually have would still remain. In such complex circumstances, decisions must be based on fundamentally incorrect information, and inefficient decisions must be expected.

The incentives to attempt to influence an organization's decisions are, to some extent, endogenous. The costs and benefits of influence activities depend on an organization's information-gathering and decision-making procedures and on its reward systems. Thus, careful organizational design can at least partially control the direct costs of influence activities. For example, Holstrom and Ricart (1986) have investigated how capital budgeting practices that reward investment and growth per se and establish high internal hurdle rates for investments can help alleviate managers' natural reluctance to undertake risky but profitable investments. Milgrom (1988) and Milgrom and Roberts (1988a) have examined how compensation and promotion policies can be used to make employees more nearly indifferent about company decisions, thereby reducing resistance to change and other organizationally unproductive influence activities. As an alternative to using compensation policies and promotion criteria to control incentives to attempt influence, Milgrom and Roberts also explored limiting communication between decision makers and potentially affected parties and otherwise restricting these parties' involvement in decision making.

Even the very boundaries of the firm can become design variables used to control influence. The widespread practice of spinning off or isolating unprofitable subsidiaries can be partly interpreted in these terms: It is done to prevent the subsidiary's employees and management from imposing large influence costs on the organization through attempts to claim corporate resources to cover their losses and thereby to avoid having to become efficient or to curtail operations. Similarly, a university's policy of requiring its schools to be "tubs on their own bottoms," each individually responsible for its revenues and expenditures (subject to formula payments to or from the central administration), limits influence activities that would amount to raids on other schools' or the university's resources. For example, when universities centrally determine and fund salaries, research support, and teaching loads, faculties have incentives to try to get more for themselves from the center by invoking comparisons with other schools and departments rather than by raising their own resources. Of course, they can (and do) still make the same complaints when financial boundaries exist between schools, but they have less to gain by doing so because resources cannot easily be shifted from the envied to the envious.

Of course, such responses as these bring costs of their own. Worthwhile investments will be foregone, and managers may seek out the wrong investment opportunities; less qualified people will be assigned to key positions; too many valued employees will quit to increase their pay; bad decisions will be made because communication has been restricted and available information is not used; and desirable resource transfers between divisions will not be effected. These costs of employing policies and organizational structures that would be inefficient if influence activities were not a problem are then in themselves a third category of influence costs.

In this context, an important element of organizational design involves trading off these various costs. For example, Japanese firms make use both of wage policies and of organizational rules to facilitate extensive involvement of their employees in decision making without encouraging excessive attempts at influence. Lifetime employment for key decision makers, relatively small wage differentials within age cohorts, relatively low wages for senior executives, and promotions based largely on seniority combine to insulate employees from the effects of the firm's investment and promotion decisions and to make promotion decisions relatively immune to influence.

. . .

Taken together, the activities just described could consume a major portion of division heads', and central office personnel's, time, diverting them from more productive activities. The boundaries between independent firms reduce the possibilities for influence. Consequently, those boundaries reduce influence costs.

. . .

The validity of these arguments depends on our characterization of the firm as a centrally controlled organization considerably free from outside intervention. In capitalist economies, several institutions support executives' having much more extensive control over their firms than do courts or government agencies acting from outside. First, property rights tend to limit government interventions more than executive interventions because property rights over the firm generally reside at the executive level or higher. Thus, a court, a governmental regulatory agency, and a firm's central office can all order a plant that is polluting the environment to cease operations until the problem is fixed, but the central office can also replace the plant manager if it finds that to be the most effective way to do the job. Second, executives generally have better and more fluid information systems than courts or government agencies do. Managers in firms hear most of the important information they need in conversations and meetings where they can query sources informally to resolve ambiguities and acquire needed detail. In contrast, agencies and courts must rely on written reports or adversary proceedings. Finally, executives can deliver incentives directly where they count most – to individual employees – and can tailor the incentives to take the form either of rewards, such as pay increases, bonuses, promotions, or desirable assignments, or of punishments, such as undesirable assignments or layoffs. The incentives courts and government agencies offer consist mostly of threats to collect penalties against the firm's treasury.

. . .

173

Summary and conclusions

. . .

Whenever a central authority, whether a governmental unit or an executive in a firm, has discretion to intervene, certain identifiable costs are incurred. These include (1) a tendency for the authority to intervene excessively, both because intervening is that authority's job and because the authority may have a personal interest (licit or illicit, but in either case differing from the organization's interests) in certain decisions; (2) increased time devoted to influence activities and a corresponding reduction in organizational productivity, as interested parties seek to have the authority intervene in particular ways or to adopt their favored alternatives; (3) poorer decision making resulting from the distortion of information associated with influence activities; and (4) a loss of efficiency as the organization adapts its structure and policies to control influence activities and their costs.

We believe that these ideas about influence cost are important in analyzing organizations. For example, they might be used to examine issues of corporate control, financial structure, bankruptcy, proxy fights, and takeovers. Moreover, because influence activities are essentially political and because the theory applies equally to public and private organizations, we believe that it may also prove valuable in the more general study of political economy.

CHAPTER 13

Towards an economic theory of
the multiproduct firm

DAVID TEECE

David Teece was born in New Zealand in 1948. He received a Ph.D. in economics from the University of Pennsylvania in 1975. When this paper was published, he was Mitsubishi Bank Professor in the Haas School of Business at the University of California, Berkeley, where he is now also Director of the Institute for Management, Innovation, and Organization.

1. Introduction

"Of all outstanding characteristics of business firms, perhaps the most inadequately treated in economic analysis is the diversification of their activities" (Penrose, 1959, p. 104). Little progress has been made since Penrose registered her dismay. Accordingly, the theory of the firm has yet to accommodate one of the principal features of the modern business enterprise – its multiproduct character. The mission of this paper is to outline how this deficiency might be rectified. To accomplish this objective it turns out to be necessary to modify the neoclassical theory of the firm to emphasize the distinctive properties of organizational knowledge and the transactions cost properties of market exchange. It is also necessary to make an analytical separation between a theory of diversification and a theory of growth since growth and diversification are not inextricably linked. A central issue for a theory of multiproduct organization is to explain why firms diversify into related and unrelated product lines rather than reinvesting in traditional lines of business or transferring assets directly to stockholders.

An earlier paper (Teece, 1980) argued that the multiproduct firm could not be explained by reference to neoclassical cost functions. Panzar and Willig (1975, p. 3) have argued that economies of scope explain multiproduct organization.[1] While economies of scope explain joint production, they do not

Reprinted in abridged form from David Teece, "Towards an Economic Theory of the Multiproduct Firm," *Journal of Economic Behavior and Organization*, 3 (1982): 39–63, by permission of the publisher.

[1]Economies of scope exist when for all outputs y_1 and y_2, the cost of joint production is less than the cost of producing each output separately (Panzar and Willig, 1975). That is, it is the condition, for all y_1 and y_2: $C(y_1, y_2) < C(y_1, 0) + C(0, y_2)$.

175

explain why joint production must be organized within a single multiproduct enterprise. Joint production can proceed in the absence of multiproduct organization if contractual mechanisms can be devised to share the inputs which are yielding the scope economies. Whereas the earlier paper had the limited objective of exploring the relationship between economies of scope and the scope of the enterprise, the objective here is more ambitious – to outline a theory of multiproduct enterprise.

. . .

3. Nature of the firm

In microtheory textbooks, and in much contemporary research, it is accepted practice "to represent the business enterprise abstractly by the productive transformations of which it is capable, and to characterize these productive transformations by a production function or production set regarded as a datum" (Winter, 1982, p. 58).[2] Furthermore, production functions and hence firms can be eliminated or replicated with amazing alacrity, as when prices a whisker above competitive levels attract new entrants. New entry in turn drives profits back down to equilibrium levels. Embedded in this conceptualization is the notion that a firm's know-how is stored in symbolic form in a "book of blueprints." Implicit in this commonly used metaphor is the view that knowledge can be and is articulated. Following Winter (1982), and Nelson and Winter (1980, 1982), the appropriateness of this abstraction is examined below, and the implications for multiproduct organization explored.

3.1 Individual and organizational knowledge

Polanyi has stressed, in obvious contradiction to the book of blueprints metaphor, that individual knowledge has an important tacit dimension, in that very often know-how and skills cannot be articulated. It is a "well known fact that the aim of a skillful performance is achieved by the observance of a set of rules which are not known as such to the person following them"[3] (Polanyi, 1958, p. 49). In the exercise of individual skill, many actions are taken that

[2]In modern general equilibrium theory (Arrow, 1951; Arrow and Debreu, 1954; Debreu, 1959) "commodity outputs in amounts represented by $q = (q_1, \ldots q_m)$ may or may not be producible from input commodities in amounts represented by $X = (x_1, \ldots x_n)$. If q is producible from x, then the input/output pair (x, q) is 'in the production set'. Whatever is known or considered plausible as a property of the structure of technical knowledge is treated as a postulate about the properties of the production set" (Winter, 1982, p. 63).
[3]"The premises of a skill cannot be discovered focally prior to its performance, not even understood if explicitly stated by others, before we ourselves have experienced its performance, whether by watching it or engaging in it ourselves" (Polanyi, 1958, p. 1962).

are not the result of considered choices but rather are automatic responses that constitute aspects of the skill.[4]

Similarly, in the routine operation of an organization such as a business firm, much that could in principle be deliberated is instead done automatically in response to signals arising from the organization or its environment. Articulation of the knowledge underlying organizational capabilities is limited in the same respects and for the same reasons as in the case of individual capabilities though for other reasons as well, and to a greater extent. This routinization of activity in an organization itself constitutes the most important form of storage of the organization's specific operational knowledge. In a sense, organizations "remember by doing." Routine operation is the organizational counterpart of the exercise of skills by an individual. (Nelson and Winter, 1982, quoted in part from an earlier draft.)

Thus, routines function as the basis of organizational memory. To utilize organizational knowledge, it is necessary not only that all members know their routines, but also that all members know when it is appropriate to perform certain routines. This implies that the individual must have the ability to interpret a stream of incoming messages from other organizational members and from the environment. Once received and interpreted, the member utilizes the information contained in a message in the selection and performance of an appropriate routine from his own repertoire.[5] Thus to view organizational memory as reducible to individual member memories is to overlook, or undervalue, the linking of those individual memories by shared experiences in the past, experiences that have established the extremely detailed and specific communication system that underlies routine performance (Nelson and Winter, 1982, p. 105).

While there is abundant reason to believe that remembering-by-doing may in a wide range of circumstances surpass symbolic storage in cost effectiveness, one circumstance where complications arise is where the knowledge is

---

[4]Polanyi illustrates this point by discussing how a bicyclist keeps his balance: "I have come to the conclusion that the principle by which the cyclist keeps his balance is not generally known. The rule observed by the cyclist is this. When he starts falling to the right he turns the handlebars to the right, so that the course of the bicycle is deflected along a curve towards the right. This results in a centrifugal force pushing the cyclist to the left and offsets the gravitational force dragging him down to the right. This maneuver presently throws the cyclist out of balance to the left which he counteracts by turning the handlebars to the left; and so he continues to keep himself in balance by winding along a series of appropriate curvatures. A simple analysis shows that for a given angle of unbalance the curvature of each winding is inversely proportional to the square of the speed at which the cyclist is proceeding. But does this tell us exactly how to ride a bicycle? No. You obviously cannot adjust the curvature of your bicycle's path in proportion to the ratio of your unbalance over the square of your speed; and if you could, you would fall off the machine, for there are a number of these factors to be taken into account in practice which are left out in the formulation of this rule" (Polanyi, 1958, pp. 49–50).

[5]An organizational member's repertoire is the set of routines that could be performed in some appropriate environment (Nelson and Winter, 1982).

to enter market exchange for subsequent transfer to a different organizational context. The transfer of key individuals may suffice when the knowledge to be transferred relates to the particulars of a separable routine. The individual in such cases becomes a consultant or a teacher with respect to that routine. However, only a limited range of capabilities can be transferred if a transfer activity is focused in this fashion. More often than not, the transfer of productive expertise requires the transfer of organizational as well as individual knowledge.[6] In such cases, external transfer beyond an organization's boundary may be difficult if not impossible, since taken out of context, an individual's knowledge of a routine may be quite useless.

3.2 Fungible knowledge

Another characteristic of organizational knowledge is that it is often fungible to an important degree. That is, the human capital inputs employed by the firm are not always entirely specialized to the particular products and services which the enterprise is currently producing. This is particularly true of managerial talent, but it is also true for various items of physical equipment and for other kinds of human skills as well. Of course, various items of capital may have to be scrapped or converted if an organization's product mix is changed but these costs may in fact be quite low if the opportunity cost of withdrawing the equipment from its current use is minimal.

Accordingly, the final products produced by a firm at any given time merely represent one of several ways in which the organization could be using its internal resources (Penrose, 1959). As wartime experience demonstrated, automobile manufacturers suddenly began making tanks, chemical companies began making explosives, and radio manufacturers began making radar. In short, a firm's capability lies upstream from the end product – it lies in a generalizable capability which might well find a variety of final product applications. Economies of specialization assume a different significance when viewed from this conceptual vantage point, as specialization is referenced not to a single product but to a generalized capability. (It might be "information processing" rather than computers, "dairy products" rather than butter and cheese, "farm machinery" rather than tractors and harvesters, and "time measurement" rather than clocks and watches.) The firm can therefore be considered to have a variety of end products which it can produce with its organizational technology. Some of these possibilities may be known to it and some may not. What needs to be explained is the particular end product or configuration of end products which the firm chooses to produce.

[6]"Over the years an individual may learn a piece of the company puzzle exceptionally well, and he may even understand how the piece fits into the entire puzzle. But he may not know enough about the other pieces to reproduce the entire puzzle" (Lieberstein, 1979).

This view of the nature of the firm turns the neoclassical conceptualization on its head. Whereas the neoclassical firm selects, according to factor prices, technologies off the shelf to manufacture a given end product, the organization theoretic firm depicted here selects an end product configuration, consistent with its organizational technology, which is defined yet fungible over certain arrays of final products. In short, the firm has end product as well as technological choices to confront.

4. Dynamic considerations

4.1 General

Whether the firm's know-how is embedded in a book of blueprints or in individual and organizational routines will not explain its multiproduct scope unless other dimensions of the neoclassical model of firms and markets are modified. Thus following Schumpeter (1950) and others, the competitive process is viewed as dynamic, involving uncertainty, struggle, and disequilibrium. In particular, two fundamental characteristics of a dynamic competitive system are recognized: (a) firms accumulate knowledge through R & D and learning, some of it incidental to the production process; (b) the market conditions facing the firm are constantly changing, creating profit opportunities in different markets at different times. Furthermore, the demand curve facing a specialized firm is rarely infinitely elastic, as is assumed in the perfectly competitive model.

4.2 Learning, teaching, and "Penrose-effects"

Edith Penrose (1959) has described the growth processes of the firm in a way that is both unconventional and convincing. According to Penrose, at any time a firm has certain productive resources, the services of which are used to exploit the production opportunities facing the firm. Opportunities for growth exist because there are always unused productive services which can be placed into employment – presumably in new as well as existing lines of business. Unused resources exist not only because of indivisibilities, but also because of the learning which occurs in the normal process of operating a business. Thus, even with a constant managerial workforce, managerial services are released for expansion without any reduction in the efficiency with which existing operations are run. Not only is there continuous learning, but also as each project becomes established so its running becomes more routine and less demanding on managerial resources. The managerial workforce can also be expanded, at least within limits. Existing managers can teach new managers. However, the increment to total managerial services provided by

179

each additional manager is assumed to decrease the faster the rate at which they are reoriented. (The "Penrose-effect.")

A specialized firm's generation of excess resources, both managerial and technical, and their fungible character is critical to the theory of diversification advanced here. What has to be explained, however, is (1) why diversification is likely to lead to the productive utilization of "excess" resources and (2) the sequence in which this assignment is likely to occur.

4.3 Demand conditions

A specialized firm's excess resources can of course be reinvested in the firm's traditional business. Indeed, if the firm confronts a perfectly elastic demand curve, has a distinctive capability (lower costs) in its traditional business, and markets elsewhere are competitive, it has incentives to reinvest in its traditional line of business, both at home and abroad. Assume, however, that at some point, competitive returns can no longer be obtained through reinvestment at home or abroad, either because of a secular decline of demand due to life cycle considerations (Grabowski and Mueller, 1975; Mueller, 1972), or because the firm is facing a finite degree of elasticity to its demand curve, in which case reinvestment and expansion will serve to lower prices and profits. Confronted with this predicament, a profit-seeking firm confronts three fundamental choices:

1. It can seek to sell the services of its unused assets to other firms in other markets.
2. It can diversify into other markets, either through acquisition or de novo entry.
3. If the unused resource is cash, it can be returned to stockholders though higher dividends or stock repurchase.

A theory of diversification for a profit-seeking enterprise emerges when conditions are established under which the second option appears the more profitable. The first option involves the use of markets for capturing the employment value of the unused assets. Multiproduct diversification (option 2) will be selected by profit-seeking firms over the market alternative (option 1) when transaction cost problems are likely to confound efficient transfer. Accordingly, an assessment of the efficiency properties of factor and financial markets is warranted.

4.4 Market failure considerations: physical and human capital

If excess resources are possessed by a single product firm, there is the possibility of disposal in factor markets, i.e., sale and transfer to other specialized firms. This strategy permits standard specialization economies to be obtained, and if transaction costs are zero, ought to usurp incentives for diversification. Consider, therefore, whether efficient employment of these resources is likely to involve multiproduct organization. Assume, furthermore, that the excess resources are either indivisible or fungible, so that scope economies exist.[7] Four classes of scope economies are identified and analyzed.

Class 1. Indivisible but *nonspecialized* physical capital as a common input into two or more products:

Scope economies may arise because some fixed item of capital equipment is indivisible. It may be a machine – such as heavy gauge sheet metal shears – which is needed occasionally in the production process for product A but is otherwise idle. Assume that the machine could be used to manufacture both products A and B. Even if this is the case it need not indicate that an efficient solution is for the manufacturer of A to diversify into the manufacture of B. There are at least two other options. The manufacturer of A could rent the services of another firm's machine, or it could acquire its own machine and lease access to it when it would otherwise remain idle.

To the extent that there is not a thin market for the services of the machinery in question – which will often be the case – there does not appear to be a compelling reason for diversification on account of the hazards of exposure to opportunism (Williamson, 1975; Klein, Crawford, and Alchian, 1978). Market solutions would appear to be superior.[8]

Class II. Indivisible *specialized* physical capital as a common input to two or more products:

Assume that the piece of equipment is specialized but not entirely so. Assume specifically that it can only be used for making products A and B, that there is some idle capacity if it is only used to manufacture A, and that the market for A and B will only support a small number of producers. In these circumstances there may be incentives for the manufacturer of A to also

---

[7]As a general matter, "economies of scope arise from inputs that are shared, or utilized jointly without complete congestion. The shared factor may be imperfectly divisible, so that the manufacture of a subset of the goods leaves excess capability in some stage of production, or some human or physical capital may be a public input which, when purchased for use in one production process, is then freely available to another" (Willig, 1979, p. 346).

[8]A related example would be the provision of air services between points A and B. An airport will be needed at both A and B and in the absence of complete congestion, service can also be provided from both points to C (which has an airport) once airport terminals A and B are constructed. Hence $C(AB, BC, AC) < C(AB, 0, 0) + C(0, BC, 0) + C(0, 0, AC)$. While economies of scope exist, it need not imply that one airline ought provide services AB, BC and CA. Individual airlines could specialize on each route and access to terminals (the source of the assumed indivisibility) could be shared via contracts. Only in the extent to which transactional difficulties can be expected in writing, executing, and enforcing contracts will common ownership be necessary to capture the scope of economies.

manufacture B because of the transactional difficulties which might otherwise be encountered in the small numbers markets assumed. Since the fixed asset is highly specialized, and the number of potential lessees is assumed to be quite small, markets for the services of the fixed assets will be thin. Bilateral monopoly situations can then arise in which lessees may attempt to extract the quasi rents associated with the utilization of the leasor's fixed and specialized asset[9] (Williamson, 1975, 1979; Klein, Crawford, and Alchian, 1978; Monteverde and Teece, 1982a, 1982b). In order to avoid these hazards, intrafirm trading – that is, multiproduct diversification – can be substituted for market exchange. Internal trading changes the incentives of the parties and enables the firm to bring managerial control devices to bear on the transaction, thereby attenuating costly haggling and other manifestations of noncooperative behavior. Exchange can then proceed more efficiently because of lower transactions costs.

Class III. Human capital as a common input to two or more products:

To the extent that know-how has fungible attributes, it can represent a common input into a variety of products. Know-how may also display some of the characteristics of a public good in that it may be used in many different noncompeting applications without its value in any one application being substantially impaired. Furthermore, the marginal cost of employing know-how in a different endeavor is likely to be much less than the average cost of production and dissemination (transfer). Accordingly, the transfer and application of proprietary information to alternative production activities is likely to generate important economies.

However, internal organization (multiproduct enterprise) is generally needed for these economies to be realized. Markets do not work well as the institutional mode for trading know-how. One reason is that an important component of organizational knowledge is tacit. As discussed above, the transfer of tacit knowledge from one enterprise to another is likely to be difficult and costly. A temporary if not permanent transfer of employees may be needed, especially if the technology involved is state of the art and has not as yet been stabilized and formalized. If this is the case, multiproduct organization is likely to have appeal because it provides a more efficient technology transfer mode.

Besides the logistical problems surrounding the transfer of tacit knowledge, technology transfer must confront an important class of transactions cost problems. These can be summarized in terms of (1) recognition, (2) disclosure, and (3) team organization (Teece, 1980; Williamson and Teece, 1982). Thus consider a firm which has accumulated know-how which can

[9]The quasi rents will be the difference between the asset value if the equipment is used to produce multiple products and its value when it is used to produce the single product.

potentially find application in the fields of industrial activity beyond its existing product line(s). If there are other firms in the economy which can apply this know-how with profit, then according to received microtherapy, trading will ensue until Pareto optimality conditions are satisfied. Or, as Calabresi has put it, "if one assumes rationality, no transactions costs, and no legal impediments to bargaining, all misallocations of resources would be fully cured in the market by bargains" (Calabresi, 1968). However, one cannot in general expect this result in the market for proprietary know-how. Not only are there high costs associated with obtaining the requisite information but there are also organizational and strategic impediments associated with using the market to effectuate transfer.

Consider, to begin with, the information requirements associated with using markets. In order to carry out a market transaction it is necessary to discover who it is that one wishes to deal with, to inform people that one wishes to deal and on what terms, to conduct negotiations leading up to the bargain, to draw up the contract, to undertake the inspection needed to make sure that the terms of the contract are being observed, and so on (Coase, 1960, p. 15). Furthermore, the opportunity for trading must be identified. As Kirzner (1973, pp. 215–16) has explained:

. . . for an exchange transaction to be completed it is not sufficient merely that the conditions for exchange which prospectively will be mutually beneficial be present; it is necessary also that each participant be aware of his opportunity to gain through exchange. . . . It is usually assumed . . . that where scope for (mutually beneficial) exchange is present, exchange will in fact occur. . . . In fact of course exchange may fail to occur because knowledge is imperfect, in spite of conditions for mutually profitable exchange.

The transactional difficulties identified by Kirzner are especially compelling when the commodity in question is proprietary information, be it of a technological or managerial kind. This is because the protection of the ownership of technological know-how often requires suppressing information on exchange possibilities. For instance, by its very nature industrial R & D requires disguising and concealing the activities and outcomes of R & D establishment. As Marquis and Allen (1966, p. 1055) point out, industrial laboratories, with their strong mission orientation, must

. . . cut themselves off from interaction beyond the organizational perimeter. This is to a large degree intentional. The competitive environment in which they operate necessitates control over the outflow of messages. The industrial technologist or scientist is thereby essentially cut off from free interaction with his colleagues outside of the organization.

Except as production or marketing specialists within the firm perceive the transfer opportunity, transfer may fail by reason of nonrecognition.

Even where the processor of the technology recognizes the opportunity, market exchange may break down because of the problems of disclosing value to buyers in a way that is both convincing and does not destroy the basis for exchange. A very severe information impactedness problem exists, on which account the less informed party (in this instance the buyer) must be wary of opportunistic representations by the seller. If, moreover, there is insufficient disclosure, including veracity checks thereon, to assure the buyer that the information possesses great value, the "fundamental paradox" of information arises: "its value for the purchaser is not known until he has the information, but then he has in effect acquired it without cost" (Arrow, 1971, p. 152).

Suppose that recognition is no problem, that buyers concede value, and are prepared to pay for information in the seller's possession. Occasionally that may suffice. The formula for a chemical compound or the blueprints for a special device may be all that is needed to effect the transfer. However, more is frequently needed. As discussed above, know-how has a strong tacit and learning-by-doing character, and it may be essential that human capital in an effective team configuration accompany the transfer. Sometimes this can be effected through a one-time contract (a know-how agreement) to provide a "consulting team" to assist start-up. Although such contracts will be highly incomplete, and the failure to reach a comprehensive agreement may give rise to dissatisfaction during execution, this may be an unavoidable, which is to say irremediable, result. Plainly, multiproduct organization is an extreme response to the needs of a one-time exchange. In the absence of a superior organizational alternative, reliance on market mechanisms is thus likely to prevail.

Where a succession of proprietary exchanges seems desirable, reliance on repeated contracting is less clearly warranted. Unfettered two-way communication is needed not only to promote the recognition and disclosure of opportunities for information transfer but also to facilitate the execution of the actual transfer itself. The parties in these circumstances are joined in a small numbers trading relation and as discussed by Williamson, such contracting may be shot through with hazards for both parties (Williamson, 1975, 1979). The seller is exposed to hazards such as the possibility that the buyer will employ the know-how in subtle ways not covered by the contract, or the buyer might "leap frog" the licensor's technology and become an unexpected competitive threat. The buyer is exposed to hazards such as the seller asserting that the technology has better performance or cost reducing characteristics than is actually the case; or the seller might render promised transfer assistance in a perfunctory fashion. While bonding or the execution of performance guarantees can minimize these hazards, they need not be eliminated since costly haggling might ensue when measurement of the performance characteristics of the technology is open to some ambiguity. Furthermore, when a lateral transfer is contemplated and the technology has not therefore been previously commercialized by either party in the new application, the execution of performance guarantees is likely to be especially hazardous to the seller because of the uncertainties involved (Teece, 1977). In addition, if a new application of a generic technology is contemplated, recurrent exchange and continuous contact between buyer and seller will be needed. These requirements will be extremely difficult to specify *ex ante*. Hence, when the continuous exchange of proprietary know-how between the transferor and transferee is needed, and where the end use application of the know-how is idiosyncratic in the sense that it has not been accomplished previously by the transferor, it appears that something more than a classical market contracting structure is required. As Williamson notes "The nonstandardized nature of (these) transactions makes primary reliance on market governance hazardous, while their recurrent nature permits the cost of the specialized governance structure to be recovered" (Williamson, 1979, p. 250). What Williamson refers to as "relational contracting" is the solution; this can take the form of bilateral governance, where the autonomy of the parties is maintained; or unified structures, where the transaction is removed from the market and organized within the firm subject to an authority relation (Williamson, 1979, p. 250). Bilateral governance involves the use of "obligational contracting" (Wachter and Williamson, 1978; Williamson, 1979). Exchange is conducted between independent firms under obligational arrangements, where both parties realize the paramount importance of maintaining an amicable relationship as overriding any possible short-run gains either might be able to achieve. But as transactions become progressively more idiosyncratic, obligational contracting may also fail, and internal organization (intrafirm transfer) is the more efficient organizational mode. The intrafirm transfer of know-how avoids the need for repeated negotiations and ameliorates the hazards of opportunism. Better disclosure, easier agreement, better governance, and therefore more effective execution of know-how transfer are likely to result. Here lies an incentive for multiproduct organization.

The above arguments are quite general and extend to the transfer of many different kinds of proprietary know-how. Besides technological know-how, the transfer of managerial (including organizational) know-how, and goodwill (including brand loyalty) represent types of assets for which market transfer mechanisms may falter and for which the relative efficiency of intrafirm as against interfirm trading is indicated.

Class IV. External economies:

George Stigler has cast the Coase theorem (Coase, 1960) in the following form: "Under perfect competition and any assignment of property rights, market transactions between a firm producing a nuisance and one consuming it will bring about the same composition of output as would have been determined by a single firm engaged in both activities. That is, market transactions will have the same consequences as internal management no matter what the property structure, *provided transactions costs are negligible*" (Stigler, 1966, p. 113, emphasis added). The converse of this is that external economies – which can generate economies of scope – will dictate multiproduct organization when there are significant transaction costs.

External economies in the production of various goods are quite common. For instance, there are locational externalities if a new airport opens up a previously remote area and stimulates tourism.[10] There are also externalities if a cost saving innovation in one industry lowers costs in another. If these externalities can be captured at low cost by common ownership, then multiproduct organization is suggested.

Of course there are limits to the economies which can be captured through diversification. If diversification is based on scope economies, then there will eventually be a problem of congestion associated with accessing the common input. For instance, if the common input is know-how, then while the value of the know-how may not be impaired by repeated transfer, the costs of assessing it may increase if the simultaneous transfer of the information to a number of different applications is attempted. This is because know-how is generally not embodied in blueprints alone; the human factor is critically important in technology transfer. Accordingly, as the demands for sharing know-how increase, bottlenecks in the form of overextended scientists, engineers, and managers can be anticipated.[11] Congestion associated with assessing common inputs will thus clearly limit the amount of diversification which can be profitably engaged. However, if the transfers are arranged so that they occur in a sequential fashion, then the limits imposed by congestion are relieved, at least in part (Teece, 1977).

Control loss considerations may also come into play. However, the establishment of a decentralized divisionalized "M-Form" (Williamson, 1975) structure is likely to minimize control loss problems. In fact Chandler argues that the M-Form innovation made diversification a viable strategy (Chandler, 1969). It is also important to note that diversification need not represent abandonment of specialization. It is simply that a firm's particular advantage is defined not in terms of products but in terms of capabilities. The firm is seen as possessing a specialized know-how or asset base from which it ex-

---

[10]Common ownership may also be needed if the external economies are in the form of skills. Suppose firm X_1 is a monopolist in industry A. A new industry Y emerges which requires labor skills developed in industry X. Because of the transactional difficulties which confront X_1 in appropriating the skills with which it has imbued its employees, X_1 may generate an externality in industry Y. Diversification of X_1 into Y enables the externality to be internalized.

[11]The "Penrose-effect" discussed earlier focuses on the problem with respect to managerial resources.

tends its operations in response to competitive conditions. This element of commonality simplifies the control problem, at least compared to other forms of diversification.

4.5 Market failure considerations and financial capital

Suppose that cash is the only excess capacity possessed by a specialized firm. Assuming, for the moment, that taxation of dividends and capital gains is unimportant, I wish to investigate whether allocative efficiency and/or a firm's market value can possibly be improved by diversification if financial markets are "efficient." Oliver Williamson, among others, has postulated that multidivisional firms can establish internal capital markets with resource allocation properties superior to those obtained by the (external) capital market. In particular, he postulates "a tradeoff between breadth of information, in which respect the banking system may be presumed to have the advantage, and depth of information, which is the advantage of the specialized firm" (Williamson, 1975, p. 162). Inferior access to inside information and the weak control instruments exercised by financial intermediaries and the stock market provides the foundation for Williamson's assertion that the "miniature capital market" within the firm has distinctive efficiency properties.

Financial theorists, however, are often quick to reply that since the financial markets have been shown to be "efficient," no improvement in allocative efficiency or market value can possibly derive from managers usurping the role of financial markets. Myers (1968), Schall (1972), and Mossin (1973) have all argued that value is conserved (value additivity obtains) under the addition of income streams, as would occur with diversification by merger. However, the notions of "efficiency" as used by financial theorists is highly specialized and do not accord with the concept of allocative efficiency used in welfare economics. Nor does it deny that stockholder wealth can be improved through the operations of the firm's internal capital markets. These issues are critical to the analysis to follow and so are examined below.

In the finance literature, the term "efficient markets" has taken on a specialized and misleading meaning. One widely employed definition refers to informational efficiency. For example, according to Fama (1970a, p. 383) "A market in which prices fully reflect available information is called 'efficient,'"[12] and according to Jensen (1978), "A market is efficient with respect

---

[12]Fama (1970a, 1976) actually defines three types of efficiency, each of which is based on a different notion or the type of information understood to be relevant in the phrase "prices fully reflect available information." Specifically, he recognizes:

(1) *Weak-form efficiency*. No investor can earn excess returns if he develops trading rules based on historical price of return information. In other words, the information in past prices or returns is not useful or relevant in achieving excess returns.

(2) *Semistrong-form efficiency*. No investor can earn excess returns from trading rules based

to information set Θ_t if it is impossible to make economic profits by trading on the basis of information set Θ_t." The other widely employed definition is what can be called mean–variance efficiency. The market is mean–variance efficient if capital market prices correspond to an equilibrium in which all individuals evaluate portfolios in terms of their means and variances, about which they all have identical beliefs. Unfortunately, these concepts have nothing to do with allocative efficiency. As Stiglitz (1981) has shown, neither informational efficiency or mean–variance efficiency are necessary or sufficient conditions for the Pareto optimality of the economy. In short, "there is no theoretical presumption simply because the financial markets appear to be competitive, or 'pass' the standard finance literature tests concerning efficiency, that they are efficient" (Stiglitz, 1981, p. 237).

One reason for this result is that it is costly to obtain and transmit information about investment opportunities. Since managers are obviously more informed about investment opportunities available to the firm, they must somehow convey this information to potential investors if efficient outcomes are to be obtained solely through utilization of the (external) capital market. However, capital markets in which it is costly to obtain and transmit information look substantially different from those in which information is assumed to be perfect, and they fail to possess the standard optimality properties (Stiglitz, 1981, p. 244).

The capital market clearly does not fully reflect all information – which is what is necessary for Pareto optimality to obtain.[13] If markets were perfectly efficient in transmitting information from the informed to the uninformed, informed individuals wouldn't obtain a return on their investment in information; thus, the only information which can, in equilibrium, be efficiently transmitted is costless information. With costly information, markets cannot be fully arbitraged (Grossman and Stiglitz, 1976, 1980).

The above considerations indicate why a useful economic function can be performed by the internal allocation of capital within the firm. If managers have access to an information set which is different from investors, and if it is difficult and costly to transmit the content of this information set to investors,

on any publicly available information. Examples of publicly available information are: annual reports of companies, investment advisory data such as "Heard on the street" in *The Wall Street Journal,* or ticker tape information.

(3) *Strong-form efficiency.* No investor can earn excess returns using any information, whether publicly available or not.

Obviously, the last type of market efficiency is very strong indeed. If markets were efficient in their strong form, prices would fully reflect all information even though it might be held exclusively by a corporate insider. Suppose, for example, he knows that his company has just discovered how to control nuclear fusion. Even before he has a chance to trade based on the news, the strong form of market efficiency predicts that prices will have adjusted so that he cannot profit.

[13]Strong-form efficiency, defined in the previous footnote, would be necessary for Pareto optimality to hold.

then managers may be able to increase stockholder wealth by making investment decisions on behalf of the stockholders. In the process, resource allocation is likely to be improved over a situation in which all earnings are returned to
stockholders who then make all reinvestment decisions. The transactions cost
properties of such an arrangement render it absurd in most circumstances.
Accordingly, the existence of internal capital markets and the (partial) internalization of the capital allocation process within the firm appear to possess a
compelling rationale – both in terms of stockholder wealth enhancement and
allocative efficiency.

In this context it is possible to recognize that if a specialized firm possesses
financial resources beyond reinvestment opportunities in its traditional business, there are circumstances under which both stockholder wealth and allocative efficiency can be served if managers allocate funds to new products.
However, the domain within which an efficiency gain is likely swings on
empirical factors, and is likely to be quite narrow, given the relative efficiencies within which managers and stockholders can scan investment opportunities. It is generally only with respect to related businesses – businesses
related functionally, technologically, and geographically – that a relative advantage seems likely. It is for those investment opportunities in which the firm
has a decided information advantage that managers are likely to possess such
an advantage. Broader investment opportunities are better assessed by mutual
funds which specialize in that function and can make portfolio investments at
low transactions costs.

. . .

5.4 Some historical observations

The economic theory of the multiproduct firm outlined above has firms adopt-
ing multiproduct features due to the coupling of market failures and the
emergence of excess capacity. Implicit in the analysis is a conviction that this
model explains a substantial portion of the diversification activity which has
occurred in the American economy. To demonstrate this convincingly would
involve a major empirical effort. I settle here for a more limited objective – to
establish that the historical trends appear broadly consistent with the theory.

Diversification has unquestionably made for great changes in the profile of
American industry during the last half century (Chandler, 1969, p. 247).
Furthermore, the Depression apparently triggered the trend towards diversification. Historians point out that the purpose of diversification was not to
reduce portfolio risk or to pursue managerial motives but rather to put slack
resources to work. Furthermore, it was the technologically sophisticated firms
which led the way. As Chandler (1969, p. 275) observed:

189

DAVID TEECE

Precisely because these firms had accumulated vast resources in skilled manpower, facilities, and equipment, their executives were under even greater pressure than those of smaller firms to find new markets as the old ones ceased to grow. In the 1920s, the chemical companies, each starting from a somewhat different technological base, began to widen their product lines into new industries. In the same decade, the great electrical manufacturers –General Electric and Westinghouse – which had concentrated primarily on the manufacture of light and power equipment, diversified into production of a wide variety of household appliances. They also entered electronics with radios and X-ray equipment. During the Depression General Motors (and to a lesser extent other firms in the auto industry) moved into diesels, appliances, tractors, and airplanes. Some makers of primary metals, particularly aluminum and copper, turned to consumer products like kitchenware and household fittings, while rubber firms developed the possibilities of rubber chemistry to compensate for declining tire sales. In the same period food companies employed their existing distribution organizations to market an increasing variety of products.

Whereas the Depression triggered diversification by generating excess capacity, the Second World War stimulated the demand for new products because the world market for many raw materials was severely disrupted while the war effort generated demand for a wide range of military products. The synthetic rubber program caused both rubber and petroleum firms to make far greater use of chemical technologies than they had ever done before. Similarly, the demand for radar and other electronic equipment carried the electrical, radio, and machinery firms farther into this new field, and the production of tanks, high-speed aircraft, and new drugs all created skills and resources (Chandler, 1969, p. 275). Once these capabilities were created, they were applied, where possible, in the production of civilian goods for the peace time economy. Thus, "the modern diversified enterprise represents a calculated rational response of technically trained professional managers to the needs and opportunities of changing technologies and markets" (Chandler, 1969, p. 279).[14]

. . .

[14]While Chandler's original focus was on managerial and technological considerations, his more recent writings indicate that he has been able to identify additional sources of underutilized resources – such as marketing and purchasing know-how – which could also provide the foundation for an efficient diversification strategy. In the years after the First World War, "many American companies . . . added lines that permitted them to make more effective use of their marketing and purchasing organizations and to exploit the by-products of their manufacturing and processing operations" (Chandler, 1977, p. 473).

PART III

The employment relation, the human factor, and internal organization

CHAPTER 14

Production, information costs, and economic organization

ARMEN ALCHIAN AND
HAROLD DEMSETZ

Armen Alchian is Professor Emeritus at the University of California, Los Angeles. See also the chapter by Alchian with Benjamin Klein and Robert Crawford.

Harold Demsetz was born in Chicago, Illinois in 1930. He received a Ph.D. in economics at Northwestern University in 1959. This article was written during his last months at the University of Chicago and his first months at the University of California, Los Angeles, where he has been Professor of Economics since 1971.

The mark of a capitalistic society is that resources are owned and allocated by such nongovernmental organizations as firms, households, and markets. Resource owners increase productivity through cooperative specialization and this leads to the demand for economic organizations which facilitate cooperation. When a lumber mill employs a cabinetmaker, cooperation between specialists is achieved within a firm, and when a cabinetmaker purchases wood from a lumberman, the cooperation takes place across markets (or between firms). Two important problems face a theory of economic organization – to explain the conditions that determine whether the gains from specialization and cooperative production can better be obtained within an organization like the firm or across markets, and to explain the structure of the organization.

It is common to see the firm characterized by the power to settle issues by fiat, by authority, or by disciplinary action superior to that available in the conventional market. This is delusion. The firm does not own all its inputs. It has no power of fiat, no authority, no disciplinary action any different in the slightest degree from ordinary market contracting between any two people. I can "punish" you only by withholding future business or by seeking redress in the courts for any failure to honor our exchange agreement. That is exactly all that any employer can do. He can fire or sue, just as I can fire my grocer by

Reprinted with minor abridgements from Armen Alchian and Harold Demsetz, "Production, Information Costs, and Economic Organization," *"The American Economic Review*, 62 (1972): 777–95, by permission of the publisher.

stopping purchases from him or sue him for delivering faulty products. What then is the content of the presumed power to manage and assign workers to various tasks? Exactly the same as one little consumer's power to manage and assign his grocer to various tasks. The simple consumer assigns his grocer to the task of obtaining whatever the customer can induce the grocer to provide at a price acceptable to both parties. That is precisely all that an employer can do to an employee. To speak of managing, directing, or assigning workers to various tasks is a deceptive way of noting that the employer continually is involved in renegotiation of contracts on terms that must be acceptable to both parties. Telling an employee to type this letter rather than to file that document is like my telling a grocer to sell me this brand of tuna rather than that brand of bread. I have no contract to continue to purchase from the grocer and neither the employer nor the employee is bound by any contractual obligations to continue their relationship. Long-term contracts between employer and employee are not the essence of the organization we call a firm. My grocer can count on my returning day after day and purchasing his services and goods even with the prices not always marked on the goods – because I know what they are – and he adapts his activity to conform to my directions to him as to what I want each day . . . he is not my employee.

   Wherein then is the relationship between a grocer and his employee different from that between a grocer and his customers? It is in a *team* use of inputs and a centralized position of some party in the contractual arrangements of *all* other inputs. It is the *centralized contractual agent in a team productive process* – not some superior authoritarian directive or disciplinary power. Exactly what is a team process and why does it induce the contractual form, called the firm? These problems motivate the inquiry of this paper.

I. The metering problem

The economic organization through which input owners cooperate will make better use of their comparative advantages to the extent that it facilitates the payment of rewards in accord with productivity. If rewards were random, and without regard to productive effort, no incentive to productive effort would be provided by the organization; and if rewards were negatively correlated with productivity the organization would be subject to sabotage. Two key demands are placed on an economic organization – metering input productivity and metering rewards.[1]

---

[1]Meter means to measure and also to apportion. One can meter (measure) output and one can also meter (control) the output. We use the word to denote both; the context should indicate which.

Metering problems sometimes can be resolved well through the exchange of products across competitive markets, because in many situations markets yield a high correlation between rewards and productivity. If a farmer increases his output of wheat by 10 percent at the prevailing market price, his receipts also increase by 10 percent. This method of organizing economic activity meters the *output directly,* reveals the marginal product, and apportions the *rewards* to resource owners in accord with that direct measurement of their outputs. The success of this decentralized, market exchange in promoting productive specialization requires that changes in market rewards fall on those responsible for changes in *output.*[2]

The classic relationship in economics that runs from marginal productivity to the distribution of income implicitly *assumes* the existence of an organization, be it the market or the firm, that allocates rewards to resources in accord with their productivity. The problem of economic organization, the economical means of metering productivity and rewards, is not confronted directly in the classical analysis of production and distribution. Instead, that analysis tends to assume sufficiently economic – or zero cost – means, as if productivity automatically created its reward. We conjecture the direction of causation is the reverse – the specific system of rewarding which is relied upon stimulates a particular productivity response. If the economic organization meters poorly, with rewards and productivity only loosely correlated, then productivity will be smaller; but if the economic organization meters well, productivity

---

[2] A producer's wealth would be reduced by the present capitalized value of the future income lost by loss of reputation. Reputation, i.e., credibility, is an asset, which is another way of saying that reliable information about expected performance is both a costly and a valuable good. For acts of God that interfere with contract performance, both parties have incentives to reach a settlement akin to that which would have been reached if such events had been covered by specific contingency clauses. The reason, again, is that a reputation for "honest" dealings – i.e., for actions similar to those that would probably have been reached had the contract provided this contingency – is wealth.

Almost every contract is open-ended in that many contingencies are uncovered. For example, if a fire delays production of a promised product by *A* to *B*, and if *B* contends that *A* has not fulfilled the contract, how is the dispute settled and what recompense, if any, does *A* grant to *B*? A person uninitiated in such questions may be surprised by the extent to which contracts permit either party to escape performance or to nullify the contract. In fact, it is hard to imagine any contract, which, when taken solely in terms of its stipulations, could not be evaded by one of the parties. Yet that is the ruling, viable type of contract. Why? Undoubtedly the best discussion that we have seen on this question is by Stewart Macaulay (1963).

There are means not only of detecting or preventing cheating but also for deciding how to allocate the losses or gains of unpredictable events or quality of items exchanged. Sales contracts contain warranties, guarantees, collateral, return privileges, and penalty clauses for specific nonperformance. These are means of assignment of *risks* of losses of cheating. A lower price without warranty – an "as is" purchase – places more of the risk on the buyer while the seller buys insurance against losses of his "cheating." On the other hand, a warranty or return privilege or service contract places more risk on the seller with insurance being bought by the buyer.

will be greater. What makes metering difficult and hence induces means of economizing on metering costs?

II. Team production

Two men jointly lift heavy cargo into trucks. Solely by observing the total weight loaded per day, it is impossible to determine each person's marginal productivity. With team production it is difficult, solely by observing total output, to either define or determine *each* individual's contribution to this output of the cooperating inputs. The output is yielded by a team, by definition, and it is not a *sum* of separable outputs of each of its members. Team production of Z involves at least two inputs, X_i and X_j, with $\partial^2 Z/\partial X_i \partial X_j \neq 0$.[3] The production function is *not* separable into two functions each involving only inputs X_i or only inputs X_j. Consequently there is no *sum* of Z of two separable functions to treat as the Z of the team production function. (An example of a *separable* case is $Z = aX_i^2$ and $Z_j = bX_j^2$, and $Z = Z_i + Z_j$. This is not team production.) There exist production techniques in which the Z obtained is greater than if S_i and X_j had produced separable Z. Team production will be used if it yields an output enough larger than the sum of separable production of Z to cover the costs of organizing and disciplining team members – the topics of this paper.[4]

Usual explanations of the gains from cooperative behavior rely on exchange and production in accord with the comparative advantage specialization principle with separable additive production. However, as suggested above there is a source of gain from cooperative activity involving working as a *team*, wherein individual cooperating inputs do not yield identifiable, separate products which can be *summed* to measure the total output. For this cooperative productive activity, here called "team" production, measuring *marginal* productivity and making payments in accord therewith is more expensive by an order of magnitude than for separable production functions.

Team production, to repeat, is production in which (1) several types of resources are used and (2) the product is not a sum of separable outputs of each cooperating resource. An additional factor creates a team organization problem – (3) not all resources used in team production belong to one person.

We do not inquire into why all the jointly used resources are not owned by one person, but instead into the types of organization, contracts, and informational and payment procedures used among owners of teamed inputs. With respect to the one-owner case, perhaps it is sufficient merely to note that (a)

[3]The function is separable into additive functions if the cross partial derivative is zero, i.e., if $\partial 2Z/\partial X_i \partial X_j = 0$.

[4]With sufficient generality of notation and conception, this team production function could be formulated as a case of the generalized production function interpretation given by our colleague, E. A. Thompson (1970).

slavery is prohibited, (b) one might assume risk aversion as a reason for one person's not borrowing enough to purchase all the assets or sources of services rather than renting them, and (c) the purchase–resale spread may be so large that costs of short-term ownership exceed rental costs. Our problem is viewed basically as one of organization among different people, not of the physical goods or services, however much there must be selection and choice of combination of the latter.

How can the members of a team be rewarded and induced to work efficiently? In team production, marginal products of cooperative team members are not so directly and separably (i.e., cheaply) observable. What a team offers to the market can be taken as the marginal product of the team but not of the team members. The costs of metering or ascertaining the marginal products of the team's members is what calls forth new organizations and procedures. Clues to each input's productivity can be secured by observing *behavior* of individual inputs. When lifting cargo into the truck, how rapidly does a man move to the next piece to be loaded, how many cigarette breaks does he take, does the item being lifted tilt downward toward his side?

If detecting such behavior were costless, neither party would have an incentive to shirk, because neither could impose the cost of his shirking on the other (if their cooperation was agreed to voluntarily). But since costs must be incurred to monitor each other, each input owner will have more incentive to shirk when he works as part of a team than if his performance could be monitored easily or if he did not work as a team. If there is a net increase in productivity available by team production, net of the metering cost associated with disciplining the team, then team production will be relied upon rather than a multitude of bilateral exchanges of separable individual outputs.

Both leisure and higher income enter a person's utility function.[5] Hence, each person should adjust his work and realized reward so as to equate the marginal rate of substitution between leisure and production of real output to his marginal rate of substitution in consumption. That is, he would adjust his rate of work to bring his demand prices of leisure and output to equality with their true costs. However, with detection, policing, monitoring, measuring, or metering costs, each person will be induced to take more leisure, because the effect of relaxing on *his realized* (reward) rate of substitution between output and leisure will be less than the effect on the *true* rate of substitution. His realized cost of leisure will fall more than the true cost of leisure, so he "buys" more leisure (i.e., more nonpecuniary reward).

If his relaxation cannot be detected perfectly at zero cost, part of its effects will be borne by others in the team, thus making *his* realized cost of relaxation

---

[5]More precisely: "if anything other than pecuniary income enters his utility function." Leisure stands for all nonpecuniary income for simplicity of exposition.

less than the true total cost to the team. The difficulty of detecting such actions permits the private costs of his actions to be less than their full costs. Since each person responds to his private realizable rate of substitution (in production) rather than the true total (i.e. social) rate, and so long as there are costs for other people to detect his shift toward relaxation, it will not pay (them) to force him to readjust completely by making him realize the true cost. Only enough efforts will be made to equate the marginal gains of detection activity with the marginal costs of detection, and that implies a lower rate of productive effort and more shirking than in a costless monitoring, or measuring, world.

In a university, the faculty use office telephones, paper, and mail for personal uses beyond strict university productivity. The university administrators could stop such practices by identifying *the* responsible person in each case, but they can do so only at higher costs than administrators are willing to incur. The extra costs of identifying each party (rather than merely identifying the presence of such activity) would exceed the savings from diminished faculty "turpitudinal peccadilloes." So the faculty is allowed some degree of "privileges, perquisites, or fringe benefits." And the total of the pecuniary wages paid is lower because of this irreducible (at acceptable costs) degree of amenity-seizing activity. Pay is lower in pecuniary terms and higher in leisure, conveniences, and ease of work. But still every person would prefer to see detection made more effective (if it were somehow possible to monitor costlessly) so that he, as part of the now more effectively producing team, could thereby realize a higher pecuniary pay and less leisure. If everyone could, at zero cost, have his reward-realized rate brought to the true production possibility real rate, all could achieve a more preferred position. But detection of the responsible parties is costly; that cost acts like a tax on work rewards.[6] Viable shirking is the result.

What forms of organizing team production will lower the cost of detecting "performance" (i.e., marginal productivity) and bring personally realized rates of substitution closer to true rates of substitution? Market competition, in principle, could monitor some team production. (It already *organizes* teams.) Input owners who are not team members can offer, in return for a smaller share of the team's rewards, to replace excessively (i.e., overpaid) shirking members. Market competition among potential team members would determine team membership and individual rewards. There would be no team

---

[6]Do not assume that the sole result of the cost of detecting shirking is one form of payment (more leisure and less take-home money). With several members of the team, each has an incentive to cheat against each other by engaging in more than the average amount of such leisure if the employer can not tell at zero cost which employee is taking more than average. As a result the total productivity of the team is lowered. Shirking detection costs thus change the form of payment and also result in lower total rewards. Because the cross partial derivatives are positive, shirking reduces other people's marginal products.

leader, manager, organizer, owner, or employer. For such decentralized organizational control to work, outsiders, possibly after observing each team's total output, can speculate about their capabilities as team members and, by a market competitive process, revised teams with greater production ability will be formed and sustained. Incumbent members will be constrained by threats of replacement by outsiders offering services for lower reward shares or offering greater rewards to the other members of the team. Any team member who shirked in the expectation that the reduced output effect would not be attributed to him will be displaced if his activity is detected. Teams of productive inputs, like business units, would evolve in apparent spontaneity in the market – without any central organizing agent, team manager, or boss.

But completely effective control cannot be expected from individualized market competition for two reasons. First, for this competition to be completely effective, new challengers for team membership must know where, and to what extent, shirking is a serious problem, i.e., know they can increase net output as compared with the inputs they replace. To the extent that this is true it is probably possible for existing fellow team members to recognize the shirking. But, by definition, the detection of shirking by observing team output is costly for team production. Secondly, assume the presence of detection costs, and assume that in order to secure a place on the team a new input owner must accept a smaller share of rewards (or a promise to produce more). Then his incentive to shirk would still be at least as great as the incentives of the inputs replaced, because he still bears less than the entire reduction in team output for which he is responsible.

III. The classical firm

One method of reducing shirking is for someone to specialize as a monitor to check the input performance of team members.[7] But who will monitor the monitor? One constraint on the monitor is the aforesaid market competition offered by other monitors, but for reasons already given, that is not perfectly effective. Another constraint can be imposed on the monitor: give him title to the net earnings of the team, net of payments to other inputs. If owners of cooperating inputs agree with the monitor that he is to receive any residual product above prescribed amounts (hopefully, the marginal value products of

---

[7]What is meant by performance? Input energy, initiative, work attitude, perspiration, rate of exhaustion? Or output? It is the latter that is sought – the *effect* or output. But performance is nicely ambiguous because it suggests both input and output. It is *nicely* ambiguous because as we shall see, sometimes by inspecting a team member's input activity we can better judge his output effect, perhaps not with complete accuracy but better than by watching the output of the *team*. It is not always the case that watching input activity is the only or best means of detecting, measuring, or monitoring output effects of each team member, but in some cases it is a useful way. For the moment the word performance glosses over these aspects and facilitates concentration on other issues.

the other inputs), the monitor will have an added incentive not to shirk as a monitor. Specialization in monitoring plus reliance on a residual claimant status will reduce shirking, but additional links are needed to forge the firm of classical economic theory. How will the residual claimant monitor the other inputs?

We use the term monitor to connote several activities in addition to its disciplinary connotation. It connotes measuring output performance, apportioning rewards, observing the input behavior of inputs as a means of detecting or estimating their marginal productivity, and giving assignments or instructions in what to do and how to do it. (It also includes, as we shall show later, authority to terminate or revise contracts.) Perhaps the contrast between a football coach and team captain is helpful. The coach selects strategies and tactics and sends instructions about what plays to utilize. The captain is essentially an observer and reporter of the performance at close hand of the members. The latter is an inspector-steward and the former a supervisor-manager. For the present all these activities are included in the rubric "monitoring." All these tasks are, in principle, negotiable across markets, but we are presuming that such market measurement of marginal productivities and job reassignments are not so cheaply performed for team production. And in particular our analysis suggests that it is not so much the costs of spontaneously negotiating contracts in the markets among groups for team production as it is the detection of the performance of individual members of the team that calls for the organization noted here.

The specialist *who receives the residual rewards* will be the monitor of the members of the team (i.e., will manage the use of cooperative inputs). The monitor earns his residual through the reduction in shirking that he brings about, not only by the prices that he agrees to pay the owners of the inputs, but also by observing and directing the actions or uses of these inputs. *Managing or examining the ways to which inputs are used in team production is a method of metering the marginal productivity of individual inputs to the team's output.*

To discipline team members and reduce shirking, the residual claimant must have power to revise the contract terms and incentives of *individual* members without having to terminate or alter every other input's contract. Hence, team members who seek to increase their productivity will assign to the monitor not only the residual claimant right but also the right to alter individual membership and performance on the team. Each team member, of course, can terminate his own membership (i.e., quit the team), but only the monitor may unilaterally terminate the membership of any of the other members without necessarily terminating the team itself or his association with the team; and he alone can expand or reduce membership, alter the mix of membership, or sell the right to be the residual claimant-monitor of the team. It is this entire bundle of rights: (1) to be a residual claimant, (2) to observe input behavior, (3) to be the central party common to all contracts with inputs, (4) to alter the membership of the team, and (5) to sell these rights, that defines the *ownership* (or the employer) of the *classical* (capitalist, free-enterprise) firm. The coalescing of these rights has arisen, our analysis asserts, because it resolves the shirking-information problem of team production better than does the noncentralized contractual arrangement.

The relationship of each team member to the *owner* of the firm (i.e., the party common to all input contracts *and* the residual claimant) is simply a "quid pro quo" contract. Each makes a purchase and sale. The employee "orders" the owner of the team to pay him money in the same sense that the employer directs the team member to perform certain acts. The employee can terminate the contract as readily as can the employer, and long-term contracts, therefore, are not an essential attribute of the firm. Nor are "authoritarian," "dictational," or "fiat" attributes relevant to the conception of the firm or its efficiency.

In summary, two necessary conditions exist for the emergence of the firm on the prior assumption that more than pecuniary wealth enter utility functions: (1) It is possible to increase productivity through team-oriented production, a production technique for which it is costly to directly measure the marginal outputs of the cooperating inputs. This makes it more difficult to restrict shirking through simple market exchange between cooperating inputs. (2) It is economical to estimate marginal productivity by observing or specifying input behavior. The simultaneous occurrence of both these preconditions leads to the contractual organization of inputs, known as the *classical capitalist firms* with (a) joint input production, (b) several input owners, (c) one party who is common to all the contracts of the joint inputs, (d) who has rights to renegotiate any input's contract independently of contracts with other input owners, (e) who holds the residual claim, and (f) who has the right to sell his central contractual residual status.[8]

Other theories of the firm

At this juncture, as an aside, we briefly place this theory of the firm in the contexts of those offered by Ronald Coase and Frank Knight.[9] Our view of the firm is not necessarily inconsistent with Coase's; we attempt to go further and identify refutable implications. Coase's penetrating insight is to make more of the fact that markets do not operate costlessly, and he relies on the cost of using markets to *form* contracts as his basic explanation for the existence of

[8]Removal of (b) converts a capitalist proprietary firm to a socialist firm.
[9]Recognition must also be made to the seminal inquiries by Morris Silver and Richard Auster (1969) and by H. B. Malmgren (1961).

firms. We do not disagree with the proposition that, *ceteris paribus*, the higher is the cost of transacting across markets the greater will be the comparative advantage of organizing resources within the firm; it is a difficult proposition to disagree with or to refute. We could with equal ease subscribe to a theory of the firm based on the cost of managing for surely it is true that, *ceteris paribus*, the lower is the cost of managing the greater will be the comparative advantage of organizing resources within the firm. To move the theory forward, it is necessary to know what is meant by a firm and to explain the circumstances under which the cost of "managing" resources is low relative to the cost of allocating resources through market transaction. The conception of and rationale for the classical firm that we propose takes a step down the path pointed out by Coase toward that goal. Consideration of team production, team organization, difficulty in metering outputs, and the problem of shirking are important to our explanation but, so far as we can ascertain, not in Coase's. Coase's analysis insofar as it had heretofore been developed would suggest open-ended contracts but does not appear to imply anything more – neither the residual claimant status nor the distinction between employee and subcontractor status (nor any of the implications indicated below). And it is not true that employees are generally employed on the basis of long-term contractual arrangements any more than on a series of short-term or indefinite length contracts.

The importance of our proposed additional elements is revealed, for example, by the explanation of why the person to whom the control monitor is responsible receives the residual, and also by our later discussion of the implications about the corporation, partnerships, and profit sharing. These alternative forms for organization of the firm are difficult to resolve on the basis of market transaction costs only. Our exposition also suggests a definition of the classical firm – something crucial that was heretofore absent.

In addition, sometimes a technological development will lower the cost of market transactions while, at the same time, it expands the role of the firm. When the "putting out" system was used for weaving, inputs were organized largely through market negotiations. With the development of efficient central sources of power, it became economical to perform weaving in proximity to the power source and to engage in team production. The bringing in of weavers surely must have resulted in a reduction in the cost of negotiating (forming) contracts. Yet, what we observe is the beginning of the factory system, in which inputs are organized within a firm. Why? The weavers did not simply move to a common source of power that they could tap like an electric line, purchasing power while they used their own equipment. Now team production in the joint use of equipment became more important. The measurement of marginal productivity, which now involved interactions between workers, especially through their joint use of machines, became more difficult though contract negotiating cost was reduced, while managing the *behavior* of inputs became easier because of the increased centralization of activity. The firm as an organization expanded even though the cost of transactions was reduced by the advent of centralized power. The same could be said for modern assembly lines. Hence the emergence of central power sources expanded the scope of productive activity in which the firm enjoyed a comparative advantage as an organizational form.

Some economists, following Knight, have identified the bearing of risks of wealth changes with the director or central employer without explaining why that is a viable arrangement. Presumably, the more risk-averse inputs become employees rather than owners of the classical firm. Risk averseness and uncertainty *with regard to the firm's fortunes* have little, if anything, to do with our explanation although it helps to explain why all resources in a team are not owned by one person. That is, the role of risk taken in the sense of absorbing the windfalls that buffet the firm because of unforeseen competition, technological change, or fluctuations in demand are not central to our theory, although it is true that imperfect knowledge and, therefore, risk, in *this* sense of risk, underlie the problem of monitoring team behavior. We deduce the system of paying the manager with a residual claim (the equity) from the desire to have efficient means to reduce shirking so as to make team production economical and not from the smaller aversion to the risks of enterprise in a dynamic economy. We conjecture that "distribution-of-risk" is not a valid rationale for the *existence* and organization of the *classical* firm.

Although we have emphasized team production as creating a costly metering task and have treated team production as an essential (necessary?) condition for the firm, would not other obstacles to cheap metering also call forth the same kind of contractual arrangement here denoted as a firm? For example, suppose a farmer produces wheat in an easily ascertained quantity but with subtle and difficult to detect quality variations determined by how the farmer grew the wheat. A vertical integration could allow a purchaser to control the farmer's behavior in order to more economically estimate productivity. But this is not a case of joint or team production, unless "information" can be considered part of the product. (While a good case could be made for that broader conception of production, we shall ignore it here.) Instead of forming a firm, a buyer can contract to have his inspector on the site of production, just as home builders contract with architects to supervise building contracts; that arrangement is not a firm. Still, a firm might be organized in the production of many products wherein no team production or jointness is involved.

This possibility rather clearly indicates a broader, or complementary, approach to that which we have chosen. (1) As we do in this paper, it can be argued that the firm is the particular policing device utilized when joint team production is present. If other sources of high policing costs arise, as in the wheat case just indicated, some other form of contractual arrangement will be used. Thus to each source of informational cost there may be a different type of policing and contractual arrangement. (2) On the other hand, one can say that where policing is difficult across markets, various forms of contractual arrangements are devised, but there is no reason for that known as the firm to be uniquely related or even highly correlated with team production, as defined here. It might be used equally probably and viably for other sources of high policing cost. We have not intensively analyzed other sources, and we can only note that our current and readily revisable conjecture is that (1) is valid, and has motivated us in our current endeavor. In any event, the test of the theory advanced here is to see whether the conditions we have identified are necessary for firms to have long-run viability rather than merely births with high infant mortality. Conglomerate firms or collections of separate production agencies into one owning organization can be interpreted as an investment trust or investment diversification device – probably Knight's interpretation. A holding company can be called a firm, because of the common association of the word firm with any ownership unit that owns income sources. The term firm as commonly used is so turgid of meaning that we can not hope to explain every entity to which the name is attached in common or even technical literature. Instead, we seek to identify and explain a particular contractual arrangement induced by the cost of information factors analyzed in this paper.

IV. Types of firms

A. Profit-sharing firms

Explicit in our explanation of the capitalist firm is the assumption that the cost of *managing* the team's inputs by a central monitor, who disciplines himself because he is a residual claimant, is low relative to the cost of metering the marginal outputs of team members.

If we look within a firm to see who monitors – hires, fires, changes, promotes, and renegotiates – we should find him being a residual claimant or, at least, one whose pay or reward is more than any others correlated with fluctuations in the residual value of the firm. They more likely will have options or rights or bonuses than will inputs with other tasks.

An implicit "auxiliary" assumption of our explanation of the firm is that the cost of team production is increased if the residual claim is not held entirely by the central monitor. That is, we assume that if profit sharing had to be relied upon for *all* team members, losses from the resulting increase in central

204

monitor shirking would exceed the output gains from the increased incentives of other team members not to shirk. If the optimal team size is only two owners of inputs, then an equal division of profits and losses between them will leave each with stronger incentives to reduce shirking than if the optimal team size is large, for in the latter case only a smaller percentage of the losses occasioned by the shirker will be borne by him. Incentives to shirk are positively related to the optimal size of the team under an equal profit-sharing scheme.[10]

The preceding does not imply that profit sharing is never viable. Profit sharing to encourage self-policing is more appropriate for small teams. And, indeed, where input owners are free to make whatever contractual arrangements suit them, as generally is true in capitalist economies, profit sharing seems largely limited to partnerships with a relatively small number of *active*[11] partners. Another advantage of such arrangements for smaller teams is that it permits more effective reciprocal monitoring among inputs. Monitoring need not be entirely specialized.

Profit sharing is more viable if small team size is associated with situations where the cost of specialized management of inputs is large relative to the increased productivity potential in team effort. We conjecture that the cost of managing team inputs increases if the productivity of a team member is difficult to correlate with his behavior. In "artistic" or "professional" work, watching a man's activities is not a good clue to what he is actually thinking or doing with his mind. While it is relatively easy to manage or direct the loading of trucks by a team of dock workers where input activity is so highly related in an obvious way to output, it is more difficult to manage and direct a lawyer in the preparation and presentation of a case. Dock workers can be directed in detail without the monitor himself loading the truck, and assembly line workers can be monitored by varying the speed of the assembly line, but detailed direction in the preparation of a law case would require in much greater degree that the monitor prepare the case himself. As a result, artistic or professional inputs, such as lawyers, advertising specialists, and doctors, will be given relatively freer reign with regard to individual behavior. If the management of inputs is relatively costly, or ineffective, as it would seem to be in these cases, but, nonetheless if team effort is more productive than separable

---

[10]While the degree to which residual claims are centralized will affect the size of the team, this will be only one of many factors that determine team size, so as an approximation, we can treat team size as exogenously determined. Under certain assumptions about the shape of the "typical" utility function, the incentive to avoid shirking with unequal profit sharing can be measured by the Herfindahl index.

[11]The use of the word active will be clarified in our discussion of the corporation, which follows below.

production with exchange across markets, then there will develop a tendency to use profit-sharing schemes to provide incentives to avoid shirking.[12]

B. Socialist firms

We have analyzed the classical proprietorship and the profit-sharing firms in the context of free association and choice of economic organization. Such organizations need not be the most viable when political constraints limit the forms of organization that can be chosen. It is one thing to have profit sharing when professional or artistic talents are used by small teams. But if political or tax or subsidy considerations induce profit-sharing techniques when these are not otherwise economically justified, then additional management techniques will be developed to help reduce the degree of shirking.

For example, most, if not all, firms in Jugoslavia are owned by the employees in the restricted sense that all share in the residual. This is true for large firms and for firms which employ nonartistic, or nonprofessional, workers as well. With a decay of political constraints, most of these firms could be expected to rely on paid wages rather than shares in the residual. This rests on our auxiliary assumption that general sharing in the residual results in losses from enhanced shirking by the monitor that exceed the gains from reduced shirking by residual-sharing employees. If this were not so, profit sharing with employees should have occurred more frequently in Western societies where such organizations are neither banned nor preferred politically. Where residual sharing by employees is politically imposed, as in Jugoslavia, we are led to expect that some management technique will arise to reduce the shirking by the central monitor, a technique that will not be found frequently in Western societies since the monitor retains all (or much) of the residual in the West and profit sharing is largely confined to small, professional-artistic team production situations. We do find in the larger scale residual-sharing firms in Jugoslavia that there are employee committees that can recommend (to the state) the termination of a manager's contract (veto his continuance) with the enterprise. We conjecture that the workers' committee is given the right to recommend the termination of the manager's contract precisely because the general sharing of the residual increases "excessively" the manager's incentive to shirk.[13]

---

[12]Some sharing contracts, like crop sharing, or rental payments based on gross sales in retail stores, come close to profit sharing: However, it is gross output sharing rather than profit sharing. We are unable to specify the implications of the difference. We refer the reader to S. N. Cheung (1969).

[13]Incidentally, investment activity will be changed. The inability to capitalize the investment value as "take-home" private property *wealth* of the members of the firm means that the benefits of the investment must be taken as annual income by those who are employed at the time of the

C. The corporation

All firms must initially acquire command over some resources. The corporation does so primarily by selling promises of future returns to those who (as creditors or owners) provide financial capital. In some situations resources can be acquired in advance from consumers by promises of future delivery (for example, advance sale of a proposed book). Or where the firm is a few artistic or professional persons, each can "chip in" with time and talent until the sale of services brings in revenues. For the most part, capital can be acquired more cheaply if many (risk-averse) investors contribute small portions to a large investment. The economies of raising large sums of equity capital in this way suggest that modifications in the relationship among corporate inputs are required to cope with the shirking problem that arises with profit sharing among large numbers of corporate stockholders. One modification is limited liability, especially for firms that are large relative to a stockholder's wealth. It serves to protect stockholders from large losses no matter how they are caused.

If every stock owner participated in each decision in a corporation, not only would large bureaucratic costs be incurred, but many would shirk the task of becoming well informed on the issue to be decided, since the losses associated with unexpectedly bad decisions will be borne in large part by the many other corporate shareholders. More effective control of corporate activity is achieved for most purposes by transferring decision authority to a smaller group, whose main function is to negotiate with and manage (renegotiate with) the other inputs of the team. The corporate stockholders retain the authority to revise the membership of the management group and over major decisions that affect the structure of the corporation or its dissolution.

As a result a new modification of partnerships is induced – the right to sale of corporate shares without approval of any other stockholders. Any share holder can remove his wealth from control by those with whom he has differences of opinion. Rather than try to control the decisions of the management, which is harder to do with many stockholders than with only a few, unrestricted salability provides a more acceptable escape to each stockholder from continued policies with which he disagrees.

Indeed, the policing of managerial shirking relies on across-market competition from new groups of would-be managers as well as competition from members within the firm who seek to displace existing management. In addi-

income. Investment will be confined more to those with shorter life and with higher rates or payoffs if the alternative of investing is paying out the firm's income to employees to take home and use as private property. For a development of this proposition, see the papers by Eirik Furubota and Svetozar Pejovich (1974) and by Pejovich (1969).

tion to competition from outside and inside managers, control is facilitated by the temporary congealing of share votes into voting blocs owned by one or a few contenders. Proxy battles of stock purchases concentrate the votes required to displace the existing management or modify managerial policies. But it is more than a change in policy that is sought by the newly formed financial interests whether of new stockholders or not. It is the capitalization of expected future benefits into stock prices that concentrates on the innovators the wealth gains of their actions if they own large numbers of shares. Without capitalization of future benefits, there would be less incentive to incur the costs required to exert informed decisive influence on the corporation's policies and managing personnel. Temporarily, the structure of ownership is reformed, moving away from diffused ownership into decisive power blocs, and this is a transient resurgence of the classical firm with power again concentrated in those who have title to the residual.

In assessing the significance of stockholders' power it is not the usual diffusion of voting power that is significant but instead the frequency with which voting congeals into decisive changes. Even a one-man owned company may have a long term with just one manager – continuously being approved by the owner. Similarly a dispersed voting power corporation may be also characterized by a long-lived management. The question is the probability of replacement of the management if it behaves in ways not acceptable to a majority of the stockholders. The unrestricted stability of stock and the transfer of proxies enhances the probability of decisive action in the event current stockholders or any outsider believes that management is not doing a good job with the corporation. We are not comparing the corporate responsiveness to that of a single proprietorship; instead, we are indicating features of the corporate structure that are induced by the problem of delegated authority to manager-monitors.[14]

[14]Instead of thinking of shareholders as joint *owners,* we can think of them as investors, like bondholders, except that the stockholders are more optimistic than bondholders about the enterprise prospects. Instead of buying bonds in the corporation, thus enjoying smaller risks, shareholders prefer to invest funds with a greater realizable return if the firm prospers as expected, but with smaller (possibly negative) returns if the firm performs in a manner closer to that expected by the more pessimistic investors. The pessimistic investors, in turn, regard only the bonds as likely to pay off.

If the entrepreneur-organizer is to raise capital on the best terms to him, it is to his advantage, as well as that of prospective investors, to recognize these differences in expectations. The residual claim on earnings enjoyed by shareholders does not serve the function of enhancing their efficiency as monitors in the general situation. The stockholders are "merely" the less risk-averse or the more optimistic member of the group that finances the firm. Being more optimistic than the average and seeing a higher mean value future return, they are willing to pay more for a certificate that allows them to realize gain on their expectations. One method of doing so is to buy claims to the distribution of returns that "they see," while bondholders, who are more pessimistic, purchase a claim to the distribution that they see as more likely to emerge. Stockholders are then comparable to warrant holders. They care not about the voting rights (usually not attached to warrants);

D. Mutual and nonprofit firms

The benefits obtained by the new management are greater if the stock can be purchased and sold, because this enables *capitalization* of anticipated future improvements into present *wealth* of new managers who bought stock and created a larger capital by their management changes. But in nonprofit corporations, colleges, churches, country clubs, mutual savings banks, mutual insurance companies, and "coops," the future consequences of improved

they are in the same position in so far as voting rights are concerned as are bondholders. The only difference is in the probability distribution of rewards and the terms on which they can place their bets.

If we treat bondholders, preferred and convertible preferred stockholders, and common stockholders and warrant holders as simply different classes of investors – differing not only in their risk averseness but in their beliefs about the probability distribution of the firm's future earnings, why should stockholders be regarded as "owners" in any sense distinct from the other financial investors? The entrepreneur-organizer, who let us assume is the chief operating officer and sole repository of control of the corporation, does not find his authority residing in common stockholders (except in the case of a take-over). Does this type of control make any difference in the way the firm is conducted? Would it make any difference in the kinds of behavior that would be tolerated by competing managers and investors (and we here deliberately refrain from thinking of them as owner-stockholders in the traditional sense)?

Investment old timers recall a significant incidence of nonvoting common stock, now prohibited in corporations whose stock is traded on listed exchanges. (Why prohibited?) The entrepreneur in those days could hold voting shares while investors held nonvoting shares, which in every other respect were identical. Nonvoting share holders were simply investors devoid of ownership connotations. The control and behavior of inside owners in such corporations has never, so far as we have ascertained, been carefully studied. For example, at the simplest level of interest, does the evidence indicate that nonvoting shareholders fared any worse because of not having voting rights? Did owners permit the nonvoting holders the normal return available to voting shareholders? Though evidence is prohibitively expensive to obtain, it is remarkable that voting and nonvoting shares sold for essentially identical prices, even during some proxy battles. However, our casual evidence deserves no more than interest-initiating weight.

One more point. The facade is deceptive. Instead of nonvoting shares, today we have warrants, convertible preferred stocks, all of which are solely or partly "equity" claims without voting rights, though they could be converted into voting shares.

In sum, is it the case that the stockholder–investor relationship is one emanating from the *division of ownership* among several people, or is it that the collection of investment funds from people of varying anticipations is the underlying factor? If the latter, why should any of them be thought of as the owners in whom voting rights, whatever they may signify or however exercisable, should reside in order to enhance efficiency? Why voting rights in any of the outside, participating investors?

Our initial perception of this possibly significant difference in interpretation was precipitated by Henry Manne (1976). A reading of his paper makes it clear that it is hard to understand why an investor who wishes to back and "share" in the consequences of some new business should necessarily have to acquire voting power (i.e., power to change the manager-operator) in order to invest in the venture. In fact, we invest in some ventures in the hope that no other stockholders will be so "foolish" as to try to toss out the incumbent management. We want him to have the power to stay in office, and for the prospect of sharing in his fortunes we buy nonvoting common stock. Our willingness to invest is enhanced by the knowledge that we can act legally via fraud, embezzlement and other laws to help assure that we outside investors will not be "milked" beyond our initial discounted anticipations.

management are not capitalized into present wealth of stockholders. (As if to make more difficult that competition by new would-be monitors, multiple shares of ownership in those enterprises cannot be bought by one person.) One should therefore, find greater shirking in nonprofit, mutually owned enterprises. (This suggests that nonprofit enterprises are especially appropriate in realms of endeavor where more shirking is desired and where redirected use of the enterprise in response to market-revealed values is less desired.)

E. Partnerships

Team production in artistic or professional intellectual skills will more likely be by partnerships than other types of team production. This amounts to market-organized team activity and to a nonemployer status. Self-monitoring partnerships, therefore, will be used rather than employer–employee contracts, and these organizations will be small to prevent an excessive dilution of efforts through shirking. Also, partnerships are more likely to occur among relatives or long-standing acquaintances, not necessarily because they share a common utility function, but also because each knows better the other's work characteristics and tendencies to shirk.

F. Employee unions

Employee unions, whatever else they do, perform as monitors for employees. Employers monitor employees and similarly employees monitor an employer's performance. Are correct wages paid on time and in good currency? Usually, this is extremely easy to check. But some forms of employer performance are less easy to meter and are more subject to employer shirking. Fringe benefits often are in nonpecuniary, contingent form; medical, hospital, and accident insurance, and retirement pensions are contingent payments or performances partly in *kind* by employers to employees. Each employee cannot judge the character of such payments as easily as money wages. Insurance is a contingent payment – what the employee will get upon the contingent event may come as a disappointment. If he could easily determine what other employees had gotten upon such contingent events he could judge more accurately the performance by the employer. He could "trust" the employer not to shirk in such fringe contingent payments, but he would prefer an effective and economic monitor of those payments. We see a specialist monitor – the union employees' agent – hired by them and monitoring those aspects of employer payment most difficult for the employees to monitor. Employees should be willing to employ a specialist monitor to administer such hard-to-detect employer performance, even though their monitor has incentives to use pension and retirement funds not entirely for the benefit of employees.

V. Team spirit and loyalty

Every team member would prefer a team in which no one, not even himself, shirked. Then the true marginal costs and values could be equated to achieve more preferred positions. If one could enhance a common interest in non-shirking in the guise of a team loyalty or team spirit, the team would be more efficient. In those sports where team activity is most clearly exemplified, the sense of loyalty and team spirit is most strongly urged. Obviously the team is better, with team spirit and loyalty, because of the reduced shirking – not because of some other feature inherent in loyalty or spirit as such.[15]

Corporations and business firms try to instill a spirit of loyalty. This should not be viewed simply as a device to increase profits by *over*working or misleading the employees, nor as an adolescent urge for belonging. It promotes a closer approximation to the employees' potentially available true rates of substitution between production and leisure and enables each team member to achieve a more preferred situation. The difficulty, of course, is to create economically that team spirit and loyalty. It can be preached with an aura of moral code of conduct – a morality with literally the same basis as the ten

[15]*Sports Leagues:* Professional sports contests among teams are typically conducted by a *league* of teams. We assume that sports consumers are interested not only in absolute sporting skill but also in skills *relative* to other teams. Being slightly better than opposing teams enables one to claim a major portion of the receipts; the inferior team does not release resources and reduce costs, since they were expected in the play of contest. Hence, absolute skill is developed beyond the equality of marginal investment in sporting skill with its true social marginal value product. It follows there will be a tendency to overinvest in training athletes and developing teams. "Reverse shirking" arises, as budding players are induced to overpractice hyperactively relative to the social marginal value of their enhanced skills. To prevent overinvestment, the teams seek an agreement with each other to restrict practice, size of teams, and even pay of the team members (which reduces incentives of young people to overinvest in developing skills). Ideally, if all the contestant teams were owned by one owner, overinvestment in sports would be avoided, much as ownership of common fisheries or underground oil or water reserves would prevent overinvestment. This hyperactivity (to suggest the opposite of shirking) is controlled by the league of teams, wherein the league adopts a common set of constraints on each team's behavior. In effect, the teams are no longer really owned by the team owners but are supervised by them, much as the franchisers of some product. They are not full-fledged owners of their business, including the brand name, and can not "do what they wish" as franchises. Comparable to the franchiser is the league commissioner or conference president, who seeks to restrain hyperactivity, as individual team supervisors compete with each other and cause external diseconomies. Such restraints are usually regarded as anticompetitive, antisocial, collusive-cartel devices to restrain free open competition and reduce players' salaries. However, the interpretation presented here is premised on an attempt to avoid hyperinvestment in team sports production. Of course, the team operators have an incentive, once the league is formed and restraints are placed on hyperinvestment activity, to go further and obtain the private benefits of monopoly restriction. To what extent overinvestment is replaced by monopoly restriction is not yet determinable; nor have we seen an empirical test of these two competing, but mutually consistent interpretations. (This interpretation of league-sports activity was proposed by Earl Thompson (1970) and formulated by Michael Canes (1970)). Again, athletic teams clearly exemplify the specialization of monitoring with captains and coaches; a captain detects shirkers while the coach trains and selects strategies and tactics. Both functions may be centralized in one person.

commandments – to restrict our conduct toward what we would choose if we bore our full costs.

VI. Kinds of inputs owned by the firm

To this point the discussion has examined why firms, as we have defined them, exist? That is, why is there an owner-employer who is the common party to contracts with other owners of inputs in team activity? The answer to that question should also indicate the kind of the jointly used resources likely to be owned by the central-owner-monitor and the kind likely to be hired from people who are not team-owners. Can we identify characteristics or features of various inputs that lead to their being hired or to their being owned by the firm?

How can residual-claimant, central-employer-owner demonstrate ability to pay the other hired inputs the promised amount in the event of a loss? He can pay in advance or he can commit wealth sufficient to cover negative residuals. The latter will take the form of machines, land, buildings, or raw materials committed to the firm. Commitments of labor wealth (i.e., human wealth) given the property rights in people, is less feasible. These considerations suggest that residual claimants – owners of the firm – will be investors of resalable capital equipment in the firm. The goods or inputs more likely to be invested, than rented, by the owners of the enterprise, will have higher resale values relative to the initial cost and will have longer expected use in a firm relative to the economic life of the good.

But beyond these factors are those developed above to explain the existence of the institution known as the firm – the costs of detecting output performance. When a durable resource is used it will have a marginal product and a depreciation. Its use requires payment to cover at least use-induced depreciation; unless that user cost is specifically detectable, payment for it will be demanded in accord with *expected* depreciation. And we can ascertain circumstances for each. An indestructible hammer with a readily detectable marginal product has zero user cost. But suppose the hammer were destructible and that careless (which is easier than careful) use is more abusive and causes greater depreciation of the hammer. Suppose in addition the abuse is easier to detect by observing the way it is used than by observing only the hammer after its use, or by measuring the output scored from a hammer by a laborer. If the hammer were rented and used in the absence of the owner, the depreciation would be greater than if the use were observed by the owner and the user charged in accord with the imposed depreciation. (Careless use is more likely than careful use – if one does not pay for the greater depreciation.) An absentee owner would therefore ask for a higher rental price because of the higher *expected* user cost than if the item were used by the owner. The

212

expectation is higher because of the greater difficulty of observing specific user cost, by inspection of the hammer after use. Renting is therefore in this case more costly than owner use. This is the valid content of the misleading expressions about ownership being more economical than renting – ignoring all other factors that may work in the opposite direction, like tax provision, short-term occupancy, and capital risk avoidance.

Better examples are tools of the trade. Watch repairers, engineers, and carpenters tend to own their own tools especially if they are portable. Trucks are more likely to be employee owned rather than other equally expensive team inputs because it is relatively cheap for the driver to police the care taken in using a truck. Policing the use of trucks by a nondriver owner is more likely to occur for trucks that are not specialized to one driver, like public transit busses.

The factor with which we are concerned here is one related to the costs of monitoring not only the gross product performance of an input but also the abuse or depreciation inflicted on the input in the course of its use. If depreciation or user cost is more cheaply detected when the owner can see its use than by only seeing the input before and after, there is a force toward owner use rather than renting. Resources whose user cost is harder to detect when used by someone else tend on this count to be owner used. Absentee ownership, in the lay language, will be less likely. Assume momentarily that labor service cannot be performed in the absence of its owner. The labor owner can more cheaply monitor any abuse of himself than if somehow labor services could be provided without the labor owner observing its mode of use or knowing what was happening. Also his incentive to abuse himself is increased if he does not own himself.[16]

---

[16]Professional athletes in baseball, football, and basketball, where athletes have sold their source of service to the team owners upon entering into sports activity, are owned by team owners. Here the team owners must monitor the athletes' physical condition and behavior to protect the team owners' wealth. The athlete has *less* (not, *no*) incentive to protect or enhance his athletic prowess since capital value changes have less impact on his own wealth and more on the team owners. Thus, some athletes sign up for big initial bonuses (representing present capital value of future services). Future salaries are lower by the annuity value of the prepaid "bonus" and hence the athlete has *less* to lose by subsequent abuse of his athletic prowess. Any decline in his subsequent service value would in part be borne by the team owner who owns the players' future service. This does not say these losses of future salaries have no effect on preservation of athletic talent (we are not making a "sunk cost" error). Instead, we assert that the preservation is reduced, not eliminated, because the amount of loss of wealth suffered is smaller. The athlete will spend less to maintain or enhance his prowess thereafter. The effect of this revised incentive system is evidenced in comparisons of the kinds of attention and care imposed on the athletes at the "expense of the team owner" in the case where athletes' future services are owned by the team owner with that where future labor service values are owned by the athlete himself. Why athletes' future athletic services are owned by the team owners rather than being hired is a question we should be able to answer. One presumption is cartelization and monopsony gains to team owners. Another is exactly the theory being expounded in this paper – costs of monitoring production of athletes; we know not on which to rely.

The similarity between the preceding analysis and the question of absentee landlordism and sharecropping arrangements is no accident. The same factors which explain the contractual arrangements known as a firm help to explain the incidence of tenancy, labor hiring, or sharecropping.[17]

VII. Firms as a specialized market institution for collecting, collating, and selling input information

The firm serves as a highly specialized surrogate market. Any person contemplating a joint-input activity must search and detect the qualities of available joint inputs. He could contact an employment agency, but that agency in a small town would have little advantage over a large firm with many inputs. The employer, by virtue of monitoring many inputs, acquires special superior information about their productive talents. This aids his *directive* (i.e., market hiring) efficiency. He "sells" his information to employee-inputs as he aids them in ascertaining good input combinations for team activity. Those who work as employees or who rent services to him are using him to discern superior combinations of inputs. Not only does the director-employer "decide" what each input will produce, he also estimates which heterogeneous inputs will work together jointly more efficiently, and he does this in the context of a privately owned market for forming teams. The department store is a firm and is a superior private market. People who shop and work in one town can as well shop and work in a privately owned firm.

This marketing function is obscured in the theoretical literature by the assumption of homogeneous factors. Or it is tacitly left for individuals to do themselves via personal market search, much as if a person had to search without benefit of specialist retailers. Whether or not the firm arose because of this efficient information service, it gives the director-employer more knowledge about the productive talents of the team's inputs, and a basis for superior decisions about efficient or profitable combinations of those heterogeneous resources.

In other words, opportunities for profitable team production by inputs already within the firm may be ascertained more economically and accurately than for resources outside the firm. Superior combinations of inputs can be more economically identified and formed from resources already used in the organization than by obtaining new resources (and knowledge of them) from the outside. Promotion and revision of employee assignments (contracts) will be preferred by a firm to the hiring of new inputs. To the extent that this

[17]The analysis used by Cheung (1969) in explaining the prevalence of sharecropping and land tenancy arrangements is built squarely on the same factors – the costs of detecting output performance of jointly used inputs in team production and the costs of detecting user costs imposed on the various inputs if owner used or if rented.

occurs, there is reason to expect the firm to be able to operate as a conglomerate rather than persist in producing a single product. Efficient production with heterogeneous resources is a result not of having *better* resources but in *knowing more accurately* the relative productive performances of those resources. Poorer resources can be paid less in accord with their inferiority; greater accuracy of knowledge of the potential and actual productive actions of inputs rather than having high productivity resources makes a firm (or an assignment of inputs) profitable.[18]

VIII. Summary

While ordinary contracts facilitate efficient specialization according to comparative advantage, a special class of contracts among a group of joint inputs to a team production process is commonly used for team production. Instead of multilateral contracts among all the joint inputs owners, a central common party to a set of bilateral contracts facilitates efficient organization of the joint inputs in team production. The terms of the contracts form the basis of the entity called the firm – especially appropriate for organizing team production processes.

Team productive activity is that in which a union, or joint use, of inputs yields a larger output than the sum of the products of the separately used inputs. This team production requires – like all other production processes – an assessment of marginal productivities if efficient production is to be achieved. Nonseparability of the products of several differently owned joint inputs raises the cost of assessing the marginal productivities of those resources or services of each input owner. Monitoring or metering the productivities to match marginal productivities to costs of inputs and thereby to reduce shirking can be achieved more economically (than by across market bilateral negotiations among inputs) in a firm.

---

[18]According to our interpretation, the firm is a specialized surrogate for a market for team use of inputs; it provides superior (i.e., cheaper) collection and collation of knowledge about heterogeneous resources. The greater the set of inputs about which knowledge of performance is being collated within a firm the greater are the present costs of the collation activity. Then, the larger the firm (market) the greater the attenuation of monitor control. To counter this force, the firm will be divisionalized in ways that economize on those costs – just as will the market be specialized. So far as we can ascertain, other theories of the reasons for firms have no such implications.

In Japan, employees by custom work nearly their entire lives with one firm, and the firm agrees to that expectation. Firms will tend to be large and conglomerate to enable a broader scope of input revision. Each firm is, in effect, a small economy engaging in "intranational and international" trade. Analogously, Americans expect to spend their whole lives in the United States, and the bigger the country, in terms of variety of resources, the easier it is to adjust to changing tastes and circumstances. Japan, with its lifetime employees, should be characterized more by large, conglomerate firms. Presumably, at some size of the firm, specialized knowledge about inputs becomes as expensive to transmit across divisions of the firms as it does across markets to other firms.

The essence of the classical firm is identified here as a contractual structure with: (1) joint input production, (2) several input owners, (3) one party who is common to all the contracts of the joint inputs, (4) who has rights to renegotiate any input's contact independently of contracts with other input owners, (5) who holds the residual claim, and (6) who has the right to sell his central contractual residual status. The central agent is called the firm's owner and the employer. No authoritarian control is involved; the arrangement is simply a contractual structure subject to continuous renegotiation with the central agent. The contractual structure arises as a means of enhancing efficient organization of team production. In particular, the ability to detect shirking among owners of jointly used inputs in team production is enhanced (detection costs are reduced) by this arrangement and the discipline (by revision of contracts) of input owners is made more economic.

Testable implications are suggested by the analysis of different types of organizations – nonprofit, proprietary for profit, unions, cooperatives, partnerships, and by the kinds of inputs that tend to be owned by the firm in contrast to those employed by the firm.

We conclude with a highly conjectural but possibly significant interpretation. As a consequence of the flow of information to the central party (employer), the firm takes on the characteristic of an efficient market in that information about the productive characteristics of a large set of specific inputs is now more cheaply available. Better recombinations or new uses of resources can be more efficiently ascertained than by the conventional search through the general market. In this sense inputs compete with each other within and via a firm rather than solely across markets as conventionally conceived. Emphasis on interfirm competition obscures intrafirm competition among inputs. Conceiving competition as the *revelation and exchange* of knowledge or information about qualities, potential uses of different inputs in different potential applications indicates that the firm is a device for enhancing competition among sets of input resources as well as a device for more efficiently rewarding the inputs. In contrast to markets and cities which can be viewed as publicly or nonowned market places, the firm can be considered a privately owned market; if so, we could consider the firm and the ordinary market as competing types of markets, competition between private proprietary markets and public or communal markets. Could it be that the market suffers from the defects of communal property rights in organizing and influencing uses of valuable resources?

CHAPTER 15

Contested exchange: new microfoundations for the political economy of capitalism

SAMUEL BOWLES AND
HERBERT GINTIS

Samuel Bowles was born in 1939 in New Haven, Connecticut. He received a Ph.D. in economics at Harvard University in 1965. Since 1973, he has been Professor of Economics at the University of Massachusetts at Amherst.

Herbert Gintis was born in 1940 in Philadelphia, Pennsylvania. He received a Ph.D. in economics at Harvard University in 1969. Since 1975, he has taught economics at the University of Massachusetts at Amherst, where he has held the position of Professor since 1980.

Though conflicts of interest are central to economic reasoning, they are addressed in an artificial and misleading way in the conventional neoclassical model. This treatment is apparent in the following quote from the distinguished economist Abba Lerner:

> An economic transaction is a solved political problem. Economics has gained the title of queen of the social sciences by choosing *solved* political problems as its domain.[1]

Exchanges may be solved political problems where contracts are comprehensive and enforceable at no cost to the exchanging parties. We use the term *exogenous claim enforcement* to refer to this type of comprehensive and third party (generally state) regulation of contracts; it tends to occur where the transaction is transparent in the sense that the characteristics of the goods or services exchanged are readily determined, and hence contractual transgressions are readily detected and redressed, often by resort to the courts.

Where some aspect of the object of exchange is so complex or difficult to monitor that comprehensive contracts are not feasible or enforceable by a third party, however, exogenous claim enforcement does not obtain, and the exchange is *not* a solved political problem. By comparison with the transpar-

Excerpted from Samuel Bowles and Herbert Gintis, "Contested Exchange: New Microfoundations for the Political Economy of Capitalism," *Politics and Society*, 18, no. 2 (June 1990): 165–222, with minor amendments by the authors. Reprinted with permission of the publisher.

[1]Lerner (1972).

ency of the exogenously enforceable exchange, these exchanges are characterized by opacity: Some aspect of the good or service exchanged is not readily determined. Far from being a special case, the absence of exogenous claim enforcement is quite general; the two critical exchanges of the capitalist economy – the labor and the capital markets – provide, as we will see, the archetypal examples.

In these cases which we take to be quite general, we have a *problem of agency*: In an exchange between agents A and B, B can take actions that are harmful or beneficial to A's interests, and which cannot be precluded or guaranteed by contractual agreement. Where a problem of agency exists, the *de facto* terms of an exchange result in part from the sanctions, surveillance, and other enforcement activities adopted by the parties to the exchange themselves. We refer to this process of regulation of the contract by the parties to the contract as *endogenous claim enforcement*.

A transaction characterized by both an agency problem and endogenous claim enforcement is termed a *contested exchange*. More formally, consider agent A who engages in an exchange with agent B. We call the exchange *contested* when B's good or service possesses an attribute that is valuable to A, is costly for B to provide, and yet is not fully specified in a costlessly enforceable contract.

Our key claim is that the most important exchanges in a capitalist economy are contested and that in these exchanges endogenous enforcement gives rise to a well-defined set of power relations among voluntarily participating agents even in the absence of collusion or other obstacles to perfect *competition.*

We take as uncontroversial the following *sufficient condition for the exercise of power.* Let us accept the assertion that, *for A to have power over B, it is sufficient that, by imposing or threatening to impose sanctions on B, A is capable of affecting B's actions in ways that further A's interests while B lacks this capacity with respect to A.* Because in Walrasian equilibrium the cost to B of foregoing an exchange with A is zero (B is free to deal with C on identical terms), A cannot affect B's well-being by terminating the exchange. Thus in the competitive equilibrium of a Walrasian economy, no sanctions may be imposed through the private actions of noncolluding agents. Whence flows Alchian's and Demsetz's belief that one can walk away from one's employer or creditor with as little concern as one crosses the street to shop at one supermarket rather than another.

Paul Samuelson's famous assertion "in a perfectly competitive market it really doesn't matter who hires whom; so let capital hire labor"[2] follows

2Samuelson (1957).

218

trivially. For the *boss* has no more authority over the workers than conversely (they all have none), and there is no real decision-making authority to relocate. A worker-run firm would be constrained by competition simply to replicate the structure and functioning of the capitalist firm. By a simple extension of this argument, the traditional democratic and socialist critiques of the fragmentation of tasks, deskilling, and other aspects of work experience, technology, and the division of labor in capitalist production may be shown to be without foundation. Work may be unpleasant, but a socialist economy would offer the same unless it chose to sacrifice productive efficiency.

The relationship between wage labor and capital is a contested exchange because while the worker's time can be contracted for, the amount and quality of actual work done generally cannot. The relationship of borrower to lender or of owner to the management of a firm is also a contested exchange because, while the repayment schedule of the loan can be contracted for, this is not true of the actions of the borrower that will determine the possibility of repayment. Exogenous enforcement will generally be absent and exchanges will be contested when there is no relevant third party (as when A and B are sovereign states), when the contested attribute can be measured only imperfectly or at considerable cost (work effort, for example, or the degree of risk assumed by a firm's management), when the relevant evidence is not admissible in a court of law (such as an agent's eye witness but unsubstantiated experience), when there is no possible means of redress (for example, when the liable party is bankrupt), or when the number of contingencies concerning future states of the world relevant to the exchange preclude writing a fully specified contract.

In such cases the *ex post* terms of exchange are determined by the monitoring and sanctioning mechanisms instituted by A to induce B to provide the desired level of the contested attribute. We shall here stress one extremely important endogenous enforcement mechanism: *contingent renewal*. This obtains when A elicits performance from B by promising to renew the contract in future periods if satisfied and to terminate the contract if not. For instance, a manager may promise a worker reemployment contingent upon satisfactory performance or a lender may offer a borrower a short-term loan with the promise of rolling over the loan contingent upon the borrower's prudent business behavior.

The labor market is a case in point. An employment relationship is established when, in return for a wage, the worker agrees to submit to the authority of the employer. The worker's promise to bestow an adequate level of effort and care upon the tasks assigned, even if offered, is legally unenforceable. At the level of effort expected by management, work is subjectively costly for the worker to provide, valuable to the employer, and costly to measure. The manager–worker relationship thus is a contested exchange. The endogenous enforcement mechanisms of the enterprise, not the state, are thus responsible for ensuring the delivery of any particular level of labor services per hour of labor time supplied.[3]

A simple model of the manager–worker relationship will illuminate the archetypal contested exchange. Our objective is to identify the aspects of the labor market and the labor process that determine the terms of exchange: the wage rate and the intensity of labor. Let e represent the level of work effort provided by employee B. We assume effort is costly for B to provide above some minimal level $\bar{e}$. B's employer, A, knows that B will choose e in response to both the cost of supplying effort and the penalty employer A will impose if dissatisfied with B's performance. The penalty imposed by A is the nonrenewal of employment – that is, dismissing the worker. Of course the employer may choose not to terminate the worker is the cost associated with the termination (demoralization or ill will among fellow workers, a work-to-rule slowdown, a strike, or simply the search and training costs of replacement) are excessive.

The level of work intensity is chosen in a proximate sense by the worker. But in choosing, the worker must consider both short- and long-term costs and benefits; working less hard now, for example, means more on-the-job leisure now and a probability of no job and hence less income later. To take into account this time dimension, we will consider the worker's job as an asset, the value of which depends in part on the worker's effort level.

We define the *value of employment, v(w)*, as the discounted present value of the worker's future income stream taking account of the probability that the worker will be dismissed; for obvious reasons it is an increasing function of the current wage rate w. We define the employee's *fallback position, z,* as the present value of future income for a person whose job is terminated – perhaps the present value of a future stream of unemployment benefits, the present value of some other job, or more likely a sequence of the two weighted by the expected duration of unemployment. Then A's threat of dismissal is credible only if $v(w) > z$. We call $v(w) - z$, the difference between the value of employment and the fallback position, z, the *employment rent* or the cost of job loss. We term this a *rent* as it represents a payment above and beyond the income of an identical employee without the job.[4] Workers who receive

---

[3]The analysis presented in this section is developed in Gintis (1976); Bowles (1985); Gintis and Ishikawa (1987); and Bowles and Gintis (1993a, 1993b).

[4]It is thus similar to the rents in the theory of rent-seeking behavior (James Buchanan, Robert Tollison, and Gordon Tullock, *Toward a Theory of the Rent-seeking Society* [College Station: Texas A&M University Press, 1980]) except for the important difference that contested exchange rents arise through the *lack* of effective state intervention while rent-seeking literature focuses on state intervention as the source of rents.

employment rents are not indifferent to losing their job (their cost of job loss is not zero).

Employment rents accorded to workers in labor markets are a particularly important case of the more general category, *enforcement rents,* which arise in all cases of competitively determined contested exchange under conditions of contingent renewal. Our objective will be to show that employment rents – and more generally, enforcement rents – will exist in a competitive equilibrium of a contested exchange.

A sufficiently low wage would make the job no more desirable to the worker than a spell of unemployment followed by a job search and another job. Let $\bar{w}$ be this wage that equates $v(w)$ and z. This wage rate implies a zero employment rent, hence the absence of effective sanctions by the employer, and thus induces the worker's freely chosen effort level, $\bar{e}$, the "whistle-while-you-work labor intensity." We term $\bar{w}$ the *reservation wage.* At any wage less than $\bar{w}$ the worker will refuse employment or quit if employed. The level of $\bar{w}$ depends obviously on the worker's relative enjoyment of leisure and work, the level and coverage of unemployment benefits, the expected duration of unemployment for a terminated worker, the loss of seniority associated with moving to a new job, and the availability of other income. In the Walrasian model, the equilibrium wage must be the reservation wage; otherwise workers could not be indifferent between their current transaction and their next best alternative.

We assume A has a monitoring system such that B's performance will be found adequate with a probability f, which depends positively on B's level of effort. If this effort level is found to be inadequate, B is dismissed with probability $1 - p$ (that is, is the probability that the worker found to be working inadequately will *not* be dismissed). It is the link between effort and the likelihood of job retention that induces B to provide effort above $\bar{e}$.[5]

To elicit greater effort than $\bar{e}$, A is obliged to offer a wage greater than $\bar{w}$, balancing the cost of paying the larger wage against the benefits associated with B's greater effort induced by a higher cost of job loss. For any given wage, the worker will determine how hard to work by trading the marginal disutility of additional effort against the effect that additional effort has on the probability of retaining the job and thus continuing to receive the employment rent. Noting that the fallback position z is exogenous to the exchange, we may write B's best response to w, which we call the *labor extraction function,*

---

[5]More complete models allow an endogenous selection by A of an optimal schedule of dismissal probabilities and an optimal choice of the level of surveillance underlying the function $f(e)$ (Bowles, 1985; Gintis and Ishikawa, 1987). We lose little, however, by assuming that the probability of detection is exogenously given as a function of effort.

221

simply as $e = e(w)$. In the neighborhood of the competitive equilibrium, e increases with w, though at a diminishing rate, or $e_w > 0$, $e_{ww} < 0$.[6]

The equilibrium wage and effort level illustrated in Figure 15.1 is determined as follows. Agent A knows B's best response schedule, $e(w)$, so once A selects the wage, the level of effort that will be performed is known with certainty. Agent A then optimizes – maximizes profits or, what is equivalent in this model, minimizes costs – *given the response schedule of B*. Contingent renewal equilibria are thus Stackelberg equilibria, where agent A is a Stackelberg leader, making a take it or leave it offer to B, the Stackelberg follower.[7]

The solution to A's optimum problem is to set w such that $e_w = e/w$, or the marginal effect on effort of a wage increase equals the average effort provided per unit of wage cost.[8] This solution yields the equilibrium effort level e^* and wage w^*, shown in Figure 15.1. The ray $(e/w)^*$ is one of the employer's isolabor cost loci: All points on this ray have the same effort per wage dollar, and the employer is hence indifferent amongst them. Its slope is e^*/w^*. Steeper rays are obviously preferred by the employer.

Two important results are apparent. First, $e^* > \bar{e}$, so B provides a level of

---

[6]The single and double subscripts, respectively, indicate first and second derivatives of the function e. The labor extraction function can be derived as follows. Let $u = u(w, e)$ be B's utility function, and assume $u_w > 0$, $u_e < 0$ for $(w, e) > (\bar{w}, \bar{e})$. In the simplest case, where the worker is dismissed if detected not working (that is, $p = 0$), B's value of employment is then

$$v = \{u(w, e) + f(e)v + (1 - f(e)z\}/(1 + \rho),$$

where ρ is the employee's rate of time preference: B receives $u(w, e)$ this period plus the present value v if retained, which occurs with probability $f(e)$, and plus the present value z if dismissed, which occurs with probability $1 - f(e)$. Assuming for simplicity that income and the disutility of effort are both evaluated at the end of the period, the whole expression is discounted to the present by the factor $1/(1 + \rho)$. Solving for v, we obtain

$$v = (u(w, e) - \rho z)/(1 - f(e) + \rho) + z,$$

where the first term on the right hand side is obviously the employment rent, $v - z$, or *value of employment = employment rent + fallback position*. The $e(w)$ schedule then results from B's choosing e to maximize v for given w, taking the schedule $f(e)$ as given. The resulting first order condition, to equate u_e to $-f_e(v - z)$, expresses the tradeoff mentioned in the text.

[7]This asymmetry between leader and follower that is absent in the Walrasian equilibrium. In the latter both agents make offers, and only offers (those that clear markets) are accepted. A Stackelberg equilibrium (see H. von Stackelberg, *Marktform und Gleichgewicht* [Vienna: Springer Verlag, 1934] and Hugo Sonnenschein, "Oligopoly and Game Theory," in *The New Palgrave: A Dictionary of Economics*, John Eatwell, Murray Milgate, Peter Newman, eds. [London: Macmillan, 1987], pp. 705–708) is one in which the leader, A, has no incentive to change strategy given the offer curve (response function) of the follower B, and B has no incentive to change strategy given that followed by A. B gains no strategic advantage by considering A's response function since A will choose a single cost-minimizing wage no matter what B does. (Strictly speaking B is also optimizing with respect to A's response function. In this case, however, A's response function is simply a vertical line in (e, w) space, as A's action cannot be influenced by B's choices.)

[8]This is the first order condition for the problem: Select w so as to maximize $e(w)/w$.

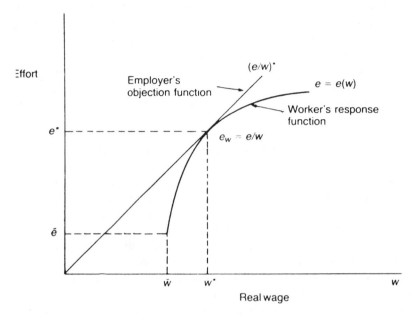

Figure 15.1. Optimal wages and labor intensity.

effort greater than would have been the case in the absence of the enforcement rent and the employer's monitoring system; and second, $w^* > \bar{w}$, so B receives a wage greater than the reservation wage. The first result indicates that A's enforcement strategy is effective; the second indicates that the labor market does not clear in competitive equilibrium: Workers holding jobs are not indifferent to losing them, and there are identical workers either involuntarily unemployed or employed in less desirable positions.

Both results are of course at variance with the Walrasian model, which can be seen to be a limiting case of contested exchange that obtains when there is either an absence of a conflict of interest between employer and employee over effort or a costless means by which A can enforce a specific level of effort. The first of these conditions can be represented in Figure 15.1 by hypothetically increasing $\bar{e}$, the level of effort B supplied independently of the wage. This might occur, for example, if work norms were to change so as to favor greater work effort. Alternatively, $\bar{e}$ might rise, for example, if the employer had some other means of extracting effort, for example through physical punishment. At some point $\bar{e}/\bar{w}$ may exceed e_w, implying that the optimal solution for A is simply to pay $\bar{w}$ and accept the effort level $\bar{e}$.[9]

---

[9]A similar result obtains if the reservation wage $\bar{w}$ is decreased sufficiently, provided $\bar{e} > 0$.

The second Walrasian case may be illustrated by *flattening out* the best response schedule $e(w)$, so the level of effort does not vary significantly with the enforcement rent. This might occur, for example, if workers were so rich that they were indifferent to additional income. At some point we again arrive at the corner solution at $(\bar{e}, \bar{w})$, implying the Walrasian result: The employer offers a wage equal to the reservation wage $\bar{w}$, abandons the attempt to apply enforcement rent sanctions to the employee, and accepts the effort level $\bar{e}$.

Perhaps significantly, the Walrasian result can be seen to require either the unalienated or perhaps conformist norm-following Stakhanovite (the first case) or the income-satiated worker who cannot be manipulated by the wage carrot (the second case). In either case, the labor process would not then be a contested exchange, the labor market would clear in equilibrium, and no agent could sanction any other. Our sufficient condition for the exercise of power would thus not obtain. One might reasonably suspect, nonetheless, that in at least the first case the exercise of power is implicated, perhaps in the prior socialization of the worker to accept hard work as a norm or the effectiveness of employer sanctions unrelated to income. We regard both cases as unrealistic: Workers are not indifferent to additional income, and they would not choose the profit-maximizing level of effort in the absence of employer sanctions.

If one were rightly to dismiss on empirical grounds either the Stakhanovite or income-satiated worker routes back to the Walrasian model of clearing markets, however, one might equally charge that our representation of the labor process and labor market fails to capture important aspects of actually existing capitalism and particularly the social nature of the work process and the welfare state. By stressing the carrot of high wages and the stick of dismissal we do not, however, abstract from other possibly important aspects of the regulation of work such as conformism, good will, and pride in work, for these determine the position of the labor extraction function. Does not the welfare state and collective bargaining offer workers some protection from job termination and a minimum living standard when unemployed? True, but the degree of worker security from firing and unemployment insurance are integral parts of the model (reflected in p and z respectively). Indeed one of the advantages of the model is that it allows an analysis of the economic effects of the welfare state that goes considerably beyond the standard treatments of the effects of taxes and transfers on the supply of factors of production and on individual saving behavior.[10]

---

[10]For example, as p approaches 1 (complete job security) or unemployment insurance coverage is extended such that z approaches v, the effectiveness of a dismissal based labor extraction system is eroded. See Bowles and Gintis (1982) and Bowles and Gintis (1982).

Short-side power in the production process

Does employer A have power over worker B? Given the sufficient condition for the exercise of power, the answer is surely yes: A may use the threat of sanction to cause B to act in A's interest, and the converse is not true. First, A may dismiss B, reducing B's present value to z. Hence A can apply sanctions to B. Second, A can use sanctions to elicit a preferred level of effort from B and thus to further A's interests.[11] Finally, while B may be capable of applying sanctions to A (for example, B may be capable of burning down A's factory), B cannot use this capacity to induce A to choose a different wage or to refrain from dismissing B should A desire to do so. Should B make A a take-it-or-leave-it offer to work at a higher than equilibrium wage or should B threaten to apply sanctions unless A offers a higher wage, A would simply reject the offer and hire another worker. For as we have seen in the previous section, in equilibrium there will exist unemployed workers identical to B who would prefer to be employed. Thus A has power over B.

This model can be extended to include many agents and firms in a system of general economic equilibrium, making explicit the centrality of nonclearing markets to contested exchange equilibrium. In particular, because such an equilibrium exhibits positive enforcement rents, it entails by definition involuntary unemployment as well. The existence of agents who are involuntarily without employment (or with less desirable employment than B) follows from the strict inequality $v(w) > z$: If B enjoys an employment rent, there must be another otherwise identical agent, C, who would be willing to fill B's position at the going, or even at a lower, wage.[12] Moreover, should C promise A to work as hard as B for a lower wage, the offer will rightly be disbelieved and hence rejected by A. The reason is that, other than their employment status, B and C are identical; A knows exactly how much effort is forthcoming for a given employment rent and has already selected a cost-minimizing wage. Agent C is thus involuntarily unemployed in equilibrium so A's threat to replace B is credible.[13]

[11]A game theorist might object that the threat to dismiss the worker is not credible so long as the dismissal imposes costs upon the employer (for example, costs of search and training). Clearly, however, if the firm's overall contingent renewal strategy is profit maximizing, and if shirking and dismissal are observed by other workers, a shirking worker must be dismissed to maintain the credibility of the employer's threat.

[12]Such agents, rather than being unemployed, may simply prefer B's position to their own at the going wage. The point is that they are quantity constrained: They would prefer to sell more of their services at the going rate but are unable to (unless B is dismissed).

[13]Does A have power over C? The negative sanction that A may impose on B (withdrawal of the employment rent) is exactly equal to a positive sanction that A might offer or refuse to extend to C. If A refuses to hire C in order to maintain a racially homogeneous workplace, for instance, we might say that A has furthered his or her interests (gratification of racial prejudice) and A has

Models in which markets fail to clear have traditionally been viewed as disequilibrium theories. In the contested exchange model, however, nonclearing markets are characteristic of competitive equilibrium defined in the standard manner: No actor is capable of improving his or her position by altering a variable over which he or she has control. Employers have no interest in changing the wage offered, employed workers have no interest in changing the level of effort supplied, and workers in search of a job can do nothing but await an offer at the equilibrium wage.

The employer's power is thus related to his or her favorable position in a nonclearing market. We say that the employer A, who can purchase any desired amount of labor and hence is not quantity constrained, is on the *short side* of the market. Where excess supply exists – as in the labor market – the demand side is the short side and conversely.[14] Suppliers of labor are on the *long side* of the market. When contingent renewal is operative and where the institutional environment is such that the threat of sanctions by the short sider may be instrumental to furthering his or her interests, the principle of short-side power holds: Agents on the short side of the market will have power over agents on the long side with whom they transact.[15] Long-side agents are of two types: those such as B who succeed in finding an employer and thus receive a rent that constrains them to accept the employer's authority and those such as C who fail to make a transaction and hence are rationed out of the market. We will sometimes refer to agents such as B as long-side transactors and those such as C as quantity constrained.

Three aspects of this result deserve to be noted. First, it might appear that A has expressed a preference for power and has simply traded away some money – the enforcement rent – to gain power. But while real world employers may act this way, it is quite unnecessary for our result: A is assumed to be indifferent to the nature of the authority relationship per se and is simply maximizing profits.

Second, it might be thought that A has intentionally generated the unemployment necessary for the maintenance of his or her short-side power. It is true that the employer's profit maximizing strategy, when it is adopted by

---

sanctioned C (refused to offer the employment rent). By contrast to the relationship of A to B, however, the sanction is incidental to the furthering of A's interests. Thus A does not have power over C in our sense.

[14]More generally, the short side of an exchange is located where the total amount of desired transactions is least; the demand side, if there is excess supply; and the supply side, if there is excess demand (Benassy, 1982).

[15]Note that being on the short side of a nonclearing market does not *in itself* ensure that an agent has short-side power. Since such a market does not clear, short sider A can indeed impose sanction on long sider B. A, however, need not have the ability to use this capacity in any way to affect B's behavior. Consumers buying on glutted markets present an example of agents whose short-side location does not confer short-side power (unless they collude).

all other employers, results in the existence of unemployed workers and that other wage-setting rules would not have this result. But we have assumed that the employer treats the level of unemployment, which figures in the determination of the workers' fallback position, z, as exogenous for the simple reason that no employer acting singly can determine the level of aggregate employment.[16]

Third, it may be argued that B has power over A, if not in our formal sense then in the sense that B has the capacity to induce A to offer an employment rent over and above the amount needed to induce B to enter into the transaction. But B's advantage does not stem from B's *power* in the sense of a capacity that can be strategically deployed towards furthering one's interests. To see this, note that A's power to dismiss B is a credible threat, while B can put forth no credible threat whatever. Rather than attributing the fact that B receives a wage in excess of the reservation wage to "B's power over A," we might better say that the employment rent derives from B's autonomy, that is from the inability of A costlessly to determine B's level of effort. The rent is a cost to A of exercising power over B.[17]

We may summarize these results in the form of two propositions:

Proposition 1 (short-side power): A competitive equilibrium of a system of contested exchanges may allocate power to agents on the short side of nonclearing markets.

Proposition 2 (the politics of production): Those in positions of decisionmaking authority in capitalist firms occupy locations on the short side of the labor market and exercise power over employees.

Let us not overstate these results. Not all contested exchanges give rise to short-side power. We analyzed an important case of contested exchange where contingent renewal strategies of endogenous enforcement are adopted by

---

[16]If employers act collectively, of course, a quite different picture emerges, as the contested exchange model demonstrates the interests of employers in the existence of unemployment and suggests that they might use their influence on the state to foster macroeconomic policies to maintain adequate levels of unemployment. An interpretation of recent U.S. macroeconomic policy along these lines is presented in Bowles, Gordon, and Weisskopf (1989). A parallel treatment of the collective action of workers is presented in Bowles and Boyer (1990).

[17]A fourth possible objection is that the employment rent could be recouped by the employer by requiring that workers post a bond – that is, to transfer a sum of money to the employer as a condition of employment, in effect paying the employer for the job. Since the present value of the job exceeds the present value of being unemployed, potential employees might be willing to post such a bond to gain access to the job. Because bonding will generally be profit enhancing for the employer, our abstraction from bonding on empirical grounds cannot be motivated theoretically within the framework of our models. But if bonding is used, its availability to workers is likely to be related to their holdings of property. Thus were we to take account of bonding, the importance of wealth in the market for managers and labor would be considerably enhanced. Reasons for the absence of bonding are explored by Eaton and White (1982); Akerlof and Katz (1988); Dickens, Katz, Lang, and Summers (1989); and Bowles and Gintis (1990).

agents on one side of the market and where the short-side agents have the strategic capacity to act as Stackelberg leaders and thus to make use of their advantageous short-side location. But there may be other important cases in which our sufficient condition for the exercise of power do not obtain. Where no costlessly enforceable contracts can be written at all, for example, both agents may engage in endogenous enforcement activities, both may receive enforcement rents, and each may thus effectively pursue their interests by threatening to sanction the other. An employer facing a group of organized workers where the cost of replacing workers is high is an example of such bilateral power.[18]

Second, we have located power in the economy, but we have not shown that the exercise of this power is socially consequential. Indeed is it not inconceivable that, while short-side agents in labor markets exercise power over long-side transactors, there are no feasible alternative institutional arrangements that would yield superior outcomes. Rendering economic power democratically accountable is an important political project only if the exercise of power has socially consequential effects. While demonstrating this point is far from trivial, we think that the power of short siders does make a difference in both moral and political senses and have explored the implications of democratic accountability.

We may extract two less obvious results from the contested exchange model of the labor process and labor market. The first concerns Milton Friedman's claim that labor market discrimination and competitive equilibrium are incompatible.

In a contested exchange framework, discriminatory hiring practices may be an equilibrium employer strategy: Paying identical workers different wages (according to race, for example) will be profitable if it contributes to racial divisions that make cooperation among workers more difficult and hence lowers the cost of identifying and terminating a nonworking employee. Because all workers receive wages above their reservation wage, paying some less than others is not precluded as it is in the Walrasian model by the lower wage workers withdrawing their labor supply. If we identify as *primary jobs* the higher-paying positions into which one racial group is hired and as *secondary jobs* the lower-paying positions into which the other is hired, the labor market then includes in addition to employed and unemployed, the new category of *job-rationed* workers: agents who may be employed in one job

---

[18]See Aoki (1984) and Williamson (1985). We doubt, however, the substantive symmetry between employers and workers on empirical grounds. A terminated worker experiences a significant reduction in net wealth, roughly equivalent to a year's income, following termination. By contrast, in all but the smallest firms, the loss inflicted upon the firm in the form of search, recruitment, and training costs is a very small percentage of net profits (Bowles and Gintis 1990 and Mitchell and Kimbell 1982).

category but are excluded from employment in another category for which they are qualified. A discriminated-against worker employed in a secondary position is thus job-rationed in the sense of being a long sider with a contract (a type B agent) with respect to the secondary market but a long sider without a contract (a type C agent) with respect to the primary job market.

The efficacy of cooperation among workers is obviously critical to this argument. But how might collusion among workers benefit workers at the expense of their employers? Most obviously a unified work force could threaten to strike if even a single worker is terminated. Of course under competitive assumptions the striking workers could be replaced, but the search, recruitment, and training costs of an entire workforce might deter the termination of any but the most recalcitrant on-the-job loafer. If racial hiring practices impede collusion among workers and if they are not costly on other grounds, they will be an equilibrium strategy for the employer who as a Stackelberg leader will design wage and working conditions packages with racial disunity as an objective and make these as take-it-or-leave-it offers to prospective employees.

Formally, an increase in collusion will raise p, the probability of *not* being terminated if observed not working up to standard. This in turn will have the effect of reducing the optimal amount of effort offered at each wage rate, yielding a downward rotation around point $(\bar{w}, \bar{e})$ of the labor extraction function as shown in Figure 15.2. The result, necessarily, is a fall in e/w, or what is the same thing, an increase in labor costs per unit of effective labor done. An analogous downward shift in the extraction function might take place if collusion among workers made the detection of nonworking workers more difficult or more costly, perhaps by workers refusing to cooperate with the surveillance system of the employer, giving false reports on the work activities of fellow workers, and the like. We thus have:

Proposition 3 (divide and rule): The competitive equilibrium of a contested exchange economy may exhibit racial, gender, and other forms of labor market discrimination among otherwise identical workers.

It is worth noting that Proposition 3 relies on the constitutive as well as the contested nature of the exchange process: The structure of wages provides a basis for feelings of solidarity or antagonism.

Our last labor market result concerns the social determination of technology or what might be termed the shaping of the forces of production by the social relations of production.[19] The production system entailed by our model in-

---

[19]Our model here is obviously inspired by, but is a drastic simplification of, primarily historical and institutionalist arguments presented in the now vast literature initiated by Marglin's treatment of this problem (1974). For a more extended contested exchange treatment of technical change with some historical examples, see Bowles (1988).

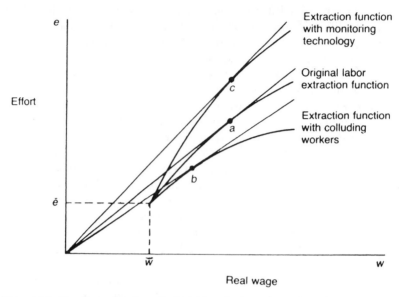

Figure 15.2. The effects of worker collusion and monitoring technologies on the labor extraction equilibrium (a, b, and c are the three equilibria corresponding to the three extraction functions).

cludes a production function, which describes the transformation of inputs into outputs, and a labor extraction function, which describes the manner in which the firm acquires work from employees whose time it has purchased on the labor market. Thus far we have assumed that the choice of the technologies that make up the production function is unrelated to the endogenous enforcement of claims arising in the labor market. But technologies differ markedly in their impact on the enforcement problem facing employers; some, like the assembly line, computerized point-of-sale terminals, or centralized word processing systems, make the detection of a laggard worker by a nonworker relatively simple while others, like team production methods, make the production process considerably more opaque to outsiders.

Thus the choice of technology will influence the cost of monitoring the work process and, for any given cost level the probability, that a nonworking worker will be detected. Formally the choice of a technology that yields an easily monitored production process may be represented as an upwards rotation of the labor extraction function, as shown in Figure 15.2. The result is a saving on the cost of extracting labor from labor power that in the technical choice decision will be compared with the possibly greater production cost of the new technology stemming from its possibly lesser efficiency in transforming inputs into outputs. Thus the efficiency of a technology in transforming inputs into outputs does not determine the course of technical change, and the choice of technique may be inefficient in the sense that production systems may be selected for their capacity to police the labor process despite their relative ineffectiveness in producing goods and services. We thus can assert:

Proposition 4 (capitalist technology): Where claim enforcement is endogenous, the profit-maximizing choice of production technologies will be made in light of both the efficiency with which technologies transform inputs into outputs and their efficacy in enforcing contested claims; the resulting technologies, though cost minimizing, will generally not be efficient.

Thus the technologies in use (and possibly technological research) will be influenced by the structure of the enforcement environments and enforcement instruments available. Because these are determined in important measure by the social institutions governing everything from civil liberties through bankruptcy law to the welfare state, we may expect social institutions and production relations in particular to influence technical choice in ways unrelated to the standard arguments concerning price and income effects.[20]

Our analysis of the employment relationship and labor markets may be extended in two ways. First, it is well known that markets are allocation mechanisms, promoting movements to and along an exogenously defined production possibility frontier. But markets are also disciplinary mechanisms, altering the supplies of inputs and technologies alike and thus shifting the production possibility frontier. Just as allocative efficiency is a sensible normative standard for economic institutions, we may reasonably inquire to what extent and under what conditions markets provide efficient disciplining mechanisms.

Second, enforcement capacities are a determinant of institutional evolution. Like markets, all important economic institutions have consequences for the enforcement of claims arising from exchange. The evolution of such institutions responds to the changing technologies of enforcement no less than to the changing technologies of production and demographic shifts stressed in the

---

[20]Analogous reasoning applies to the choice of which goods to produce. According to a number of economic historians, for example, the production of some products – like sugar – present relatively few endogenous enforcement problems while others – tobacco, for example – depend heavily on subtle variations in the quality of care that are highly costly to extract from a resistant workforce. Ortiz (1963) used this argument to construct a powerful interpretation of the modern history of Cuba. Nilsson (1989) has analyzed product-related enforcement effects in an incisive critique of the neoclassical theory of comparative advantage and international specialization.

standard treatment by neoclassical economic historians.[21] The workings and larger consequences of economically important institutions (schooling and the welfare state come to mind) may also be fruitfully analyzed from the standpoint of their effects on endogenous enforcement environments.[22]

[21]Here North's recent work (1981) represents a major contribution to the post-Walrasian theory of institutional structure and evolution (see also Levi [1988] and Pagano [1988]), while his earlier work is closer to the Walrasian tradition.

[22]Failure to analyze the effect of schooling on the labor market enforcement environment was our main critique of human capital theory. See Bowles and Gintis (1975); and Bowles and Gintis (1976). On the effect of the welfare state on enforcement environments see Bowles and Gintis (1982a); Bowles and Gintis (1982b); and Schor and Bowles (1987).

CHAPTER 16

Understanding the employment relation: the analysis of idiosyncratic exchange

OLIVER WILLIAMSON,
MICHAEL WACHTER, AND
JEFFREY HARRIS

Oliver Williamson is Professor of Business, Economics, and Law at the University of California, Berkeley. See also the previous papers by Williamson.

Michael Wachter was born in New York City in 1943. He received a Ph.D. in economics from Harvard University in 1970. When this paper was published, he was Associate Professor of Economics at the University of Pennsylvania. He is currently William B. Johnson Professor of Law and Economics and Director of the Institute for Law and Economics at the University of Pennsylvania.

Jeffrey Harris was born in 1948. He earned an M.D. and a Ph.D. in economics from the University of Pennsylvania in 1974 and 1975, respectively. At the time of publication of this paper, he was a Resident in Medicine at Massachusetts General Hospital. Since 1982, he has been Associate Professor of Economics at the Massachusetts Institute of Technology and a staff physician at the Massachusetts General Hospital.

. . .

2. Background

A brief review of the literature. The internal labor market literature has its roots in the industrial relations – labor economics literature of the 1950s and early 1960s. The important contributions in this area include the work of Dunlop, Kerr, Livernash, Meij, Raimon, and Ross.[1] This work, which is

Reprinted with abridgements from Oliver Williamson, Michael Wachter, and Jeffrey Harris, "Understanding the Employment Relation: The Analysis of Idiosyncratic Exchange," *The Bell Journal of Economics*, 6 (1975): 250–78. Copyright © 1975. Reprinted with permission of the Rand Corporation. (A variant of this paper also appears as Chapter 4 of Williamson's *Markets and Hierarchies: Analysis and Antitrust Implications*. New York: The Free Press, 1975.)

[1]See Dunlop (1957, 1958), Kerr (1954), Livernash (1957), Meij (1963), Raimon (1953), and Ross (1958).

O. WILLIAMSON, M. WACHTER, AND J. HARRIS

descriptively oriented, has since been developed and extended by Doeringer and Piore.[2]

The distinction between structured and structureless labor markets is especially notable. Whereas spot market contracting characterizes the latter (as Kerr puts it, the "only nexus is cash"),[3] structured markets are ones for which a large number of institutional restraints have developed. Outside access to jobs in structured markets is limited to specific "ports of entry" into the firm, these generally being lower level appointments. Higher level jobs within the firm are filled by the promotion or transfer of employees who have previously secured entry. Training for these jobs involves the acquisition of task-specific and firm-specific skills, occurs in an on-the-job context, and often involves a team element. The internal due process rules which develop in these internal markets "are thought to effectuate standards of equity that a competitive market cannot or does not respect."[4]

Though coming from a somewhat more theoretical tradition, the study of human capital represents a second and related approach to labor market analysis. It likewise makes the distinction between specific and general training. Incumbent employees who have received specific training become valuable resources to the firm. Turnover is costly, since a similarly qualified but inexperienced employee would have to acquire the requisite task-specific skills before he would reach a level of productivity equivalent to that of an incumbent. A premium is accordingly offered to specifically trained employees to discourage turnover, although in principle a long-term contract would suffice.[5]

The present analysis is both similar to and different from both of these traditions. It relies extensively on the institutional literature for the purpose of identifying the structural elements associated with internal labor markets. Also, our interpretation of the institutional restraints that have developed in such markets is consonant with much of this literature. What distinguishes our treatment from prior institutional discussions is that it is more microanalytic, in that it expressly identifies and evaluates alternative contracting modes, and it employs the proposed organizational failures framework apparatus throughout.

Like Becker, we are much concerned with the organizational implications of task-specific training. But whereas he finds that long-term contracts are

[2]Although acknowledging some of the efficiency aspects of the internal labor market, Doeringer and Piore also stress nonneoclassical attributes. Subsequent work in this tradition moves even further away from an efficiency orientation. Harrison (1972), Piore (1973), Thurow (1971), and Wachtel and Betsy (1972) have pushed this nonneoclassical interpretation to the point that efficiency considerations become, at most, a minor theme and at times disappear altogether in the study of collective organization.
[3]Kerr (1959), p. 95.   [4]Doeringer and Piore (1971), p. 29.
[5]See Becker (1962), pp. 10–25.

234

vitiated because the courts regard them as a form of involuntary servitude[6]; we emphasize that the transaction costs of writing, negotiating, and enforcing such contracts are prohibitive.[7]

Technology. It is widely felt that technology has an important, if not fully determinative, influence on the employment relationship. We agree, but take exception with the usual view in several respects. First, we argue that indivisibilities (of the usual kinds) are neither necessary nor sufficient for market contracting to be supplanted by internal organization. Second, we contend that nonseparabilities at most explain small group organization. Third, and most important, we find that the leading reason why an internal labor market supplants spot contracting is because of small numbers exchange relations.

Conventional treatment – indivisibilities

Indivisibilities of both physical capital and informational types are said to lead to the substitution of internal for market organization. The former involves scale economies associated with physical assets and is reasonably familiar. Larger scale units, provided they are utilized at design capacity, permit lower average costs to be realized. The group may thus be formed so as to assure that utilization demands will be sufficient.

Somewhat less familiar are the indivisibilities associated with information. Radner observes in this connection that "the acquisition of information often involves a 'set up cost'; i.e., the resources needed to obtain the information may be independent of the scale of the production process in which the information is used."[8] Consequently, groups may also be formed so as to economize on information costs.

That there are economies of either of these types to be realized, however, does not clearly imply, as a technological imperative, collective organization. Thus, technologically speaking, there is nothing that prevents one individual from procuring the physical asset in requisite size to realize the economies in question and contracting to supply the services of this asset to all of the members of the group. Similarly, there is no technological bar that prevents one individual from assuming the information gathering and dissemination function. All parties, suppliers of the specialized services and users alike, could be independent, yet scale economies of both types could be fully realized. If, therefore, such specialization fails to materialize, it is not because

---

[6]See Becker (1962), p. 23.

[7]Becker hints at this in his remark that "any enforceable contract could at best specify the hours required on a job, not the quality of performance" (1962), p. 24. But rather than develop this line of analysis, and address the underlying transactional factors that explain such a condition, he merely notes that workers could always secure a release from long term contracts by "sabotaging" operations (p. 24). The implications for collective organization are nowhere addressed.

[8]Radner (1970), p. 457.

235

monopoly ownership of the physical assets and information services in question is impeded in technological respects. Rather, the problems are to be traced to transactional difficulties that predictably attend market exchange in these circumstances. Accordingly, the incentive to collectivize activities for which indivisibilities are large in relation to the market is ultimately of a transactional kind.

Conventional treatments – nonseparabilities

Alchian and Demsetz[9] contend that normal sales relationships are supplanted by an employment relation on account of nonseparabilities. The standard example is the manual loading of freight into a truck by two men, both of whom must work coordinately to lift the cargo in question. The inability to impute marginal products to each man on the basis of observed output is what, in Alchian and Demsetz' scheme of things, warrants hierarchical organization. A "boss" is introduced who monitors the work of both, thereby checking malingering and yielding a larger team output.

We agree, but make two further points. First, it is not the nonseparability by itself that occasions the problem. Rather, it is this in conjunction with what we shall refer to below as "opportunism" and a condition of "information impactedness" that poses the difficulties. Absent these transactional considerations, the purported metering problems associated with nonseparability vanish. Second, and more important, we contend that most tasks are separable in the sense that – provided that successive stages of production are in balance – it is possible to sever the connection between stages by introducing buffer inventories.

Consider Adam Smith's pin-making example.[10] Pin manufacture involved a series of technologically distinct operations (wire straightening, cutting, pointing, grinding, etc.). In principle, each of these activities could be performed by an independent specialist and work passed from station to station by contract. Autonomous contracting would be facilitated, moreover, by introducing buffer inventories at each station, since coordination requirements and hence contractual complexity would thereby be reduced. Each worker could then proceed at his own pace, subject only to the condition that he maintain his buffer inventory at some minimum level. A series of independent entrepreneurs rather than a group of employees, each subject to an authority relation, could thus perform the tasks in question.

Transaction costs militate against such an organization of tasks, however. For one thing, it may be possible to economize on buffer inventories by

[9]Alchian and Demsetz (1972). [10]Smith (1937), p. 457.

designating someone to act as a coordinator,[11] which entails, albeit in limited degree, a shift toward hierarchy. But more germane to our purposes here are the economies attributable to the structure of internal labor markets – provided that the jobs in question are idiosyncratic in nontrivial degree. The ways in which the structured bargaining features of internal labor markets permit such economies to be realized are developed below. We nevertheless take this opportunity to emphasize that small numbers exchange relations *evolve* much more frequently than is usually acknowledged and that the prospect of costly haggling among autonomous agents is a consequence. The interesting institutional design question that is thereby posed is, how can such haggling be attenuated? Examining the structural bargaining attributes of alternative contracting modes is plainly relevant in this connection.

Small numbers – general

Arrow illustrates the problem of small numbers exchange with the lighthouse example. Indivisibility is no problem, since the light can be either on or off. He furthermore abstracts from uncertainty, by assuming that the lighthouse keeper knows exactly when each ship will need its services, and assumes that exclusion is possible since only one ship will be within lighthouse range at any one time. A trading problem nevertheless arises, because "there would be only one buyer and one seller and no competitive forces to drive the two of them into competitive equilibrium."[12] As will be evident, this condition, together with the stipulation that the firm is confronted with changing internal and market circumstances, is what we mainly rely on to explain the employment relation.

Small numbers – task idiosyncracies

Doeringer and Piore describe idiosyncratic tasks in the following way[13]:

Almost every job involves some specific skills. Even the simplest custodial tasks are facilitated by familiarity with the physical environment specific to the workplace in which they are being performed. The apparently routine operation of standard machines can be importantly aided by familiarity with the particular piece of operating equipment. . . . In some cases workers are able to anticipate trouble and diagnose its source by subtle changes in the sound or smell of the equipment. Moreover, performance in some production or managerial jobs involves a team element, and a critical skill is the ability to operate effectively with the given members of the team. This ability is dependent upon the interaction skills of the personalities of the members, and

---

[11]For a discussion of some of the ways in which buffer inventory savings can be realized, see Williamson (1964a), pp. 1454–5.
[12]Arrow (1969), p. 58.   [13]Doeringer and Piore (1971), pp. 15–16.

the individual's work "skills" are specific in the sense that skills necessary to work on one team are never quite the same as those required on another.

Hayek describes the consequences of idiosyncracy as follows[14]:

. . . practically every individual has some advantage over all others in that he possesses unique information of which beneficial use might be made, but of which use can be made only if the decisions depending on it are left to him or are made with his active cooperation. We need to remember only how much we have to learn in any occupation after we have completed our theoretical training, how big a part of our working life we spend learning particular jobs, and how valuable an asset in all walks of life is knowledge of people, of local conditions, and special circumstances.

More generally, task idiosyncracies can arise in at least four ways: (1) equipment idiosyncracies, due to incompletely standardized, albeit common, equipment, the unique characteristics of which become known through experience; (2) process idiosyncracies, which are fashioned or "adopted" by the worker and his associates in specific operating contexts; (3) informal team accommodations, attributable to mutual adaptation among parties engaged in recurrent contact but which are upset, to the possible detriment of group performance, when the membership is altered; and (4) communication idiosyncracies with respect to information channels and codes that are of value only within the firm. Given that "technology is [partly] unwritten and that part of the specificity derives from improvements which the work force itself introduces, workers are in a position to perfect their monopoly over the knowledge of the technology should there be an incentive to do so."[15]

Training for idiosyncratic jobs ordinarily takes place in an on-the-job context. Classroom training is unsuitable both because the *uniqueness* attributes associated with particular operations, machines, the work group, and, more generally, the atmosphere of the workplace may be impossible to replicate in the classroom, and because job incumbents, who are in possession of the requisite skills and knowledge with which the new recruit or candidate must become familiar, may be unable to describe, demonstrate, or otherwise impart this information except in an operational context.[16] Teaching by doing thus facilitates the learning by doing process. Where such uniqueness and teaching attributes are at all important, specific exposure in the workplace at some stage becomes essential. Outsiders who lack specific experience can thus achieve parity with insiders only by being hired and incurring the necessary start up costs.

The success of on-the-job training is plainly conditional on the information disclosure attitudes of incumbent employees. Both individually and as a group, incumbents are in possession of a valuable resource (knowledge) and

[14]Hayek (1945), pp. 521–2.   [15]Doeringer and Piore (1971), p. 84.
[16]See Doeringer and Piore (1971), p. 20.

can be expected to reveal it fully and candidly only in exchange for value. The way the employment relation is structured turns out to be important in this connection. The danger is that incumbent employees will hoard information to their personal advantage and engage in a series of bilateral monopolistic exchanges with the management – to the detriment of both the firm and other employees as well.

An additional feature of these tasks not described above but nevertheless important to an understanding of the contractual problems associated with the employment relation is that the activity in question is subject to periodic disturbance by environmental changes.[17] Shifts in demand due to changes in the prices of complements or substitutes or to changes in consumer incomes or tastes occur; relative factor price changes appear; and technological changes of both product design and production technique types take place. Successive adaptations to changes of each of these kinds are typically needed if efficient production performance is to be realized. In addition, life cycle changes in the workforce occur which occasion turnover, upgrading, and continuous training. The tasks in question are thus to be regarded in moving equilibrium terms. Put differently, they are not tasks for which a once-for-all adaptation by workers is sufficient, thereafter to remain unchanged.

· · ·

4. Individualistic bargaining models

Four types of individualistic contracting modes can be distinguished.[18] (1) Contract now for the specific performance of x in the future; (2) contract now for the delivery of x_i contingent on event e_i obtaining in the future; (3) wait until the future materializes and contract for the appropriate (specific) x at the

---

[17]Omitted from the discussion of the framework in this paper is a systems related condition referred to as "atmosphere." Failure to include atmosphere does not imply that we think it unimportant. But the concept is somewhat difficult to explicate in what is already a rather long paper.

[18]Lest the ensuing discussion of autonomous bargaining modes be thought to be contrived and/or unnecessary, since "everyone knows" such bargaining modes are inapposite, we make the following observations. First, though it is widely recognized that complex contingent claims contracting is infeasible (e.g., Radner notes that the Arrow–Debreu contracting model "requires that the economic agents possess capabilities of imagination and calculation that exceed reality by many orders of magnitude" (1970, p. 457), the reasons for this are rarely fully spelled out – either in general or, even less, with respect to labor market contracting. We attempt to rectify this condition in Section 4 below. Second, as our discussion of Alchian and Demsetz below reveals, it is plainly not the case that everyone appreciates that idiosyncratic tasks need to be distinguished from tasks in general and that sequential spot contracting is singularly unsuited for jobs of the idiosyncratic kind. Third, so as to correct the widely held belief that the authority relation represents a well defined alternative to "normal" market contracting (as recently illustrated by Arrow's (1974, pp. 25, 63–64) reliance on Simon's treatment of the authority relation), we think it important that the ambiguities of the authority relation be exposed.

time; and (4) contract now for the right to select a specific x from within an admissible set X, the determination of the particular x to be deferred until the future. Simon's study of the employment relation[19] treats contracts of the first type, which he characterizes as sales contracts, as the main alternative to the so-called authority relation (type 4). This, however, is unfortunate because type 1 contracts, being rigid, are singularly unsuited to permit adaptation in response to changing internal and market circumstances. By contrast, contingent claims contracts (type 2) and sequential spot sales contract (type 3) both permit adaptation. If complexity/uncertainty is held to be a central feature of the environment with which we are concerned, which it is, the deck is plainly stacked against contracts of type 1 from the outset. Accordingly, type 1 contracts will hereafter be disregarded.

Contingent claims contracts. Suppose that the efficient choice of x on each date depends on how the future unfolds. Suppose furthermore that the parties are instructed to negotiate a once-for-all labor contract in which the obligations of both employer and employee are fully stipulated at the outset. A complex contingent claims contract would then presumably result. The employer would agree to pay a particular wage now in return for which the employee agrees to deliver stipulated future services of a contingent kind, the particular services being dependent upon the circumstances which eventuate.

Contracting problems of several kinds can be anticipated. First, can the complex contract be written? Second, even if it can, is a meaningful agreement between the parties feasible? Third, can such agreements be implemented in a low cost fashion? The issues posed can all usefully be considered in the context of the framework sketched out above.

The feasibility of writing complex contingent claims contracts reduces fundamentally to a bounded rationality issue. The discussion by Feldman and Kanter of complex decision trees is instructive in this connection[20]:

For even moderately complex problems . . . the entire decision trees cannot be generated. There are several reasons why this is so: one is the size of the tree. The number of alternative paths in complex decision problems is very large. . . . A second reason is that in most decision situations, unlike chess, neither the alternative paths nor a rule for generating them is available. . . . A third reason is the problem of estimating consequences. . . . For many problems, consequences of alternatives are difficult, if not impossible to estimate. The comprehensive decision model is not feasible for most interesting decision problems.

Plainly, the complex labor agreements needed to describe the idiosyncratic tasks in question are of this kind. Not only are changing market circumstances (product demand, rivalry, factor prices, technological conditions, and the

[19]Simon (1957), pp. 183–195.   [20]Feldman and Kanter (1965), p. 615.

like) impossibly complex to enumerate, but the appropriate adaptations thereto cannot be established with any degree of confidence *ex ante*. Changing life cycle conditions with respect to the internal labor force compound the complexities.

The enumeration problems referred to are acknowledged by Meade in his discussion of contingent claims contracts: "When environmental uncertainties are so numerous that they cannot all be considered . . . or, what comes perhaps to much the same thing, when any particular environmental risks are so hard to define and to distinguish from each other that it is impossible to base a firm betting or insurance contract upon the occurrence or nonoccurrence of any of them, then for this reason alone it is impossible to have a system of contingency . . . markets."[21] But for bounded rationality, Meade's concerns with excessive numbers, undefinable risks, and indistinguishable events would vanish.

But suppose, *arguendo,* that exhaustive complex contracts could be written at reasonable expense. Would such contracts be acceptable to the parties? We submit that a problem of incomprehensibility will frequently arise and impede reaching agreement. At least one of the parties, probably the worker, will be unable meaningfully to assess the implications of the complex agreement to which he is being asked to accede. Sequential contracting, in which experience permits the implications of various contingent commitments to be better understood, is thus apt to be favored instead.

Assume, however, that *ex ante* understanding poses no bar to contracting. *Ex post* enforcement issues then need to be addressed. First, there is the problem of declaring what state of the world has obtained. Meade's remarks that contingent claims contracts are infeasible in circumstances where it is impossible, on the contract execution date, "to decide precisely enough for the purposes of a firm legal contract" what state of the world has eventuated bear on this.[22] While it is easy to agree with Meade's contentions, we think it noteworthy to observe that, were it not for opportunism and information impactedness, the impediments to contracting to which he refers vanish. Absent these conditions, the responsibility for declaring what state of the world had obtained could simply be assigned to the "best informed" party. Once he has made the determination, the appropriate choice of x is found by consulting the contract. Execution then follows directly.

It is hazardous, however, to permit the best informed party unilaterally to make state of the world declarations where opportunism can be anticipated. If the worker is not indifferent between supplying services of type x_j rather than x_k, and if the declaration of the state of the world were to be left to him, he will be inclined, when circumstances permit, to represent the state of the

[21]Meade (1971), p. 183.   [22]Meade (1971), p. 183.

world in terms most favorable to him. Similar problems are to be expected for those events for which the employer is thought to be the best informed party and unilaterally declares, from among a plausible set, which e_i has eventuated.[23] Moreover, mediation by a third party is no answer since, by assumption, an information impactedness condition prevails with respect to the observations in question.

Finally, even were it that state of the world issues could be settled conclusively at low cost, there is still the problem of execution. Did the worker really supply x_i in response to condition e_i, as he should, or did he (opportunistically) supply x_j instead? If the latter, how does the employer show this in a way that entitles him to a remedy? These are likewise information impactedness issues. Problems akin to moral hazard are posed.

Ordinarily, bounded rationality renders the description of once-for-all contingent claims employment contracts strictly infeasible. Occasions to examine the negotiability and enforcement properties of such contracts thus rarely develop. It is sufficient for our purposes here, however, merely to establish that problems of any of these kinds impair contingent claims contracting. In consideration of these difficulties, alternatives to the once-for-all supply relation ought presumably to be examined.

Sequential spot contracts. Alchian and Demsetz take the position that it is delusion to characterize the relation between employer and employee by reference to fiat, authority, or the like. Rather, it is their contention that the relation between an employer and his employee is identical to that which exists between a shopper and his grocer in fiat and authority respects[24]:

> The single consumer can assign his grocer to the task of obtaining whatever the customer can induce the grocer to provide at a price acceptable to both parties. That is precisely all that an employer can do to an employee. To speak of managing, directing, or assigning workers to various tasks is a deceptive way of noting that the employer continually is involved in renegotiation of contracts on terms that must be acceptable to both parties. . . . Long-term contracts between employer and employee are not the essence of the organization we call a firm.

Implicit in their argument, we take it, is an assumption that the transition costs associated with employee turnover are negligible. Employers, therefore,

---

[23]The issue here is somewhat more subtle, however. The employer, when he assumes the role of the best informed party, will not wish to declare a false state of the world *unless,* at the time he got the worker to agree to a wage w, he represented to the worker that services of type x_i would be called for when event e_i obtained when in fact x_i' services, which the worker dislikes, yield a greater e_i gain. The worker, being assured that he would be called on to perform x, ne'_i services only when the unlikely event e_i' occurred, agreed to a lower wage than he would have if he realized that an x_i' response would be called for in both e_i and e_i' situations – because the employer will falsely declare e_i to be e_i' so as to get x_i' performed.

[24]Alchian and Demsetz (1972), p. 777.

are able easily to adapt to changing market circumstances by filling jobs on a spot market basis. Although job incumbents may continue to hold jobs for a considerable period of time, and may claim to be subject to an authority relationship, all that they are essentially doing is continuously meeting bids for their jobs in the spot market. This is option number three, among the contracting alternatives described at the beginning of this section, done repeatedly.

That adaptive, sequential decision making can be effectively implemented in sequential spot labor markets which satisfy the low transition cost assumption (as some apparently do, e.g., migrant farm labor),[25] without posing issues that differ in kind from the usual grocer–customer relationship, seems uncontestable. We submit, however, that many jobs do not satisfy this assumption. In particular, the tasks of interest here are not of this primitive variety. Where tasks are idiosyncratic, in nontrivial degree, the worker–employer relationship is no longer contractually equivalent to the usual grocer–customer relationship and the feasibility of sequential spot market contracting breaks down.

Whereas the problems of contingent claims contracts were attributed to bounded rationality and opportunism conditions, sequential spot contracts are principally impaired only by the latter. (Bounded rationality poses a less severe problem because no effort is made to describe the complex decision tree from the outset. Instead, adaptations to uncertainty are devised as events unfold.) Wherein does opportunism arise and how is sequential spot contracting impaired?

Recall from the discussion of opportunism in Section 3 that opportunism poses a contractual problem only to the extent that it appears in a small numbers bargaining context. Otherwise, large numbers bidding effectively checks opportunistic inclinations and competitive outcomes result. The problem with the tasks in question is that while large numbers bidding conditions obtain at the outset, before jobs are first assigned and the work begun, the idiosyncratic nature of the work experience effectively destroys parity at the contract renewal interval. Incumbents who enjoy nontrivial advantages over similarly qualified but inexperienced bidders are well situated to demand some fraction of the cost savings which their idiosyncratic experience has generated.

One possible adaptation is for employers to avoid idiosyncratic technologies and techniques in favor of more well-standardized operations. Although least-cost production technologies are sacrificed in the process, pecuniary gains may nevertheless result since incumbents realize little strategic advantage over otherwise qualified but inexperienced outsiders. Structuring the initial bidding in such a way as to permit the least-cost technology and

---

[25]See Doeringer and Piore (171), pp. 4–5; also Kerr (1954), p. 95.

techniques to be employed without risking untoward contract renewal outcomes is, however, plainly to be preferred. Two possibilities warrant consideration: (1) extract a promise from each willing bidder at the outset that he will not use his idiosyncratic knowledge and experience in a monopolistic way at the contract renewal interval or (2) require incumbents to capitalize the prospective monopoly gains that each will accrue and extract corresponding lump-sum payments from winning bidders at the outset.

The first of these can be dismissed as utopian. It assumes that promises not to behave opportunistically are either self-enforcing or can be enforced in the courts. Self-enforcement is tantamount to denying that human agents are prone to be opportunists and fails for want of reality testing. Enforcement of such promises by the courts is likewise unrealistic. Neither case by case litigation nor simple rule-making disposition of the issues is feasible. Litigation on the merits of each case is prohibitively costly, while rules to the effect that "all workers shall receive only competitive wages" fail because courts cannot, for information impactedness reasons, determine whether workers put their energies and inventiveness into the job in a way which permits task-specific cost savings to be fully realized – in which case disaffected workers can counter such rules by withholding effort.

The distinction between consummate and perfunctory cooperation is important in this connection. Consummate cooperation is an affirmative job attitude – to include the use of judgment, filling gaps, and taking initiative in an instrumental way.[26] Perfunctory cooperation, by contrast, involves job performance of a minimally acceptable sort. Incumbents, who through experience have acquired task-specific skills, need merely to maintain a slight margin over the best available inexperienced candidate (whose job attitude, of necessity, is an unknown quantity). The upshot is that workers, by shifting to a perfunctory performance mode, are in a position to "destroy" idiosyncratic efficiency gains. Reliance on preemployment promises as a means by which to deny workers from participating in such gains is accordingly self-defeating.

Consider, therefore, the second alternative in which, though worker participation in realized cost savings is assumed to be normal, workers are required to submit lump-sum bids for jobs at the outset. Assuming that large numbers

---

[26]Consummate cooperation involves working in a fully functional, undistorted mode. Efforts are not purposefully withheld; neither is behavior of a knowingly inapt kind undertaken. Blau and Scott are plainly concerned with the difference between perfunctory and consummate cooperation in the following passage (1962, p. 140):

the contract obligates employees to perform only a set of duties in accordance with minimum standards and does not assure their striving to achieve optimum performance . . . [L]egal authority does not and cannot command the employee's willingness to devote his ingenuity and energy to performing his tasks to the best of his ability. . . . It promotes compliance with directives and discipline, but does not encourage employees to exert effort, to accept responsibilities, or to exercise initiative.

of applicants are qualified to bid for these jobs at the outset, will such a scheme permit employers fully to appropriate the expected, discounted value of future cost savings by awarding the job to whichever worker offers to make the highest lump-sum payment?

Such a contracting scheme amounts to long-term contracting in which many of the details of the agreement are left unspecified. As might be anticipated, numerous problems are posed. For one thing, it assumes that workers are capable of assessing complex future circumstances in a sophisticated way and of making a determination of what the prospective gains are. Plainly, a serious bounded rationality issue is raised. Second, even if workers had the competence to complete such an exercise, it is seriously to be doubted that they could raise the funds, if their personal assets were deficient, to make the implied full valuation bids. As Malmgren has observed, in a somewhat different but nevertheless related context, "some [individuals] will see opportunities, but be unable to communicate their own information and expectations favorably to bankers, and thus be unable to acquire finance, or need to pay a higher charge for the capital borrowed."[27] The communication difficulties referred to are due to language limitations (attributable to bounded rationality) that the parties experience. That bankers are unwilling to accept the representations of loan-seekers at face value is because of the risks of opportunism.

Third, and crucially, the magnitude of the estimated future gains to be realized by workers often depends not merely on exogenous events and/or activities that each worker fully controls but also on the posture of coworkers and the posture of the employer. Problems with co-workers arise if, despite steady state task separability, the consent or active cooperation of workers who interface with the task in question must be secured each time an adaptation is proposed. This effectively means that related sets of workers must enter bids as teams, which complicates the bidding scheme greatly and offers opportunities for free-riding. Problems also arise if gains cannot be realized independently of the decisions taken by management with respect, for example, to the organization of production, complementary new asset acquisitions, equipment repair policy, etc. Lump sum bidding is plainly hazardous where workers are entering bids on life cycle earnings streams that are repeatedly exposed to rebargaining.[28]

[27]Malmgren (1961), p. 46.

[28]There is the related problem of comparing the bids of workers who have different age, health, and other characteristics. Possibly this could be handled by stipulating that winners have claims to jobs in perpetuity, so that a job can be put up for rebidding by the estate of a worker who dies or retires. Such rebidding, however, is hazardous if the new worker must secure anew the cooperation of his colleagues. Established workers are then in a position strategically to appropriate some of the gains. (This assumes that coalition asymmetries exist which favor old workers in relation to the new.)

Finally, but surely of negligible importance in relation to the issues already raised, there is a question of efficient risk bearing: which party is best situated to bear the risks of future uncertainties, individual workers or the firm? That individual workers may be poorly suited to bear such risks and, as a group, can pool risks only with difficulty, seems evident and further argues against the bidding scheme proposed.

Transactional difficulties thus beset both contingent claims and sequential spot market contracting for the idiosyncratic tasks of interest in this chapter. Consider, therefore, the so-called authority relation as the solution to the contracting problems in question.

The authority relation. Simon has made one of the few attempts to assess the employment relation formally. Letting B designate the employer (or boss), W be the employee (or worker), and x be an element in the set of possible behavior patterns of W, he defines an authority relation as follows[29]:

We will say that B exercises *authority* over W if W permits B to select x. That is, W accepts authority when his behavior is determined by B's decision. In general, W will accept authority only if x_o, the x chosen by B, is restricted to some subset (W's "area of acceptance") of all the possible values.

An employment contract is then said to exist whenever W agrees to accept the authority of B in return for which B agrees to pay W a stated wage.[30]

Simon then asks when will such an employment relationship be preferred to a sales contract, and offers the following two conjectures[31]:

(1) W will be willing to enter into an employment contract with B only if it does not matter to him "very much" which x (within the agreed upon area of acceptance) B will choose, or if W is compensated in some way for the possibility that B will choose x that is not desired by W (i.e., that B will ask W to perform an unpleasant task).

(2) It will be advantageous to B to offer W added compensation for entering into an employment contract if B is unable to predict with certainty, at the time the contract is made, which x will be the optimum one, from his standpoint. That is, B will pay for the privilege of postponing, until some time after the contract is made, the selection of x.

He then goes on to develop a formal model in which he demonstrates that the employment contract commonly has attractive properties, under conditions of uncertainty, *provided that the alternatives are* (1) the promise of a particular x in exchange for a given wage w (what he considers to be the sales contract option) or (2) a set of X from which a particular x will subsequently be chosen in exchange for a given wage w' (the employment contract option).

Put differently, the deterministic sales contract is shown to be inferior to an incompletely specified employment relation in which W and B do not agree on

[29]Simon (1957), p. 184.   [30]See Simon (1957), p. 184.   [31]Simon (1957), p. 185.

all terms *ex ante,* but "agree to agree later" – or better, "agree to tell and be told." But plainly the terms are rigged from the outset. As noted previously, the particular type of sales contract to which Simon refers in attempting to establish the rationale for an authority relation is the only one of the three types of sales contracts described at the beginning of this section that lacks for adaptability in response to changing market circumstances. Since employment contracts of both the contingent claim and sequential spot marketing kinds are not similarly flawed, a better test of the authority relation would be to compare it with either of these instead.

Simon's modeling apparatus, unfortunately, does not lend itself to such purposes. It is simply silent with respect to the efficiency properties of alternative contracts in which adaptability is featured. Not only is it unable to discriminate between the authority relation, contingent claims contract, and spot market contracting in adaptability respects, but Simon's model fails to raise transaction cost issues of the types described here.

This is not, however, to suggest that the authority relation had nothing to commend it. To the contrary, such a relation does not require that the complex decision tree be generated in advance, and thus does not pose the severe bounded rationality problems to which the contingent claims contracting model is subject. The authority relation also, presumably, reduces the frequency with which contracts must be negotiated in comparison with the sequential spot contracting mode. Adaptations in the small can be costlessly accomplished under an authority relation because such changes, to the worker, do not matter "very much."

Assuming, however, that the parties are prospectively joined in a long-term association and the jobs in question are of the idiosyncratic kind, most of the problems of sequential spot contracting still need to be faced. Thus how are wage and related terms of employment to be adjusted through time in response to either small, but cumulative, or large, discrete changes in the data? What happens when hitherto unforeseen and unforeseeable contingencies eventuate? How are differences between the parties regarding state of the world determinations, the definition of the task, and job performance to be reconciled? Substantially all of the problems that are posed by idiosyncratic tasks in the sequential spot contracting mode appear, we submit, under the authority relation as well.

5. The efficiency implications of internal labor market structures

The upshot is that none of the above contracting schemes has acceptable properties for tasks of the idiosyncratic variety. Contingent claims contracting[32] fails principally on account of bounded rationality. Spot marketing contracting[33] is impaired by first mover advantages and problems of opportunism. The authority relation[34] is excessively vague and, ultimately, is confronted with the same types of problems as is spot market contracting. Faced with this result, the question of alternative contracting schemes naturally arises. Can more effective schemes be designed? Do more efficient contracting modes exist?

Our analysis here is restricted to the latter of these questions, which we answer in the affirmative. Although we do not contend that the internal labor market structures which we describe are optimally efficient with respect to idiosyncratic tasks, we think it significant that their efficiency properties have been little noted or understated by predominantly nonneoclassical interpretations of these markets in the past.

Our assessment of the efficiency implications of internal labor market structures is in three parts. The occasion for and purposes of collective organization are sketched first. The salient structural attributes of internal labor markets are then described and the efficiency implications of each, expressed in terms of the language of the organizational failures framework, are indicated. Several caveats follow.

Collective organization. To observe that the pursuit of perceived individual interests can sometimes lead to defective collective outcomes is scarcely novel. Schelling has treated the issue extensively in the context of the "ecology of micromotives."[35] The individual in each of his examples is both small in relation to the system – and thus his behavior, by itself, has no decisive influence on the system – and is unable to appropriate the collective gains that would obtain were he voluntarily to forego individual self-interest seeking. Schelling then observes that the remedy involves collective action. An enforceable social contract which imposes a cooperative solution on the system is needed.[36]

Although it is common to think of collective action as state action, this is plainly too narrow. As Arrow and Schelling[37] emphasize, both private collective action (of which the firm, with its hierarchical controls, is an example) and norms of socialization are also devices for realizing cooperative solutions. The internal labor market, we contend, is usefully interpreted in this same spirit.

Thus, although it is in the interest of each worker, bargaining individually or as a part of a small team, to acquire and exploit monopoly positions, it is plainly not in the interest of the *system* that employees should behave in this way. Opportunistic bargaining not only itself absorbs real resources, but effi-

---

[32]See Meade (1971), Chapter 10.   [33]See Alchian and Demsetz (1972), p. 777.
[34]See Simon (1957), pp. 183–95.   [35]Schelling (1971).
[36]See Schelling (1971), p. 69.   [37]See Arrow (1969), p. 62, and Schelling (1971), p. 69.

cient adaptations will be delayed and possibly foregone altogether. What this suggests, accordingly, is that the employment relation be transformed in such a way that systems concerns are made more fully to prevail and the following objectives are realized: (1) bargaining costs are made lower, (2) the internal wage structure is rationalized in terms of objective task characteristics, (3) consummate rather than perfunctory cooperation is encouraged, and (4) investments of idiosyncratic types, which constitute a potential source of monopoly, are undertaken without risk of exploitation. For the reasons and in the ways developed below, internal labor markets can have, and some do have, the requisite properties to satisfy this prescription.[38]

Structural attributes and their efficiency consequences

Wage bargaining. A leading difficulty with individual contracting schemes where jobs are idiosyncratic is that workers are strategically situated to bargain opportunistically. The internal labor market achieves a fundamental transformation by shifting to a system where wage rates attach mainly to jobs rather than to workers. Not only is individual wage bargaining thereby discouraged, but it may even be legally foreclosed.[39] Once wages are expressly removed from individual bargaining, there is really no occasion for the worker to haggle over the incremental gains that are realized when adaptations of degree are proposed by the management. The incentives to behave opportunistically, which infect individual bargaining schemes, are correspondingly attenuated.

Moreover, not only are affirmative incentives lacking, but there are disincentives, of group disciplinary and promotion ladder types, which augur against resistance to authority on matters that come within the range customarily covered by the authority relation.[40] Promotion ladder issues are taken up in conjunction with the discussion of ports of entry below; consider, therefore, group disciplinary effects.

Barnard observes in this connection[41]:

[38]Commons' discussion with Sidney Hillman concerning the transformation of membership attitudes among the Amalgamated Clothing Workers illustrates some of the systems attributes of collective agreements (1970, p. 130):

Ten years after World War I, I asked Sidney Hillman . . . why his members were less revolutionary than they had been when I knew them twenty-five years before in the sweatshop. . . . Hillman replied, "They know now that they are citizens of the industry. They know that they must make the corporation a success on account of their own jobs." They were citizens because they had an arbitration system which gave them security against arbitrary foremen. They had an unemployment system by agreement with the firm which gave them security of earnings. This is an illustration of the meaning of part-whole relations.

[39]See Summers (1969), pp. 538, 573.

[40]Authority relation is used here in the *qualified* short-run sense suggested in our discussion of Simon in Section 4 above.

[41]Barnard (1962), p. 169.

Since the efficiency of organization is affected by the degree to which individuals assent to orders, denying the authority of an organization communication is a threat to the interests of all individuals who derive a net advantage from their connection with the organization, unless the orders are unacceptable to them also. Accordingly, at any given time there is among most of the contributors an active personal interest in the maintenance of the authority of all orders which to them are within the zone of indifference. The maintenance of this interest is largely a function of informal organization.

The application of group pressures thus combines with promotional incentives to facilitate adaptations in the small.[42] Even individuals who have exhausted their promotional prospects can thereby be induced to comply. System interests are made more fully to prevail. This concern with viability possibly explains the position taken in labor law that those orders which are ambiguous with respect to, and perhaps even exceed, the scope of authority, are to be fulfilled first and disputed later.[43]

Contractual incompleteness/arbitration. Internal labor market agreements are commonly reached through collective bargaining. Cox observes in this connection that the collective bargaining agreement should be understood as an instrument of government as well as an instrument of exchange: "the collective agreement governs complex, many-sided relations between large numbers of people in a going concern for very substantial periods of time."[44]Provision for unforeseeable contingencies is made by writing the contract in general and flexible terms and supplying the parties with a special arbitration machinery: "One simply cannot spell out every detail of life in an industrial establishment, or even of that portion which both management and labor agree is a matter of mutual concern."[45] Such contractual incompleteness is an implicit concession to bounded rationality. Rather than attempt to anticipate all bridges that might conceivably be faced, which is impossibly ambitious and excessively costly, bridges are crossed as they appear.

But however attractive adaptive, sequential decision making is in bounded rationality respects, admitting gaps into the contract also poses hazards: where parties are not indifferent with respect to the manner in which gaps are to be

[42]Of course informal organization does not operate exclusively in the context of a collectivized wage bargain. Autonomous bargainers, however, are ordinarily expected to behave in autonomous ways. The extent to which group powers serve as a check on challenges to authority is accordingly much weaker where the individual bargaining mode prevails (see March and Simon, 1958, pp. 59, 66). By contrast, the individual in the collectivized system who refuses to accede to orders on matters that fall within the customarily defined zone of acceptance is apt to be regarded as cantankerous or malevolent, since there is no private pecuniary gain to be appropriated, and will be ostracized by his peers.

[43]See Summers (1969), pp. 538, 573.   [44]Cox (1958), p. 22.   [45]Cox (1958), p. 23.

filled, fractious bargaining or litigation commonly results. It is for the purpose of forestalling worst outcomes of this kind that the special arbitration apparatus is devised.

Important differences between commercial and labor arbitration are to be noted in this connection. For one thing, "the commercial arbitrator finds facts – did the cloth meet the sample – while the labor arbitrator necessarily pours meaning into the general phrases and interstices of a document."[46] In addition, the idiosyncratic practices of the firm and its employees also constitute "shop law" and, to the labor arbitrator, are essential background for purposes of understanding a collective agreement and interpreting its intent.[47]

In the language of Section 3, the creation of such a special arbitration apparatus serves to overcome information impactedness, in that the arbitrator is able to explore the facts in greater depth and with greater sensitivity to idiosyncratic attributes of the enterprise than could judicial proceedings. Furthermore, once it becomes recognized that the arbitrator is able to apprise himself of the facts in a discerning and low cost way, opportunistic misrepresentations of the data are discouraged as well.

Grievances. Also of interest in relation to the above is the matter of who is entitled to activate the arbitration machinery when an individual dispute arises. Cox takes the position that[48]

. . . giving the union control over all claims arising under the collective agreement comports so much better with the functional nature of a collective bargaining agreement. . . . Allowing an individual to carry a claim to arbitration whenever he is dissatisfied with the adjustment worked out by the company and the union . . . discourages the kind of day-to-day cooperation between company and union which is normally the mark of sound industrial relations – a relationship in which grievances are treated as problems to be solved and contracts are only guideposts in a dynamic human relationship. When . . . the individual's claim endangers group interests, the union's function is to resolve the competition by reaching an accommodation or striking a balance.

---

[46]Cox (1958), p. 23.   [47]Cox (1958), p. 24.

[48]Cox (1958), p. 24. We are informed that this practice is changing and offer three comments in this regard. First, institutional change does not always promote efficiency outcomes; backward steps will sometimes occur – possibly because the efficiency implications are not understood. Second, relegating control to the union as to whether a grievance is to be submitted to arbitration can sometimes lead to capricious results. Disfavored workers can be unfairly disadvantaged by those who control the union decision-making machinery. Some form of appeal may therefore be a necessary corrective. Third, that workers are given rights to bring grievances on their own motion does not imply that this will happen frequently. Grievances that fail to secure the support of peers are unlikely to be brought unless they represent egregious conditions on which the grievant feels confidently he will prevail. The bringing of trivial grievances not only elicits the resentment of peers but impairs the grievant's standing when more serious matters are posed.

The practice described by Cox of giving the union control over arbitration claims plainly permits group interests, whence concern for system viability, to supersede individual interests, thereby curbing small numbers opportunism.

Internal promotion/ports of entry. Acceding to authority on matters that fall within the zone of acceptance[49] merely requires that the employee respond in a minimally acceptable, even perfunctory way. This may be sufficient for tasks that are reasonably well structured. In such circumstances, the zeal with which an instruction to "do this" or "do that" is discharged may have little effect on the outcome. As indicated, however, consummate cooperation is valued for the tasks of interest here. But how is cooperation of this more extensive sort to be realized?

A simple answer is to reward cooperative behavior by awarding incentive payments on a transaction-specific basis. The employment relation would then revert to a series of haggling encounters over the nature of the quid pro quo, however, and would hardly be distinguishable from a sequential spot contract. Moreover, such payments would plainly violate the nonindividualistic wage bargaining attributes of internal labor markets described above.

The internal promotion practices in internal labor markets are of special interest in this connection. Access to higher level positions on internal promotion ladders is not open to all comers on an unrestricted basis. Rather, as part of the internal incentive system, higher level positions (of the prescribed kinds)[50] are filled by promotion from within whenever this is feasible. This practice, particularly if it is followed by other enterprises to which the worker might otherwise turn for upgrading opportunities, ties the interests of the worker to the firm in a continuing way.[51] Given these ties, the worker looks to internal promotion as the principal means of improving his position.[52]

The practice of restricting entry to lower level jobs and promoting from within has interesting experience-rating implications. It permits firms to protect themselves against low productivity types, who might otherwise successfully represent themselves to be high productivity applicants, by bringing employees in at low level positions and then upgrading them as experience warrants.[53] Furthermore, employees who may have been incorrectly upgraded

[49]The zone of acceptance is discussed in the quotation from Barnard in Section 5 above.

[50]For a discussion, see Doeringer and Piore (1971), pp. 42–47.

[51]Since access to idiosyncratic types of jobs is limited by requiring new employees to accept a lower job at the bottom of promotion ladders, individuals can usually not shift laterally between firms without cost: "employees in nonentry jobs in one enterprise often have access only to entry-level jobs in other enterprises. The latter will often pay less than those which the employees currently hold" (Doeringer and Piore, 1971, p. 78).

[52]Assuming that unit costs are equalized across rival enterprises (as a condition of competitive viability), the internal wage structure will be everywhere lower, including port of entry wages, if straight seniority is adopted.

[53]For a more general discussion of the special powers of internal organization in auditing and

252

but later have been "found out," and hence barred from additional internal promotions, are unable to move to a new organization without penalty.[54] Were unpenalized lateral moves possible, workers might, considering the problems of accurately transmitting productivity valuations between firms, be able to disguise their true productivity attributes from new employers sufficiently long to achieve additional promotions. Restricting access to low level positions serves to protect the firm against exploitation by opportunistic types who would, if they could, change jobs strategically for the purpose of compounding errors between successive independent organizations.

Were it, however, that markets could equally well perform these experience-rating functions, the port of entry restrictions described would be unnecessary. The (comparative) limitations of markets in experience-rating respects accordingly warrant attention. The principal impediment to effective interfirm experience-rating is one of communication.[55] By comparison with the firm, markets lack a rich and common rating language. The language problem is particularly severe where the judgments to be made are highly subjective. The advantages of hierarchy in these circumstances are especially great if those who are the most familiar with an agent's characteristics, usually his immediate supervisor, also do the experience-rating. The need to rationalize subjective assessments that are confidently held but, by reason of bounded rationality, difficult to articulate is reduced. Put differently, interfirm experience-rating is impeded in information impactedness respects.

Reliance on internal promotion has affirmative incentive properties in that workers can anticipate that differential talent and degrees of cooperativeness will be rewarded. Consequently, although the attachment of wages to jobs rather than to individuals may result in an imperfect correspondence between wages and marginal productivity at ports of entry, productivity differentials will be recognized over time and a more perfect correspondence can be expected for higher level assignments in the internal labor market job hierarchy.

. . .

experience rating respects, see Williamson (1975). The treatment in the text is keyed to an efficiency interpretation of the Doeringer and Piore (1971) discussion of ports of entry limitation.

[54]Agents seeking transfer may have gotten ahead in an organization by error. Experiencing rating, after all, is a statistical inference process and is vulnerable to "Type II" error. When a mistake has been discovered and additional promotions are not forthcoming, the agent might seek transfer in the hope that he can successfully disguise his true characteristics in the new organization and thereby secure further promotions. Alternatively, the agent may have been promoted correctly, but changed his work attitudes subsequently – in which case further promotion is denied. Again, he might seek transfer in the hope of securing additional promotion in an organization that, because of the difficulty of interfirm communication about agent characteristics, is less able to ascertain his true characteristics initially.

[55]Interfirm experience-rating may also suffer in veracity respects, since firms may choose deliberately to mislead rivals. The major impediment, however, is one of communication.

CHAPTER 17

Multitask principal–agent analyses: incentive contracts, asset ownership, and job design

BENGT HOLMSTROM AND
PAUL MILGROM

Bengt Holmstrom was born in 1949 in Helsinki, Finland. He earned his Ph.D. in economics from the Graduate School of Business, Stanford University, in 1978. When this article was published, he was Edwin J. Beinecke Professor of Management Studies, Yale School of Management. He is currently Professor of Economics and Management, Department of Economics, Massachusetts Institute of Technology.

Paul Milgrom is Professor of Humanities and Sciences and Professor of Economics at Stanford University. See also the previous chapter coauthored by Milgrom.

1. Introduction

In the standard economic treatment of the principal–agent problem, compensation systems serve the dual function of allocating risks and rewarding productive work. A tension between these two functions arises when the agent is risk averse, for providing the agent with effective work incentives often forces him to bear unwanted risk. Existing formal models that have analyzed this tension, however, have produced only limited results.[1] It remains a puzzle for this theory that employment contracts so often specify fixed wages and more generally that incentives within firms appear to be so muted, especially compared to those of the market. Also, the models have remained too intractable to effectively address broader organizational issues such as asset ownership, job design, and allocation of authority.

In this article, we will analyze a principal–agent model that (i) can account for paying fixed wages even when good, objective output measures are available and agents are highly responsive to incentive pay; (ii) can make recom-

Excerpted from Bengt Holmstrom and Paul Milgrom, "Multitask Principal–Agent Analyses: Incentive Contracts, Asset Ownership, and Job Design," *Journal of Law, Economics, and Organization* 7 (1991): 24–52, with permission of the publisher.
[1]Some of the predictive weaknesses of standard agency models are discussed in the surveys by MacDonald, Hart and Holmstrom, and Baker, Jensen, and Murphy.

mendations and predictions about ownership patterns even when contracts can take full account of all observable variables and court enforcement is perfect; (iii) can explain why employment is sometimes superior to independent contracting even when there are no productive advantages to specific physical or human capital and no financial market imperfections to limit the agent's borrowings; (iv) can explain bureaucratic constraints; and (v) can shed light on how tasks get allocated to different jobs.

The distinguishing mark of our model is that the principal either has several different tasks for the agent or agents to perform, or the agent's single task has several dimensions to it. Some of the issues raised by this modeling are well illustrated by the current controversy over the use of incentive pay for teachers based on their students' test scores. Proponents of the system, guided by a conception very like the standard one-dimensional incentive model, argue that these incentives will lead teachers to work harder at teaching and to take greater interest in their students' success. Opponents counter that the principal effect of the proposed reform would be that teachers would sacrifice such activities as promoting curiosity and creative thinking and refining students' oral and written communication skills in order to teach the narrowly defined basic skills that are tested on standardized exams. *It would be better, these critics argue, to pay a fixed wage without any incentive scheme than to base teachers' compensation only on the limited dimensions of student achievement that can be effectively measured.*[2]

Multidimensional tasks are ubiquitous in the world of business. As simple examples, production workers may be responsible for producing a *high volume* of *good quality* output, or they may be required both to produce output and to care for the machines they use. In the first case, if volume of output is easy to measure but the quality is not, then a system of piece rates for output may lead agents to increase the volume of output at the expense of quality. Or, if quality can be assured by a system of monitoring or by a robust product design, then piece rates may lead agents to abuse shared equipment or to take inadequate care of it. In general, when there are multiple tasks, incentive pay serves not only to allocate risks and to motivate hard work, it also serves to direct the allocation of the agents' attention *among* their various duties. This represents the first fundamental difference between the multidimensional theory and the more common one-dimensional principal–agent models.

There is a second fundamental difference as well, and it, too, can be illustrated by reference to the problem of teaching basic skills: If the task of teaching basic skills could be separated from that of teaching higher-level

---

[2]As a concrete illustration of the distortions that testing can cause, in 1989 a ninth-grade teacher in Greenville, South Carolina, was caught having passed answers to questions on the statewide tests of basic skills to students in her geography classes in order to improve her performance rating (*Wall Street Journal*, November 2, 1989).

thinking, then these tasks could be carried out by different teachers at different times during the day. Similarly, in the example of the production worker, when the care and maintenance of a productive asset can be separated from the use of that asset in producing output, the problem that a piece-rate system would lead to inadequate care can be mitigated or even eliminated. In general, in multitask principal–agent problems, *job design is an important instrument for the control of incentives.* In the standard model, when each agent can engage in only one task, the grouping of tasks into jobs is not a relevant issue.

Our formal modeling of these issues utilizes our linear principal–agent model (Holmstrom and Milgrom, 1987), mainly specialized to the case where the agent's costs depend only on the *total* effort or attention the agent devotes to all of his tasks. This modeling assures that an increase in an agent's compensation in any one task will cause some reallocation of attention away from other tasks. First, we show that an optimal incentive contract can be to pay a fixed wage independent of measured performance, just as the opponents of incentives based on educational testing have argued. More generally, the desirability of providing incentives for any one activity decreases with the difficulty of measuring performance in any other activities that make competing demands on the agent's time and attention. This result may explain a substantial part of the puzzle of why incentive clauses are so much less common than one-dimensional theories would predict.

Second, we specialize our model to the case where the unmeasurable aspect of performance is how the value of a productive asset changes over time. The difficulties of valuing assets are well recognized, and the vast majority of accounting systems value assets using fixed depreciation schedules based on historical costs, deviating from this procedure only in exceptional circumstances. Under these conditions, when the principal owns the returns from the asset, the optimal incentive contract will provide only muted incentives for the agent to produce output, in order to mitigate any abuse of the asset or any substitution of effort away from asset maintenance. However, when the agent owns the asset returns, the optimal incentive contract will provide more intensive incentives to engage in production, in order to alleviate the reverse problem that the agent may use the asset too cautiously or devote too much attention to its care and improvement. This analysis supports Williamson's observation that "high-powered" incentives are more common in market arrangements than within firms, without relying on any assumptions about specific investments. Moreover, it provides a rudimentary theory of ownership, according to which the conditions that favor the agent owning the assets are (i) that the agent is not too risk averse, (ii) that the variance of asset returns is low, and (iii) that the variance of measurement error in other aspects of the agent's performance is low. Thus, it emphasizes measurement cost as an important determinant of integration in contrast to the leading approaches, which stress asset specificity.[3]

. . .

Third, we explore how a firm might optimally set policies limiting personal business activities on company time. Again, it is not just the characteristics of the "outside activities" themselves that determine whether these activities should be permitted. We find that outside activities should be most severely restricted when performance in the tasks that benefit the firm – the "inside activities" – are hard to measure and reward. Thus, a salesperson whose pay is mostly in the form of commissions will optimally be permitted to engage in more personal activities during business hours than a bureaucrat who is paid a fixed wage, because the commissions direct the salesperson toward inside activities in a way that cannot be duplicated for the bureaucrat. Our theory also predicts that home office work should be accompanied by a stronger reliance on performance-based pay incentives, a prediction that seems to fit casual observation.

Our analysis of restrictions on outside activities underscores the fact that incentives for a task can be provided in two ways: either the task itself can be rewarded or the marginal opportunity cost for the task can be lowered by removing or reducing the incentives on competing tasks. Constraints are substitutes for performance incentives and are extensively used when it is hard to assess the performance of the agent. We believe this opens a new avenue for understanding large-scale organization. It also offers an alternative interpretation of the Anderson–Schmittlein evidence. It is inefficient to let a salesperson, whose performance is poorly measured, divert his time into commission selling of competing products. If the employer has an advantage in restricting the employees' other activities, as both Simon and Coase have argued, then problems with measuring sales performance will lead to employing an in-house sales force.

Finally, we obtain a series of results in the theory of job design, using a model in which the employer can divide responsibility for many small tasks between two agents and can determine how performance in each task will be compensated. The resulting optimization problem is a fundamentally nonconvex one, and we have had to make some extra assumptions to keep the

[3]Alchian and Demsetz argued that monitoring difficulties account for the formation of firms, but their theory was subsequently rejected in favor of the view that asset specificity and *ex post* bargaining problems drive integration (Grossman and Hart; Williamson). We are reintroducing measurement cost as a key factor but in a way that differs from the original Alchian–Demsetz theory. In particular, we do not argue that owners can better monitor the workforce. Our approach is more closely related to Barzel's work.

analysis tractable. Nevertheless, the results we obtain seem intriguing and suggestive. First, we find that each task should be made the responsibility of just one agent. To our knowledge, this is the first formal derivation in the incentive literature of the principle of unity of responsibility, which underlies the theory of hierarchy. Second, we find that tasks should be grouped into jobs in such a way that the tasks in which performance is most easily measured are assigned to one worker and the remaining tasks are assigned to the other worker. This conclusion squares nicely with the intuition that it is the *differences* between the measurability of quantity and quality in production, or of the so-called basic skills and higher-order thinking skills in education, that make those incentive problems difficult. The theory indicates that even when the agents have identical *ex ante* characteristics, the principal should still design their jobs to have measurement characteristics that differ as widely as possible. The principal should then provide more intensive incentives and require more work effort from the jobholder whose performance is more easily measured.

Our results are variations on the general theme of second best, which stresses that when prices cannot allocate inputs efficiently, then optimal incentives will typically be provided by subsidizing or taxing all inputs. For instance, Greenwald and Stiglitz, in a vivid metaphor, point out the value of a government subsidy for home fire extinguishers, since homeowners with fire insurance have too little incentive to invest in all forms of fire prevention and to fight fires once they have started. This mechanism has been most extensively analyzed in the theory of optimal taxation and in welfare theory.

However, the study of interdependencies among incentives and the use of instruments other than compensation to alleviate incentive problems have entered agency analyses more recently. Lazear argues that where cooperation among workers is important, we should expect to see less wage differentiation, that is, "lower-powered" incentives. Holmstrom and Ricart i Costa have observed how a firm's capital budgeting policy, including the hurdle rate and the way the firm assesses idiosyncratic risks, can affect the willingness of risk-averse managers to propose risky investment projects. Milgrom and Milgrom and Roberts have studied how organizational decision processes affect the allocation of effort between politicking and directly productive work. Farrell and Shapiro show that a price clause may be worse than no contract at all, because it reduces incentives to supply quality; this is similar to our result that it may be optimal to provide no quantity incentives when quality is poorly measured.

Some articles containing related ideas have been developed contemporaneously. Itoh (1991), in an analysis complementary to ours, studies conditions under which an employer might induce workers to work separately on their tasks, and those in which it is best for them to spend some effort helping one another. Laffont and Tirole show that concerns for quality help explain the use of cost plus contracting in procurement. Baker investigates a model in which observable proxies of marginal product are imperfect in a way that causes the agent to misallocate effort across contingencies and therefore leads to incentives that are not as powerful as standard theory would suggest. Minahan reports a result on task separation that suggests a job design similar to ours but based on a different argument, as we will later explain.

The remainder of this article is organized as follows. In Section 2, we recapitulate our basic principal–agent theory, upon which the entire analysis is based. In Section 3, we specialize the analysis to the case where the agent's costs depend only on the total attention supplied and prove the various propositions about the optimality of fixed wages, the factors determining the assignment of ownership, and the optimal limits on outside business activities. In Section 4, we consider restrictions on private tasks. In Section 5, we offer a summary and suggest directions in which this line of research can be taken.

. . .

3. Allocation incentives for effort and attention

3.1 The effort and attention allocation model

We now move to a group of models in which the agent's effort or attention is a homogeneous input that can be allocated among tasks however the agent likes. We shall suppose that effort in the various tasks is perfectly substitutable in the agent's cost function. More formally, we suppose that the agent chooses a vector $t = (t_1, \ldots, t_m)$ at a personal (strictly convex) cost $C(t_1 + \cdots + t_m)$, leading to expected profits $B(t)$ and generating signals $x(t) = \mu(t) + \epsilon$. Then, if the agent increases the amount of time or attention devoted to one activity, the marginal cost of attention to the other activities will grow larger.

Contrary to most earlier principal–agent models, we shall not suppose that all work is unpleasant. . . . A worker on the job may take pleasure in working up to some limit; incentives are only required to encourage work beyond that limit. Formally, we assume that there is some number $\bar{t} > 0$ such that $C'(t) \leq 0$ for $t \leq \bar{t}$ and $C(\bar{t}) = 0$. This is important, because it means that contracts that provide for fixed wages may still elicit some effort, though more may be elicited by providing positive incentives. It also means that there is a range of effort allocations among which the agent is indifferent and willing to follow the principal's preference.

3.2 Missing incentive clauses in contracts

One of the most puzzling and troubling failures of incentive models has been their inability to account for the paucity of explicit incentive provisions in actual contracts. For example, it is surprisingly uncommon in contracts for home remodeling to incorporate explicit incentives for timely completion of construction, even though construction delays arise frequently and can be profoundly disruptive to the homeowner. There can be little doubt that such clauses could be written into the contracts; similar clauses are common in commercial construction contracts. We shall argue that these facts can best be understood as a result of the greater standardization of commercial construction and the consequent ability of commercial buyers to specify and monitor quality standards. The innovation in our analysis is that our explanation of the presence or absence of the timely completion clause lies in an examination of the principal's ability to monitor *other aspects* of the agent's performance.[4]

Thus, suppose that some desirable attributes of the contractor's performance (such as courtesy, attention to detail, or helpful advice) are unmeasurable but are enhanced by attention t_1 spent on that activity, while other aspects of quality (such as timely completion) are measurable (perhaps imperfectly) and enhanced by attention t_2 devoted to this second activity. Supposing that the measured quality is one dimensional, we may write $\mu(t_1,t_2) = \mu(t_2)$, $x = \mu + \epsilon$. As we have seen, the agent's efficient compensation contract pays an amount $S = \alpha x + \beta$.

Suppose that the overall value of the job to the homeowner is determined by the function $B(t_1,t_2)$. To model the idea that the first activity is "very important" and that both activities are valuable, we assume that B is increasing and that $B(0,t_2) = 0$, for all $t_2 \geq 0$.

Proposition 1. For the home contractor model specified in the last paragraph, the efficient linear compensation rule pays a fixed wage and contains no incentive component ($\alpha = 0$), even if the contractor is risk neutral.

. . .

The ideas that underlie this analysis have many applications. For example, piece rates are relatively rare in manufacturing and, where they are used, they are frequently accompanied by careful attention to monitoring the quality of the work. Our analysis indicates that if quality were poorly measured, it would be expensive or impossible to maintain good quality while using a piece-rate scheme. Similarly, where individuals spend part of their efforts on individual projects and part on team production, and assuming that individual contributions to the team effort are difficult to assess, it would be dangerous to provide incentives for good performance on the individual projects. The problem, of course, is that individuals may shift their attention from the team

---

[4]Another plausible explanation is that home construction contracts are frequently changed to reflect design modifications, and timely completion clauses would be nullified by these changes.

activity where their individual contributions are poorly measured to the better measured and well-compensated individual activity. For this reason, piece-rate schemes may be especially dysfunctional in large hierarchies.

3.3 "Low-powered incentives" in firms

A similar model can be used to explain Williamson's observation that the incentives offered to employees in firms are generally "low-powered" com-pared to the "high-powered" incentives offered to independent contractors. Like Williamson, we distinguish employees from independent contractors by the condition of asset ownership: Employees use and develop assets that are owned by others while contractors use and develop their own assets.

Once again, the heart of our modeling is our assumption that there are multiple activities to be undertaken and that the allocation of time and atten-tion between them is crucial. Thus, let the expected gross profit from the enterprise be the sum of two parts, $B(t_1) + V(t_2)$, where B represents the expected net receipts and V the expected change in the net asset value. We assume that B and V are increasing, concave, and twice continuously differen-tiable and that $B(0) = V(0) = 0$. The actual change in asset value, $V + \epsilon_v$, accrues to whomever owns the asset. Assets are notoriously hard to value (that is why accountants generally use historical cost as a valuation basis), so we assume that there is no performance indicator for the asset enhancement activity t_2. The primary activity t_1 is to produce output for sale in the current period: its indicator is $x = \mu(t_1) + \epsilon_x$, where μ is increasing and concave. We assume that ϵ_x and ϵ_v are independent.

We consider two alternative organizational modes – *contracting,* in which the change in asset value accrues to the agent, and *employment,* in which the change in asset value accrues to the firm or principal. The crucial difference between these lies in the incentives for the agent to engage in the two kinds of activities. To focus on the most interesting case, we will assume that it is highly desirable to induce the agent to devote a positive amount of effort to both activities. Let

$$\pi^1 = \underset{t_1}{\text{Max}}\, B\,(t_1) - C\,(t_1),$$

$$\pi^2 = \underset{t_2}{\text{Max}}\, V\,(t_2) - C\,(t_2),$$

$$\pi^{12} = \underset{t_1}{\text{Max}}\, B\,(t_1) + V(\bar{t} - t_1) - C(\bar{t}).$$

Proposition 2. Assume that $\pi^{12} \geq \text{Max}(\pi^1, \pi^2)$. Then, the optimal employ-ment contract always entails paying a fixed wage ($\alpha = 0$). Whenever the

261

independent contracting relation is optimal, it involves "high-powered incentives" ($\alpha > 0$). Furthermore, there exist values of the parameters r, σ_v^2, σ_x^2 [ed.: risk aversion and the variances associated with V and x, respectively] for which employment contracts are optimal and others for which independent contracting is optimal. If employment contracting is optimal for some fixed parameters $(r, \sigma_v^2, \sigma_x^2)$, then it is also optimal for higher values of these parameters. Similarly, if independent contracting is optimal, then it is also optimal for lower values of these parameters.

. . .

[A] piece of evidence consistent with our model comes from the fast-food industry. Firms such as McDonald's and Burger King own about 30% of their stores and franchise the rest. The difference in incentives between franchisees and owner-managed firms is striking. Franchisees pay royalties that are at most 10% of sales, corresponding to at least a 90% commission, whereas managers of company-owned stores typically receive no explicit incentives either on profit or sales (Krueger, Brickley, and Dark). The difference in incentives is all the more remarkable, considering how similar the two types of stores are in all other aspects. According to our theory, the discontinuous shift in residual returns [$V(t_2)$] associated with franchising and the attendant shift in attention toward long-term asset values and cost containment, forces the franchise contract to increase short-term incentives sharply. Or, looked upon the other way, short-term incentives for employed managers must be muted to prevent them from allocating their attention away from important, but hard to measure, asset values.

4. Limits on outside activities

Our previous analysis emphasizes the importance of studying the full range of the agent's activities for analyzing incentives. If activities interact in the agent's cost function, incentive strength can be predicted only once the agent's whole portfolio of tasks is known. An equally important implication is that the principal can influence the agent's incentives by choosing the agent's portfolio of tasks. In the next section, we will study the optimal allocation of tasks between two agents. In this section, we consider how the principal might try to manage the agent's access to outside (private) activities.

Even casual observation makes it clear that the rules governing outside activities depend on the job. It is a commonplace observation that employees in "responsible positions" are allowed more freedom of action than other employees and that they use that freedom in part to pursue personally beneficial activities. To analyze the issues that this observation raises, we begin with the assumption that it is easier for an employer to exclude an activity entirely than to monitor it and limit its extent. For example, a rule against personal telephone calls during business hours is found in many offices and seems to be motivated in part by its ease of enforcement compared, say, to a rule that limits the percentage of business hours devoted to personal calls to 2%. Although generalizations about employment all seem to have exceptions, a common feature of employment contracts is that the employer has authority to restrict the employee's outside activities during business hours, and sometimes after hours as well.

Assume then that the agent has a finite pool $K = \{1, \ldots, N\}$ of potential activities, which the principal can control only by exclusion. The returns to these tasks, which we will refer to as the agent's *personal business* for short, are assumed nonstochastic and to benefit the agent alone (in principle, these tasks could benefit the principal, too, but the analytics would be more complicated). The principal controls the agent's personal business by allowing the agent to engage only in a subset of tasks $A \subset K$. Within the *set of allowable tasks, A*, the agent can engage in as much or as little personal business as he pleases, but none outside A. To focus on the interactions between the agent's workplace activities and personal business, we represent workplace activities simply as a single task in which performance is imperfectly measured.

. . .

[Proposition 4.] (ii) If it becomes easier to measure the agent's performance (σ^2 decreases), or the agent becomes less risk averse (r decreases), then the agent's marginal reward will be raised and his personal business activities will be less curtailed.

. . .

[Thus], there will be more constraints on an agent's activities in situations where performance rewards are weak because of measurement problems. The rigid rules and limits that characterize bureaucracy, in this view, constitute an optimal response to difficulties in measuring and rewarding performance. Among the "personal business" activities that bureaucracies try to limit are collusion (Tirole; Holmstrom and Milgrom, 1990; Itoh, 1989) and influence activities (Milgrom; Milgrom and Roberts). The restrictions on trade between employees that Holmstrom and Milgrom (1990) recommend and the restrictions on communications that Milgrom and Roberts propose are examples of optimal exclusion of activities that would be permitted or perhaps even encouraged in a first-best world.

. . .

5. Allocating tasks between two agents

In the single-agent model, the commission rates α_i serve three purposes: they allocate risk, motivate work, and direct the agent's efforts among his various activities. A trade-off arises when these objectives are in conflict with each other: Optimal risk sharing may be inconsistent with motivating work, and motivating hard work may distort the agent's allocation of efforts across tasks. Among the instruments available to the principal to alleviate these problems are job restructuring and relative performance evaluation: The former allows the principal to reduce the distortions in how attention is allocated among activities, while the latter enables the principal to lower the cost of incentives by using a more sensitive measure of actual performance.

5.1 Optimal groupings of tasks into jobs

Here we initiate the study of how incentive considerations might affect the grouping of tasks into jobs. We use a model that eliminates other important effects, such as differences among the agents and complementarities among task assignments. There are two identical agents, indexed $i = 1,2$, who allocate their attention across a continuum of tasks indexed by $k \in [0,1]$. Let $t_i(k)$ denote the attention agent i devotes to task k. We assume that the two agents can share a task and that their labor inputs are perfect substitutes. Thus, profit $B(t)$ is a function of the total time vector $t \equiv \{t(k): k \in [0,1]\}$, where $t(k) = t_1(k) + t_2(k)$. Likewise, the performance signal from task k, $\mu(t(k),k)$, only depends on the total attention $t(k)$ devoted to it. The error variance of task k is $\sigma^2(k) > 0$ and the errors are assumed independent.

. . .

Proposition 5. In the model described above, it is never optimal for the two agents to be jointly responsible for any task k.

. . .

This proposition reflects our earlier observation that providing incentives for an agent in any task incurs a fixed cost as the agent assumes some nontrivial fraction of the risk associated with that task (or its measurement). Since we have assumed that the tasks are small relative to the agent's capabilities, assigning joint responsibility for any task would incur two fixed costs unnecessarily. As the proof demonstrates, if one begins with an arrangement in which some tasks are shared, it is possible to split the same tasks among the agents without affecting either the total effort required of either agent or the total effort allocated to any task. This rearrangement makes it possible to eliminate some of each agent's responsibilities [setting $\alpha_i(k) = 0$], thereby reducing the risk that the agent must bear and so increasing the total surplus of the three parties.

Having established that each task will be assigned to just one employee, we next turn to the issue of how the tasks will be grouped. With this in mind, it is convenient to redefine our variables. We reinterpret $\alpha_i(k)$ to be the *hypothetical* commission rate that the principal would need to pay in order to elicit the desired level of effort $t(k)$ from agent i if he were assigned task k.

. . .

Proposition 6. Suppose that the two agents devote different amounts of total attention to their tasks (i.e., $\bar{t}_1 < \bar{t}_2$). Then, tasks are optimally assigned in this model so that all the hardest-to-monitor tasks are undertaken by agent 1 and all the easiest-to-monitor tasks are undertaken by agent 2. That is, agent 1 is assigned all the tasks k for which $\rho(k) \geq \rho$, and agent 2 is assigned all those with $\rho(k) < \rho$, where ρ is defined in (23) [ed.: as an indicator of task measurability].

. . .

These results provide, in purely incentive-theoretic terms, an account of how activities might be grouped, with some employees specializing in activities that are hard to monitor and others in activities that are easily monitored. Separating tasks according to their measurability characteristics [$\rho(k)$] allows the principal to give strong incentives for tasks that are easy to measure without fearing that the agent will substitute efforts away from other, harder-to-measure tasks. The present model oversimplifies these issues by assuming that there are no restrictions on how the principal may group tasks. In the case of piece rates discussed in Section 3, it might not be possible to separate the tasks of providing high output from those of providing high quality: The worker might always be able to substitute speed for attention to details. Nevertheless, the results of Proposition 6 are suggestive.

. . .

6. Conclusion

The problem of providing incentives to agents and employees is far more intricate than is represented in standard principal–agent models. The performance measures upon which rewards are based may aggregate highly disparate aspects of performance into a single number and omit other aspects of rate aspects of performance into a single number and omit other aspects of performance that are essential if the firm is to achieve its goals. Commonly, the principal–agent problem boils down to this: Given a highly incomplete set of performance measures and a highly complex set of potential responses from the agent, how can the agent be motivated to act in the social interest?

Our approach emphasizes that incentive problems must be analyzed in totality; one cannot make correct inferences about the proper incentives for an activity by studying the attributes of that activity alone. Moreover, the range of instruments that can be used to control an agent's performance in one activity is much wider than just deciding how to pay for performance. One can also shift ownership of related assets, vary restrictions on the ways a job can be done, vary limits and incentives for competing activities, group related tasks into a single job, and so on.

In a related article (Holmstrom and Milgrom, 1991), we study the simultaneous use of various instruments for controlling agents to derive new, testable results from the theory of organization. Our emphasis there is on how cross-sectional variations in the parameters that determine the optimal design of jobs, the optimal intensity of incentives, and the optimal allocation of ownership lead to covariations among endogenous variables that are similar to the patterns we find in actual firms.

Most past models of organization focus only on one instrument at a time for determining incentives and a single activity to be motivated. Newer theories, such as ours, that explicitly recognize connections between instruments and activities, offer new promise to explain the richer patterns of actual practice.

266

The prisoners' dilemma in the invisible hand: an analysis of intrafirm productivity

HARVEY LEIBENSTEIN

Harvey Leibenstein (1922–1994) was born in Russia. He received a Ph.D. in economics at Princeton University in 1951. In 1967, after serving for many years on the faculty of the University of California at Berkeley, he moved to Harvard University, where he was Andelot Professor of Economics and Population when the present article was published.

This paper attempts to show that it is useful to view productivity as a prisoners' dilemma problem, that conventions are alternative solutions to the prisoners' dilemma, that effort conventions are usually nonoptimal, and that a "shock" is necessary in order to shift from one nonoptimal solution to another. Within this framework the invisible hand does *not* produce a Pareto optimal result. It is consistent with any number of nonoptimal effort conventions.

I. Effort discretion and the game theory view of production

Under neoclassical assumptions, decision units follow parametric maximization; they control all the variables, and they view other influences as parameters. Game theory takes a different view: no single decision unit controls all the variables; the outcome depends on decisions made by two or many parties. I argue that once we look at productivity from the viewpoint of X-efficiency theory postulates, effort discretion is implied, and productivity becomes a game theoretic problem. Two X-efficiency theory postulates concern us: incomplete firm membership contracts and frequent nonoptimal "conventional" behavior. Employment contracts are incomplete since remuneration is usually well specified but effort is not. Agents (employees), in principal–agent relations, need not behave exactly as the principals wish. As a consequence some effort discretion exists. Hence, firm members can choose, within bounds, the amount of effort they put forth. The productivity outcome depends in part on effort choices made by firm members, and in part on the wage and work

Reprinted from Harvey Leibenstein, "The Prisoners' Dilemma in the Invisible Hand: An Analysis of Intrafirm Productivity," *The American Economic Review (Papers and Proceedings),* 72 (1982): 92–7, by permission of the editors.

condition choices made by the firm. Note: I distinguish "firm decisions" from the decisions of firm members whether or not the latter are managers or other employees.

I now turn to the basic behavioral postulate which relaxes the usual maximization assumption. It can be seen in terms of three-stage process. First, people behave in terms of habits or conventions. A convention is a routine that has an interpersonal component. Second, when pressure is increased, the individual shifts to a more calculating mode of behavior. Third, under a high degree of pressure, individuals are complete calculators, that is, maximizers. Related to conventional behavior is the assumption of inert areas; that is, the existence of upper and lower bounds within which behavior does not change. Thus, routine behavior continues unaltered unless some variable changes so that the value of this variable goes beyond the upper or lower bounds of the inert area. Essentially, we visualize a process whereby external variables change the amount of pressure on the individual so that the pressure goes beyond the inert area bounds, which in turn results in a new type of behavior – say a new convention or a shift to partial calculation. We will see that conventions play an essential role in determining the outcome of the prisoners' dilemma problem.

Now consider an illustration which looks at productivity from a game theory viewpoint. Suppose all employees make the same effort choice, but they have two options: a "Golden Rule" effort option and a maximizing private satisfaction option. Under the Golden Rule every employee acts in the best interest of the firm. He treats the firm as he would like the firm to treat him and puts forth effort as if the enterprise was his own. The alternative option is at the other extreme: the individual works as little as possible in the firm's interest and does other things (on the job) to pursue his own private interests.

The firm has two similar symmetrical options. It could behave in a Golden Rule fashion in which it provides employees with the maximal conditions, salaries, and security, consistent with "sustainable profits"; it is as if the firm operates *almost* entirely in the interest of the employees. The other alternative is parametric maximization, which implies cost minimization. That is, the firm *attempts* to minimize working conditions and wages cost while trying to get the most effort from employees. In the payoff table (Table 18.1) the payoffs to each side are shown in the four corners of the table in terms of utilities of the two types of options. As illustrated the symmetrical choices give higher values for the mutual Golden Rule choice than to the individual maximizing choice.

Given the numbers in Table 18.1 we can readily see that it involves a prisoners' dilemma situation. First, consider the choice problem from the firm's viewpoint. If employees operate according to the Golden Rule, then it

TABLE 18.1

		Firm Options		
		W_1	W_2	W_3
	Employee Options	Golden Rule	Peer Group Standard	Indiv Maxi
π_1	Golden Rule	15 \\ 15	17 \\ 6	20 \\ 3
π_2	Peer Group Standard	6 \\ 17	10 \\ 10	12 \\ 4
π_3	Indiv Max	3 \\ 20	4 \\ 12	5 \\ 5

certainly pays for the firm to choose maximization. Similarly, if the firm assumes that employees are private maximizers, it also makes sense for the firm to choose maximization. A very similar argument can be made for employees. They also choose maximization under both cases of the choices by the firm. As a consequence, the joint choice is maximization. But this joint choice is clearly inferior to the cooperative choice of the dual Golden Rule. Thus, if each side attempts to behave "rationally" and maximize given the other's behavior, then the result is the prisoners' dilemma outcome.

Now consider the 3 × 3 payoff table reflecting a slightly more complicated productivity game. Two of the options are the same as before: the Golden Rule and maximization. In between we indicate a "peer group standard" effort option. Under this option, employees consider the average effort level in terms of pace, quality, and choice of activities, and perform (as a group) according to the established average. Individual effort levels are distributed more or less symmetrically around the average level. This average is a *convention* determined and supported by peer group pressures. I consider later how such conventions are formed. From the point of view of the firm, the same choices exist. In between the Golden Rule and maximization there is a third option under which the employer recognizes the existing peer group effort standard and provides wages and working conditions in accordance with the average peer group effort.

In Table 18.1 the utilities associated with the various joint choices are shown. As the utilities are listed, we can readily see that what we have is a prisoners' dilemma situation. As in the 2 × 2 case, the choices made by the two parties will be those under parametric maximization, and, as a result, the prisoners' dilemma outcome occurs. However, by introducing the peer group standard, we add a new possibility. "Rational" choice still leads to the prisoners' dilemma outcome. In practice, however, the prisoners' dilemma outcome frequently does not occur; and a peer group standard frequently is chosen. Most of what follows is to explain why this should be the case.

We may view the three diagonal outcomes as the symmetrical cooperative choices. If these were the *only* alternatives, then obviously the choice made would be the joint Golden Rule. However, if we add the adversarial options, and since both sides can do better through adversarial behavior when the other does not choose an adversary position, then the joint adversarial choices dominate. Is productivity, in general, really a prisoners' dilemma problem? A basic criterion is that a prisoners' dilemma occurs wherever there are possibilities for adversarial behavior between the parties, and by all parties, which reduces the joint cooperative outcome. Now, it seems reasonable to presume that adversarial behavior between employees and the firm will usually decrease productivity, while cooperative behavior will increase it. This is certainly not the case in all types of games. But this is the case for the particular "game" set where productivity is the outcome.

II. Effort conventions as solutions

An alternative way of finding a solution to prisoners' dilemma problems is for an individual to behave in a not necessarily maximizing fashion: that is, to use conventions or conventionlike elements such as ethics. It is important to distinguish (a) the rationale behind a convention and (b) behavior given a convention. The rationale behind conventions has been developed by D. Lewis (1969), Edna Ullman-Margalit (1978), and reviewed by Andrew Schotter (1981). The basic idea is that conventions represent solutions to game theory coordination problems. Special interest is attached to those cases that involve multiple equilibria, and hence a multiplicity of possible conventions, any one of which, *includes nonoptimal ones,* are better than none.

Let me give a few examples. Consider the choice on which side of the road to drive. Individuals should be indifferent whether everyone drives on the left, or on the right; but the payoffs for all individuals driving on the left, or the right, are the same. The payoffs are negative if one drives on the left and others drive on the right, or vice versa. Thus we have multiple solutions (everyone driving on the left or on the right). The choice of either convention is superior to none. Similarly, languages and writing systems are conventions. There is a multiplicity of possible connections between sounds and meanings. Hence many possible languages. Thus, the reason for a convention (say a specific language) lies in the fact that once the convention exists, dropping the convention may have a very high cost. Recall the biblical Tower of Babel story. Thus a writing or spelling system which is clearly nonoptimal may

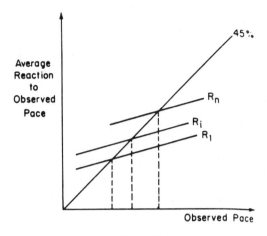

Figure 18.1

persist. Hence conventions are solutions to multiple equilibria problems. However, such latent equilibria need not all be equally good. It is only required that not having the convention (any equilibrium point) makes people worse off.

Once a convention exists people do not normally reappraise it; rather behavior becomes part of a *stimulus–response* mechanism. When the context (i.e., the stimulus) for the use of a convention arises, people employ the convention. Thus, people who know many languages will normally speak in the language of the community once they determine that it is appropriate for the context.

In the same spirit we can think of an effort convention as determined by a peer group standard. Entrants to the firm observe the average effort level and set their own effort approximately at or fairly close to the observed average. If the observed level were higher, many would simply shift their own level to a higher level, and similarly if it were somewhat lower. The general notion is illustrated in Figure 18.1. The abscissa indicates alternative pace levels. The ordinate indicates the average of individual reactions to each alternative. The reaction curves indicate the reactions of individuals to various observed rates and is denoted by the letter R_i. There is a large set of possible reactions to a given observed rate; and, hence, each reaction curve depends on some initial (or historical) observed rate, so that the reaction curves range from R_1 to R_n. Different histories yield different reaction curves. The 45° line indicates the set of possible equilibria between observed rates and reactions to them. The distance between R_1, R_n on the 45° line indicates all the possible equilibrium effort levels. Clearly, if the convention is R_1, it need not be an optimal

271

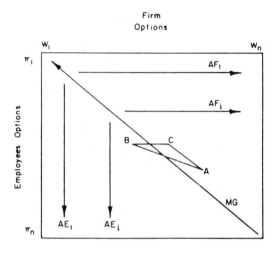

Figure 18.2

solution, but once chosen it will continue to be the solution in question. In the illustration I choose "pace" to signify effort. However, other components of effort, such as the quality levels of the activities carried out, are implicit in the example. The main point is that individual reactions to the observed *components* of effort determine the equilibrium effort *convention*.

An effort convention need not depend only on the peer group standard. It is also possible that some type of work ethic, or the Japanese consensus system, creates conventions which are superior to some or all possible peer group standards. Thus there may exist a wide range of alternative latent solutions along the cooperative diagonal. (See Figure 18.2.)

Note especially that an effort convention solves (i.e., avoids) the prisoners' dilemma.[1] The convention is clearly superior to permitting the latent prisoners' dilemma solution to assert itself. Thus, what may appear as an inferior convention to other alternatives will turn out to be stable. If that convention was not supported, the result (the latent prisoners' dilemma outcome) could be worse.[2]

---

[1]This general notion is spelled out in a paper I wrote in 1978 (published 1980). Ullman-Margalit's book (1978), which I was not aware of when I wrote my paper, explores these matters very carefully.

[2]Despite the repeated game aspect of the problem a nonoptimal convention can be stable since (1) convention followers can agree implicitly to police deviants, (2) to police those who might be tempted by free-rider low-effort incentives, and (3) to continually reinforce veneration for the convention. These elements can be sufficiently strong so that it takes a large perturbation (shock) to generate a movement out of a nonoptimal cooperative position.

272

III. The continuous model

Let us now consider a model which generalizes the 3×3 options case to continuous option sets. Certainly effort is a continuous variable. Wages and working conditions offered by the firm are also continuous. This is illustrated in Figure 18.2. From the top (the NW corner), we have a set of wage-working condition options given by the range W_1 to W_n, and a set of effort options which imply productivity levels given by the range π_1 to π_n. Note: $W_1 > W_2 > \cdots > W_n$ and $\pi_1 > \pi_2 > \cdots > \pi_n$.

The cooperative possibilities are indicated along the cooperative mutual gain diagonal marked MG. Assume that as we move from a lower to a higher effort level, there is an increase in output value which is divided between a higher W and a higher firm profit. Thus, a movement along the diagonal MG leads to successively Pareto-superior points since both employees and the firm gain by such movements. We must keep in mind that there are many cooperative diagonals approximately parallel to the one in the figure. However, a shift along any of the horizontal option sets (say along AF_1) involves adversarial movements for which the firm gains at the expense of employees. Similarly, vertical movements from top to bottom are adversarial movements (say along AE_1) for which the employees gain at the expense of the firm. What makes this general case a prisoners' dilemma case is the postulate that joint choices which are adversarial lead to smaller joint payoffs than would otherwise be the case.

If we consider horizontal movements away from the cooperative diagonal or vertical movements (towards the bottom), then we obtain adversarial behavior under which one party gains and the other loses. But it is the possibility of such shifts in options which creates the lower values along the cooperative diagonal as we move from west to east and from north to south simultaneously.

There is the possibility of shifts which combine both a change in distribution and a change in the cooperative valuation. For example, in the figure the shift from A to B is a shift under which the distribution shifts towards employees. At the same time it represents a move towards a higher cooperative level and, hence, a higher joint output. We can decompose this movement into two segments shown by the sides of the triangle AC and CB. The net effect can still be beneficial to both parties even if some redistribution also takes place.

IV. Example and implications

The view of a convention as a solution to a prisoners' dilemma problem requires that we focus on the stability of the convention. This is related to a concept of inert areas. Each convention is embedded in an inert area. Only if the values of certain variables get beyond the inert area bounds is the convention destabilized. Thus, to obtain a desirable change requires two elements: a necessary "shock" in order to destabilize the operating effort convention and a movement towards a new convention. A purely static theory does not allow us to determine whether the movement is to a superior convention, an inferior one, or to the prisoners' dilemma solution.

A recent article in the *New York Times* (October 13, 1981) compared two identically designed plants, with identically designed labor requirements, producing the same Ford automobiles; but the plant in Germany produced 50 percent more cars per day with 22 percent *less* labor. Obviously, despite the design, the effort conventions in the two countries are extremely different.

Now consider (without proof) a few of the implications of nonoptimal effort conventions in our model. Firms operate within, and not on, their production frontier. For a given output, costs are generally not minimized. Innovations are not introduced when it optimally pays to do so. Firm equilibrium is not Pareto optimal. Less output is not necessarily associated with more desired leisure. Firms do not necessarily maximize profits.

V. The prisoners' dilemma and the invisible hand – interrelations

This paper suggests that the invisible hand theory has to be reconsidered. Even if we assume decreasing returns to scale, and no externalities, we can still end up with nontraditional conclusions. The invisible hand theorem which leads to an optimal exchange situation no longer represents an unalloyed optimum in the sense that the *produced* commodities exchanged could have been produced under an infinity of different conventions, some of which are very much inferior to others. Thus, two countries with identical inputs, identical knowledge, identical capital accumulation, and the same level of employment may yet produce significantly different outputs because production takes place on the basis of very different effort conventions.

In addition to visualizing the prisoners' dilemma *in* the invisible hand, as it were, we must also take note that the invisible hand is embedded in a wider *latent* prisoners' dilemma framework. At any specific time the latent prisoners' dilemma possibilities are held in abeyance by conventions, institutions, and laws, involving trust, enforcement of contracts, etc. In other words, we can view a set of cooperative diagonals as exchange options available under a market mechanism. If the adversarial portions are absent, then the mutual choice is the optimal position on the cooperative diagonal. Adversarial portions of the payoff table may be made essentially nonaccessible through nonmarket conventions, such as trust, honesty, fairness, legal recourse for misunderstanding or fraud, emphasis on reputation for fair dealings, etc. Thus, a convention of honesty in contractual relations eliminates adversarial behavior in which both sides attempt to cheat the other. Similarly, an effective low-cost system of laws which enforces contracts may minimize the inducement to use other types of adversarial behavior. To the extent that such conventions are absent, the invisible hand is weakened, the exchange mechanism flawed, and the outcome is no longer optimal.

CHAPTER 19

Labor contracts as partial gift exchange

GEORGE AKERLOF

George Akerlof was born in 1940 in New Haven, Connecticut. He earned a Ph.D. in economics at the Massachusetts Institute of Technology in 1966. When the present article was published, he was Professor of Economics at the University of California at Berkeley. Since 1994, he has, in addition, been Senior Fellow at the Brookings Institution.

I. Introduction

In a study of social relations among workers at a utility company in the eastern United States, George Homans (1953, 1954) observed that a small group of young women (doing a job called "cash posting") exceeded the minimum work standards of the firm by a significant margin (i.e., on average by 15 percent). Most of these women neither desired nor expected promotion in the firm in return for their troubles. Why did they do it?

Section II shows that the standard neoclassical model cannot simultaneously explain both the behavior of the firm and the behavior of the cash posters. But, as shown in Section III, application of a standard sociological model does explain the behavior of both the young women and their employer. According to this model, in their interaction, workers acquire sentiment for each other and also for the firm. As a consequence of sentiment for the firm, the workers acquire utility for an exchange of "gifts" with the firm – the amount of utility depending upon the so-called norms of gift exchange. On the worker's side, the "gift" given is work in excess of the minimum work standard and on the firm's side, the "gift" given is wages in excess of what these women could receive if they left their current jobs. As a consequence of worker sentiment for one another, the firm cannot deal with each worker individually, but rather must, at least to some extent, treat the group of workers with the same norms, collectively.

Norm–gift-exchange models have been used in many sociological studies to explain the behavior of workers. And these explanations are simple; proper-

Excerpt reprinted from George Akerlof, "Labor Contracts as Partial Gift Exchange," *Quarterly Journal of Economics* 47, 4 (1982): 543–69 by permission of The MIT Press, Cambridge, Mass.

ly understood, they are in tune with everyone's personal experiences of human behavior, so that they can be taken to have considerable generality. For that reason I feel confident in extrapolating such behavior beyond the narrow and particular instance of the "cash posters" to concern wage bargains and work conditions in some generality. Sections IV and V verbally explore the consequences of such behavior for wage determination; Sections VI and VII build formal mathematical models; and Section VIII gives conclusions.

This model of the microeconomics of the labor market is used to explain two phenomena that have not been successfully analyzed by more conventional economic theory. First, in most other analyses of unemployment, such as that of search theory (Phelps et al., 1970), all unemployment is voluntary. In my analysis there are primary labor markets in which unemployed workers are unable to obtain jobs at the prevailing market wages. Second, the theory of dual labor markets (Doeringer and Piore, 1971) brings up the question as to which markets will be primary and which markets secondary. In the formal models developed in this paper, it is endogenously determined whether a market will be primary or secondary. Primary markets are those in which the gift component of labor input and wages is sizeable, and therefore wages are not market clearing. Secondary labor markets are those in which wages are market clearing.

The major feature of the usual model of implicit contracts due to Azariadis (1975) and Baily (1974) is risk-sharing agreements by the contracting agents over a span of time. These models have been taken as a vehicle for Okun's (1981, p. 133) description of labor and customer markets. This paper offers an alternative microfoundation for implicit contracts. Its emphasis is sociological. It focuses on the gift-exchange nature of employment arrangements, where the exchange is based partially on norms of behavior that are endogenously determined. This dependence of implicit contracts on *norms* of behavior (rather than on risk sharing) captures important aspects of Okun's description (1975, 1981) that have not been analyzed in the Azariadis–Baily framework.

According to this paper, norms of work effort are a major determinant of output. In emphasizing effort, it carries further the work of Liebenstein (1976) on X-efficiency. The focus on effort could also be expressed in Marxian terminology via the distinction between *labor-power* and *labor* as in Edwards' recent book (1979) on the inevitable conflict between labor and management over the use of labor-power.[1] In Edwards' terms this paper gives equilibrium models of the resolution of this conflict. Finally, it should be mentioned, Hirschman's concepts of *Exit, Voice,* and *Loyalty* (1970) can be expressed in terms of norms and gift exchange.

[1]For a review of the Marxian literature on this distinction, also see Edwards (1979).

II. The Nonneoclassical behavior of the cash posters or of the eastern utilities co.

Economists usually assume that labor is hired as a factor of production and is put to work like capital. There is, however, one fundamental difference between labor and capital that is ignored by this assumption. Once a capitalist has hired capital, he is, over a fairly wide latitude, free to use it (or abuse it) as he wishes. However, having hired a laborer, management faces considerable restriction on how it can use its labor. Not only are there legal restrictions (such as OSHA regulations, child labor laws, etc.), but the willing cooperation of labor itself must usually be obtained for the firm to make the best use of the labor services.

Of course, standard economic theory does describe the nature of contracts when there are many possible standards of performance. According to standard theory, when a firm hires a laborer, there is an understanding by both parties that certain minimum standards of performance must be met. Furthermore, the contract may be *implicit* in the sense that workers need not be currently rewarded for their current performance but may earn chances for promotion with higher pay in the future in return for good performance in their current jobs. If this is the case, the firm need not have tight rules regarding work and compensation that very carefully specify the quid pro quo of pay for work, since injustices in the present can be compensated later. So standard theory can serve as a good approximation to reality even where very specific contracts relating effort or output to compensation would be quite expensive.

Against this background let us consider the study by Homans of "The Cash Posters." In this study a group of ten young women working as cash posters for a utility company in a New England city were interviewed and closely observed over a period of six months. The duty of a cash poster at Eastern Utilities was to record customers' payments on ledger cards at the time of receipt. The company's standard for such cash posting was 300 per hour, and careful records were made of the speed at which individual cash posters variously worked. Anyone who worked below the rate of 300 per hour received a mild rebuke from the supervisor. Table 19.1 adapted from Homans' article, "The Cash Posters," shows both the number of cash postings per hour of different workers and their rate of error.

Note from Table 19.1 that the average number of cash postings per hour (353) was 17.7 percent greater than the standard set by the company. The simple neoclassical theory of contracts cannot simultaneously explain why the faster persons did not reduce their speed to the standard; or, alternatively, why the firm did not increase the speed expected of its faster workers. The possibility that the faster workers worked harder than the standard for either in-

Labor Contracts as Partial Gift Exchange

TABLE 19.1.

WORK PERFORMANCE OF INDIVIDUAL CASH POSTERS

	Age in years	Time on job in years–months	Mean cards per hour	Mean errors per hour
Asnault	22	3–5	363	0.57
Burke	26	2–5	306	0.66
Coughlin	20	2–0	342	0.40
Donovan	20	1–9	308	0.79
Granara	21	1–3	438	0.65
Lo Presti	25	–11	317	0.03
Murphy	19	–7	439	0.62
Rourk	17	–4	323	0.82
Shaugnessy	23	–2	333	0.44
Urquhart	18	–2	361	0.49
Average	21.1	1–4	353	0.55

creased pay or promotion was belied by the uniformity of wage for all cash posters and by the refusal of promotion by two cash posters. When promotion did occur, it was normally to a job considered more responsible than cash posting but nevertheless paying the same wage. In addition, voluntary quits among the cash posters were quite frequent (with most of the young women leaving to be married), so that in most cases promotion was not a relevant consideration. Since pay was not dependent on effort and promotion was rarely a consideration, the standard economic model of contract would predict that workers set their work habits to meet the company's minimum standards of performance as long as they have marginal disutility for work at that level. On the other hand, if workers do have positive utility for work at this level, the lack of incentives for effort given by the firm should lead them to choose to work to the point where the marginal disutility of additional effort is just zero. But in that case the firm could increase its profits by increasing work standards for the faster workers. Unless their utility function is discontinuous, they would still prefer their current jobs to what they could obtain elsewhere at somewhat faster speeds of work.

Since output is easily observable, it is at least a bit surprising from the point of view of the neoclassical theory of contracts that workers are not paid wages proportional to their outputs. This constitutes another puzzlement regarding the system of industrial relations among the cash posters at Eastern Utilities, although a potential answer has been suggested by Etzioni (1971). According to Etzioni, workers find pecuniary incentives, such as piece rates, "alienating."

The mysterious behavior of the cash posters and of Eastern Utilities in terms of neoclassical theory can be posed a bit more formally. Suppose for whatever reason (perhaps Etzioni's) that the firm has decided to pay the same wage $w = \bar{w}$ to all cash posters. Further, suppose that workers have a utility function $u(w,e)$, where w is the wage rate and e is effort. Workers, mindful of the firm's work rules, should choose their effort e to maximize.

$$u(w,e), \tag{1}$$

subject to the constraints,

$$w = \bar{w}, \tag{2}$$

$$e \geq e_{min}, \tag{3}$$

where $\bar{w} = \$1.05$ per hour, the wage fixed for all cash posters, and e_{min} is the minimum effort necessary to accomplish the required 300 cash postings per hour.

Solution of this trivial maximization problem yields

$$e = e_{min} \tag{4}$$

as long as $u_e < 0$ for $e \geq e_{min}$. On the assumption that utility is convex, there are two potential types of solutions. Each poses an empirical problem. If u_e $(\bar{w},e_{min}) < 0$, the question arises – why did the workers not reduce their effort to 300 per hour? On the other hand, if $u_e (\bar{w},e_{min}) > 0$, so that workers choose $u_e = 0$, why did the firm not raise the minimum standards for different workers above the point where $u_e = 0$? In either case the observation obtained is inconsistent with the neoclassical model.[2]

Of course, each cash poster may have a different utility function, and for some reason the firm may find it optimal to set the same minimum standard for all workers. For example, the rate perhaps cannot be set higher than 300 per hour in deference to the two workers who find the standard a bit onerous (as shown by Burke's and Donovan's performance in Table 19.1, only 2 percent above the 300 minimum). But the question of why the same standard should be set for all workers can be answered only in terms of the interactions of workers among themselves and also with the firm. It is precisely in such terms that the next section poses the solution to the cash poster mystery.

Other potential objections such as the nonobservability of output and risk aversion by workers can be all but ruled out. Workers kept records of their outputs so output was easily observable; and the workers did not work faster than the minimum out of fear of being sacked for falling below the minimum;

---

[2]The argument is just a bit subtle. If a worker with convex utility and positive marginal product for effort has a positive utility for wage income and zero disutility for added effort, the firm can increase his compensation and force him to work harder, to the advantage of both. If the worker was satisfied with his job before this additional trade, he will be even more satisfied afterwards and therefore less willing to quit.

as already mentioned, falling below the minimum occasioned no more than mild rebuke.

An explanation for either the firm's behavior of the workers' behavior must depend either on maximization of something other than profits by the firm or on interaction of the workers with each other and with the firm that alters their utility functions. It is to such a theory that we now turn.

III. Sociological explanation of cash posters' – eastern utilities' behavior

The previous section showed behavior by the cash posters inconsistent with a simple neoclassical theory of worker utility maximization and firm profit maximization. I do not doubt that there is some neoclassical model involving turnover costs or difficulty of observation[3] which can explain the behavior of the firm and the cash posters, but given the failure of the simple model, the adequate model must of necessity be complicated. In contrast, this section presents a simple sociological explanation of the joint behavior of the cash posters and the Eastern Utilities Company.

According to a prominent school of sociological thought, the determinant of workers' effort is the norm of the work group. According to Elton Mayo (1949, p. 70), referring to the famous studies at the Hawthorne plant in the Bank Wiring Observation Room, "the working group as a whole actually determined the output of individual workers by reference to a standard, predetermined but clearly stated, that represented the group's conception of a fair day's work. The standard was rarely, if ever, in accord with the standards of the efficiency engineers."

According to an alternative, but equivalent, view of the cash posters' performance, they give a *gift* to the firm of work in excess of the minimum work required of 300 per hour. Offhand, it may seem absurd to view the workers as giving the firm a gift of any part of his work. Of course, the worker does not strictly give his labor as a gift to the firm; he expects a wage in return and, if not paid, will almost certainly sue in court. Likewise, the firm does not give the wage strictly as a gift. If the worker consistently fails to meet certain minimum standards, he will almost surely be dismissed. But above these minimum standards the worker's performance is freely determined. The norm (or "standard" as Mayo termed it) for the proper work effort is quite like the norm that determines the standards for gift giving at Christmas. Such gift giving is a trading relationship – in the sense that if one side of the exchange

---

[3]For an interesting explanation of unemployment due to imperfect information, see Stoft (1980). Solow (1980) supports the view that involuntary unemployment must be explained by sociological models of behavior.

does not live up to expectations, the other side is also likely to curtail its activities.

The classic anthropological literature on the gift, particularly the essay by Marcel Mauss (1954), emphasizes this reciprocal nature of gift giving.[4] Mauss points out that, in the two major branches of Western European languages, the root for *poison* is the same as the root for *gift,* since in ancient German the word *gift* means both gift and poison, and the Greek word δόσισ for poison, which is the root of the English *dose,* has the same root as the Greek word to *give.* The reason for the close association of the words for *gift* and *poison* in these ancient languages comes from the obligatory nature of reciprocity of a gift, or, equivalently, the threat of harm that was believed to befall a recipient who failed to reciprocate. Although the magic has gone out of the sanctions behind repayment of most gifts, there are probably few in modern times who have never received a gift they did not want or who have not given a gift they considered to be inadequately appreciated.[5]

Why should there be any portion of labor that is given as a gift by the firm or of treatment of the worker by the firm that can be considered a gift? The answer to this question is at once trivial and profound. Persons who work for an institution (a firm in this case) tend to develop sentiment for their co-workers and for that institution; to a great extent they anthropomorphize these institutions (e.g., "the friendly bank"). For the same reasons that persons (brothers, for example) share gifts as showing sentiment for each other, it is natural that persons have utility for making gifts to institutions for which they have sentiment. Furthermore, if workers have an interest in the welfare of their co-workers, they gain utility if the firm relaxes pressure on the workers who are hard pressed; in return for reducing such pressure, better workers are often willing to work harder.

The giving of gifts is almost always determined by norms of behavior. In most cases the gift given is approximately in the range of what the recipient expects, and he reciprocates in kind. The norms of gift giving are determined by the relationship between the parties; thus, for example, it is expected that an increase in workers' productivity will be rewarded by increased wages to the workers. Much of union wage negotiations concerns the question of what constitutes a *fair* wage. To an economist who believes that wages are market

---

[4]A good, although not recent, review of the anthropology and sociology of gift exchange is Belshaw (1965). See also Titmuss (1971).

[5]It has been suggested to me by one referee that the analysis of labor contracts as partial gift exchange relates to the Freeman–Medoff argument (1979) on trade unions as collective voice. Reciprocal gift giving induces union formation because discontented workers find it more difficult to quit and find another job with gift giving than without. As in Mauss's analysis it is suggested that reciprocal giving, i.e., mutual benevolence and dependence, go together with mutual hostility and militancy.

clearing or only determined by the relative bargaining power of the contractual parties, long discussions about the "fair wage" should have no bearing on the final settlement. But this notion neglects the fact that the average worker works harder than necessary according to the firm's work rules, and in return for this donation of goodwill and effort, he expects a fair wage from the firm.

This view of wages-effort as mutually reciprocal *gifts* leaves several unanswered questions. The firm decides not only work rules but also wages for each and every worker. Why should not Eastern Utilities set high standards of minimum effort and terminate all workers who are not capable of meeting or who are not willing to meet that standard (for example, Burke and Donovan in Table 19.1)? Again there is a simple answer. In working together, workers acquire sentiment for each other. An increase in minimum standards that would put pressure on Burke and Donovan might easily be considered by the group as a whole as failure by the firm to reciprocate the group's collective donation of productivity 17.7 percent in excess of the minimum requirements. Indeed, although the details are unclear in Homans' account, there is indication that such a situation had arisen with respect to the cash posters. As Homans reports, "a couple of years before, when relations between the posters and a former division head were strained, there may have been some restriction on output."

In a different context, that of a soldier in basic training in World War II, it is revealed most clearly why better workers come to the aid of their fellows:

If one is so favored by nature or training that he gets much more done, or done better, than his neighbor, he shows up that neighbor. The neighbor then gets rebukes or extra work. One cannot do this to any decent fellow who is trying his best, especially when you have to live side by side with him and watch his difficulties and sufferings. Therefore, the superior person – if he has any heart at all and if he is sensitive to the attitudes of his barracks mates – will help his less able neighbor to get along (Stouffer et al., 1949, vol. 2, p. 414).

Of course the cash posters were working under less extreme conditions. Nevertheless, they undoubtedly could have expressed their own reasons for helping each other in similar terms.

I have indicated the nature of the trade between firms and workers that is exemplified in the case study of the cash posters and that gives a consistent and plausible explanation for the behavior of both the firm and the workers; this explanation tells why workers exceed the minimum standards of work on the one hand, and why the firm does not raise these minimum standards on the other hand. But work standards are only one dimension of the treatment of workers. Another dimension is wages. For reasons similar to why minimum work standards are not necessarily set at the limit that workers will bear before leaving the firm, the optimal contract may not set wages at the minimum acceptable: if part of worker effort is a *gift,* likewise, part of wages paid should be a *gift.*

IV. Reference groups

With the cash posters (or any other work group whose effort is determined not by the work rules but by the group's norms) the question arises: What does the group receive in return for working more than prescribed by the work rules? In the first place, the worker may receive leniency in the work rules. Even if the worker habitually works at a speed in excess of work rules, he still benefits from leniency in two ways. First, he derives positive utility from the *gift* by the firm of potential leniency should he slacken his pace; second, as already mentioned, if he has sympathy for other members of the work group, he derives utility from the firm's generous treatment of other members of the group for whom the work rules are a binding constraint. Additionally, the firm may give remuneration in excess of that needed to obtain another worker of similar skills. Thus, excess remuneration and leniency of work rules constitute the major gifts by the firm to its workers.

Presumably, the gift of the worker to the firm, effort in excess of the work rules, is linked to the gift of the firm to the worker. Following Mauss and others, reciprocity is a major feature of gift exchange (as also of market exchange).

The quid pro quo in gift exchange is, however, established at least slightly differently from market exchange. The norms for effort are established according to the conception of a fair day's work. (Note that Mayo described the work standard in precisely those terms.) In return, the workers expect to be treated "fairly" by the firm. The conception of fair treatment has been the subject of considerable work by social psychologists and sociologists. For the most part it is not based on absolute standards but, rather, on comparison of one's own situation with that of other persons.

According to Festinger (1954), persons have an innate psychological need to compare their actions and treatment with those of others. Persons use comparison with others as a guide to how they ought to behave or how they ought to be treated. The point should be clear to any parent with a young child. Consider the young child who has fallen but not hurt himself/herself. Such situations usually produce that momentary pause before the child decides whether she/he should cry. If the surrounding adults act as if the situation calls for crying, the child is likely to behave accordingly; however, if adults act as if she/he should not cry, the child is likely not to do so. In the context of this paper I wish to note that the child's behavior is not determined by the real phenomenon of being hurt, but rather by the social definition of the

284

situation given by the norms of the surrounding adults. In this way the child calibrates his/her actions by the social standards set by others.

How do people decide that they are fairly treated? There is no natural measure (just as there is no natural language). Merton (1957) has constructed a theory of how people determine the fairness of their treatment by reference to the treatment of reference individuals and treatment of reference groups.

. . .

V. The fair wage

The gift of the firm to the worker (in return for the worker's gift of hard work for the firm) consists in part of a wage that is fair in terms of the norms of this gift giving. Using reference-individual–reference-group theory, the fairness of this wage depends on how other persons in the worker's reference set are similarly treated. Although persons do sometimes have reference groups, or reference individuals, who are dissimilar (Hyman, 1942), in matters of fairness it is probably safe to suppose that most persons compare themselves to persons who are *similar*. In that case, one argument of the perceived fairness of the wage will be the wages received by other similar workers. Such workers, of course, include workers who are employed; but, in addition, it includes workers in the reference set who are unemployed. While empirically unemployment at any moment is a fairly small fraction of the labor force, flows in and out of unemployment are large, and most workers have many friends and close relatives. The probability that a whole reference set be free of unemployment for a significant period (say a year) is not large for most persons.

There is one other argument to the reference wage. To the psychologist or sociologist, to say that persons compare their own behavior or treatment with that in the past is probably neither useful nor profound. But persons certainly do that, and some economic theory (for example, the Modigliani–Duesenberry peak income hypothesis) does depend on such behavior. Thus, one additional argument to the reference wage, in addition to the remuneration of similar employed and unemployed persons and their respective weights in the reference set, is past wages.

Consistent with this observation is the role of past wages in all labor negotiations. Labor disputes often concern the level of past wages, which are the benchmark for current negotiations. To cite a case in point, consider the General Motors strike of 1970. In the 1967–70 contract, wages were indexed, but an eight-cent-per-hour limit was placed on raises due to increases in the cost of living. The cost of living increased relative to wages by considerably more than eight cents per hour with a resultant level of wages twenty-six cents below the fully indexed level (Pearlstine, 1970). The union claimed that the corporation had already received a windfall gain for the three years of the contract during which period wages were not fully indexed, and the negotiations should concern growth of the real wage from the fully indexed level; the company claimed negotiations should concern growth from the actual 1970 level. This matter was the most contentious issue in the settlement of a long strike.

Summing up all our discussion of the fair wage, the fair wage received by the worker depends on the effort he expends in excess of the work rules, the work rules themselves, the wages of other workers, the benefits of unemployed workers, as well as the number of such workers, and the worker's wages received in previous periods.

. . .

VII. Two examples

According to the standard neoclassical model of the labor market, the firm purchases labor services in an optimal amount, *given the market wage*. This statement does not completely describe the firm's choice set, although in the *neoclassical* model the inaccuracy is of no importance. The neoclassical firm can purchase all the labor services it wishes if it pays a wage *at least as great as* the market wage. The firm chooses the wage and its purchases of labor services subject to this constraint. If the firm chooses a wage below the market-clearing level, it receives no labor. As far as its choice is concerned, it would be making the same decision if it demanded no labor and paid the market wage; and there is no advantage to choosing a wage in excess of the market rate. The firm's choice of wage therefore is always at the boundary: it will choose the optimal quantity of labor at the market-clearing wage.

However, once labor contracts are viewed in the context of gift exchange, it is not necessarily true that the firm will always choose wages on the boundary. In gift exchange the usual norm is that gifts should be more than the minimum required to keep the other party in the exchange relationship. In terms of the labor market this means that the worker who does no more than necessary to keep his job is the subject of at least some slight loss of reputation; reciprocally, the firm that pays its workers no more than the minimum necessary to retain them will also lose some reputation. In the neoclassical model the firm *never* chooses to pay more than the market-clearing wage because there is no advantage to doing so. In the gift-exchange model, however, the interior solution, in which the firm finds it advantageous to pay a wage in excess of the one at which it can acquire labor, may occur because there are some benefits (as well as costs) from paying a higher wage. Doubtless, this interior solution need not occur. Where it does occur, the labor market is primary. A worker entering the labor market will not automatically find work at the wage received by equally qualified employed persons. If the boundary solution occurs, in contrast, the labor market clears; the market is secondary, and a person in that market can readily obtain work at the wage received by current employees of similar qualifications.

The purpose of this section is to demonstrate by two specific examples the characteristics of the labor market in which gift exchange occurs in the sense that the workers' norm for effort depends upon their treatment by the firm. One example assumes that the firm's work rules are fixed, and with this assumption the equilibrium wage and unemployment are derived. The second example assumes that the real wage is fixed and demonstrates that work rules do not equilibrate supply and demand for labor in the sociological model (with norms) as they do in the neoclassical model. This model is specifically constructed with the behavior of the cash posters in mind.

· · ·

VIII. Conclusion

This paper has explored the idea that labor contracts are partial gift exchanges. According to this idea, at least in part, wages are determined by, and in turn also influence, the norms of workers' effort; similarly, workers' effort is determined, at least in part, by these norms. A relation between the terms of exchange and norms is in our view what differentiates gift exchange from pure market exchange.

Indeed, while the norms may be greatly influenced by the same things as market prices, there is still a major difference between pure market exchange and gift exchange. In pure market exchange the maximum price at which a buyer is willing to purchase a commodity or factor service is the minimum at which the respective commodity or factor service is obtainable. Obversely, the minimum price at which a seller is willing to sell a commodity or factor service is the maximum at which the respective commodity or factor service can be sold. In gift exchange, buyers may be willing to pay more than the minimum at which they can purchase a commodity or factor service because of the effect of the terms of exchange on the norms. Similarly, sellers may be willing to accept less than the maximum at which they can sell a commodity or factor service because of the effects of the terms of exchange on the norms. It has been shown that due to this behavior with gift exchange, markets need not clear. Thus, the gift-exchange economy and the neoclassical economy differ in at least one fundamental respect. Future papers will explore further differences between the two models of exchange.

287

CHAPTER 20

Profit sharing and productivity

MARTIN WEITZMAN AND
DOUGLAS KRUSE

Martin Weitzman was born in 1942 in New York City. He received a
Ph.D. in economics at Massachusetts Institute of Technology in 1967.
When the paper from which this chapter is excerpted was published, he
was Ernest E. Monrad Professor of Economics at Harvard University, a
position he continues to occupy.

Douglas Kruse was born in Kearney, Nebraska, in 1959. He received a
Ph.D. in economics from Harvard University in 1988. At the time of
publication of this chapter, he was assistant professor at the Institute of
Management and Labor Relations at Rutgers University, where he is
now Associate Professor.

Recently there has been a strong growth of interest in profit sharing and
related forms of pay for group performance. Many reasons undoubtedly exist
for this heightened attention. The primary motive probably has to do with the
perception that by giving workers a partial stake in their company's performance, profit sharing may, under certain circumstances, lead to desirable
outcomes that ultimately increase productivity. If this perception contains an
element of truth, widespread profit sharing might conceivably improve national "competitiveness," with consequent policy implications. In such a context, but also for more general reasons, it becomes important to sort out and
evaluate as systematically as possible the evidence on a possible link between
profit sharing and productivity.

   The purpose of this paper is to bring together the partial strands of eclectic
evidence from a wide variety of fields and perspectives, including considerations of economic theory.

. . .

In general, economic theory can provide a powerful organizing framework for
thinking consistently about certain economic issues. And it often suggests the
outlines of an answer to some specific question. But pure theory rarely pro-

Excerpted from Martin Weitzman and Douglas Kruse, "Profit Sharing and Productivity,"
pp. 95–114 in Alan Blinder, ed., *Paying for Productivity*, Washington, D.C.: The Brookings
Institution by permission of the publisher.

vides a definitive answer. Every model has a countermodel, and judgments about which models apply to which situations are ultimately empirical. The particular issue under examination here – the relation between profit sharing and productivity – is no exception to this generalization. The subject involves a particularly complicated interplay of economic and other motivations that rubs awkwardly against the confines of conventional theorizing. Nevertheless, we think that economic theory can be used here both to frame the main theoretical issues and to offer some explanatory power. We begin with the simplest conventional model and work our way up to more complicated contemporary models that incorporate increasingly sophisticated considerations. Throughout, the emphasis is on talking through a particular application – what the models might say about the real world connection between profit sharing and productivity – not on modeling per se.

The prototype

The simple one-person case is what most people have in mind as the prototype of the advantages of profit sharing. It illustrates nicely many of the principal issues and can serve as a point of departure for more sophisticated models.

Suppose that a person produces a single output from a single input according to some well-defined production function. The input is most easily thought of as a generic combination of hours of work and effort. The hours part of labor input can be measured, but the effort part largely cannot be. Effort might stand for all sorts of unobservable things like working harder, working smarter, taking initiative, and taking advantage of unforeseen opportunities of time and place. Individual small-scale farming might be a good example of this kind of paradigm, but there are many others.

A "wage system" in the present context would pay the hired farmer-worker a fixed wage in return for a fixed number of hours of labor. The fixed hours, in conjunction with a certain verifiable level of effort set by implicit or explicit standards, would yield some level of output. Unfortunately, there is no guarantee that this output level is efficient. In particular, with effort both unpleasurable and difficult or otherwise costly to monitor (at least beyond a certain point), the wage system would result in too little output being produced relative to what is socially optimal. In other words, a wage system tends to result in low productivity equilibria, where the marginal value of an extra unit of effort exceeds its marginal cost.

The obvious solution is to pay the hired farmer the value of his output over some fixed amount accounting for economic rent. This kind of profit sharing will automatically guarantee an efficient outcome, where the marginal value of an extra unit of output is equal to the marginal effort-cost of producing it.

When the farmer-worker is paid for what he produces, he will automatically adjust his effort to the optimal degree. Here, then, a switch from a wage system to a profit-sharing system would increase productivity.

Such a simple example of a farmer-worker is what most people have in mind when they assume that a profit-sharing system can be expected to increase productivity relative to a wage system. Common sense tells them that a worker will work harder and produce more output under profit sharing than under a rigid wage system because he or she has some stake in the outcome. Even though the basic message of this example can be diluted by more sophisticated formulations, a germ of truth remains. The key insight is that under profit sharing, high productivity is rewarded with more pay, so there tends to be *some* pressure to move toward modes of behavior that increase output.

As applied to an individual farmer-worker, the proposition that profit sharing increases productivity is one of the more spectacular examples of simple theory giving an essentially correct insight that is confirmed by experience. One may fairly generalize that throughout the world, other things being equal, agriculture run on a decentralized "responsibility system" with rewards directly linked to output is more efficient than agriculture run on a centralized, labor-for-hire type system with rewards far removed from performance.[1]

This simple model, however, omits certain aspects of reality. In the next three subsections we treat what we consider to be the three most important deviations from the basic model. These are: the free-rider problem of individual incentives that become diluted in a group setting where rewards are linked to group effort, risk-bearing issues associated with profit sharing that expose workers to an unacceptable degree of pay variation, and the possible weakening of capitalist property rights under profit sharing through some form of codetermination.

The free rider problem

Some difficult issues are connected with understanding what extension, if any, of the single farmer-worker model applies to a multiworker setting, where profit sharing is naturally tied to group performance. A dilution or free-rider problem seems to arise whenever it is hard to monitor a single person's contribution, as is presumably frequently the case. An externality is present because any one person's reward depends on everyone else's effort. With n members of the group, the extra profit-sharing reward associated with marginal effort on any single worker's part is diluted by a factor of $1/n$. The result is an inefficiently low level of effort, which is lower as n is larger. Following the

---

[1] Of course there are exceptions that prove the rule, such as, perhaps, some aspects of California agribusiness.

logic of the static Nash equilibrium framework, profit sharing might not have very much effect on a large organization, since every member would hold back effort while trying to free ride off the others.

Such a free-rider scenario is often used to argue that group incentives will be ineffective for any reasonably large value of n, and therefore, by default, relatively greater emphasis should be placed on individual incentives. This argument doubtless has some truth. Yet there is an important caveat. In a repeated game setting the conclusions may be quite different.

The profit-sharing "game" is a form of prisoner's dilemma. All members of the collective are potentially better off if everyone works harder. Yet there is always a temptation for any single individual to shirk, because per capita output and the reward of any member of the group will not be much affected when one person's effort is reduced. (Hence the conclusion in a static context that one-shot profit sharing will not have much effect on effort and output.) But when the game is repeated, which corresponds to a long-term relationship among the workers, a much richer set of strategies emerges in the resulting noncooperative "supergame." Depending on the specifics of how the technology of observation and production is molded, workers may punish shirking workers by withholding their own effort or, if feasible, ostracizing the offending antisocial shirkers. In such a setting an enormous number of dynamic equilibrium strategies can exist. Among the equilibria, if the participants' discount rate is sufficiently small, is the cooperative strategy in which all participants choose to work at the socially optimal level. (This is a particular application of the so-called folk theorem of noncooperative game theory.)[2] Thus there is a rigorous sense in which profit sharing *may* defeat the prisoner's dilemma free-rider problem and induce greater productivity in a multiperson setting. By contrast, a rigid wage system does not have a chance to improve productivity, because rewards are independent of effort. With profit sharing, as opposed to a rigid wage system, there are modes of behavior that can make everyone better off, and it may be individually rational to pursue such modes for the long-term benefits they yield.

The theory we have outlined – that repetition allows for the possibility of self-enforcing socially desirable outcomes when rewards are linked to group performance – is not without its problems. Profit sharing *may* induce greater productivity, so that the single farmer-worker model can be extended to groups, but other outcomes like narrowly self-interested shirking are possible as well.

Equilibrium is a state of rest from which no agent has an incentive to deviate, given that all other agents are at equilibrium in the same state of rest.

---

[2]See Fudenberg and Maskin (1986), pp. 533–54. For a readable account of a broad series of related issues, see Axelrod (1984).

When there are multiple equilibria (in this case an uncountable infinity of them), the relevant equilibrium depends on a complex, typically unspecified interaction between the underlying dynamic process and initial conditions. At present, theory does not offer much guidance on which equilibria are more likely to emerge under what conditions. In a way, the theory can be interpreted as highlighting considerations of history, chance, culture, exhortation, institutional detail, and the like.[3]

In the end, repeated game theory delivers a complicated message about the likely effects of profit sharing on productivity in a multiperson organization. It is possible that profit sharing will lead to increased productivity. But it is possible that it will not. The outcome would seem to depend on whether an organization can convince its members that everyone pulling together is essentially a better idea than everyone pulling separately. In some equilibria it may be in my long-term self-interest to pull together because everyone else is pulling together, and if I do not I risk the danger of unraveling the social compact. In some other self-fulfilling equilibria it may not be in my long-term interest to pull together because no one else is pulling together, and I do not think my good behavior is going to influence anyone else.

An attempt to sum up the implications of this particular application of theoretical research to the effect of profit sharing on productivity might go as follows. To some extent the door is open for believing that, by comparison with an unresponsive wage system, a group-based reward system can improve productivity. But it appears to be not enough for management just to install a profit-sharing system and walk out the door. To get the productivity-enhancing effects, something more may be needed – something akin to developing a corporate culture that emphasizes company spirit, promotes group cooperation, encourages social enforcement mechanisms, and so forth.

Risk issues

Another problem with our original farmer-worker model is that it abstracts away from risk. In a deterministic context, linking a worker's pay to his or her output makes good sense because it will encourage the socially optimal degree of effort. But what happens in the presence of uncertainty? Then the correct contract is not so clear. A higher degree of profit sharing relative to the base wage will elicit more effort from the worker but will also expose him to greater risk. Sometimes this risk-exposure argument is put forth as if it were a compelling reason that workers should be paid only base wages without any profit shares. But on closer examination, the argument is not decisive.

[3]For related interpretations, see Kreps (1984) and Roy Radner (1986).

This set of issues has been extensively examined in the theoretical literature under the heading of the so-called principal–agent problem.[4] In the present setting the agent is the farmer-worker, while the principal is the hiring party who is ultimately interested in output. On the one hand, an efficient contract should link the agent's reward closely to output because that will elicit greater, or more attentive, work effort. On the other hand, in a world of uncertainty the agent's pay should be made relatively stable, because the agent is typically more averse to risk than the principal. (A company can diversify risks more easily than a worker, whose pay constitutes the main component of his income portfolio.) The optimal contract balances these two opposing considerations of effort and exposure to risk.

The theory can be used to derive a formula for the optimal mix of base wage and profit share.[5] The formula for the optimal profit share is typically a complicated function inversely related to the degree of risk aversion or the amount of uncertainty and directly related to the elasticity response of output to increased effort. Explicit modeling of risk considerations does not, per se, eliminate the argument for profit sharing, though it probably lowers the degree of profit sharing in the optimal pay formula (from 100 percent) to soften the exposure to risk. More important, the theory shows that under standard assumptions it is quite difficult to derive a corner solution where the efficient pay contract involves only straight wages and no profit sharing.

An additional consideration in any analysis of the risk aspect of a profit-sharing contract is the effect on employment. Standard principal–agent theory evades this issue. The theory is, in essence, about the individual high-seniority worker who already has job tenure, not about the aggregate of all would-be workers. In a world of sticky pay parameters, profit sharing may help to reduce employment fluctuations. If that is so – and this interpretation is controversial – the argument for profit sharing might be somewhat stronger than what is suggested by standard principal–agent theory.[6]

. . .

Codetermination issues

The repeated prisoner's dilemma argument previously outlined shows that, other things being equal, profit sharing may improve effort and productivity despite a dilution or free-rider problem. In effect, it may be in the self-interest of each member of the work collective to act over time like one artificially

---

[4]For a survey see Hart and Holmstrom (1987) and the references cited here.
[5]See, for example, Weitzman (1980).
[6]For an advocate's argument of this case, see Weitzman (1984) and Weitzman (1986). See Kruse (1988) for some empirical evidence in favor of this interpretation.

aggregated worker and therefore to work harder under profit sharing. However, this argument neglects one potentially significant element.

If workers share more profits, then capitalists of necessity share less. One must therefore worry about whether diluting the capitalists' incentives might not weaken or fatally compromise their motivation, discretion, power, or authority. For example, increased worker profit sharing may lead to increased worker demands for codetermination in enterprise decision making.

The theoretical arguments, pro and con, on this set of issues are complex because the applicable models are usually concerned only with partial aspects, and in any event they are not fully developed. A complete model would be very messy, technically, including as it should considerations of information, monitoring, supervision, dynamic gaming, risk sharing, insider versus outsider workers, and many other issues. At present, economists do not fully understand on a theoretical level the possible connection between increased worker profit sharing and increased codetermination in enterprise decision making.

At a practical level, the connection between profit sharing and codetermination is also poorly understood. There are many examples of profit sharing without codetermination. Indeed, that would appear to be the typical pattern in the United States. It seems possible to believe that some profit sharing is basically productive, whereas the more extreme forms of European-style legislated codetermination are essentially counterproductive. Thus we are admittedly on uncomfortable ground in this paper when we try to concentrate on profit sharing per se while blurring the already murky boundary with issues of worker control.[7] The critiques and defenses that have arisen are really of worker management rather than of profit sharing per se. No one, so far as we can tell, has attempted to disentangle the two issues carefully.

In the extreme case of perfectly costless monitoring and supervision, an efficient outcome requires that management be given all the residual claims on profits and all decision making power. This basic insight underlies the claims of some members of the "property rights" school that profit sharing, insofar as it involves worker management, is likely to be inefficient because it diverts vesting of property rights from the capitalist central monitors to individualistically oriented workers whose motivation is diluted by the free-rider problem.[8] In this view, profit sharing would be associated with lower productivity because of more shirking, increased enjoyment of on-the-job leisure, slowed or incorrect managerial decisions, a too-short time horizon, an excessively risk-averse attitude due to a nondiversified pay portfolio, and the like. Although there are many variations, the basic theme of the critique of codeter-

[7]For more on the latter, see Levine and Tyson (1990).
[8]See Alchian and Demsetz (1972) and Jensen and Meckling (1979).

mination by the property rights school revolves around the idea that (1) the essence of the firm concerns monitoring because otherwise labor does not work well, (2) capital can effectively monitor labor, and, therefore, (3) efficiency requires that capital be given all residual claims on profits and all decision-making power.

The defense of profit sharing and worker participation largely involves challenging the basic assumptions of the property rights school.[9] In less extreme settings than perfectly costless monitoring and supervision, finding the optimal degree of profit sharing becomes an extraordinarily complicated problem in the theory of the second or third best. Some profit sharing may be desirable in a world where workers can sometimes monitor, supervise, and motivate each other more effectively than management can, or where workers are able to provide technical information to management that would otherwise be costly or time consuming to obtain. For what it is worth, the popular literature is full of talk about the importance of corporate culture, cooperative work environments, team spirit, peer pressure, and the like.[10] Proponents of profit sharing and worker participation stress the potential for improved channels of information processing, better conflict resolution, greater possibilities for acquiring on-the-job human capital from other workers, a more positive attitude toward the introduction of new technology, and other good things.

This survey of the worker control issue is a necessarily brief review of some subtle and complicated arguments, whose connection with profit sharing is poorly understood.[11] The main element of the debate seems to center on the appropriate model of monitoring, supervision, and incentives to shirk. Explicit consideration of property rights does not, per se, eliminate the argument for profit sharing, though it may well affect one's view of the optimal degree of profit sharing. We think the appropriate application of the theory of property rights indicates that quite extreme assumptions are needed to derive a corner solution in which the efficient pay contract would consist entirely of base wages, with zero profit sharing. In that sense our conclusions are analogous to those we drew from the principal–agency theory.

Summary

One could go further in applying modern economic theory to analyze the likely effect of profit sharing on productivity but we believe the main themes have been covered.

If we take all considerations into account, what does contemporary economic theory say about the relation between profit sharing and productivity?

[9]For well-developed arguments see, for example, Putterman (1984) and Nalbantian (1987).
[10]See, for example, O'Dell and McAdams (1987) and Kanter (1987).
[11]For more detail see the works cited in notes 8 and 9.

The message is complicated and incomplete. Certainly theory does not rule out the possibility that, even in a multiperson context, profit sharing may increase productivity. Whether this happens may depend largely on historical and institutional factors in the workplace. On balance, the theoretical considerations point more toward a positive than a negative effect of profit sharing on productivity. When all relevant considerations are factored in, it seems unlikely that a corner solution consisting of all base wages and zero profit sharing can be an efficient contract. Such an extreme outcome would have a probability measure close to zero, given reasonable probability distributions on underlying model parameters. Although we are far from being able to give an operational formula for the optimal degree of profit sharing, on theoretical grounds alone a value of exactly zero seems implausible. We think that, taken as a whole, economic theory is suggesting the plausible existence of a positive relation between some modest degree of profit sharing and some modest degree of productivity enhancement. But, as usual, theory gives us few hints about quantitative magnitudes.

. . .

PART IV

Finance and the control
of the firm

CHAPTER 21

Mergers and the market for corporate control

HENRY MANNE

Henry Manne was born in 1928 in New Orleans, Louisiana. He received a J.D. at the University of Chicago in 1952 and a J.S.D. at Yale University in 1966. He was Professor at George Washington University Law School when this paper was published. In 1986, he became Dean of the School of Law and University Professor at George Mason University.

The corporate-control market

The conventional approach to a merger problem takes corporations merely as decision-making units or firms within the classical market framework. This approach dictates a ban on many horizontal mergers almost by definition. The basic proposition advanced in this paper is that the control of corporations may constitute a valuable asset, that this asset exists independent of any interest in either economies of scale or monopoly profits, that an active market for corporate control exists, and that a great many mergers are probably the result of the successful workings of this special market.

Basically this paper will constitute an introduction to a study of the market for corporation control. The emphasis will be placed on the antitrust implications of this market, but the analysis to follow has important implications for a variety of economic questions. Perhaps the most important implications are those for the alleged separation of ownership and control in large corporations. So long as we are unable to discern any control relationship between small shareholders and corporate management, the thrust of Berle and Means's famous phrase remains strong. But, as will be explained below, the market for corporate control gives to these shareholders both power and protection commensurate with their interest in corporate affairs.

A fundamental premise underlying the market for corporate control is the existence of a high positive correlation between corporate managerial efficien-

Excerpted from Henry Manne, "Mergers and the Market for Corporate Control," *Journal of Political Economy,* 73 (1965): 110–20. Copyright © 1965. Reprinted with the permission of the University of Chicago Press.

cy and the market price of shares of that company.[1] As an existing company is poorly managed – in the sense of not making as great a return for the shareholders as could be accomplished under other feasible managements – the market price of the shares declines relative to the shares of other companies in the same industry or relative to the market as a whole. This phenomenon has a dual importance for the market for corporate control.

In the first place, a lower share price facilitates any effort to take over high-paying managerial positions. The compensation from these positions may take the usual forms of salary, bonuses, pensions, expense accounts, and stock options. Perhaps more important, it may take the form of information useful in trading in the company's shares; or, if that is illegal, information may be exchanged and the trading done in other companies' shares. But it is extremely doubtful that the full compensation recoverable by executives for managing their corporations explains more than a small fraction of outsider[2] attempts to take over control. Takeovers of corporations are too expensive generally to make the "purchase" of management compensation an attractive proposition.[3]

It is far more likely that a second kind of reward provides the primary motivation for most takeover attempts. The market price of shares does more than measure the price at which the normal compensation of executives can be "sold" to new individuals. Share price, or that part reflecting managerial efficiency, also measures the potential capital gain inherent in the corporate stock. The lower the stock price, relative to what it could be with more

[1]The claim of a positive correlation between managerial efficiency and the market price of shares would seem at first blush to raise an empirical question. In fact, however, the concept of corporate managerial efficiency, with its overtones of an entrepreneurial function, is one for which there are no objective standards. But there are compelling reasons, apart from empirical data, for believing that this correlation exists. Insiders, those who have the most reliable information about corporate affairs, are strongly motivated financially to perform a kind of arbitrage function for their company's stock. That is, given their sense of what constitutes efficient management, they will cause share prices to rise or decline in accordance with that standard. The contention is often made that stock-market prices are not accurate gauges, since far more trades take place without reliable information than with it. But there is reason to believe that intelligence rather than ignorance ultimately determines the course of individual share prices. Stock-market decisions tend to be of the one-out-of-two-alternatives variety, such as buy or not buy, hold or sell, or put or call. To the extent that decisions on these questions are made by shareholders or potential shareholders operating without reliable information, over a period of time the decisions will tend to be randomly distributed and the effect will therefore be neutral. Decisions made by those with a higher degree of certainty will to that extent not meet a canceling effect since they will not be made on a random basis. Over some period of time it would seem that the average market price of a company's shares must be the "correct" one.

[2]"Outsider" here refers to anyone not presently controlling the affairs of the corporation, even though it may include one or more individuals on the corporation's board of directors.

[3]To the extent that executive compensation increases with higher share prices, the takeover is most attractive at the time when it is also most expensive. Indeed, the danger of a takeover may account for managers' voluntarily decreasing their compensation when the company's share price is down.

efficient management, the more attractive the takeover becomes to those who believe that they can manage the company more efficiently. And the potential return from the successful takeover and revitalization of a poorly run company can be enormous.

Additional leverage in this operation can be obtained by borrowing the funds with which the shares are purchased, although American commercial banks are generally forbidden to lend money for this purpose. A comparable advantage can be had from using other shares rather than cash as the exchange medium. Given the fact of special tax treatment for capital gains, we can see how this mechanism for taking over control of badly run corporations is one of the most important "get rich quick" opportunities in our economy today.

But the greatest benefits of the takeover scheme probably inure to those least conscious of it. Apart from the stock market, we have no objective standard of managerial efficiency. Courts, as indicated by the so-called business-judgment rule, are loath to second-guess business decisions or re-move directors from office. Only the takeover scheme provides some assurance of competitive efficiency among corporate managers and thereby affords strong protection to the interests of vast numbers of small, noncontrolling shareholders. Compared to this mechanism, the efforts of the SEC and the courts to protect shareholders through the development of a fiduciary duty concept and the shareholder's derivative suit seem small indeed. It is true that sales by dissatisfied shareholders are necessary to trigger the mechanism and that these shareholders may suffer considerable losses. On the other hand, even greater capital losses are prevented by the existence of a competitive market for control.[4]

. . .

[4]Unfortunately the suppression of this market would be the consequence of proposals made by several writers in the field. For a review and a criticism of this literature see Henry G. Manne, (1962), 399–432. For another defense of this market see Harry G. Johnson (1963), pp. xvii–xviii.

CHAPTER 22

Agency problems and the theory
of the firm

EUGENE FAMA

Eugene Fama was born in 1939 in Boston, Massachusetts. He received
a Ph.D. in business from the University of Chicago in 1964. When this
paper was published, he was Theodore O. Yntema Professor of Finance
in the Graduate School of Business at the University of Chicago. He is
currently Robert R. McCormick Distinguished Service Professor of
Finance in the same school.

Economists have long been concerned with the incentive problems that arise
when decision making in a firm is the province of managers who are not the
firm's security holders.[1] One outcome has been the development of "behavioral" and "managerial" theories of the firm which reject the classical model
of an entrepreneur, or owner-manager, who single-mindedly operates the firm
to maximize profits, in favor of theories that focus more on the motivations of
a manager who controls but does not own and who has little resemblance to
the classical "economic man." Examples of this approach are Baumol (1959),
Simon (1959), Cyert and March (1963), and Williamson (1964b).

More recently the literature has moved toward theories that reject the classical model of the firm but assume classical forms of economic behavior on the
part of agents within the firm. The firm is viewed as a set of contracts among
factors of production, with each factor motivated by its self-interest. Because
of its emphasis on the importance of rights in the organization established by
contracts, this literature is characterized under the rubric "property rights."
Alchian and Demsetz (1972) and Jensen and Meckling (1976b) are the best
examples. The antecedents of their work are in Coase (1937, 1960).

The striking insight of Alchian and Demsetz (1972) and Jensen and Meckling (1976b) is in viewing the firm as a set of contracts among factors of
production. In effect, the firm is viewed as a team whose members act from
self-interest but realize that their destinies depend to some extent on the
survival of the team in its competition with other teams. This insight, however, is not carried far enough. In the classical theory, the agent who personi-

Reprinted with abridgements from Eugene Fama, "Agency Problems and the Theory of the
Firm," *Journal of Political Economy*, 88 (1980): 288–307. Copyright © 1980. Reprinted with
the permission of the University of Chicago Press.
[1]Jensen and Meckling (1967b) quote from Adam Smith (1776). The modern literature on the
problem dates back at least to Berle and Means (1932).

fies the firm is the entrepreneur who is taken to be both manager and residual risk bearer. Although his title sometimes changes – for example, Alchian and Demsetz call him "the employer" – the entrepreneur continues to play a central role in the firm of the property rights literature. As a consequence, this literature fails to explain the large modern corporation in which control of the firms is in the hands of managers who are more or less separate from the firm's security holders.

The main thesis of this paper is that separation of security ownership and control can be explained as an efficient form of economic organization within the "set of contracts" perspective. We first set aside the typical presumption that a corporation has owners in any meaningful sense. The attractive concept of the entrepreneur is also laid to rest, at least for the purposes of the large modern corporation. Instead, the two functions usually attributed to the entrepreneur, management and risk bearing, are treated as naturally separate factors within the set of contracts called a firm. The firm is disciplined by competition from other firms, which forces the evolution of devices for efficiently monitoring the performance of the entire team and of its individual members. In addition, individual participants in the firm, and in particular its managers, face both the discipline and opportunities provided by the markets for their services, both within and outside of the firm.

The irrelevance of the concept of ownership of the firm

To set a framework for the analysis, let us first describe roles for management and risk bearing in the set of contracts called a firm. Management is a type of labor but with a special role – coordinating the activities of inputs and carrying out the contracts agreed among inputs, all of which can be characterized as "decision making." To explain the role of the risk bearers, assume for the moment that the firm rents all other factors of production and that rental contracts are negotiated at the beginning of each production period with payoffs at the end of the period. The risk bearers then contract to accept the uncertain and possibly negative difference between total revenues and costs at the end of each production period.

When other factors of production are paid at the end of each period, it is not necessary for the risk bearers to invest anything in the firm at the beginning of the period. Most commonly, however, the risk bearers guarantee performance of their contracts by putting up wealth *ex ante,* with this front money used to purchase capital and perhaps also the technology that the firm uses in its production activities. In this way the risk-bearing function is combined with ownership of capital and technology. We also commonly observe that the joint functions of risk bearing and ownership of capital are repackaged and sold in different proportions to different groups of investors. For example, when front money is raised by issuing both bonds and common stock, the bonds involve a combination of risk bearing and ownership of capital with a low amount of risk bearing relative to the combination of risk bearing and ownership of capital inherent in the common stock. Unless the bonds are risk free, the risk-bearing function is in part borne by the bondholders, and ownership of capital is shared by bondholders and stockholders.

However, ownership of capital should not be confused with ownership of the firm. Each factor in a firm is owned by somebody. The firm is just the set of contracts covering the way inputs are joined to create outputs and the way receipts from outputs are shared among inputs. In this "nexus of contracts" perspective, ownership of the firm is an irrelevant concept. Dispelling the tenacious notion that a firm is owned by its security holders is important because it is a first step toward understanding that control over a firm's decisions is not necessarily the province of security holders. The second step is setting aside the equally tenacious role in the firm usually attributed to the entrepreneur.

Management and risk bearing: a closer look

The entrepreneur (manager–risk bearer) is central in both the Jensen–Meckling and Alchian–Demsetz analyses of the firm. For example, Alchian–Demsetz state: "The essence of the classical firm is identified here as a contractual structure with: (1) joint input production, (2) several input owners, (3) one party who is common to all the contracts of the joint inputs, (4) who has the right to renegotiate any input's contract independently of contracts with other input owners, (5) who holds the residual claim, and (6) who has the right to sell his central contractual residual status. The central agent is called the firm's owner and the employer" (1972, p. 794).

To understand the modern corporation, it is better to separate the manager, the agents of points 3 and 4 of the Alchian–Demsetz definition of the firm, from the risk bearer described in points 5 and 6. The rationale for separating these functions is not just that the end result is more descriptive of the corporation, a point recognized in both the Alchian–Demsetz and Jensen–Meckling papers. The major loss in retaining the concept of the entrepreneur is that one is prevented from developing a perspective on management and risk bearing as separate factors of production, each faced with a market for its services that provides alternative opportunities and, in the case of management, motivation toward performance.

Thus, any given set of contracts, a particular firm, is in competition with other firms, which are likewise teams of cooperating factors of production. If there is a part of the team that has a special interest in its viability, it is not obviously the risk bearers. It is true that if the team does not prove viable, factors like labor and management are protected by markets in which rights to their future services can be sold or rented to other teams. The risk bearers, as residual claimants, also seem to suffer the most direct consequences from the failings of the team. However, the risk bearers in the modern corporation also have markets for their services – capital markets – which allow them to shift among teams with relatively low transaction costs and to hedge against the failings of any given team by diversifying their holdings across teams.

Indeed, portfolio theory tells us that the optimal portfolio for any investor is likely to be diversified across the securities of many firms.[2] Since he holds the securities of many firms precisely to avoid having his wealth depend too much on any one firm, an individual security holder generally has no special interest in personally overseeing the detailed activities of any firm. In short, efficient allocation of risk bearing seems to imply a large degree of separation of security ownership from control of a firm.

On the other hand, the managers of a firm rent a substantial lump of wealth – their human capital – to the firm, and the rental rates for their human capital signaled by the managerial labor market are likely to depend on the success or failure of the firm. The function of management is to oversee the contracts among factors and to ensure the viability of the firm. For the purposes of the managerial labor market, the previous associations of a manager with success and failure are information about his talents. The manager of a firm, like the coach of any team, may not suffer any immediate gain or loss in current wages from the current performance of his team, but the success or failure of the team impacts his future wages, and this gives the manager a stake in the success of the team.

The firm's security holders provide important but indirect assistance to the managerial labor market in its task of valuing the firm's management. A security holder wants to purchase securities with confidence that the prices paid reflect the risks he is taking and that the securities will be priced in the future to allow him to reap the rewards (or punishments) of his risk bearing. Thus, although an individual security holder may not have a strong interest in directly overseeing the management of a particular firm, he has a strong interest in the existence of a capital market which efficiently prices the firm's securities. The signals provided by an efficient capital market about the values of a firm's securities are likely to be important for the managerial labor market's revaluations of the firm's management.

We come now to the central question. To what extent can the signals

---

[2]Detailed discussions of portfolio models can be found in Fama and Miller (1972, chaps. 6 and 7), Jensen (1972), and Fama (1976, chaps. 7 and 8).

provided by the managerial labor market and the capital market, perhaps along with other market-induced mechanisms, discipline managers? We first discuss, still in general terms, the types of discipline imposed by managerial labor markets, both within and outside of the firm. We then analyze specific conditions under which this discipline is sufficient to resolve potential incentive problems that might be associated with the separation of security ownership and control.

The viability of separation of security ownership and control of the firm: general comments

The outside managerial labor market exerts many direct pressures on the firm to sort and compensate managers according to performance. One form of pressure comes from the fact that an ongoing firm is always in the market for new managers. Potential new managers are concerned with the mechanics by which their performance will be judged, and they seek information about the responsiveness of the system in rewarding performance. Moreover, given a competitive managerial labor market, when the firm's reward system is not responsive to performance the firm loses managers, and the best are the first to leave.

There is also much internal monitoring of managers by managers themselves. Part of the talent of a manager is his ability to elicit and measure the productivity of lower managers, so there is a natural process of monitoring from higher to lower levels of management. Less well appreciated, however, is the monitoring that takes place from bottom to top. Lower managers perceive that they can gain by stepping over shirking or less competent managers above them. Moreover, in the team or nexus of contracts view of the firm, each manager is concerned with the performance of managers above and below him since his marginal product is likely to be a positive function of theirs. Finally, although higher managers are affected more than lower managers, all managers realize that the managerial labor market uses the performance of the firm to determine each manager's outside opportunity wage. In short, each manager has a stake in the performance of the managers above and below him and, as a consequence, undertakes some amount of monitoring in both directions.

All managers below the very top level have an interest in seeing that the top managers choose policies for the firm which provide the most positive signals to the managerial labor market. But by what mechanism can top management be disciplined? Since the body designated for this function is the board of directors, we can ask how it might be constructed to do its job. A board dominated by security holders does not seem optimal or endowed with good survival properties. Diffuse ownership of securities is beneficial in terms of an optimal allocation of risk bearing, but its consequence is that the firm's security holders are generally too diversified across the securities of many firms to take much interest in a particular firm.

If there is competition among the top managers themselves (all want to be the boss of bosses), then perhaps they are the best ones to control the board of directors. They are most directly in the line of fire from lower managers when the markets for securities and managerial labor give poor signals about the performance of the film. Because of their power over the firm's decisions, their market-determined opportunity wages are also likely to be most affected by market signals about the performance of the firm. If they are also in competition for the top places in the firm, they may be the most informed and responsive critics of the firm's performance.

Having gained control of the board, top management may decide that collusion and expropriation of security holder wealth are better than competition among themselves. The probability of such collusive arrangements might be lowered, and the viability of the board as a market-induced mechanism for low-cost internal transfer of control might be enhanced, by the inclusion of outside directors. The latter might best be regarded as professional referees whose task is to stimulate and oversee the competition among the firm's top managers. In a state of advanced evolution of the external markets that buttress the corporate firm, the outside directors are in their turn disciplined by the market for their services which prices them according to their performance as referees. Since such a system of separation of security ownership from control is consistent with the pressures applied by the managerial labor market, and since it likewise operates in the interests of the firm's security holders, it probably has good survival properties.[3]

This analysis does not imply that boards of directors are likely to be composed entirely of managers and outside directors. The board is viewed as a market-induced institution, the ultimate internal monitor of the set of contracts called a firm, whose most important role is to scrutinize the highest decision makers within the firm. In the team or nexus of contracts view of the firm, one cannot rule out the evolution of boards of directors that contain many different factors of production (or their hired representatives), whose common trait is that their marginal products are affected by those of the top decision makers. On the other hand, one also cannot conclude that all such factors will naturally show up on boards since there may be other market-

---

[3]Watts and Zimmerman (1978) provide a similar description of the market-induced evolution of "independent' outside auditors whose function is to certify and, as a consequence, stimulate the viability of the set of contracts called the firm. Like the outside directors, the outside auditors are policed by the market for their services which prices them in large part on the basis of how well they resist perverting the interests of one set of factors (e.g., security holders) to the benefit of other factors (e.g., management). Like the professional outside director, the welfare of the outside auditor depends largely on "reputation."

induced institutions, for example, unions, that more efficiently monitor managers on behalf of specific factors. All one can say is that in a competitive environment lower-cost sets of monitoring mechanisms are likely to survive. The role of the board in this framework is to provide a relatively low-cost mechanism for replacing or reordering top managers; lower cost, for example, than the mechanism provided by an outside takeover, although, of course, the existence of an outside market for control is another force which helps to sensitize the internal managerial labor market.

The perspective suggested here owes much to, but is nevertheless different from, existing treatments of the firm in the property rights literature. Thus, Alchian (1969) and Alchian and Demsetz (1972) comment insightfully on the disciplining of management that takes place through the inside and outside markets for managers. However, they attribute the task of disciplining management primarily to the risk bearers, the firm's security holders, who are assisted to some extent by managerial labor markets and by the possibility of outside takeover. Jensen and Meckling (1976b) likewise make control of management the province of the firm's risk bearers, but they do not allow for any assistance from the managerial labor market. Of all the authors in the property-rights literature, Manne (1965, 1967) is most concerned with the market for corporate control. He recognizes that with diffuse security ownership, management and risk bearing are naturally separate functions. But for him, disciplining management is an "entrepreneurial job" which in the first instance falls on a firm's organizers and later on specialists in the process of outside takeover.

When management and risk bearing are viewed as naturally separate factors of production, looking at the market for risk bearing from the viewpoint of portfolio theory tells us that risk bearers are likely to spread their wealth across many firms and so not to be interested in directly controlling the management of any individual firm. Thus, models of the firm, like those of Alchian–Demsetz and Jensen–Meckling, in which the control of management falls primarily on the risk bearers, are not likely to allay the fears of those concerned with the apparent incentive problems created by the separation of security ownership and control. Likewise, Manne's approach, in which the control of management relies primarily on the expensive mechanism of an outside takeover, offers little comfort. The viability of the large corporation with diffuse security ownership is better explained in terms of a model where the primary disciplining of managers comes through managerial labor markets, both within and outside of the firm, with assistance from the panoply of internal and external monitoring devices that evolve to stimulate the ongoing efficiency of the corporate form, and with the market for outside takeovers providing discipline of last resort.

The viability of separation of security ownership
and control: details

The preceding is a general discussion of how pressure from managerial labor markets helps to discipline managers. We now examine somewhat more specifically conditions under which the discipline imposed by managerial labor markets can resolve potential incentive problems associated with the separation of security ownership and control of the firm.

To focus on the problem we are trying to solve, let us first examine the situation where the manager is also the firm's sole security holder, so that there is clearly no incentive problem. When he is sole security holder, a manager consumes on the job, through shirking, perquisites, or incompetence, to the point where these yield marginal expected utility equal to that provided by an additional dollar of wealth usable for consumption or investment outside of the firm. The manager is induced to make this specific decision because he pays directly for consumption on the job; that is, as manager he cannot avoid a full *ex post* settling up with himself as security holder.

In contrast, when the manager is no longer sole security holder, and in the absence of some form of full *ex post* settling up for deviations from contract, a manager has an incentive to consume more on the job than is agreed in his contract. The manager perceives that, on an *ex post* basis, he can beat the game by shirking or consuming more perquisites than previously agreed. This does not necessarily mean that the manager profits at the expense of other factors. Rational managerial labor markets understand any shortcomings of available mechanisms for enforcing *ex post* settling up. Assessments of *ex post* deviations from contract will be incorporated into contracts on an *ex ante* basis; for example, through an adjustment of the manager's wage.

Nevertheless, a game which is fair on an *ex ante* basis does not induce the same behavior as a game in which there is also *ex post* settling up. Herein lie the potential losses from separation of security ownership and control of a firm. There are situations where, with less than complete *ex post* settling up, the manager is induced to consume more on the job than he would like, given that on average he pays for his consumption *ex ante*.

Three general conditions suffice to make the wage revaluation imposed by the managerial labor market a form of full *ex post* settling up which resolves the managerial incentive problem described above. The first condition is that a manager's talents and his tastes for consumption on the job are not known with certainty, are likely to change through time, and must be imputed by managerial labor markets at least in part from information about the manager's current and past performance. Since it seems to capture the essence of the

309

task of managerial labor markets in a world of uncertainty, this assumption is no real restriction.

The second assumption is that managerial labor markets appropriately use current and past information to revise future wages and understand any enforcement power inherent in the wage revision process. In short, contrary to much of the literature on separation of security ownership and control, we impute efficiency or rationality in information processing to managerial labor markets. In defense of this assumption, we note that the problem faced by managerial labor markets in revaluing the managers of a firm is much entwined with the problem faced by the capital market in revaluing the firm itself. Although we do not understand all the details of the process, available empirical evidence (e.g., Fama, 1976, chaps. 5 and 6) suggests that the capital market generally makes rational assessments of the value of the firm in the face of imprecise and uncertain information. This does not necessarily mean that information processing in managerial labor markets is equally efficient or rational, but it is a warning against strong presumption to the contrary.

The final and key condition for full control of managerial behavior through wage changes is that the weight of the wage revision process is sufficient to resolve any potential problems with managerial incentives. In this general form, the condition amounts to assuming the desired result. More substance is provided by specific examples.

. . .

Example: stochastic processes for marginal products

The next example of *ex post* settling up through the wage revision process is somewhat more formal than that described above. We make specific assumptions about the stochastic evolution of a manager's measured marginal product and about how the managerial labor market uses information from the process to adjust the manager's future wages – in a manner which amounts to precise, full *ex post* settling up for the results of past performance.

Suppose the manager's measured marginal product for any period t is composed of two terms: (i) an expected value, given his talents, effort exerted during t, consumption of perquisites, etc.; and (ii) random noise. The random noise may in part result from measurement error, that is, the sheer difficulty of accurately measuring marginal products when there is team production, but it may also arise in part from the fact that effort exerted and talent do not yield perfectly certain consequences. Moreover, because of the uncertain evolution of the manager's talents and tastes, the expected value of his marginal product is itself a stochastic process. Specifically, we assume that the expected value,

310

$\bar{z}_t$, follows a random walk with steps that are independent of the random noise, ϵ_t, in the manager's measured marginal product, z_t. Thus, the measured marginal product,

$$z_t = \bar{z}_t + \epsilon_t, \tag{1}$$

is a random walk plus white noise. For simplicity, we also assume that this process describes the manager's marginal product both in his current employment and in the best alternative employment.

The characteristics (parameters) of the evolution of the manager's marginal product depend to some extent on endogenous variables like effort and perquisites consumed, which are not completely observable. Our purpose is to set up the managerial labor market so that the wage revision process resolves any potential incentive problems that may arise from the endogeneity of z_t in a situation where there is separation of security ownership and control of the firm.

Suppose next that risk bearers are all risk neutral and that 1-period market interest rates are always equal to zero. Suppose also that managerial wage contracts are written so that the manager's wage in any period t is the expected value of his marginal product, $\bar{z}_t$, conditional on past measured values of his marginal product, with the risk bearers accepting the noise ϵ_t, in the *ex post* measurement of the marginal product. We shall see below that this is an optimal arrangement for our risk-neutral risk bearers. However, it is not necessarily optimal for the manager if he is risk averse. A risk-averse manager may want to sell part of the risk inherent in the uncertain evolution of his expected marginal product to the risk bearers, for example, through a long-term wage contract.

We avoid this issue by assuming that, perhaps because of the more extreme moral hazard problems in long-term contracts (remember that $\bar{z}_t$ is in part under the control of the manager) and the contracting costs to which these moral hazard problems give rise, simple contracts in which the manager's wage is reset at the beginning of each period are dominant, at least for some nontrivial subset of firms and managers.[4] If we could also assume away any remaining moral hazard (managerial incentive) problems, then with risk-averse managers, risk-neutral risk bearers, and the presumed fixed recontracting period, the contract which specifies *ex ante* that the manager will be paid

[4]Institutions like corporations, that are subject to rapid technological change with a large degree of uncertainty about future managerial needs, may find that long-term managerial contracts can only be negotiated at high cost. On the other hand, institutions like governments, schools, and universities may be able to forecast more reliably their future needs for managers (and other professionals) and so may be able to offer long-term contracts at relatively low cost. These institutions can then be expected to attract the relatively risk-averse members of the professional labor force, while the riskier employment offered by corporations attracts those who are willing to accept shorter-term contracts.

311

EUGENE FAMA

the current expected value of his marginal product dominates any contract where the manager also shares the *ex post* deviation of his measured marginal product from its *ex ante* expected value (see, e.g., Spence and Zeckhauser, 1971).

However, contracts which specify *ex ante* that the manager will be paid the current expected value of his marginal product seem to leave the typical moral hazard problem that arises when there is less than complete *ex post* enforcement of contracts. The noise ϵ_t in the manager's marginal product is borne by the risk bearers. Once the manager's expected marginal product $\bar{z}_t$ (= his current wage) has been assessed, he seems to have an incentive to consume more perquisites and provide less effort than are implied in $\bar{z}_t$.

A mechanism for *ex post* enforcement is, however, built into the model. With the expected value of the manager's marginal product wandering randomly through time, future assessments of expected marginal products (and thus of wages) will be determined in part by ϵ_t, the deviation of the current measured marginal product from its *ex ante* expected value. In the present scenario, where $\bar{z}_t$ is assumed to follow a random walk, Muth (1960) has shown that the expected value of the marginal product evolves according to

$$\bar{z}_t = \bar{z}_{t-1} + (1 - \phi)\epsilon_{t-1}, \tag{2}$$

where the parameter ϕ ($0 < \phi < 1$) is closer to zero the smaller the variance of the noise term in the marginal product equation (1) relative to the variance of the steps in the random walk followed by the expected marginal product.

In fact, the process by which future expected marginal products are adjusted on the basis of past deviations of marginal products from their expected values leads to a precise form of full *ex post* settling up. This is best seen by writing the marginal product z_t in its inverted form, that is, in terms of past marginal products and the current noise. The inverted form for our model, a random walk embedded in random noise is

$$z_t = (1 - \phi)z_{t-1} + \phi(1 - \phi)z_{t-2} + \phi^2(1 - \phi)z_{t-3} + \cdots + \epsilon_t, \tag{3}$$

so that

$$\bar{z}_t = (1 - \phi)z_{t-1} + \phi(1 - \phi)z_{t-2} + \phi^2(1 - \phi)z_{t-3} + \cdots \tag{4}$$

(see, e.g., Nelson, 1973, chap. 4; or Muth, 1960).

For our purposes, the interesting fact is that, although he is paid his *ex ante* expected marginal product, the manager does not get to avoid his *ex post* marginal product. For example, we can infer from (4) that z_{t-1} has weight $1 - \phi$ in $\bar{z}_t$; then it has weight $\phi(1 - \phi)$ in $\bar{z}_{t+1}$, $\phi^2(1 - \phi)$ in $\bar{z}_{t+2}$, and so on. In the end, the sum of the contributions of z_{t-1} to future expected marginal products, and thus to future wages, is exactly z_{t-1}. With zero interest rates, this means that the risk bearers simply allow the manager to smooth his

312

marginal product across future periods at the going opportunity cost of all such temporal wealth transfers. As a consequence, the manager has no incentive to try to bury shirking or consumption of perquisites in his *ex post* measured marginal product.

Since the managerial labor market is presumed to understand the weight of the wage revision process, which in this case amounts to precise full *ex post* settling up, any potential managerial incentive problems in the separation of risk bearing, or security ownership, from control are resolved. The manager can contract for and take an optimal amount of consumption on the job. The wage set *ex ante* need not include any allowance for *ex post* incentives to deviate from the contract since the wage revision process neutralizes any such incentives. Note, moreover, that the value of φ in the wage revision process described by (4) determines how the observed marginal product of any given period is subdivided and spread across future periods; but whatever the value of φ, the given marginal product is fully accounted for in the stream of future wages. Thus, it is now clear what was meant by the earlier claim that although the parameter φ in the process generating the manager's marginal product is to some extent under his control, this is not a matter of particular concern to the managerial labor market.

A somewhat evident qualification is in order. The smoothing process described by (4) contains an infinite number of terms, whereas any manager has a finite working life. For practical purposes, full *ex post* settling up is achieved as long as the manager's current marginal product is "very nearly" fully absorbed by the stream of wages over his future working life. This requires a value of φ in (4) which is sufficiently far from 1.0, given the number of periods remaining in the manager's working life. Recall that φ is closer to 1.0 the larger the variance of the noise in the manager's measured marginal product relative to the variance of the steps of the random walk taken by the expected value of his marginal product. Intuitively, when the variance of the noise term is large relative to that of the changes in the expected value, the current measured marginal product has a weak signal about any change in the expected value of the marginal product, and the current marginal product is only allocated slowly to expected future marginal products.

Some extensions

Having qualified the analysis, let us now indicate some ways in which it is robust to changes in details of the model.

1. More complicated models for the manager's marginal product.

The critical ingredient in enforcing precise full *ex post* settling up through wage revisions on the basis of reassessments of expected marginal products is that when the marginal product and its expected value are expressed in inverted form, as in (3) and (4), the sum of the weights on past marginal products is exactly 1.0. This will be the case (see, e.g., Nelson, 1973, chap. 4) whenever the manager's marginal product conforms to a nonstationary stochastic process, but the changes from period to period in the marginal product conform to some stationary ARMA (mixed autoregressive moving average) process. The example summarized in equations (1)–(4) is the interesting but special case where the expected marginal product follows a random walk so that the differences of the marginal product are a stationary, first-order moving average process. The general case allows the expected value of the marginal product to follow any more complicated nonstationary process which has the property that the differences of the marginal product are stationary, so that the marginal product and its expected value can be expressed in inverted form as

$$z_t = \pi_1 z_{t-1} + \pi_2 z_{t-2} + \cdots + \epsilon_t \qquad (5)$$

$$\bar{z}_t = \pi_1 z_{t-1} + \pi_2 z_{t-2} + \cdots \qquad (6)$$

with

$$\sum_{i=1}^{\infty} \pi_i = 1. \qquad (7)$$

These can be viewed as the general conditions for enforcing precise full *ex post* settling through the wage revision process when the manager's wage is equal to the current expected value of his marginal product.[5]

. . .

---

[5]When $\bar{z}_t$ follows a stationary process, the long-run average value toward which the process always tends will eventually be known with near perfect certainty. Thus, the case of a stationary expected marginal product is of little interest, at least for the purpose of *ex post* settling up enforced by the wage revision process.

CHAPTER 23

Theory of the firm: managerial behavior, agency costs and ownership structure

MICHAEL JENSEN AND
WILLIAM MECKLING

Michael Jensen was born in 1939 in Rochester, New York. He received a Ph.D. in finance from the University of Chicago in 1968. When this paper was published, he was Associate Professor at the University of Rochester. Since 1989, he has been Edsel Bryant Ford Professor of Business Administration at the Business School of Harvard University.

William Meckling was born in 1921 in McKeesport, Pennsylvania. He received an M.B.A. degree at the University of Denver in 1947 and did postgraduate work at the University of Chicago from 1949 to 1952. When this paper was published, he was Dean of the Graduate School of Management, University of Rochester, where he is now Dean Emeritus.

The directors of such [joint stock] companies, however, being the managers rather of other people's money than of their own, it cannot well be expected that they should watch over it with the same anxious vigilance with which the partners in a private copartnery frequently watch over their own. Like the stewards of a rich man, they are easily apt to consider attention to small matters as not for their master's honour and very easily give themselves a dispensation from having it. Negligence and profusion, therefore, must always prevail, more or less, in the management of the affairs of such a company.

Adam Smith, *The Wealth of Nations*, 1776, Cannan Edition
(Modern Library, New York, 1937), p. 700.

1. Introduction and summary

1.1. Motivation of the paper

In this paper we draw on recent progress in the theory of (1) property rights, (2) agency, and (3) finance to develop a theory of ownership structure[1] for the

Reprinted in abridged form from Michael Jensen and William Meckling, "Theory of the Firm: Managerial Behavior, Agency Costs and Ownership Structure," *The Journal of Financial Economics*, 3 (1976): 305–60, by permission of the publisher.

[1] We do not use the term "capital structure" because that term usually denotes the relative quantities of bonds, equity, warrants, trade credit, etc., which represent the liabilities of a firm. Our theory implies there is another important dimension to this problem – namely the relative amounts of ownership claims held by insiders (management) and outsiders (investors with no direct role in the management of the firm).

firm. In addition to tying together elements of the theory of each of these three areas, our analysis casts new light on and has implications for a variety of issues in the professional and popular literature such as the definition of the firm, the "separation of ownership and control," the "social responsibility" of business, the definition of a "corporate objective function," the determination of an optimal capital structure, the specification of the content of credit agreements, the theory of organizations, and the supply side of the completeness of markets problem.

Our theory helps explain:

1. why an entrepreneur or manager in a firm which has a mixed financial structure (containing both debt and outside equity claims) will choose a set of activities for the firm such that the total value of the firm is *less* than it would be if he were the sole owner and why this result is independent of whether the firm operates in monopolistic or competitive produce or factor markets;
2. why his failure to maximize the value of the firm is perfectly consistent with efficiency;
3. why the sale of common stock is a viable source of capital even though managers do not literally maximize the value of the firm;
4. why debt was relied upon as a source of capital before debt financing offered any tax advantage relative to equity;
5. why preferred stock would be issued;
6. why accounting reports would be provided voluntarily to creditors and stockholders, and why independent auditors would be engaged by management to testify to the accuracy and correctness of such reports;
7. why lenders often place restrictions on the activities of firms to whom they lend, and why firms would themselves be led to suggest the imposition of such restrictions;
8. why some industries are characterized by owner-operated firms whose sole outside source of capital is borrowing;
9. why highly regulated industries such as public utilities or banks will have higher debt equity ratios for equivalent levels of risk than the average nonregulated firm;
10. why security analysis can be socially productive even if it does not increase portfolio returns to investors.

1.2. Theory of the firm: an empty box?

While the literature of economics is replete with references to the "theory of the firm," the material generally subsumed under that heading is not a theory of the firm but actually a theory of markets in which firms are important actors. The firm is a "black box" operated so as to meet the relevant marginal conditions with respect to inputs and outputs, thereby maximizing profits, or more accurately, present value. Except for a few recent and tentative steps, however, we have no theory which explains how the conflicting objectives of the individual participants are brought into equilibrium so as to yield this result. The limitations of this black box view of the firm have been cited by Adam Smith and Alfred Marshall, among others. More recently, popular and professional debates over the "social responsibility" of corporations, the separation of ownership and control, and the rash of reviews of the literature on the "theory of the firm" have evidenced continuing concern with these issues.[2]

A number of major attempts have been made during recent years to construct a theory of the firm by substituting other models for profit or value maximization; each attempt motivated by a conviction that the latter is inadequate to explain managerial behavior in large corporations.[3] Some of these reformulation attempts have rejected the fundamental principle of maximizing behavior as well as rejecting the more specific profit maximizing model. We retain the notion of maximizing behavior on the part of all individuals in the analysis to follow.[4]

1.3. Property rights

An independent stream of research with important implications for the theory of the firm has been stimulated by the pioneering work of Coase and extended by Alchian, Demsetz, and others.[5] A comprehensive survey of this literature is given by Furubotn and Pejovich (1972). While the focus of this research has

---

[2]Reviews of this literature are given by Peterson (1965), Alchian (1965, 1968), Machlup (1967), Shubik (1970), Cyert and Hedrick (1972), Branch (1973), Preston (1975).

[3]See Williamson (1964b, 1970, 1975), Marris (1964), Baumol (1959), Penrose (1958), and Cyert and March (1963). Thorough reviews of these and other contributions are given by Machlup (1961) and Alchian (1965).

Simon (1955) developed a model of human choice incorporating information (search) and computational costs which also has important implications for the behavior of managers. Unfortunately, Simon's work has often been misinterpreted as a denial of maximizing behavior and misused, especially in the marketing and behavioral science literature. His later use of the term "satisficing" (Simon, 1959) has undoubtedly contributed to this confusion because it suggests rejection of maximizing behavior rather than maximization subject to costs of information and of decision making.

[4]See Meckling (1976) for a discussion of the fundamental importance of the assumption of resourceful, evaluative, maximizing behavior on the part of individuals in the development of theory. Klein (1976) takes an approach similar to the one we embark on in this paper in his review of the theory of the firm and the law.

[5]See Coase (1937, 1959, 1960), Alchian (1965, 1968), Alchian and Kessel (1962), Demsetz (1967), Alchian and Demsetz (1972), Monsen and Downs (1965), Silver and Auster (1969), and McManus (1975).

been "property rights,"[6] the subject matter encompassed is far broader than that term suggests. What is important for the problems addressed here is that specification of individual rights determines how costs and rewards will be allocated among the participants in any organization. Since the specification of rights is generally effected through contracting (implicit as well as explicit), individual behavior in organizations, including the behavior of managers, will depend upon the nature of these contracts. We focus in this paper on the behavioral implications of the property rights specified in the contracts between the owners and managers of the firm.

1.4. Agency costs

Many problems associated with the inadequacy of the current theory of the firm can also be viewed as special cases of the theory of agency relationships in which there is a growing literature.[7] This literature has developed independently of the property rights literature even though the problems with which it is concerned are similar; the approaches are in fact highly complementary to each other.

We define an agency relationship as a contract under which one or more persons (the principal(s)) engage another person (the agent) to perform some service on their behalf which involves delegating some decision making authority to the agent. If both parties to the relationship are utility maximizers there is good reason to believe that the agent will not always act in the best interests of the principal. The *principal* can limit divergences from his interest by establishing appropriate incentives for the agent and by incurring monitoring costs designed to limit the aberrant activities of the agent. In addition in some situations it will pay the *agent* to expend resources (bonding costs) to guarantee that he will not take certain actions which would harm the principal or to ensure that the principal will be compensated if he does take such actions. However, it is generally impossible for the principal or the agent at zero cost to ensure that the agent will make optimal decisions from the principal's viewpoint. In most agency relationships the principal and the agent will incur positive monitoring and bonding costs (nonpecuniary as well as pecuniary), and in all there will be some divergence between the agent's decisions[8] and those decisions which would maximize the welfare of the principal. The dollar equivalent of the reduction in welfare experienced by the principal due to this divergence is also a cost of the agency relationship, and

---

[6]Property rights are of course human rights, i.e., rights which are possessed by human beings. The introduction of the wholly false distinction between property rights and human rights in many policy discussions is surely one of the all time great semantic flimflams.

[7]Cf. Berhold (1972), Ross (1973, 1974), Wilson (1968, 1969), and Heckerman (1975).

[8]Given the optimal monitoring and bonding activities by the principal and agent.

we refer to this latter cost as the "residual loss." We define *agency costs* as the sum of:

1. the monitoring expenditures by the principal,[9]
2. the bonding expenditures by the agent,
3. the residual loss.

Note also that agency costs arise in any situation involving cooperative effort (such as the coauthoring of this paper) by two or more people even though there is no clear cut principal–agent relationship. Viewed in this light it is clear that our definition of agency costs and their importance to the theory of the firm bears a close relationship to the problem of shirking and monitoring of team production which Alchian and Demsetz (1972) raise in their paper on the theory of the firm.

Since the relationship between the stockholders and manager of a corporation fit the definition of a pure agency relationship, it should be no surprise to discover that the issues associated with the "separation of ownership and control" in the modern diffuse ownership corporation are intimately associated with the general problem of agency. We show below that an explanation of why and how the agency costs generated by the corporate form are born leads to a theory of the ownership (or capital) structure of the firm.

Before moving on, however, it is worthwhile to point out the generality of the agency problem. The problem of inducing an "agent" to behave as if he were maximizing the "principal's" welfare is quite general. It exists in all organizations and in all cooperative efforts – at every level of management in firms,[10] in universities, in mutual companies, in cooperatives, in governmental authorities and bureaus, in unions, and in relationships normally classified as agency relationships such as are common in the performing arts and the market for real estate. The development of theories to explain the form which agency costs take in each of these situations (where the contractual relations

---

[9]As it is used in this paper the term monitoring includes more than just measuring or observing the behavior of the agent. It includes efforts on the part of the principal to "control" the behavior of the agent through budget restrictions, compensation policies, operating rules etc.

[10]As we show below, the existence of positive monitoring and bonding costs will result in the manager of a corporation possessing control over some resources which he can allocate (within certain constraints) to satisfy his own preferences. However, to the extent that he must obtain the cooperation of others in order to carry out his tasks (such as divisional vice presidents) and to the extent that he cannot control their behavior perfectly and costlessly, they will be able to appropriate some of these resources for their own ends. In short, there are agency costs generated at every level of the organization. Unfortunately, the analysis of these more general organizational issues is even more difficult than that of the "ownership and control" issue because the nature of the contractual obligations and rights of the parties are much more varied and generally not as well specified in explicit contractual arrangements. Nevertheless, they exist and we believe that extensions of our analysis in these directions show promise of producing insights into a viable theory of organization.

differ significantly) and how and why they are born will lead to a rich theory of organizations which is now lacking in economics and the social sciences generally. We confine our attention in this paper to only a small part of this general problem – the analysis of agency costs generated by the contractual arrangements between the owners and top management of the corporation.

Our approach to the agency problem here differs fundamentally from most of the existing literature. That literature focuses almost exclusively on the normative aspects of the agency relationship, that is, how to structure the contractual relation (including compensation incentives) between the principal and agent to provide appropriate incentives for the agent to make choices which will maximize the principal's welfare given that uncertainty and imperfect monitoring exist. We focus almost entirely on the positive aspects of the theory. That is, we assume individuals solve these normative problems, and given that only stocks and bonds can be issued as claims, we investigate the incentives faced by each of the parties and the elements entering into the determination of the equilibrium contractual form characterizing the relationship between the manager (i.e., agent) of the firm and the outside equity and debt holders (i.e., principals).

1.5. Some general comment on the definition of the firms

Ronald Coase (1937) in his seminal paper on "The Nature of the Firm" pointed out that economics had no positive theory to determine the bounds of the firm. He characterized the bounds of the firm as that range of exchanges over which the market system was suppressed and resource allocation was accomplished instead by authority and direction. He focused on the cost of using markets to effect contracts and exchanges and argued that activities would be included within the firm whenever the costs of using markets were greater than the costs of using direct authority. Alchian and Demsetz (1972) object to the notion that activities within the firm are governed by authority, and correctly emphasize the role of contracts as a vehicle for voluntary exchange. They emphasize the role of monitoring in situations in which there is joint input or team production.[11] We sympathize with the importance they attach to monitoring, but we believe the emphasis which Alchian–Demsetz place on joint input production is too narrow and therefore misleading. Contractual relations are the essence of the firm, not only with employees but with suppliers, customers, creditors, etc. The problem of agency costs and mon-

[11]They define the classical capitalist firm as a contractual organization of inputs in which there is "(a) joint input production, (b) several inputs owners, (c) one party who is common to all the contracts of the joint inputs, (d) who has rights to renegotiate any input's contract independently of contracts with other input owners, (e) who holds the residual claim, and (f) who has the right to sell his contractual residual status."

itoring exists for all of these contracts, independent of whether there is joint production in their sense; i.e., joint production can explain only a small fraction of the behavior of individuals associated with a firm. A detailed examination of these issues is left to another paper.

It is important to recognize that most organizations are simply *legal fictions*[12] *which serve as a nexus for a set of contracting relationships among individuals.* This includes firms; nonprofit institutions such as universities, hospitals, and foundations; mutual organizations such as mutual savings banks and insurance companies; and cooperatives; some private clubs; and even governmental bodies such as cities, states and the Federal government, government enterprises such as TVA, the Post Office, transit systems, etc.

The private corporation or firm is simply one form of *legal fiction which serves as a nexus for contracting relationships and which is also characterized by the existence of divisible residual claims on the assets and cash flows of the organization which can generally be sold without permission of the other contracting individuals.* While this definition of the firm has little substantive content, emphasizing the essential contractual nature of firms and other organizations focuses attention on a crucial set of questions – why particular sets of contractual relations arise for various types of organizations, what the consequences of these contractual relations are, and how they are affected by changes exogenous to the organization. Viewed this way, it makes little or no sense to try to distinguish those things which are "inside" the firm (or any other organization) from those things that are "outside" of it. There is in a very real sense only a multitude of complex relationships (i.e., contracts) between the legal fiction (the firm) and the owners of labor, material, and capital inputs and the consumers of output.[13]

Viewing the firm as the nexus of a set of contracting relationships among individuals also serves to make it clear that the personalization of the firm implied by asking questions such as "what should be the objective function of the firm," or "does the firm have a social responsibility" is seriously misleading. *The firm is not an individual.* It is a legal fiction which serves as a focus for a complex process in which the conflicting objectives of individuals (some of whom may "represent" other organizations) are brought into equilibrium within a framework of contractual relations. In this sense the "behavior" of the firm is like the behavior of a market, i.e., the outcome of a complex equilibri-

---

[12]By legal fiction we mean the artificial construct under the law which allows certain organizations to be treated as individuals.

[13]For example, we ordinarily think of a product as leaving the firm at the time it is sold, but implicitly or explicitly such sales generally carry with them continuing contracts between the firm and the buyer. If the product does not perform as expected the buyer often can and does have a right to satisfaction. Explicit evidence that such implicit contracts do exist is the practice we occasionally observe of specific provision that "all sales are final."

um process. We seldom fall into the trap of characterizing the wheat or stock market as an individual, but we often make this error by thinking about organizations as if they were persons with motivations and intentions.[14]

1.6. An overview of the paper

We develop the theory in stages. Sections 2 and 4 provide analyses of the agency costs of equity and debt respectively. These form the major foundation of the theory. Section 3 poses some unanswered questions regarding the existence of the corporate form of organization and examines the role of limited liability. Section 5 provides a synthesis of the basic concepts derived in sections 2–4 into a theory of the corporate ownership structure which takes account of the trade-offs available to the entrepreneur-manager between inside and outside equity and debt. Some qualifications and extensions of the analysis are discussed in section 6, and section 7 contains a brief summary and conclusions.

2. The agency costs of outside equity

2.1. Overview

In this section we analyze the effect of outside equity on agency costs by comparing the behavior of a manager when he owns 100 percent of the residual claims on a firm to his behavior when he sells off a portion of those claims to outsiders. If a wholly owned firm is managed by the owner, he will make operating decisions which maximize his utility. These decisions will involve not only the benefits he derives from pecuniary returns but also the utility generated by various nonpecuniary aspects of his entrepreneurial activities such as the physical appointments of the office, the attractiveness of the secretarial staff, the level of employee discipline, the kind and amount of charitable contributions, personal relations ("love," "respect," etc.) with employees, a larger than optimal computer to play with, purchase of production inputs from friends, etc. The optimum mix (in the absence of taxes) of the

---

[14]This view of the firm points up the important role which the legal system and the law play in social organizations, especially, the organization of economic activity. Statutory law sets bounds on the kinds of contracts into which individuals and organizations may enter without risking criminal prosecution. The police powers of the state are available and used to enforce performance of contracts or to enforce the collection of damages for nonperformance. The courts adjudicate conflicts between contracting parties and establish precedents which form the body of common law. All of these government activities affect both the kinds of contracts executed and the extent to which contracting is relied upon. This in turn determines the usefulness, productivity, profitability, and viability of various forms of organization. Moreover, new laws as well as court decisions often can and do change the rights of contracting parties *ex post,* and they can and do serve as a vehicle for redistribution of wealth. An analysis of some of the implications of these facts is contained in Jensen and Meckling (1976b) and we shall not pursue them here.

various pecuniary and nonpecuniary benefits is achieved when the marginal utility derived from an additional dollar of expenditure (measured net of any productive effects) is equal for each nonpecuniary item and equal to the marginal utility derived from an additional dollar of after tax purchasing power (wealth).

If the owner-manager sells equity claims on the corporation which are identical to his (i.e., share proportionately in the profits of the firm and have limited liability), agency costs will be generated by the divergence between his interest and those of the outside shareholders, since he will then bear only a fraction of the costs of any nonpecuniary benefits he takes out in maximizing his own utility. If the manager owns only 95 percent of the stock, he will expend resources to the point where the marginal utility derived from a dollar's expenditure of the firm's resources on such items equals the marginal utility of an additional 95 cents in general purchasing power (i.e., *his* share of the wealth reduction) and not one dollar. Such activities, on his part, can be limited (but probably not eliminated) by the expenditure of resources on monitoring activities by the outside stockholders. But as we show below, the owner will bear the entire wealth effects of these expected costs so long as the equity market anticipates these effects. Prospective minority shareholders will realize that the owner-manager's interests will diverge somewhat from theirs, hence the price which they will pay for shares will reflect the monitoring costs and the effect of the divergence between the manager's interest and theirs. Nevertheless, ignoring for the moment the possibility of borrowing against his wealth, the owner will find it desirable to bear these costs as long as the welfare increment he experiences from converting his claims on the firm into general purchasing power[15] is large enough to offset them.

As the owner-manager's fraction of the equity falls, his fractional claim on the outcomes falls and this will tend to encourage him to appropriate larger amounts of the corporate resources in the form of perquisites. This also makes it desirable for the minority shareholders to expend more resources in monitoring his behavior. Thus, the wealth costs to the owner of obtaining additional cash in the equity markets rise as his fractional ownership falls.

We shall continue to characterize the agency conflict between the owner-manager and outside shareholders as deriving from the manager's tendency to appropriate perquisites out of the firm's resources for his own consumption. However, we do not mean to leave the impression that this is the only or even the most important source of conflict. Indeed, it is likely that the most important conflict arises from the fact that as the manager's ownership claim falls, his

---

[15]For use in consumption, for the diversification of his wealth, or more importantly, for the financing of "profitable" projects which he could not otherwise finance out of his personal wealth. We deal with these issues below after having developed some of the elementary analytical tools necessary to their solution.

incentive to devote significant effort to creative activities such as searching out new profitable ventures falls. He may, in fact, avoid such ventures simply because it requires too much trouble or effort on his part to manage or to learn about new technologies. Avoidance of these personal costs and the anxieties that go with them also represent a source of on the job utility to him and it can result in the value of the firm being substantially lower than it otherwise could be.

2.2. A simple formal analysis of the sources of agency costs of equity and who bears them

In order to develop some structure for the analysis to follow, we make two sets of assumptions. The first set (permanent assumptions) are those which shall carry through almost all of the analysis in section 2–5. The effects of relaxing some of these are discussed in section 6. The second set (temporary assumptions) are made only for expositional purposes and are relaxed as soon as the basic points have been clarified.

Permanent assumptions

P.1. All taxes are zero.
P.2. No trade credit is available.
P.3. All outside equity shares are nonvoting.
P.4. No complex financial claims such as convertible bonds or preferred stock or warrants can be issued.
P.5. No outside owner gains utility from ownership in a firm in any way other than through its effect on his wealth or cash flows.
P.6. All dynamic aspects of the multiperiod nature of the problem are ignored by assuming there is only one production–financing decision to be made by the entrepreneur.
P.7. The entrepreneur-manager's money wages are held constant throughout the analysis.
P.8. There exists a single manager (the peak coordinator) with ownership interest in the firm.

Temporary assumptions

T.1. The size of the firm is fixed.
T.2. No monitoring or bonding activities are possible.
T.3. No debt financing through bonds, preferred stock, or personal borrowing (secured or unsecured) is possible.

T.4.   All elements of the owner-manager's decision problem involving portfolio considerations induced by the presence of uncertainty and the existence of diversifiable risk are ignored.

Define:

X = $\{x_1, x_2, \ldots, x_n\}$ = vector of quantities of all factors and activities within the firm from which the manager derives nonpecuniary benefits;[16] the x_i are defined such that this marginal utility is positive for each of them;

$C(X)$ = total dollar cost of providing any given amount of these items;

$P(X)$ = total dollar value to the firm of the productive benefits of X;

$B(X)$ = $P(X) - C(X)$ = net dollar benefit to the firm of X ignoring any effects of X on the equilibrium wage of the manager.

Ignoring the effects of X on the manager's utility and therefore on his equilibrium wage rate, the optimum levels of the factors and activities X are defined by X^* such that

$$\frac{\partial B(X^*)}{\partial X^*} = \frac{\partial P(X^*)}{\partial X^*} - \frac{\partial C(X^*)}{\partial X^*} = 0$$

Thus for any vector $X \geq X^*$ (i.e., where at least one element of X is greater than its corresponding element of X^*), $F \equiv B(X^*) - B(X) > 0$ measures the dollar cost to the firm (net of any productive effects) of providing the increment $X - X^*$ of the factors and activities which generate utility to the manager. We assume henceforth that for any given level of cost to the firm, F, the vector of factors and activities on which F is spent are those, $\hat{X}$, which yield the manager maximum utility. Thus $F \equiv B(X^*) - B(\hat{X})$.

We have thus far ignored in our discussion the fact that these expenditures on X occur through time and therefore there are trade-offs to be made across time as well as between alternative elements of X. Furthermore, we have ignored the fact that the future expenditures are likely to involve uncertainty (i.e., they are subject to probability distributions) and therefore some allowance must be made for their riskiness. We resolve both of these issues by defining C, P, B, and F to be the *current market values* of the sequence of probability distributions on the period by period cash flows involved.[17]

Given the definition of F as the current market value of the stream of manager's expenditures on nonpecuniary benefits we represent the constraint

---

[16]Such as office space, air conditioning, thickness of the carpets, friendliness of employee relations, etc.

[17]And again we assume that for any given market value of these costs, F, to the firm, the allocation across time and across alternative probability distribution is such that the manager's current expected utility is at a maximum.

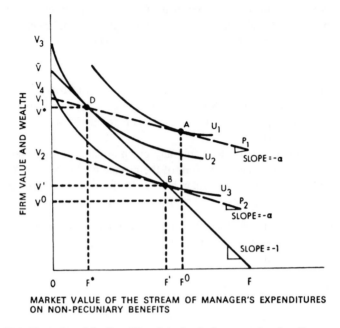

Figure 23.1. The value of the firm (V) and the level of nonpecuniary benefits consumed (F) when the fraction of outside equity is $(1 - \alpha)V$, and U_j ($j = 1, 2, 3$) represents owner's indifference curves between wealth and nonpecuniary benefits.

which a single owner-manager faces in deciding how much nonpecuniary income he will extract from the firm by the line $\bar{V}F$ in Figure 23.1. This is analogous to a budget constraint. The market value of the firm is measured along the vertical axis and the market value of the manager's stream of expenditures on nonpecuniary benefits, F, are measured along the horizontal axis. $0\bar{V}$ is the value of the firm when the amount of nonpecuniary income consumed is zero. By definition $\bar{V}$ is the maximum market value of the cash flows generated by the firm for a given money wage for the manager when the manager's consumption of nonpecuniary benefits are zero. At this point all the factors and activities within the firm which generate utility for the manager are at level X^* defined above. There is a different budget constraint $\bar{V}F$ for each possible scale of the firm (i.e., level of investment, I) and for alternative levels of money wage, W, for the manager. For the moment we pick an arbitrary level of investment (which we assume has already been made) and hold the scale of the firm constant at this level. We also assume that the manager's money wage is fixed at the level W^* which represents the current

326

market value of his wage contract[18] in the optimal compensation package which consists of both wages, W^*, and nonpecuniary benefits, F^*. Since one dollar of current value of nonpecuniary benefits withdrawn from the firm by the manager reduces the market value of the firm by \$1, by definition, the slope of $\bar{V}F$ is -1.

The owner-manager's tastes for wealth and nonpecuniary benefits is represented in Figure 23.1 by a system of indifference curves, U_1, U_2, etc.[19] The indifference curves will be convex as drawn as long as the owner-manager's marginal rate of substitution between nonpecuniary benefits and wealth diminishes with increasing levels of the benefits. For the 100 percent owner-manager, this presumes that there are not perfect substitutes for these benefits available on the outside, i.e., to some extent they are job specific. For the fractional owner-manager this presumes the benefits cannot be turned into general purchasing power at a constant price.[20]

When the owner has 100 percent of the equity, the value of the firm will be V^* where indifference curve U_2 is tangent to VF, and the level of nonpecuniary benefits consumed is F^*. If the owner sells the entire equity but remains as manager, and if the equity buyer can, at zero cost, force the old owner (as manager) to take the same level of nonpecuniary benefits as he did as owner, then V^* is the price the new owner will be willing to pay for the entire equity.[21]

---

[18]At this stage when we are considering a 100% owner-managed firm the notion of a "wage contract" with himself has no content. However, the 100% owner-managed case is only an expositional device used in passing to illustrate a number of points in the analysis, and we ask the reader to bear with us briefly while we lay out the structure for the more interesting partial ownership case where such a contract does have substance.

[19]The manager's utility function is actually defined over wealth and the future time sequence of vectors of quantities of nonpecuniary benefits, X_t. Although the setting of his problem is somewhat different, Fama (1970b, 1972) analyzes the conditions under which these preferences can be represented as a derived utility function defined as a function of the money value of the expenditures (in our notation F) on these goods conditional on the prices of goods. Such a utility function incorporates the optimization going on in the background which define $\hat{X}$ discussed above for a given F. In the more general case where we allow a time series of consumption, $\hat{X}_t$, the optimization is being carried out across both time and the components of X_t for fixed F.

[20]This excludes, for instance, (a) the case where the manager is allowed to expend corporate resources on anything he pleases, in which case F would be a perfect substitute for wealth; or (b) the case where he can "steal" cash (or other marketable assets) with constant returns to scale – if he could, the indifference curves would be straight lines with slope determined by the fence commission.

[21]Point D defines the fringe benefits in the optimal pay package since the value to the manager of the fringe benefits F^* is greater than the cost of providing them as is evidenced by the fact that U_2 is steeper to the left of D than the budget constraint with slope equal to -1.

That D is indeed the optimal pay package can easily be seen in this situation since if the conditions of the sale to a new owner specified that the manager would receive no fringe benefits after the sale, he would require a payment equal to V_3 to compensate him for the sacrifice of his claims to V^* and fringe benefits amounting to F^* (the latter with total value to him of $V_3 - V^*$). But if $F = 0$, the value of the firm is only $\bar{V}$. Therefore, if monitoring costs were zero, the sale

In general, however, we would not expect the new owner to be able to enforce identical behavior on the old owner at zero costs. If the old owner sells a fraction of the firm to an outsider, he, as manager, will no longer bear the full cost of any nonpecuniary benefits he consumes. Suppose the owner sells a share of the firm, $1 - \alpha$, $(0 < \alpha < 1)$ and retains for himself a share, α. If the prospective buyer believes that the owner-manager will consume the same level of nonpecuniary benefits as he did as full owner, the buyer will be willing to pay $(1 - \alpha)V^*$ for a fraction $(1 - \alpha)$ of the equity. Given that an outsider now holds a claim to $(1 - \alpha)$ of the equity, however, the *cost* to the owner-manager of consuming \$1 of nonpecuniary benefits in the firm will no longer be \$1. Instead, it will be $\alpha \times \$1$. If the prospective buyer actually paid $(1 - \alpha)V^*$ for his share of the equity, and if thereafter the manager could choose whatever level of nonpecuniary benefits he liked, his budget constraint would be $V_1 P_1$ in Figure 23.1 and has a slope equal to $-\alpha$. Including the payment the owner receives from the buyers as part of the owner's postsale wealth, his budget constraint $V_1 P_1$, must pass through D, since he can if he wishes have the same wealth and level of nonpecuniary consumption he consumed as full owner.

But if the owner-manager is free to choose the level of perquisites, F, subject only to the loss in wealth he incurs as a part owner, his welfare will be maximized by increasing his consumption of nonpecuniary benefits. He will move to point A where $V_1 P_1$ is tangent to U_1 representing a higher level of utility. The value of the firm falls from V^* to V^0, i.e., by the amount of the cost to the firm of the increased nonpecuniary expenditures, and the owner-manager's consumption of nonpecuniary benefits rises from F^* to F^0.

If the equity market is characterized by rational expectations the buyers will be aware that the owner will increase his nonpecuniary consumption when his ownership share is reduced. If the owner's response function is known or if the equity market makes unbiased estimates of the owner's response to the changed incentives, the buyer will not pay $(1 - \alpha)V^*$ for $(1 - \alpha)$ of the equity.

Theorem. For a claim of the firm of $(1 - \alpha)$ the outsider will pay only $(1 - \alpha)$ times the value he expects the firm to have given the induced change in the behavior of the owner-manager.

would take place at V^* with provision for a pay package which included fringe benefits of F^* for the manager.

This discussion seems to indicate there are two values for the "firm," V_3 and V^*. This is not the case if we realize that V^* is the value of the right to be the residual claimant on the cash flows of the firm and $V_3 - V^*$ is the value of the managerial rights, i.e., the right to make the operating decisions which include access to F^*. There is at least one other right which has value which plays no formal role in the analysis as yet – the value of the control right. By control right we mean the right to hire and fire the manager, and we leave this issue to a future paper.

Theory of the Firm

Proof. For simplicity we ignore any element of uncertainty introduced by the lack of perfect knowledge of the owner-manager's response function. Such uncertainty will not affect the final solution if the equity market is large as long as the estimates are rational (i.e., unbiased) and the errors are independent across firms. The latter condition assures that this risk is diversifiable and therefore equilibrium prices will equal the expected values.

Let W represent the owner's total wealth after he has sold a claim equal to $1 - \alpha$ of the equity to an outsider. W has two components. One is the payment, S_0, made by the outsider for $1 - \alpha$ of the equity; the rest, S_i, is the value of the owner's (i.e., insider's) share of the firm, so that W, the owner's wealth, is given by

$$W = S_0 + S_i = S_0 + \alpha V(F,\alpha),$$

where $V(F,\alpha)$ represents the value of the firm given that the manager's fractional ownership share is α and that he consumes perquisites with current market value of F. Let $V_2 P_2$, with a slope of $-\alpha$, represent the trade-off the owner-manager faces between nonpecuniary benefits and his wealth after the sale. Given that the owner has decided to sell a claim $1 - \alpha$ of the firm, his welfare will be maximized when $V_2 P_2$ is tangent to some indifference curve such as U_3 in Figure 23.1. A price for a claim of $(1 - \alpha)$ on the firm that is satisfactory to both the buyer and the seller will require that this tangency occur along $\bar{V}F$, i.e., that the value of the firm must be V'. To show this, assume that such is not the case – that the tangency occurs to the left of the point B on the line $\bar{V}F$. Then, since the slope of $V_2 P_2$ is negative, the value of the firm will be larger than V'. The owner-manager's choice of this lower level of consumption of nonpecuniary benefits will imply a higher value both to the firm as a whole and to the fraction of the firm $(1 - \alpha)$ which the outsider has acquired; that is, $(1 - \alpha)V' > S_0$. From the owner's viewpoint, he has sold $1 - \alpha$ of the firm for less than he could have, given the (assumed) lower level of nonpecuniary benefits he enjoys. On the other hand, if the tangency point B is to the right of the line $\bar{V}F$, the owner-manager's higher consumption of nonpecuniary benefits means the value of the firm is less than V', and hence $(1 - \alpha)V(F,\alpha) < S_0 = (1 - \alpha)V'$. The outside owner then has paid more for his share of the equity than it is worth. S_0 will be a mutually satisfactory price if and only if $(1 - \alpha)V' = S_0$. But this means that the owner's postsale wealth is equal to the (reduced) value of the firm V', since

$$W = S_0 + \alpha V' = (1 - \alpha)V' + \alpha V' = V'. \qquad \text{Q.E.D.}$$

The requirement that V^* and F' fall on $\bar{V}F$ is thus equivalent to requiring that the value of the claim acquired by the outside buyer be equal to the amount he pays for it and conversely for the owner. *This means that the decline in the total value of the firm ($V^* - V'$) is entirely imposed on the owner-manager.*

329

His total wealth after the sale of $(1 - \alpha)$ of the equity is V', and the decline in his wealth is $V^* - V'$.

The distance $V^* - V'$ is the reduction in the market value of the firm engendered by the agency relationship and is a measure of the "residual loss" defined earlier. In this simple example the residual loss represents the total agency costs engendered by the sale of outside equity because monitoring and bonding activities have not been allowed. The welfare loss the owner incurs is less than the residual loss by the value to him of the increase in nonpecuniary benefits $(F' - F^*)$. In Figure 23.1 the difference between the intercepts on the Y axis of the two indifference curves U_2 and U_3 is a measure of the owner-manager's welfare loss due to the incurrence of agency costs,[22] and he would sell such a claim only if the increment in welfare he achieves by using the cash amounting to $(1 - \alpha)V'$ for other things was worth more to him than this amount of wealth.

. . .

2.4. The role of monitoring and bonding activities in reducing agency costs

In the above analysis we have ignored the potential for controlling the behavior of the owner-manager through monitoring and other control activities. In practice it is usually possible by expending resources to alter the opportunity the owner-manager has for capturing nonpecuniary benefits. These methods include auditing, formal control systems, budget restrictions, and the establishment of incentive compensation systems which serve to more closely identify the manager's interests with those of the outside equity holders, etc. Figure 23.2 portrays the effects of monitoring and other control activities in the simple situation portrayed in Figure 23.1. Figures 23.1 and 23.2 are identical except for the curve BCE in Figure 23.2 which depicts a "budget constraint" derived when monitoring possibilities are taken into account. Without monitoring, and with outside equity of $(1 - \alpha)$, the value of the firm will be V' and nonpecuniary expenditures F'. By incurring monitoring costs, M, the equity holders can restrict the manager's consumption of perquisites to amounts less than F'. Let $F(M,\alpha)$ denote the maximum perquisites the manager can consume for alternative levels of monitoring expenditures, M, given his ownership share, α. We assume that increases in monitoring reduce F and reduce it at a decreasing rate, i.e., $\partial F/\partial M < 0$ and $\partial^2 F/\partial M^2 > 0$.

[22]The distance $V^* - V'$ is a measure of what we will define as the gross agency costs. The distance $V_3 - V_4$ is a measure of what we call net agency costs, and it is this measure of agency costs which will be minimized by the manager in the general case where we allow investment to change.

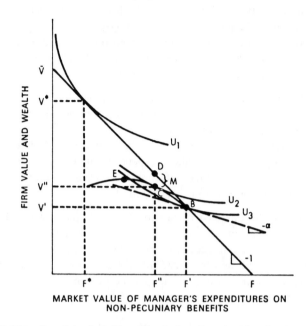

Figure 23.2. The value of the firm (V) and level of nonpecuniary benefits (F) when outside equity is $(1 - \alpha)$, U_1, U_2, U_3 represent owner's indifference curves between wealth and nonpecuniary benefits, and monitoring (or bonding) activities impose opportunity set BCE as the tradeoff constraint facing the owner.

Since the current value of expected future monitoring expenditures by the outside equity holders reduce the value of any given claim on the firm to them dollar for dollar, the outside equity holders will take this into account in determining the maximum price they will pay for any given fraction of the firm's equity. Therefore, given positive monitoring activity, the value of the firm is given by $V = \bar{V} - F(M,\alpha) - M$, and the locus of these points for various levels of M and for a given level of α lie on the line BCE in Figure 23.2. The vertical difference between the $\bar{V}F$ and BCE curves is M, the current market value of the future monitoring expenditures.

If it is possible for the outside equity holders to make these monitoring expenditures and thereby to impose the reductions in the owner-manager's consumption of F, he will voluntarily enter into a contract with the outside equity holders which gives them the rights to restrict his consumption of nonpecuniary items to F''. He finds this desirable because it will cause the value of the firm to rise to V''. Given the contract, the optimal monitoring expenditure on the part of the outsiders, M, is the amount $D - C$. The entire increase in the value of the firm that accrues will be reflected in the owner's

331

wealth, but his welfare will be increased by less than this because he forgoes some nonpecuniary benefits he previously enjoyed.

If the equity market is competitive and makes unbiased estimates of the effects of the monitoring expenditures on F and V, potential buyers will be indifferent between the following two contracts:

(i) Purchase of a share $(1 - \alpha)$ of the firm at a total price of $(1 - \alpha)V'$ and no rights to monitor or control the manager's consumption of perquisites.

(ii) Purchase of a share $(1 - \alpha)$ of the firm at a total price of $(1 - \alpha)V''$ and the right to expend resources up to an amount equal to $D - C$ which will limit the owner-manager's consumption of perquisites to F.

Given contract (ii) the outside shareholders would find it desirable to monitor to the full rights of their contract because it will pay them to do so. However, if the equity market is competitive the total benefits (net of the monitoring costs) will be capitalized into the price of the claims. Thus, not surprisingly, the owner-manager reaps all the benefits of the opportunity to write and sell the monitoring contract.

An analysis of bonding expenditures. We can also see from the analysis of Figure 23.2 that it makes no difference who actually makes the monitoring expenditures – the owner bears the full amount of these costs as a wealth reduction in all cases. Suppose that the owner-manager could expend resources to guarantee to the outside equity holders that he would limit his activities which cost the firm F. We call these expenditures "bonding costs," and they would take such forms as contractual guarantees to have the financial accounts audited by a public accountant, explicit bonding against malfeasance on the part of the manager, and contractual limitations on the manager's decisionmaking power (which impose costs on the firm because they limit his ability to take full advantage of some profitable opportunities as well as limiting his ability to harm the stockholders while making himself better off).

If the incurrence of the bonding costs were entirely under the control of the manager and if they yielded the same opportunity set BCE for him in Figure 23.2, he would incur them in amount $D - C$. This would limit his consumption of perquisites to F'' from F', and the solution is exactly the same as if the outside equity holders had performed the monitoring. The manager finds it in his interest to incur these costs as long as the net increments in his wealth which they generate (by reducing the agency costs and therefore increasing the value of the firm) are more valuable than the perquisites given up. This optimum occurs at point C in both cases under our assumption that the bonding expenditures yield the same opportunity set as the monitoring expenditures. In general, of course, it will pay the owner-manager to engage in bonding activities and to write contracts which allow monitoring as long as the marginal benefits of each are greater than their marginal cost.

. . .

2.5. Pareto optimality and agency costs in manager-operated firms

In general we expect to observe both bonding and external monitoring activities, and the incentives are such that the levels of these activities will satisfy the conditions of efficiency. They will not, however, result in the firm being run in a manner so as to maximize its value. The difference between V^*, the efficient solution under zero monitoring and bonding costs (and therefore zero agency costs), and V'', the value of the firm given positive monitoring costs, are the total gross agency costs defined earlier in the introduction. These are the costs of the "separation of ownership and control" which Adam Smith focused on in the passage quoted at the beginning of this paper and which Berle and Means (1932) popularized 157 years later. The solutions outlined above to our highly simplified problem imply that agency costs will be positive as long as monitoring costs are positive – which they certainly are.

The reduced value of the firm caused by the manager's consumption of perquisites outlined above is "nonoptimal" or inefficient only in comparison to a world in which we could obtain compliance of the agent to the principal's wishes at zero cost or in comparison to a *hypothetical* world in which the agency costs were lower. But these costs (monitoring and bonding costs and "residual loss") are an unavoidable result of the agency relationship. Furthermore, since they are borne entirely by the decision maker (in this case the original owner) responsible for creating the relationship, he has the incentives to see that they are minimized (because he captures the benefits from their reduction). Furthermore, these agency costs will be incurred only if the benefits to the owner-manager from their creation are great enough to outweigh them. In our current example these benefits arise from the availability of profitable investments requiring capital investment in excess of the original owner's personal wealth.

In conclusion, finding that agency costs are nonzero (i.e., that there are costs associated with the separation of ownership and control in the corporation) and concluding therefore that the agency relationship is nonoptimal, wasteful, or inefficient is equivalent in every sense to comparing a world in which iron ore is a scarce commodity (and therefore costly) to a world in which it is freely available at zero resource cost, and concluding that the first world is "nonoptimal" – a perfect example of the fallacy criticized by Coase

(1964) and what Demsetz (1969) characterizes as the "Nirvana" form of analysis.[23]

2.6. Factors affecting the size of the divergence from ideal maximization

The magnitude of the agency costs discussed above will vary from firm to firm. It will depend on the tastes of managers, the ease with which they can exercise their own preferences as opposed to value maximization in decision making, and the costs of monitoring and bonding activities.[24] The agency costs will also depend upon the cost of measuring the manager's (agent's) performance and evaluating it, the cost of devising and applying an index for compensating the manager which correlates with the owner's (principal's) welfare, and the cost of devising and enforcing specific behavioral rules or policies. Where the manager has less than a controlling interest in the firm, it will also depend upon the market for managers. Competition from other potential managers limits the costs of obtaining managerial services (including the extent to which a given manager can diverge from the idealized solution which would obtain if all monitoring and bonding costs were zero). The size of the divergence (the agency costs) will be directly related to the cost of replacing the manager. If his responsibilities require very little knowledge specialized to the firm, if it is easy to evaluate his performance, and if replacement search costs are modest, the divergence from the ideal will be relatively small and vice versa.

The divergence will also be constrained by the market for the firm itself, i.e., by capital markets. Owners always have the option of selling their firm, either as a unit or piecemeal. Owners of manager-operated firms can and do sample the capital market from time to time. If they discover that the value of the future earnings-stream to others is higher than the value of the firm to them given that it is to be manager-operated, they can exercise their right to sell. It is conceivable that other owners could be more efficient at monitoring or even that a single individual with appropriate managerial talents and with sufficiently large personal wealth would elect to buy the firm. In this latter case the purchase by such a single individual would completely eliminate the agency costs. If there were a number of such potential owner-manager pur-

---

[23]If we could establish the existence of a feasible set of alternative institutional arrangements which would yield net benefits from the reduction of these costs, we could legitimately conclude the agency relationship engendered by the corporation was not Pareto optimal. However, we would then be left with the problem of explaining why these alternative institutional arrangements have not replaced the corporate form of organization.

[24]The monitoring and bonding costs will differ from firm to firm depending on such things as the inherent complexity and geographical dispersion of operations, the attractiveness of perquisites available in the firm (consider the mint), etc.

Theory of the Firm

chasers (all with talents and tastes identical to the current manager), the owners would receive in the sale price of the firm the full value of the residual claimant rights including the capital value of the eliminated agency costs plus the value of the managerial rights.

Monopoly, competition, and managerial behavior. It is frequently argued that the existence of competition in product (and factor) markets will constrain the behavior of managers to idealized value maximization, i.e., that monopoly in product (or monopsony in factor) markets will permit larger divergences from value maximization.[25] Our analysis does not support this hypothesis. The owners of a firm with monopoly power have the same incentives to limit divergences of the manager from value maximization (i.e., the ability to increase their wealth) as do the owners of competitive firms. Furthermore, competition in the market for managers will generally make it unnecessary for the owners to share rents with the manager. The owners of a monopoly firm need only pay the supply price for a manager.

Since the owner of a monopoly has the same wealth incentives to minimize managerial costs as would the owner of a competitive firm, both will undertake that level of monitoring which equates the marginal cost of monitoring to the marginal wealth increment from reduced consumption of perquisites by the manager. Thus, the existence of monopoly will not increase agency costs.

Furthermore the existence of competition in product and factor markets will not eliminate the agency costs due to managerial control problems as has often been asserted [cf. Friedman (1970)]. If my competitors all incur agency costs equal to or greater than mine, I will not be eliminated from the market by their competition.

The existence and size of the agency costs depends on the nature of the monitoring costs, the tastes of managers for nonpecuniary benefits and the supply of potential managers who are capable of financing the entire venture out of their personal wealth. If monitoring costs are zero, agency costs will be zero; or if there are enough 100 percent owner-managers available to own and run all the firms in an industry (competitive or not), then agency costs in that industry will also be zero.

. . .

[25]"Where competitors are numerous and entry is easy, persistent departures from profit maximizing behavior inexorably leads to extinction. Economic natural selection holds the stage. In these circumstances, the behavior of the individual units that constitute the supply side of the product market is essentially routine and uninteresting and economists can confidently predict industry behavior without being explicitly concerned with the behavior of these individual units. "When the conditions of competition are relaxed, however, the opportunity set of the firm is expanded. In this case, the behavior of the firm as a distinct operating unit is of separate interest. Both for purposes of interpreting particular behavior within the firm as well as for predicting responses of the industry aggregate, it may be necessary to identify the factors that influence the firm's choices within this expanded opportunity set and embed these in a formal model." (Williamson, 1964, p. 2).

CHAPTER 24

Organizational forms and investment decisions

EUGENE FAMA AND MICHAEL JENSEN

Eugene Fama is Professor of Finance in the Graduate School of Business at the University of Chicago. See also the previous paper by Fama.

Michael Jensen is Professor of Business Administration at the Business School of Harvard University. When this paper was published, he was LaClare Professor of Finance and Business Administration at the University of Rochester. See also the previous paper coauthored by Jensen.

1. Introduction

Different organizational forms are distinguished by the characteristics of their residual claims on net cash flows, for example, restrictions on the extent to which residual claimant status is separable from decision roles, or restrictions on the alienability of the residual claims. Different restrictions on residual claims imply different rules for optimal investment decisions. This paper analyzes the relations between characteristics of residual claims and investment decision rules in open and closed corporations, partnerships, proprietorships, financial mutuals, and nonprofits. Our purpose is to determine whether the decisions of each of these organizations can be modeled "as if" they come from the maximization of an objective function – for example, the value maximization rule of the financial economics literature. We focus on investment decisions, but the rules are applicable to all decisions. We ignore the effects of taxes.

We first analyze the investment decision rule implied by the common stock residual claims of open corporations. We compare this rule to the decision rules implied by the more restricted residual claims of proprietorships, partnerships, and closed corporations, and we discuss aspects of the choice of organizational form. Finally, we analyze the investment decision rules implied by the even more specialized residual claims of financial mutuals and nonprofits.

Excerpted from Eugene Fama and Michael Jensen, "Organizational Forms and Investment Decisions," *Journal of Financial Economics* 14 (1985): 101–119, by permission of the publisher.

2. The decision rule implied by the common stock of open corporations

The least restricted residual claims in common use are the common stocks of large corporations. These residual claims have property rights in net cash flows for an indefinite horizon. They are separable in that stockholders are not required to have any other role in the organization. The residual claim of open corporations are also alienable without restriction. We call these organizations open corporations to distinguish them from closed corporations that are generally smaller and have residual claims that are largely restricted to decision agents.

The unrestricted nature of the residual claims of open corporations fosters the development of a capital market that specializes in pricing such claims and transferring them among investors at low cost. Suppose the capital market is perfectly competitive, that is, suppose there are perfect substitutes for the unrestricted residual claims of any open corporation, and both investors and open corporations are price takers in the capital market. Suppose also that unrestricted residual claims can be traded costlessly among investors and that the capital market is efficient or rational in the sense that the prices of residual claims correctly reflect available information. In this situation, a corporation's stockholders all agree that all decisions, including investments with payoffs in future periods, should be evaluated according to their contribution to the current market value of their residual claims. (See, for example, Fama, 1978).

The logic of the market value of maximum wealth rule is straightforward. The existence of perfect substitute securities that are always correctly priced and can be traded without transactions costs in a perfectly competitive market means the consumption streams that an investor can realize in future periods are constrained only by current wealth, that is, the market value of current and future resources. When the stream of payoffs implied by the wealth or value maximizing investment decisions of an open corporation does not correspond to an investor's optimal consumption stream, the capital market can be used to exchange residual claims in the corporation for other claims with the same market value but with a stream of payoffs that better matches the investor's desired consumption stream.

Because most residual claimants in open corporations have no direct role in the decision process, and because there are conflicts of interest with managers, there are agency problems between managers and residual claimants. As a consequence, an important investment choice in open corporations is the decision control process. As for other investment decisions, maximizing market value involves extending decision control mechanisms to the point where the incremental market value of improved decisions is just offset by the market value of the cost of improved decision control. This means some decisions that nominally reduce value will be taken when the cost of preventing them exceeds the value reduction they cause. It is obvious, but worth emphasizing, that market value reflects all costs, including agency costs – the costs incurred because contracts with decision agents are not costlessly written and enforced. These issues are discussed in detail in Jensen and Meckling (1976) and Fama and Jensen (1983a, 1983b).

One can quarrel with the perfect capital market assumptions needed to obtain the conclusion that all investors prefer the market value rule for investment decisions by open corporations. However, this case is a useful point of reference for judging the effects of restrictions on residual claims on rules for investment decisions.

3. Decision rules implied by the restricted residual claims of proprietorships, partnerships, and closed corporations

Unlike the unrestricted common stock of open corporations, the residual claims of proprietorships, partnerships, and closed corporations are generally restricted to the organization's important decision agents. We are concerned with the effects of this restriction on investment decisions.

3.1. Proprietorship investment decisions under certainty

Many issues central to the analysis of investment decisions involve risk-bearing and agency problems that are somewhat artificial in a world of certainty. We begin the analysis with the certainty case because it allows simple derivation of many major results.

Consider a proprietorship faced with a two-period perfectly certain world and the investment opportunities summarized in Figure 24.1 by the function $F(K,P)$, where K is the amount of resources invested in the venture in period 1, and P indicates that the organizational form is a proprietorship. A proprietorship is an organization in which the primary decision agent holds 100% of the residual claim on net cash flows. Open corporations are distinguished from proprietorships by the outside ownership of residual claims.

Proprietorships and open corporations can finance with debt as well as residual claims. For the moment, we only consider unlevered proprietorships, which means the organization is financed entirely from the proprietor's wealth. This restriction is dropped shortly, without major effects, when we extend the analysis to partnerships and closed corporations in which there are multiple residual claimants. The certainty assumption is relaxed in section 3.3 where the capital structure issue is addressed.

At time 1 the proprietor puts up K_1 units of resources. His opportunities for transforming current resources into future resources through investment in

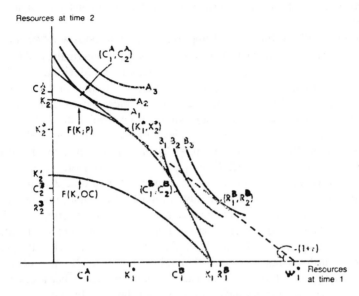

Figure 24.1. Investment decisions under certainty for two unlevered proprietorships. . . .

plant, equipment, etc., are given by the function $F(K,P)$. The proprietor can also acquire resources at time 2 by buying the securities of open corporations. The capital market interest rate for such claims is r, and we continue to assume that they are traded without cost in a perfectly competitive capital market.

Suppose the indifference curves, A_j, $j = 1, 2, \ldots$, represent the proprietor's tastes for combinations of resources consumed at time 1 and time 2. The proprietor optimally invests $K_1^* K_1$ within the proprietorship and $C_1^* K_1^*$ in the securities of open corporations. He then consumes C_1^A at time 1 and C_2^A at time 2. The proprietor stops investment within the proprietorship at $K_1^* K_1$ because further investment has a marginal return less than the rate of interest available on the securities of open corporations. An open corporation with investment opportunities summarized by the same function $F(K,P)$ would also invest $K_1^* K_1$ since this decision produces the maximum possible current wealth, W_1^*.

Although proprietor A in Figure 24.1 makes the same investment decision as an open corporation with the same opportunity set, a proprietor with tastes summarized by the indifference curves, B_j, $j = 1, 2, \ldots$, chooses to invest less. The essence of an unlevered proprietorship is that the proprietor is sole residual claimant. Thus, if proprietor B invests $K_1^* K_1$ internally at time 1, he cannot sell off part of the resulting claim to the payoff K_2^* generated at time 2. As a result, proprietor B maximizes utility by investing only the amount $C_1^B K_1$

339

which generates the resource combination (C_1^B, C_2^B) for consumption at time 1 and time 2.

Proprietor B's welfare would improve if he could borrow $K_1^*R_1^B$, of if he could reorganize as an open corporation, invest $K_1^*K_1$ internally, and then sell his residual claim for $K_1^*W_1^*$. However, as Jensen and Meckling (1979) and Fama and Jensen (1983a,b) emphasize, differences in the contract structures of different organizational forms are likely to affect the costs of delivering products. Because alternative organizational forms involve different costs and thus different net payoffs for the same level of investment, the production or transformation function for a venture depends on organizational form. In Figure 24.1, the function $F(K,P)$ shows the maximum payoffs net of all costs that can be generated by an unlevered proprietorship at time 2 with different amounts of wealth invested internally at time 1. If the unlevered proprietorship is the optimal form of organization for the investment activities underlying Figure 24.1, the transformation function for the same venture undertaken by an open corporation (OC) might be $F(K,OC)$, which lies below the proprietorship transformation function.[1] Similarly, if proprietor B issues debt, conflicts of interest with debtholders lead to contracting and other agency costs that also cause the transformation function (not shown in Figure 24.1) to shift downward by an amount that depends on the amount of debt issued. We compare here only open corporations and unlevered proprietorships.

In our certain world the dominance of the proprietorship transformation function for the venture in Figure 24.1 can be thought of as due to higher contracting costs in open corporations associated with writing and administering contracts with external residual claimants and internal decision agents. In a world of uncertainty these costs would be balanced against the efficiencies in risk sharing allowed by the open corporate form. A realistic situation where the analysis in Figure 24.1 is relevant occurs when the personal human capital of the primary decision agent is the important resource in an organization. Because human capital is difficult to sell, the decision maker is in a situation like that of proprietor B who cannot sell residual claims on the project.

Proprietors like Mr. A evaluate investment opportunities according to the maximum wealth or market value rule because they also purchase claims for resources to be delivered at time 2 in the open capital market. The restriction of the proprietorship residual claim to an investor like Mr. A is not a binding constraint on his portfolio decisions. Thus, the market interest rate, r, on external investments provides the relevant opportunity cost for internal investments. On the other hand, a proprietor like Mr. B is not also a net investor in the outside capital market. The marginal rate of time preference implied by

[1]Wolfson (1983) documents examples of the dependence of cost functions on organizational form in various forms of oil and gas limited partnerships. In particular, he provides evidence on how the choice of organizational form affects agency costs.

the slope of his indifference curve at (C_1^B, C_2^B) is higher than the market interest rate, r. Thus, it is rational for proprietor B to assign lower value to future resources generated from internal investment than is implied by the market interest rate on the unrestricted common stocks of open corporations.

If "diversified" proprietors like Mr. A are sufficient to absorb all the proprietorships that exist in a general equilibrium, the market price for the rights to the transformation function $F(K,P)$ is $K_1 W_1^*$ and Mr. B sells his rights to the venture to a Mr. A type proprietor. After purchasing residual claims on open corporations in the amount $R_1^B W_1^*$, Mr. B then consumes R_1^B at time 1 and R_2^B at time 2 and achieves utility $B_3 > B_1$.

If "diversified" proprietors like Mr. A are not sufficient to absorb all the proprietorships that will exist in a general equilibrium, that is, if, like Mr. B, the marginal proprietor in the activity only invests internally, the market price for the transformation function $F(K,P)$ is less than $K_1 W_1^*$. Proprietors like Mr. B do not use the market value rule for decisions and they invest less than open corporations faced with the same investment opportunities.

3.2. Partnerships and closed corporations

The analysis extends to partnerships and closed corporations in which residual claims are again generally restricted to decision agents. If all residual claimants in these organizations also invest in the residual claims of open corporations, that is, if they have tastes similar to Mr. A in Figure 24.1, then in a world of certainty, partnerships and closed corporations make the same decisions as open corporations faced with the same investment opportunities. However, partnerships or closed corporations whose residual claimants have consumption preferences like Mr. B do not use the market value decision rule and invest less than an open corporation with the same opportunity set. A partnership or closed corporation with a mix of Mr. A's and Mr. B's, with differing demands for current vs. future resources, faces a difficult contracting problem in making investment decisions. Such conflicts over investment and payout policies are common, for example, in family corporations and partnerships. Unlike open corporations, where all residual claimants agree on the maximum wealth or market value rule for investment decisions, in partnerships and closed corporations, investment decision rules that satisfy the interests of all residual claimants require either that all residual claimants are "diversified" (like Mr. A in Figure 24.1) or that they have identical tastes.

The residual claims in partnerships and closed corporations are generally restricted to important decision agents and to outsiders acceptable to the important decision agents. The residual claims of these organizations generally specify rules for compensating residual claimants when they retire or otherwise leave the organization. The difficulties in designing valuation processes to substitute for the capital market that continuously revalues the unrestricted residual claim of open corporations means that partnerships and closed corporations will not generally follow the value maximizing decision rule. They will tend to underinvest in assets with long-term payoffs whose current values are not easily established.

We do not expect to see voluntary contractual restrictions on the alienability of residual claims in activities where the capital value problem described above is important, that is, where decisions present major opportunities to substitute between present and future cash flows. This occurs in activities optimally carried out with large quantities of long-term assets that are difficult to value and that are more efficiently purchased by residual claimants rather than rented, for example, plant and equipment, and reputation and goodwill that can be transferred from one generation of residual claimants to the next. For example, organizations in business and financial consulting, like brokerage houses and underwriters, that were partnerships with restricted residual claims are tending to reorganize as open corporations. We hypothesize that this is largely due to changes in the nature of these activities that increase capital value problems, for example, increased demand for wealth from residual claimants to purchase risky assets that are difficult to value, and pressure to transfer the rights to the net cash flows from such assets from one generation of residual claimants to the next.

In contrast, we hypothesize that when the important asset in an activity is the human capital of existing decision agents, the activity can be efficiently supplied by partnerships with restricted residual claims. This will be true when there are no important patents, specialized assets, or technologies to be passed from one generation of partners to the next. It will also be true when the reputation and goodwill that are important in some professional service activities, such as law, public accounting, and business consulting, are tied to the human capital currently in the organization. In such cases rather extreme restrictions on residual claims can survive. For example, professional partnership residual claims often limit a partner's rights in net cash flows to period of service in the organization. (See Fama and Jensen, 1983a).

3.3. Choice of organizational form

Figure 24.2 shows a situation in which the contracting costs of the open corporate form are low enough relative to its advantages that it pays the proprietor, Mr. B, to organize the venture as an open corporation. In Figure 24.2, $F(K,OC)$ is the transformation function for an open corporation undertaking the venture. Mr. B realizes the amount $K_1W^*_{OC}$ from sale to the corporation of his rights to the venture and $K^*_{OC}K_1$ is the value maximizing level of investment by the corporation. Mr. B achieves welfare level B_3 by purchasing

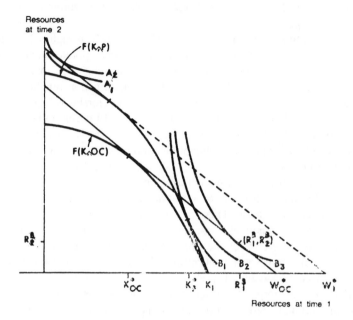

Figure 24.2. Choice of organizational form and investment under certainty when the consumption preferences of the marginal proprietor make it desirable to incur the costs of the open corporate form of organization.

shares of other open corporations amounting to $R_1^B W_{OC}^*$ and consuming (R_1^B, R_2^B) at times 1 and 2. If Mr. B organized the venture as a proprietorship he would realize utility of $B_1 < B_3$ by investing $K_P^* K_1 < K_{OC}^* K_1$.[2]

The open corporate form is optimal for Mr. B in Figure 24.2 even though the corporate transformation function $F(K,OC)$ is everywhere below the proprietorship transformation function $F(K,P)$. Mr. B's strong preference for current consumption causes him to incur the costs associated with the open corporate form. The unrestricted alienability and separability of open corporate claims allow him to rearrange his consumption pattern by selling his claims in the capital market and devoting part or all of the proceeds to current consumption. Of course, the corporate firm is optimal for Mr. B only if there are no other potential proprietors willing to purchase his rights to the venture for more than $K_1 W_{OC}^*$. In particular, if the marginal proprietorship is "well

[2]If Mr. B both manages the corporation and owns shares in it, the corporate opportunity set $F(K,OC)$ depends on Mr. B's stock ownership fraction. Figure 24.2 portrays the polar case in which he sells off all his claims on the corporation. Jensen and Meckling (1976b) analyze the intermediate cases in which the proprietor maintains both management and stock ownership interests in the corporation.

343

diversified" like Mr. A, Mr. B will sell his rights to the venture to Mr. A for $K_1W_1^* > K_1W_{OC}^*$.

While the optimal corporate investment level $K_{OC}^*K_1$ in Figure 24.2 maximizes value, $K_1W_{OC}^*$, conditional on choice of the corporate organizational form, this is obviously not equivalent to the value, $K_1W_1^*$, that could be obtained (at investment level $K_P^{**}K_1$) if the transformation function $F(K,P)$ applied to open corporations as well as to proprietorships. The distance, $W_{OC}^*W_1^*$, is what Jensen and Meckling (1976, p. 320) define to be the gross agency costs of the corporate form, the difference between the maximum value attainable if the proprietorship production function were available to the open corporation and the maximum value attainable from the production function actually available to the corporation.

The transformation function for a proprietorship does not always dominate that for an open corporation. This is illustrated in Figure 24.3 [ed.: not shown here] where scale economies cause the transformation function for the open corporation to cross that for the proprietorship. Moreover, in an uncertain world the gains from specialization of risk-bearing and decision functions discussed in Fama and Jensen (1983a) can become so large with increasing scale that the open corporate form dominates the proprietorship. In general at each point in time there is a set of transformation functions for each venture, one for each possible organizational form.

At various stages in the life of a venture it may be best carried out under different organizational forms. For example, it might first be organized as a proprietorship and then, with increasing demands for financing risky investments, converted to a partnership or a closed corporation, and then to an open corporation. At a later time, conditions can indicate reconversion to a closed corporation, partnership, or even proprietorship form.

· · ·

CHAPTER 25

The structure of ownership and the theory of the firm

HAROLD DEMSETZ

Harold Demsetz is Professor of Economics at the University of California at Los Angeles. See also the previous article coauthored by
Demsetz.

The separation of ownership and control in the modern corporation, an issue
brought to the fore so effectively by Berle and Means fifty years ago, retains a
central position in recent writings about the economic theory of the firm. The
problem is stated succinctly by Berle and Means:

> The separation of ownership from control produces a condition where the interests
> of owner and of ultimate manager may, and often do, diverge, and where many of the
> checks which formerly operated to limit the use of power disappear. . . .
>
> In creating these new relationships, the quasi-public corporation may fairly be said
> to work a revolution. It . . . has divided ownership into nominal ownership and the
> power formerly joined to it. Thereby the corporation has changed the nature of profit-
> seeking enterprise.[1]

The holder of corporate stock experiences a loss of control over his resources
because ownership is so broadly dispersed across large numbers of shareholders that the typical shareholder cannot exercise real power to oversee
managerial performance in modern corporations. Management exercises more
freedom in the use of the firm's resources than would exist if the firm were
managed by its owner(s), or at least, if ownership interests were more concentrated. Because management and ownership interests do not naturally coincide when not housed in the same person, Berle and Means perceive a conflict
of interest, which, with ownership dispersed, is resolved in management's
favor.

To Berle and Means this signifies a serious impairment of the social function of private property. Profit maximization constrained and guided by competition is the link between private ownership and efficient resource utilization, a link presumably broken by a structure of ownership that reduces the
incentives of corporate managers to maximize profit. Corporate wealth is used

Excerpted from Harold Demsetz, "The Structure of Ownership and the Theory of the Firm,"
Journal of Law and Economics 26 (1983): 375–90. Copyright ©1983 by The University of
Chicago. All rights reserved. Published by University of Chicago Press.
[1] Berle and Means (1932).

to further ends other than profit maximization. The logical consequences of decentralization through private ownership of the means of production, then, are no longer those deduced with the aid of a theory of price based on owner-managed firms. The argument is as appealing to socialists as it is credible to noninterventionists. Indeed, businessmen themselves implicitly support the central thesis of separation. They are among the first to deny the dominance of the profit motive in business decisions, frequently appealing to the evidence that exists in the record of corporate financial support of various charitable and educational endeavors.

. . .

A closer look at the problem of ownership structure is warranted, if for no other reason than that these commentators fail to examine either the theoretical problem or the empirical premise carefully. In the discussion that follows, I will be recovering some subject matter that has emerged in recent writings by economists on organization theory,[2] but the views taken in this paper offer some difference in emphasis and mild disagreement.

I view the ownership structure of the firm as an endogenous outcome of a maximizing process in which more is at stake than just accommodating to the shirking problem. A broader perspective on the problem of the optimum ownership structure makes the fears of Berle and Means meaningless. I conclude with a discussion of evidence bearing on the empirical premise assumed by the alleged separation between ownership and control.

The firm in economic theory

Two concepts of the firm motivate Berle and Means to level the charge of social inefficiency at the modern corporation: their conception of the firm in economic theory and their contrasting conception of the real modern corporation. The first of these associates the profit-maximizing firm of economic theory with the precorporation firms that populated the business world during most of the nineteenth century. The theoretical firm is viewed as a good approximation of precorporate real firms, and the theory pictures these as lean, no-nonsense institutions devoid of managerial amenities. The second conception is a firm largely controlled by a management possessing an insig-

---

[2] See Williamson (1964b), Alchian and Demsetz (1972), Jensen and Meckling (1976b), Fama (1980). My mild disagreement with this literature revolves around the following issues: I do not believe that resorting to agency relationships reduces the value of the firm to its owners. On the contrary, it increases this value. I do not believe that on-the-job consumption is necessarily, or even probably, greater with professional management than with management by owners. The cost of agency, I believe, is borne by the firm, not by the agents. I am not prepared to presume the fact of diffuseness in the ownership of the modern corporation.

nificant interest in the profitability of the firm's activities. A la Baumol,[3] the firm may seek to keep shareholders contented with a minimum acceptable positive return, but beyond that, profit is traded off to increase the *utility* of management. Utility-maximizing managerial behavior requires the use of the firms resources to provide on-the-job amenities. These might include not only the usual amenities but also abnormally high managerial wages and excessively large firms. If the organization pictured by the firm of economic theory promotes efficiency, then, for Berle and Means, the organization they perceive as the real corporation surely does not. These two conceptions of the firm draw a contrast that remains popular and guides much of the clamor for radically reorganizing corporate law, if not the private sector.[4]

It is a mistake to confuse the firm of economic theory with its real-world namesake. The chief mission of neoclassical economics is to understand how the price system coordinates the use of resources, not to understand the inner workings of real firms.[5] There are two broad divisions of use to which resources may be put, consumption and production. One of the important tasks of the theory of price is to explain how prices influence each of these uses. To this end, the theory *defines* the household, not to approximate the activities of a family of four, but as the theoretical institution in which rational decisions about consumption take place. Correspondingly, the firm is *defined*, not to approximate the activities of a real firm, pre- or postcorporate organization, but as the theoretical institution in which production (for others) takes place. This distorts some characteristics of real families and real firms. Some family activity is devoted to production and, as such, is guided primarily by profit considerations (the family rents rooms in its house to boarders), and no doubt the persons who manage real firms consume while on the job, but this is unimportant to the theory's objective, for the theory does not seek to understand the actual loci of consumption and production. Its concern is with how these activities are affected by exogenous changes (such as a tax change) and with how the price system determines the quantities and mixtures of goods consumed and produced.

The study of these problems is simplified considerably by defining households and firms to be specialized, respectively, to consumption activity and production activity. Consumption, by definition, creates utility, so the household's decisions in theory are utility-maximizing decisions. Production is devoid of direct utility-creating activities (which are defined as consumption), so the firm's decisions are guided only by profit considerations. However, the maximization of the firm's profit delivers to its owners a maximum capability for (indirect) utility-creating consumption in their households. The entire

---

[3] Baumol (1967).
[4] See Nader, Green, and Seligman (1976) and Galbraith (1967).
[5] See Demsetz (1982) for an extended discussion of the task of neoclassical economic theory.

process really is concerned with utility maximization, but some activities, identified as production (for use by others), deliver utility indirectly to factor owners through the easing of their household budget constraints.

Real firms, whether or not they are owner-managed, are not so specialized in their activities. This does not undermine the relevance of the theoretical firm for explaining the guidance given to economic activity by prices. To see why the conclusions of economic theory remain valid in this task even when consumption, as well as production, takes place in real firms, let us consider an owner-managed firm that houses both activities. For the present discussion, let us be concerned only about *known* on-the-job consumption.

The compensation received by the owner-manager of such a firm potentially contains three components – pecuniary wages of management, known amenities of office, and profit of owner. The behavior of such an owner-manager surely is guided by utility maximinization, not simply the pursuit of profit. One owner may prefer spotlessly clean surroundings for the large part of the day he spends at the office. Another values managing a larger or faster-growing firm. A third values associating with laborers who practice a particular religion or who have a particular skin color. Nothing in the theory of the price system bars the owner from indulging these desires. The theory of competitive markets, which is based on full knowledge of such consumption, requires only that he pay for these indulgences, just as if he were purchasing them as a consumer. (This is common knowledge among students of labor markets, and it has frequently been documented quantitatively by them.)

Because a good part of a real owner-manager's life is on the job, he very well may decide in favor of on-the-job consumption. This more realistically depicted firm, because of the resources used to provide on-the-job consumption, appears to add needlessly to its cost of producing goods. This seems to be at odds with the firm of economic theory, which minimizes the cost of producing goods that its customers will consume. The appearance is a delusion. Because those who consume on the job pay for their amenities, such consumption will take place only when it *reduces* the cost of producing goods for others. Competitive markets for the firm's goods prevent its owner-manager from financing his amenities through customers' contributions to his revenue. Customers always can purchase from firms whose owners prefer to confine their consumption in greater degree to their households. Competitive markets for labor similarly block an owner-manager from taxing his workers to pay for his amenities, and finally, investors always can put their funds elsewhere if they cannot receive a competitive return (corrected for risk) from a firm whose owner-manager consumes on the job.

Because the owner-manager pays for his amenities by accepting a reduction in his implicit managerial compensation, he will not consume while on the job unless the cost of doing so, per unit of utility received, is *less* than if he consumed at home. The same must be true of all workers, including hired managers. If the owner-manager or his employees desire to consume on the job, paying for what they consume, then their services can be acquired more cheaply by allowing such consumption than by barring it, for in such a case the cost of on-the-job amenities is smaller than would be the increase in take-home pay required to maintain identical utility levels for these employees. On-the-job consumption, when known, occurs only if there is a utility advantage to consuming at the firm, because the equivalent value in larger take-home pay is more fungible than is on-the-job consumption. If consumption at home is more efficient, then it will not take place on the job; the increase in pecuniary compensation required to compensate persons for not consuming on the job will be less than the cost of providing such consumption if workers' or managers' utility level is to be unchanged.

The assumption that firms minimize the cost of producing goods for others, derived so easily from the profit-maximizing assumption, remains valid even when the firm is permitted to provide on-the-job amenities. The producing activity of the firm is carried on at least cost because such consumption possibilities are available. The neoclassical theory of the firm merely simplifies the study of the price system by implicitly assuming, or defining, consumption activity to be more efficient in households.

It follows that the claim, and presumed empirical observation, that consumption takes place on the job cannot refute either profit maximization or efficiency in the production of goods by real firms. The deployment of resources in firms may differ because of different degrees of on-the-job consumption, but firms that supply more such amenities are producing them more cheaply for their employee-consumers (or perhaps more accurately, are producing more utility per dollar expended) than if these employee-consumers were forced to consume substitute "amenities" at home. Hence, goods that are produced for employee consumption on the job and goods produced for outside consumers (which the firm of economic theory is designed to explain) are both produced at as low an opportunity cost as is possible. The firm of economic theory may be only a sketch of real firms, but it nonetheless yields useful insights about resource utilization in a decentralized economy.

Shirking

To this point, I have discussed only known consumption on the job by individual employees. In a model of the firm in which monitoring cost is zero, this would be the only possible on-the-job consumption; each quality of worker, including managers, receives his market-determined wage, but the way in which that wage is received depends on whether the worker prefers to consume on the job or at home. Once we turn to a model of the firm in which monitoring cost is positive, the inverse correlation between take-home wages and on-the-job consumption is weakened, at least in the case of the individual worker. If positive monitoring cost means anything, it certainly means the weakening of this inverse correlation.

Take-home wages for an identifiable quality grouping of workers will be inversely correlated with their *collective* on-the-job consumption even when monitoring cost is positive, but some workers in the group will consume more on the job than others, and the amount of collective consumption by the group will be higher (than with zero monitoring cost) by virtue of the fact that this inverse relationship cannot be preserved so strongly when compensating each individual. Correspondingly, the group's take-home pay will be lower. We may interpret the amount by which on-the-job consumption, given positive monitoring cost, exceeds the amount of consumption that would take place when modeled with zero monitoring cost as shirking. Shirking is a nonactivity in the zero monitoring cost model. Unlike the mutually advantageous on-the-job consumption that takes place when monitoring cost is zero, shirking can be reduced and both employer and employees made better off if the monitoring cost required to reduce shirking is less than the value of the resources consumed in shirking. Presumably, shirking is reduced to its optimal level by various pressures from within and outside the firm, but shirking nonetheless will exist.

The average quality of employees contained in an identifiable quality group determines the compensation that is paid, per employee, to this group. This compensation contains a larger fraction of on-the-job consumption than it would in a zero monitoring cost model. In firms that have more difficulty (higher cost) monitoring, this fraction will be greater. The fraction that is take-home pay will be lower than for the same quality group of employees employed in a low monitoring cost firm.

Aggregate on-the-job consumption

There are thus two sources of on-the-job consumption: known individual consumption (possibly the owner-manager's) that reflects personal taste and unknown individual consumption – shirking – that reflects the existence of positive monitoring cost. Once this is recognized, it is no longer clear that diffuse ownership gives rise to more on-the-job consumption. Where is it written that the owner-manager of a closely held firm prefers to consume only at home?

The Structure of Ownership and the Theory of the Firm

Consider an owner-manager who delights in associating with people of his religion or of his skin color. Because he spends most of his waking hours on the job, this is where he will choose to indulge his preferences. If, to indulge his taste for on-the-job consumption, he must employ workers who are less productive in supplying the goods that he sells to others, then consuming in the firm will force him to accept lower pecuniary returns. For him, this may be superior to higher income and less preferred on-the-job associations.

Imagine now that this same person becomes specialized to the task of owning, not managing, the firm. Let us suppose that the professional managers that he employs to replace him in the firm's management share his tastes in fellow workers. In his new role as specialized owner, however, he derives no utility from the composition of the labor force, for he no longer puts in time at the office. He prefers instead the higher pecuniary returns that can be had with a less homogeneous mixture of laborers. His desire for profit now leads him to search for a management that is less prone to discriminate by religion and color. Alternatively, he may insist on reducing the pecuniary compensation of his hired managers until his net return rises to what could be secured from a new and different management.

The reduction in the compensation of existing management may nonetheless be insufficient to keep this management in the managing game. The owner, when he was manager, was prepared to accept some reduction in pecuniary income because *he* consumed on-the-job amenities, and he preferred this to higher take-home compensation because his utility from such consumption is time and place specific. Because he sacrifices this specificity when he consumes at home, he will insist on a greater reduction in the compensation of hired management than he was prepared to accept when he managed the firm; now it is hired management, not he, that enjoys these time- and place-specific amenities. He will ask a greater financial sacrifice from such a management than he would have asked of himself, were he managing, if he is to be just as well off consuming at home. The net result of his becoming a specialized owner, therefore, may very well be a reduction in on-the-job consumption.

This important aspect of specialization in ownership has largely gone unnoticed. The specialized owner derives little or no direct utility from on-the-job consumption by his management. He may be unaffected by such consumption if his management is prepared to stay on the job while absorbing *enough* of a wage cut to compensate the specialized owner for the resulting increase in other costs. But because of the time and place specificity of on-the-job consumption, the required wage cut will be larger than would have been required by the owner were he managing his own firm. In general, we can expect that specialized ownership, in and of itself, cre-

351

ates pressure for less on-the-job consumption so long as monitoring cost is not a barrier to guaranteeing that what is promised by management is what is delivered.

We thus have two opposing forces at work. The "pure" effect of specialized ownership is to reduce on-the-job consumption below levels that would obtain if owners were also managers. The opposing force is the increase in monitoring cost associated with organizational structures most likely to create specialized ownership interests. The shareholder of a large publicly held corporation derives no direct utility from on-the-job consumption of management, so his interests are fixed on the bottom line of the profit and loss statement. The more broadly based is the ownership of the firm, however, the greater is the cost of monitoring management.

It is clearly an error to suppose that a firm managed by its only owner comes closest to the profit-maximizing firm postulated in the model firm of economic theory. The owner-manager of such a firm may or may not be motivated only by the search for profit. He may habitually consume on the job. This consumption can take many forms. It need not be the proclivity for association with homogeneous fellow workers described above. The senior Ford, who built the Ford Motor Company into a position of dominance in the automobile industry, is said to have had such a proclivity. But also, in his later years, he proved to be stubborn, single-minded, and without managerial flexibility. He "consumed" dominance over his fellow workers at the sacrifice of profit to himself. His lieutenants were disgruntled but helpless as they witnessed the decline of the company. Ford survived as the managerial leader of his company only because it was *his* company. Had the Ford Motor Company been a publicly held corporation, it is unlikely that he would have been allowed to indulge his taste for dominance for so long. Those who criticize the publicly held corporation for favoring on-the-job consumption may be aiming at the wrong target.

Whether on-the-job consumption finds its source in the personal tastes of owners and employees of the firm or in the cost of monitoring is irrelevant to either profit maximization or efficiency. Specialization of business activity into one set of rights that we identify as share ownership and which we may, if we insist, call ownership of the corporation, and a second that we call managerial control, surely raises the utility level achievable by those with funds to invest and those with managerial skills to sell. This division of property rights allows persons the option of combining "ownership" and control in any mixture that they wish, given the budget constraints they face. Investment funds *and* control, therefore, become available at *lower* costs to society than would be possible were fractional ownership barred. The advent of the modern corporation, organized exchanges, and corporation law have reduced the cost

352

of specializing one's interest as between the different task of owning and managing.

The equilibrium business organization

. . .

It is important to treat monitoring cost as we would treat any other cost of production if we are to develop a useful perspective for assessing the consequences of a diffuse ownership structure. The structure of ownership that emerges is an endogenous outcome of competitive selection in which various cost advantages and disadvantages are balanced to arrive at an equilibrium organization of the firm. One cannot simply assert that diffuse ownership fails to yield maximum profit or maximum value of the firm or that it fails to yield efficient resource allocation. On-the-job consumption, and even control by owners, cannot be judged independently of other aspects of the equilibrium organization.

The monitoring cost that must be incurred to reduce shirking to its optimal level is a function of the way the firm has been organized and of the technological conditions that underlie the production of its goods. The cost is borne by the firm, not its employees. Because a given quality group of employees must receive the same total compensation (although its mix may differ) whether the group works for a firm with a high or a low monitoring cost, the cost of monitoring cannot be passed on to the employees. In making its choice of business organization, the firm (or its owners) therefore must pay attention to how this choice affects the cost of monitoring and whether a higher-monitoring-cost organization will also bring with it reductions in other costs that make the higher monitoring cost worth bearing.

. . .

CHAPTER 26

An economist's perspective on the theory of the firm

OLIVER HART

Oliver Hart was born in London, England, in 1948. He received a Ph.D. in economics from Princeton University in 1974. When this article was published, he was Professor of Economics at Massachusetts Institute of Technology. Since 1993, he has been Professor of Economics at Harvard University.

An outsider to the field of economics would probably take it for granted that economists have a highly developed theory of the firm. After all, firms are the engines of growth of modern capitalistic economies, and so economists must surely have fairly sophisticated views of how they behave. In fact, little could be further from the truth. Most formal models of the firm are extremely rudimentary, capable only of portraying hypothetical firms that bear little relation to the complex organizations we see in the world. Furthermore, theories that attempt to incorporate real world features of corporations, partnerships, and the like often lack precision and rigor and have therefore failed, by and large, to be accepted by the theoretical mainstream.

This article attempts to give lawyers a sense of how economists think about firms. It does not pretend to offer a systematic survey of the area; rather, it highlights several ideas of particular importance, and then explores an alternative theoretical perspective from which to view the firm.[1] Part I introduces various established economic theories of the firm. Part II turns to a newer theory of the firm, based not upon human capital structures, but rather upon property rights. Part III synthesizes this property rights-based theory of the firm with more established theories.

Excerpted from Oliver Hart, "An Economist's Perspective on the Theory of the Firm." This article originally appeared at 89 *Columbia Law Review* 1757 (1989). Reprinted by permission.

[1] Several recent surveys provide other perspectives on this material. See, e.g., Holmstrom and Tirole (1989), Milgrom and Roberts (1988), Williamson (1988).

An economist's perspective on the theory of the firm

I. Established theories

. . .

C. Transaction cost economics

While the neoclassical paradigm, modified by principal–agent theory, progressed along the above lines, a very different approach to the theory of the firm developed under the heading of transaction cost economics. Introduced in Coase's famous 1937 article, transaction cost economics traces the existence of firms to the thinking, planning, and contracting costs that accompany any transaction, costs usually ignored by the neoclassical paradigm. The idea is that in some situations these costs will be lower if a transaction is carried out within a firm rather than in the market. According to Coase, the main cost of transacting in the market is the cost of learning about and haggling over the terms of trade; this cost can be particularly large if the transaction is a long-term one in which learning and haggling must be performed repeatedly. Transaction costs can be reduced by giving one party authority over the terms of trade, at least within limits. But, according to Coase, this authority is precisely what defines a firm: within a firm, transactions occur as a result of instructions or orders issued by a boss, and the price mechanism is suppressed.

. . .

At the same time that doubts were being expressed about the specifics of Coase's theory, Coase's major idea – that firms arise to economize on transaction costs – was increasingly accepted. The exact nature of these transaction costs, however, remained unclear. What lay beyond the learning and haggling costs that, according to Coase, are a major component of market transactions? Professor Oliver Williamson has offered the deepest and most far-reaching analysis of these costs. Williamson recognized that transaction costs may assume particular importance in situations where economic actors make relationship-specific investments – investments to some extent specific to a particular set of individuals or assets. Examples of such investments include locating an electricity generating plant adjacent to a coal mine that is going to supply it, a firm's expanding capacity to satisfy a particular customer's demands, training a worker to operate a particular set of machines or to work with a particular group of individuals, or a worker's relocating to a town where he has a new job.

In situations like these, there may be plenty of competition before the investments are made – there may be many coal mines next to which an electricity generating plant could locate or many towns to which a worker could move. But once the parties sink their investments, they are to some extent locked into each other. As a result, external markets will not provide a guide to the parties' opportunity costs once the relationship is underway.

. . .

In Williamson's view, bringing a transaction from the market into the firm – the phenomenon of integration – mitigates . . . opportunistic behavior and improves investment incentives. Agent A is less likely to hold up agent B if A is an employee of B than if A is an independent contractor. However, Williamson does not spell out in precise terms the mechanism by which this reduction in opportunism occurs. Moreover, certain costs presumably accompany integration. Otherwise, all transactions would be carried out in firms, and the market would not be used at all. Williamson, however, leaves the precise nature of these costs unclear.

. . .

II. A property rights approach to the firm

One way to resolve the question of how integration changes incentives is spelled out in recent literature that views the firm as a set of property rights. This approach is very much in the spirit of the transaction cost literature of Coase and Williamson but differs by focusing attention on the role of physical, that is, nonhuman, assets in a contractual relationship.

Consider an economic relationship of the type analyzed by Williamson, where relationship-specific investments are important and transaction costs make it impossible to write a comprehensive long-term contract to govern the terms of the relationship. Consider also the nonhuman assets that, in the postinvestment stage, make up this relationship. Given that the initial contract has gaps, missing provisions, or ambiguities, situations will typically occur in which some aspects of the use of these assets are not specified. For example, a contract between GM and Fisher might leave open certain aspects of maintenance policy for Fisher machines or might not specify the speed of the production line or the number of shifts per day.

Take the position that the right to choose these missing aspects of usage resides with the *owner* of the asset. That is, ownership of an asset goes together with the possession of residual rights of control over that asset; the owner has the right to use the asset in any way not inconsistent with a prior contract, custom, or any law. Thus, the owner of Fisher assets would have the

356

right to choose maintenance policy and production line speed to the extent that the initial contract was silent about these.

Finally, identify a firm with all the nonhuman assets that belong to it, assets that the firm's owners possess by virtue of being owners of the firm. Included in this category are machines, inventories, buildings or locations, cash, client lists, patents, copyrights, and the rights and obligations embodied in outstanding contracts to the extent that these are also transferred with ownership. Human assets, however, are not included. Since human assets cannot be bought or sold, management and workers presumably own their own human capital both before and after any merger.

We now have the basic ingredients of a theory of the firm. In a world of transaction costs and incomplete contracts, *ex post* residual rights of control will be important because, through their influence on asset usage, they will affect *ex post* bargaining power and the division of *ex post* surplus in a relationship. This division in turn will affect the incentives of actors to invest in that relationship. Hence, when contracts are incomplete, the boundaries of firms matter in that these boundaries determine who owns and controls which assets.[2] In particular, a merger of two firms does not yield unambiguous benefits: to the extent that the (owner-)manager of the acquired firm loses control rights, his incentive to invest in the relationship will decrease. In addition, the shift in control may lower the investment incentives of workers in the acquired firm. In some cases these reductions in investment will be sufficiently great that nonintegration is preferable to integration.[3]

Note that, according to this theory, when assessing the effects of integration, one must know not only the characteristics of the merging firms but also who will own the merged company. If firms *A* and *B* integrate and *A* becomes the owner of the merged company, then *A* will presumably control the residual

---

[2] This consolidation of ownership and control points to an important lacuna in the property rights approach. The approach makes no distinction between ownership and control, assuming that both rest with the same entity. In most of the formal models that have been developed, such an arrangement turns out to be optimal since agents are assumed to be risk neutral and to have sufficient wealth to buy any asset. If managers were risk averse and had limited wealth, however, this conclusion would no longer be valid. Moreover, from a descriptive point of view, the assumption that owners manage is seriously inadequate; while it may apply to small firms such as partnerships or closed corporations, it certainly does not apply to large, publicly held corporations. For how the ownership/control dichotomy might affect the property rights approach, see infranotes 58–59 [ed.: notes 5 and 6, this version] and accompanying text.

[3] It is important to emphasize that the property rights approach distinguishes between ownership in the sense of possession of residual control rights over assets and ownership in the sense of entitlement to a firm's (verifiable) profit stream. In practice, these rights will often go together, but they do not have to. The property rights approach takes the point of view that the possession of control rights is crucial for the integration decision. That is, if firm *A* wants to acquire part of firm *B*'s (verifiable) profit stream, it can always do this by contract. It is only if firm *A* wants to acquire control over firm *B*'s assets that it needs to integrate.

rights in the new firm. *A* can then use those rights to hold up the managers and workers of firm *B*. Should the situation be reversed, a different set of control relations would result in *B* exercising control over *A*, and *A*'s workers and managers would be liable to holdups by *B*.

· · ·

These ideas can be used to construct a theory of the firm's boundaries. First, as we have seen, highly complementary assets should be owned in common, which may provide a minimum size for the firm. Second, as the firm grows beyond a certain point, the manager at the center will become less and less important with regard to operations at the periphery in the sense that increases in marginal product at the periphery are unlikely to be specific either to this manager or to the assets at the center. At this stage, a new firm should be created since giving the central manager control of the periphery will increase holdup problems without any compensating gains. It should also be clear from this line of argument that, in the absence of significant lock-in effects, nonintegration is always better than integration – it is optimal to do things through the market, for integration only increases the number of potential holdups without any compensating gains.[4]

Finally, it is worth noting that the property rights approach can explain how the purchase of physical assets leads to control over human assets. To see this, consider again the GM–Fisher hypothetical. We showed that someone working with Fisher assets is more likely to improve Fisher's output in a way that is specifically of value to GM if GM owns these assets than if Fisher does. This result can be expressed more informally as follows: a worker will put more weight on an actor's objectives if that actor is the worker's boss, that is, if that actor controls the assets the worker works with, than otherwise. The conclusion is quite Coasian in spirit, but the logic underlying it is very different. Coase reaches this conclusion by assuming that a boss can tell a worker what to do; in contrast, the property rights approach reaches it by showing that it is in a worker's self-interest to behave in this way, since it puts him in a stronger bargaining position with his boss later on.

To put it slightly differently, the reason an employee is likely to be more

---

[4] In the above we have concentrated on ownership by an individual or by a homogeneous and monolithic group ("management"). However, the analysis can be generalized to include more complicated forms of group ownership, such as partnerships, or worker-, manager-, or consumer-cooperatives. It turns out that these will be efficient when increases in agents' marginal products are specific to a group of individuals of variable composition, rather than to a fixed group. For example, if the increase in an agent's marginal product can be realized only if the agent has access to a majority of the members of a management team, as well as to a particular asset, then it will be optimal to give each of the managers an equal ownership share in the asset and equal voting rights and adopt majority rule. See Hart and Moore (1988), p. 19.

responsive to what his employer wants than a grocer is to what his customer wants is that the employer has much more leverage over his employee than the customer has over his grocer. In particular, the employer can deprive the employee of the assets he works with and hire another employee to work with these assets, while the customer can only deprive the grocer of his custom and as long as the customer is small, it is presumably not very difficult for the grocer to find another customer.

. . .

III. Property rights and the established theories
of the firm

. . .

As noted previously, one of the weaknesses of the property rights approach as described here is that it does not take account of the separation of ownership and control present in large, publicly held corporations. In principle, it should be possible to extend the existing analysis to such situations. A public corporation can still be usefully considered a collection of assets, with ownership providing control rights over these assets. Now, however, the picture is more complicated. Although owners (shareholders) typically retain some control rights, such as the right to replace the board of directors, in practice they delegate many others to management, at least on a day-to-day basis.[5] In addition, some of the shareholders' rights sift to creditors during periods of financial distress. Developing a formal model of the firm that contains all these features, and that includes also an explanation of the firm's financial structure, is an important and challenging task for future research. Fortunately, recent work suggests that the task is not an impossible one.[6]

Conclusion

This article began with the observation that the portrayal of the firm in neoclassical economics is a caricature of the modern firm. It then went on to discuss some other approaches that attempt to develop a more realistic picture. The end product to date is still, in many ways, a caricature, but perhaps not such an unreasonable one. One promising sign is that the different approaches economists have used to address this issue – neoclassical, principal–

---

[5] See, e.g., Clark (1985), Easterbrook and Fischel (1983), Fama and Jensen (1983b).
[6] See, e.g., Grossman and Hart (1988), Harris and Raviv, (1988), Aghion and Bolton (1988), Kahn and Huberman (1988).

agent, transaction cost, nexus of contracts, property rights – appear to be converging. It is to be hoped that in the next few years the best aspects of each of these approaches can be drawn on to develop a more comprehensive and realistic theory of the firm. Such a theory would capture the salient features both of modern corporations and of owner-managed firms and would illuminate the issues for economists and lawyers alike.

CHAPTER 27

Ownership and the nature
of the firm

LOUIS PUTTERMAN

Louis Putterman was born in 1952 in New York City. He received a
Ph.D. in economics at Yale University in 1980. Since 1987, he has been
Professor of Economics at Brown University.

. . .

1. Ownership and its components

The production of goods and services commonly requires a large variety of
inputs, including financial resources, risk-bearing services, and decision making. Decision making is a necessary input because production takes place in
real time, and relevant events, such as mechanical failures, technical innovations, or changes in market conditions, cannot be foreseen when agreements
to undertake production are initiated.[1] Financial inputs are required because it
is usually worthwhile to employ techniques entailing a lag between the investment of resources and the completion of saleable products. Risk bearing is
required when the realizable value of the products cannot be known with
certainty at the time that costly effort, materials, and services of capital goods
are used up.

In most business firms, decision-making rights are held by persons who are
also financial risk bearers and suppliers of funds. The holders of these rights
are known as the owners of the firm. Ownership refers to a bundle of rights
that an economic agent is entitled to exercise over an asset. Its main components are the right of utilization, the right to the products of the asset, and the
right to alienate or dispose of the asset and of these rights of utilization and
return (Montias, 1976, p. 116; Ryan, 1987, p. 1029). The firm as an ownable
asset is an entity that acts as a legal agent in the marketplace, entering into

Adapted and reprinted by permission of the publisher from "Ownership and the Nature of the
Firm" by Louis Putterman in *Journal of Comparative Economics* Volume 17, pages 243–263.
Copyright ©1993 by Academic Press, Inc.
[1] The transactions cost school argues that some decisions are left to be taken by specialized
agents because renegotiating the duties and rewards of each contributor to the production process
would make products uncompetitively expensive. A more complete statement of the problem
would also refer to the costs of writing complex contingent contracts; see Williamson (1975) and
Hart (1989).

contractual agreements with other agents in order to produce and sell goods and services. With respect to a firm, the right of utilization means the right to determine what contracts the firm enters into and the right to unilaterally fill in the details of incomplete contracts with some agents, e.g., employees. Revenue rights over the firm mean both a limited or an unlimited obligation for financial liabilities incurred by it and a claim on all earnings accruing to it. The right of alienation means that the bundle of ownership rights may be transferred to another party or parties on mutually agreeable terms.

Holding residual income rights and rights of alienation makes owners of firms risk bearers as well as controllers. Why these functions are bundled together in ownership, why they are usually also linked to the provision of financial resources, and who will own the firm are the questions to which I turn next, while subsequent sections examine the question of ownership concentration, the relationship between equity and nonequity finance, implications of separating ownership from work, and the problem of public ownership. A brief summary concludes the paper.

2. Who owns the firm?

Risk bearing, provision of finance, and decision making are potentially separable functions, but they are usually found together in the firms of market economies. Risk bearing and control over decision making tend to be associated with the same individuals because moral hazard means that the cost of risk bearing is inversely proportional to the degree of control the risk bearer exercises over the risks taken. Risk bearing could be separated from provision of finance if firms could be 100% debt financed. However, as is discussed further in Section 5 [of Putterman, 1993a], risk bearers can attract fixed return financiers at more favorable interest rates if they also place some of their own funds at risk in the firm.

Who will own the firm? Suppliers of machine services, raw materials, and labor could share risk bearing, financing, and decision-making functions if collective decision-making rules were adopted and if each of the parties were to provide their services without immediate compensation and agreed to accept payment in the form of a share of whatever value is realized. But just as these individuals may not consume equal quantities of finished goods and services because of differences in their income levels and preferences, they may also not find it equally attractive to finance the production process and to bear its risks. Rather, individuals having greater wealth will, as a rule, be more inclined to supply financing and risk-bearing services to the firm. Suppliers of ordinary labor services are usually not in a good position to incur risk or to finance the provision of labor without fairly immediate compensation. In contrast, the suppliers of financial resources that are advanced to pay for wages and materials and to invest in physical capital and in product and marketing research are on average of higher wealth and in a better position to bear risk.[2] If control, risk bearing, and financing go together for the reasons given above, then we can expect to see most agents cede control rights to financiers in return for an insured return to their own participation in the production process.[3]

Pointing to wealth constraints alone constitutes an incomplete explanation of why workers do not finance their own firms to a greater degree than is typically observed. Many workers engage in life-cycle saving, and their pension and insurance funds provide a significant share of the investment funds in capitalist economies. Consideration of how the possibility of portfolio diversification interacts with risk aversion must be added to that of financing capacity.

Having low net wealth, most workers will prefer to invest their savings in a portfolio in which aggregate risk is reduced by judicious diversification. Workers already bear an unavoidable burden of risk linked to the fortunes of the enterprise employing them, since an important difference between labor and financial capital is that the former is relatively undiversifiable. When workers acquire human capital specific to their firms, or when anticipated unemployment or search costs make the prospect of job loss costly, further entanglement with these firms as financiers is particularly undesirable. The diversification motive accordingly works together with workers' relatively low abilities to supply financial resources and bear risk to help explain why most workers do not own their firms (Meade, 1972; Neuberger and James, 1973; Putterman, 1988).

A cost to workers of not providing risk-bearing and financing services to their firms is that they do not control them. This may involve both an agency cost, since owners will have to expend resources on monitoring and otherwise disciplining nonowner employees, and a direct welfare cost, if workers suffer a loss of satisfaction due, for example, to the perception that they are working for the profit of others under conditions they do not control. Whether the low financial capacities and diversification motives for not financing their firms, discussed in the previous paragraphs, in fact lead workers to forego a financial role depends upon their assessments of these costs of not financing as well as on the affirmative costs of financing their firms. High assessments of the risk-bearing costs of financing their firms, or low assessments of the monitoring

---

[2] For formal models in which the less risk averse or the less liquidity constrained become suppliers of capital and holders of enterprise control rights, see Kihlstrom and Laffont (1979) and Eswaran and Kotwal (1989).

[3] An additional consideration is that control by a subset of agents having similar objectives may make decision making easier than it would be for a set of agents with more heterogeneous goals (Hansmann, 1988). This advantage may or may not be offset by costs with respect to information sharing or lost enthusiasm for implementing the decisions taken.

and direct welfare costs of not doing so, would lead to the commonly observed outcome of nonownership by workers.

. . .

Ownership and work

A basic preoccupation of the literature on the economics of organization has been the problem of the separation of ownership and control in the modern corporation. This paper argues that revenue and alienation rights, on the one hand, and control or utilization rights, on the other, are at most only partially separated in the corporation and that the joining of these rights to the right of control and to the function of supplying risk-bearing capital has been a constant element in the evolution of the modern business firm. Compared with the separation of ownership and control, separation of ownership and work is usually far more complete. While work motivation has now been extensively studied as an agency problem, it is not often noted that the roots of the agency problem of work motivation can be seen as lying precisely in the separation of ownership from work.

A quick scan of the literature on the work motivation problem[4] can bring out the importance and implications of this point. I have suggested that the fact that workers are not ordinarily owners of their firms may be explained by workers' high demand for portfolio diversification given their low wealth, their relatively undiversifiable labor, and the fact that their incomes are already linked to the fortunes of their firms by way of the returns on that labor. Workers paid a fixed wage and able to influence their prospects of continued employment only by avoiding egregious absenteeism, insubordination, and visible acts of sabotage have little economic motivation to work to their full capabilities. Structuring rewards and penalties to motivate worker behavior that is consistent with employer goals thus becomes a central problem facing the firm.

The literature treats this incentive question in various ways depending upon its assumptions about the observability of workers' contributions. In the more relevant and interesting cases, the productive effort of individual workers is not perfectly inferable from output, either because output is a team product or because the quality of individual output, care of machinery, etc., are costly to monitor. Resources are therefore expended on attempts to measure effort and to link payment and employment outcomes to the information thereby obtained. One interesting result is the efficiency wage literature's linking of equilibrium unemployment to the employer's need to make the layoff threat an

---

[4] For example, the articles in Nalbantian (1987) and Milgrom and Roberts (1992).

364

effective deterrent to shirking (Shapiro and Stiglitz, 1984). Also of interest are the observations of Bowles (1985), Edwards (1979), and others concerning the influence of the monitoring problem on the employer's choice of production technology, on expenditure on supervision in the workplace, and on the workforce's skills and attitudes via the impact of employer needs on education and socialization systems.

To be sure, a serious challenge to the claim that it is the separation of ownership and labor that creates the characteristic motivation problem of the capitalist enterprise can be posed. It can be suggested that as long as the number of workers in a firm is large, even if workers were to be owners, their profit claims and the dependence of their individual wealth levels on the values of their shares would not suffice to significantly affect their incentives to provide effort, since the level of profits is then not notably affected by the efforts of any one worker. However, as Weitzman and Kruse (1990 [and this reader]), note, whether profit sharing significantly influences the behavior of rational, self-interested workers is theoretically indeterminate, because there is a multiplicity of equilibria to the repeated game of effort choice in a profit-sharing team. These equilibria include both a collusionlike response to profit sharing, in which the effect of that payment scheme is as if each worker's share were fully contingent on that one worker's effort, and the Cournot–Nash equilibrium, in which the free-rider problem largely negates the effect of profit sharing.[5] The conclusion reached by purely theoretical reasoning, then, is that the problem of eliciting effort from workers may be fundamentally transformed by profit sharing, or there may be no basic change, and the motivation of the individual worker may be as poorly aligned with that of the organization, as a collectivity of workers, as is that of a typical nonowner worker with respect to a conventional firm.

However, the literature on the growing phenomenon of actual profit sharing suggests that outcomes lying near the collusive end of the spectrum of possibilities are common.[6] A common explanation of these outcomes is that whereas workers in a conventional setting are indifferent to one another's behavior, workers under successful profit-sharing schemes monitor each other's effort

[5] The possibility of the collusive outcome, which follows Friedman (1971), is demonstrated in MacLeod (1988). While such an equilibrium is possible, provided that workers do not have too high a rate of pure time preference, too low an expectation of continued participation in the team, or too much heterogeneity of preferences (see Putterman and Skillman, 1992), the conditions for this possibility are not assurances that the equilibrium will in fact be selected over others. The indeterminateness of the response is an application of the folk theorem (Fudenberg and Tirole, 1991).

[6] See Weitzman and Kruse (1990) and the other papers in Blinder (1990). Evidence of the favorable effects of profit sharing is also recognized by Baker et al. (1988), who contend that economic theory is poorly equipped to explain it.

and use informal sanctions to punish slacking.[7] The increasing popularity of profit sharing validates the suggestion that separation of ownership and work be seen as a cause of the characteristic motivation problem of conventional firms. However, that same popularity raises new questions about the separability of the revenue, alienation, and control elements of ownership. Where profit sharing is implemented with favorable incentive effects in firms that remain otherwise conventional in the sense that control rights and the ownership of equity stakes continue to reside with the nonworker proprietors, partners, or shareholders, it would appear to be the case that problems created by what I have called the separation of ownership and work are at least partially addressed by linking just one element of ownership, revenue rights, to work. Whether the addition of control and alienation, i.e., share ownership, rights to profit sharing leads to further improvements in worker productivity or to gains in workplace satisfaction at given levels of productivity, why participation at the shop-floor level without control over broader business matters appears to be an effective complement to profit sharing, and how the sharing of ownership rights between workers and nonworker owners affects these outcomes are topics which are only beginning to receive serious attention.[8]

. . .

7. Nonprofits and public ownership

While businesses controlled by equity suppliers are the rule in most sectors of the market economy, some goods and services are supplied primarily by organizations to which that description does not apply. . . .

An example of an organizational form that does not make use of the institution of ownership, yet prospers in some niches of market economies, is the nonprofit organization. Candidates for nonprofit provision include partially nonrival or nonexcludable goods that are demanded by too local or specialized a constituency to command public provision. In other cases, referred to as trust goods, asymmetric information between provider and demander generates a preference for the nonprofit form, because the absence of residual claims and control of the nonprofit's board by like-minded demand-side agents provides some assurance against provider opportunism.[9] This last

---

[7] In addition to mutual monitoring, profit sharing is reported to raise productivity by making workers more willing to share with employers (or co-owners) their observations on ways to increase the efficiency of the production process. For some discussions of mutual monitoring, see Bradley and Gelb (1981) and FitzRoy and Kraft (1986). See also the related discussion of peer pressure by Kandel and Lazear (1992). A formal model of mutual monitoring which roots the incentive to monitor in a trigger strategy-type penalty in a repeated game setup resembling that of MacLeod (1988) is presented in Dong (1991) and Dong and Dow (1993).

[8] See again Blinder (1990) and Bonin et al. (1993).

[9] Ben-Ner and Van Hoomissen (1991). See also Fama and Jensen (1983b).

case is interesting in terms of the issues addressed in this paper, because, whereas the existence of a residual claimant and holder of alienation rights is regarded as the best guarantor of efficient resource use where conventional goods are concerned, it is the absence of such an agent that is called for here. Nonprofits will have controlling agents, boards of directors in principle representing those who demand their services, to whom employed managers are answerable, but they will not have owners in the sense of this paper. There is no market for control of nonprofits, and they have no salable equity value.

. . .

State ownership of enterprises or of service-providing agencies again raises interesting questions from the standpoint of this paper. If ownership is to be located in individual decision makers, then the state must be viewed as a medium for exercising the ultimate ownership interests of individuals whose identities and relative degree of control will depend upon the political system in question. A basic problem with the state as a supplier of goods and services is that, while the collective action problem of free-riding with respect to payment for the items supplied can be resolved by using state powers to enforce compulsory taxation, another collective action problem complicates the agency relationship between the citizenry and the state and is not so easily resolved. This problem is highlighted presently in a discussion of proposals for broad public ownership of capital.

In light of the failure of state socialism and the limited emergence of worker control in market economies, some economists have revived the proposal of a socialist market economy in which public funds are allocated to projects according to primarily commercial criteria, with the citizenry receiving equal dividends reflecting the return on social capital.[10] While most economists agree that the production of ordinary goods and services is not the comparative advantage of the state, the literature is unclear on why a maximally decentralized system for allocating socially owned funds in an economy characterized by competitive markets for other inputs and products could not operate as efficiently as a system in which funds are privately owned.[11] One answer that may be offered, however, is that the social ownership economy is unlikely to be as efficient as the economy with privately owned investment funds because the citizen of the socialist democracy has less incentive to monitor the performance of actual and potential projects due to her inability to

---

[10] Bardhan and Roemer (1993). In the Langean model of Ortuno-Ortin et al. (1993), noncommercial criteria influence the allocation of public funds through the setting of different interest rates for different sectors to reflect social priorities. See also Yunker (1992).

[11] Regarding the consensus on limiting the role of the state in the production sector, see World Bank (1991, pp. 128–147) and the papers in Putterman and Rueschemeyer (1992).

arrange a private portfolio whereby to benefit from the information so acquired.[12]

Whereas the individual holding private assets can rearrange her portfolio to include more of the projects found to have better prospects and less of those found to be unpromising, the citizen of the public ownership economy can at most propose a change in the composition of the public portfolio or vote for replacement of the public funds manager whose project choices are suggestive of incompetence. The comparison applies even though few investors in the private ownership world do their own securities analysis work, for in that world investors can discipline the financial intermediaries (banks, brokerage houses, mutual funds) that specialize in such monitoring by entering and exiting relationships with them as their evolving reputations suggest is warranted, whereas only the voice mechanism is open to the citizen in the public ownership democracy. Thus, one way of looking at the problem of social ownership is that it does not take sufficient advantage of one of the main properties distinguishing financial capital from other resources, that it is extraordinarily mobile in character, whereas the best candidates for allocation by the voice rather than the exit mechanism are those resources that are relatively *im*mobile.[13] The upshot seems to be that attempts to achieve greater equality in control over nonlabor resources might better be designed to retain rewards for individuals who are successful in identifying good investment projects.[14]

The aforementioned problem of public ownership may also help to illustrate an advantage of the alienability property of privately owned enterprises. When a market for ownership or control of public property is absent, a force that ideally presses managers to use resources to maximize long-term benefits in the private sector is lacking in its public counterpart. Absence of a tradable enterprise value also deprives decision makers of an indicator of the performance of incumbent managers.[15] Recall, however, that an arrangement under which tradability is absent is seen as desirable in the case of some nonprofit entities. Thus, the circumstances in which a market value indicator is beneficial on balance are not entirely general.

. . .

[12] The argument summarized here is developed at length in Putterman (1993b, 1993c).

[13] For example, the relative immobility of labor is offered by Freeman (1976), among others, as a reason for having a worker voice in the firm. Note that weak citizen incentives to monitor performance is a problem arising for all public sector functions. It is presumably offset, then, by advantages of public provision in the cases of some categories of goods and services.

[14] A suggestion along these lines is offered, for example, by Roemer (1994).

[15] The cost of capital to the enterprise *may* be a meaningful indicator in the case of public ownership, but only if the public enterprise is sufficiently autonomous that creditors cannot assume repayment by the government itself.

9. Summary

. . .

Ownership arrangements evolve to satisfy the needs of the production sector for financial, risk-bearing, and decision-making services, while reflecting the risk preferences of input suppliers and the need to address the agency problems that arise in the process of balancing these demands and preferences. In particular, firms' demands for the aggregation of funds and financiers' demands for portfolio diversification may not be easy to meet without giving rise to an agency problem of separating owners and decision makers. This conflict is addressed in different ways depending upon the scale and specificity of required capital and the difficulty or ease of monitoring decision making and other activities, but retention of ultimate control rights by the holders of residual claims and alienation rights remains an almost constant element. While concentrated and even substantial inside ownership are also among the solutions that are frequently observed, control by production workers is relatively rare, presumably due to workers' limited wealth and the high cost to them of not diversifying it. The resulting separation of ownership and work is the basic cause of the familiar agency problem between employer and employee.

Where for-profit provision suffers from public good, trust good, or other market failures, government or nonprofit providers may dominate, with interesting implications from the standpoint of ownership relations. However, public ownership of capital in sectors in which such problems are absent or less acute may be inefficient relative to private alternatives because the commonality of a public portfolio exacerbates tendencies to free-ride in the monitoring of funds management.

. . .

REFERENCES

Akerlof, George, 1982, "Labor Contracts as Partial Gift Exchange," *Quarterly Journal of Economics*, 47, no. 4: 543–69.

Akerlof, George A., and Katz, Lawrence F., 1988, "Workers' Trust Funds and the Logic of Wage Profiles," National Bureau of Economic Research Working Paper 2548.

Alchian, A. A., 1965, "The Basis of Some Recent Advances in the Theory of Management of the Firm," *Journal of Industrial Economics*, 14: 30–44.

Alchian, A. A., 1968, "Corporate Management and Property Rights," in *Economic Policy and the Regulation of Securities*. Washington, D.C.: American Enterprise Institute.

Alchian, Armen, 1983, "Specificity, Specialization, and Coalitions," draft manuscript, February.

Alchian, Armen, 1984, "Specificity, Specialization, and Coalitions," *Journal of Institutional and Theoretical Economics*, 140: 34–49.

Alchian, Armen, A. and Demsetz, Harold, 1972, "Production, Information Costs, and Economic Organization," *American Economic Review*, 62: 777–95.

Alchian, A. A., and Kessel, R. A., 1962, "Competition, Monopoly and the Pursuit of Pecuniary Gain" in National Bureau of Economic Research, *Aspects of Labor Economics*. Princeton, N.J.: Princeton University Press.

Anderson, Erin, and Schmittlein, David, 1984, "Integration of the Sales Force: An Empirical Examination," *Rand Journal of Economics* 15: 385–95.

Aoki, Masahiko, 1984, *The Co-operative Game Theory of the Firm*. London: Clarendon.

Arrow, K. J., 1951, "An Extension of the Basic Theorems of Classical Welfare Economics," in J. Neyman, ed., *Proceedings of the Second Berkeley Symposium on Mathematical Statistics and Probability*. Berkeley: University of California Press.

Arrow, K. J., 1964, "Control in Large Organizations," *Management Science*, 10: 397–408.

Arrow, K. J., 1969, "The Organization of Economic Activity," in *The Analysis and Evaluation of Public Expenditure: The PPB System*. 91st Congress, 1st session, vol. 1, JEC, 47–64.

Arrow, K. J., 1974, *The Limits of Organization*. New York: Norton.

Ashenfelter, O., and Johnson, G., 1972, "Unionism, Relative Wages, and Labor Quality in U.S. Manufacturing Industries," *International Economic Review*, 13: 488–508.

Atwood, Jane, and Kobrin, Paul, 1977, "Integration and Joint Ventures in Pipelines," Research Study No. 5, American Petroleum Institute.

Axelrod, Robert M., 1984, *The Evolution of Cooperation*. New York: Basic Books.

Azariadas, C., 1975, "Implicit Contracts and Unemployment Equilibria," *Journal of Political Economy,* 53: 1183–1202.

Bailey, M. N., 1974, "Wages and Employment under Uncertain Demand," *Review of Economic Studies,* 41: 37–50.

Baker, George, 1989, "Piece Rate Contracts and Performance Measurement Error," Graduate School of Business, Harvard University.

Baker, George, Jensen, Michael, and Murphy, Kevin, 1988, "Compensation and Incentives: Practice vs. Theory," *Journal of Finance,* 43: 593–616.

Bardhan, Pranab K., and Roemer, John E., eds., 1993, *Market Socialism: The Current Debate.* New York: Oxford University Press.

Barnard, C. I., 1962, *The Functions of the Executive,* 2nd edition. Cambridge: Harvard University Press.

Bartlett, F. C., 1932, *Remembering.* Cambridge: Cambridge University Press.

Barzel, Yoram, 1982, "Measurement Costs and the Organization of Markets," *Journal of Law and Economics,* 25: 27–48.

Batt, Francis R., 1929, *The Law of Master and Servant.* New York: Pitman Publishing Co.

Baumol, William J., 1959, *Business Behavior, Value and Growth.* New York: Macmillan.

Baumol, William J., 1967, *Business Behavior, Value and Growth* (revised edition). New York: Harcourt, Brace, and World.

Becker, G., 1962, "Investment in Human Capital: A Theoretical Analysis," *Journal of Political Economy,* 70 supplement: 9–44.

Becker, Gary S., and Stigler, George J., 1974, "Law Enforcement, Malfeasance, and Compensation of Enforcers," *Journal of Legal Studies,* 3: 1–18.

Beckman, Martin, 1983, *Tinbergen Lectures on Economic Organization.* Berlin: Springer-Verlag.

Bellers, John, 1696, *Proposals for Raising a College of Industry of All Useful Trades and Husbandry.* London.

Belshaw, C. S., 1965, *Traditional Exchange and Modern Markets.* Englewood Cliffs, N.J.: Prentice-Hall.

Benassy, Jean-Pascal, 1982, *The Economics of Market Disequilibrium.* Orlando, Fla: Academic Press.

Ben-Ner, Avner, and Van Hoomisen, Theresa, 1991, "Nonprofit Organizations in the Mixed Economy: A Demand and Supply Analysis," *Annals of Public and Cooperative Economics,* 62: 519–50.

Berhold, M., 1971, "A Theory of Linear Profit Sharing Incentives," *Quarterly Journal of Economics,* 85: 460–82.

Berle, Adolf, and Means, Gardiner, 1932, *The Modern Corporation and Private Property.* New York: Commerce Clearing House.

Blinder, Alan, ed., 1990, *Paying for Productivity: A Look at the Evidence.* Washington, D.C.: The Brookings Institution.

References

Bonin, John P., Jones, Derek C., and Putterman, Louis, 1993, "Theoretical and Empirical Research on Producers' Cooperatives: Will Ever the Twain Meet?" *Journal of Economic Literature*, 31: 1290–320.

Bork, Robert, 1954, "Vertical Integration and the Sherman Act: The Legal History of an Economic Misconception," *University of Chicago Labor Review*, 22: 157–201.

Bowles, Samuel, 1985, "The Production Process in a Competitive Economy: Walrasian, Neo-Hobbesian, and Marxian Models," *American Economic Review*, 75: 16–36.

Bowles, Samuel, 1988, "Social Institutions and Technical Choice," in M. DeMatteo, A. Vercelli, and R. Goodman, eds., *Technological and Social Factors in Long Term Economic Fluctuations*. Berlin: Springer-Verlag.

Bowles, Samuel, and Boyer, Robert, 1990, "Labour Market Flexibility and Decentralization as Barriers to High Employment," in Renato Brunetta and Carlo Dell'Aringa, eds., *Labor Relations and Economic Performance*. London: Macmillan.

Bowles, Samuel, and Gintis, Herbert, 1975, "The Problems with Human Capital Theory," *American Economic Review*, 65: 74–82.

Bowles, Samuel, and Gintis, Herbert, 1976, *Schooling in Capitalist America: Educational Reform and the Contradictions of Economic Life*. New York: Basic Books.

Bowles, Samuel, and Gintis, Herbert, 1982a, "The Crisis of Liberal Democratic Capitalism," *Politics and Society*, 10: 51–93.

Bowles, Samuel, and Gintis, Herbert, 1982b, "The Welfare State and Long-Term Economic Growth: Marxian, Neoclassical, and Keynesian Approaches," *American Economic Review*, 72: 341–345.

Bowles, Samuel, and Gintis, Herbert, 1990a, "Bonding and Dismissal in Labor Discipline Models," photocopy, University of Massachusetts.

Bowles, Samuel, and Gintis, Herbert, 1990b, "Contested Exchange: New Microfoundations of the Political Economy of Capitalism," *Politics and Society*, 18: 165–222.

Bowles, Samuel, and Gintis, Herbert, 1993a, "The Democratic Firm: An Agency Theory Evaluation," in Samuel Bowles, Herbert Gintis, and Bo Gustaffson, eds., *Markets and Democracy: Participation, Accountability, and Efficiency*. Cambridge: Cambridge University Press.

Bowles, Samuel, and Gintis, Herbert, 1993b, "The Revenge of Homo Economics: Contested Exchange and the Revival of Economy," *Journal of Economic Perspectives*, 7: 83–102.

Bowles, Samuel, Gordon, David M., and Weisskopf, Thomas E., 1989, "Business Ascendancy and Economic Impasse: A Structural Retrospective on Conservative Economics, 1979–87," *Journal of Economic Perspectives*, 3: 107–134.

Bradley, Keith, and Gelb, Alan, 1981, "Motivation and Control in the Mondragon Experiment," *British Journal of Industrial Relations*, 19: 211–231.

Branch, B., 1973, "Corporate Objectives and Market Performance," *Financial Management*, 2: 24–9.

Brickley, James and Dark, Frederick, 1987, "The Choice of Organizational Form: The Case of Franchising," *Journal of Financial Economics*, 18: 401–20.

Buchanan, James, Tollison, Robert, and Tullock, Gordon, 1990, *Toward a Theory of the Rent-Seeking Society*. College Station: Texas A&M University Press.

Burnham, James, 1941, *Managerial Revolution: What is Happening in the World*. New York: The John Day Company.

Cairnes, J. E., 1862, *The Slave Power*. London.

Calvo, Guillermo, and Wellisz, Stanislaw, 1978, "Supervision, Loss of Control, and the Optimum Size of the Firm," *Journal of Political Economy*, 86: 943–52.

Canes, M., 1970, "A Model of a Sports League," doctoral dissertation, University of California at Los Angeles.

Chandler, Alfred Dupont, 1962, *Strategy and Structure: Chapters in the History of the Industrial Enterprise*. Cambridge: MIT Press.

Chandler, A., 1969, "The Structure of American Industry in the Twentieth Century: A Historical Review," *Business History Review*, 63: 255–98.

Chandler, A., 1977, *The Visible Hand*. Cambridge, MA: Harvard University Press.

Cheung, S. N. S., 1969, "Transaction Costs, Risk Aversion, and the Choice of Contractual Arrangements," *Journal of Law and Economics*, 12: 23–42.

Cheung, Steven, 1983, "The Contractual Nature of the Firm," *Journal of Law and Economics*, 26: 1–21.

Clague, Christopher, 1993, "Rule Obedience, Organizational Loyalty, and Economic Development," *Journal of Institutional and Theoretical Economics*, 149: 393–414.

Clark, J. B., 1990, *Distribution of Wealth*. New York: Macmillan.

Clark, Robert C., 1983, *Agency Costs Versus Fiduciary Duties*. Boston: Division of Research, Harvard Business School.

Clark, Robert C., 1985, *Principals and Agents: The Structure of Business*. Boston: Harvard Business School Press.

Coase, R. H., 1937, "The Nature of the Firm," *Economica*, 4: 386–405 reprinted, pp. 331–351 in American Economic Association, *Readings in Price Theory*. Chicago: Irwin, 1952.

Coase, R. H., 1937, "The Nature of the Firm," *Economica*, 4: 386–405 reprinted, pp. 33–55 in Coase, *The Firm, the Market, and the Law*. Chicago: University of Chicago Press, 1990.

Coase, Ronald H., 1952, "The Nature of the Firm," *Economica N. S.*, 4 (1937): 386–405, reprinted in G. J. Stigler and K. E. Boulding, eds., *Readings in Price Theory*. Homewood, Ill.: Richard D. Irwin.

Coase, R. H., 1959, "The Federal Communications Commission," *Journal of Law and Economics*, 2: 1–40.

Coase, R. H., 1960, "The Problem of Social Cost," *Journal of Law and Economics*, 3: 1–44.

Coase, R. H., 1972, "Durability and Monopoly," *Journal of Law and Economics*, 15: 143–50.

Coase, Ronald, 1992, "The Institutional Structure of Production: 1991 Alfred Nobel Memorial Prize Lecture in Economic Sciences," *American Economic Review*, 82: 713–19.

References

Commons, J., 1970, *The Economics of Collective Action*. Madison, Wis.: University of Wisconsin Press.

Cox, A., 1958, "The Legal Nature of Collective Bargaining Agreements," *Michigan Law Review*, 57: 1–36.

Crocker, K. J., and Masten, S. E., 1991, *"Pretia ex Machina?* Prices and Process in Long-Term Contracts," *Journal of Law and Economics*, 34: 69–99.

Cyert, R. M., and Hedrick, C. L., 1972, "Theory of the Firm: Past, Present and Future: An Interpretation," *Journal of Economic Literature*, 10: 398–412.

Cyert, R. M., and March, J. G., 1963, *A Behavioral Theory of the Firm*. Englewood Cliffs, N.J.: Prentice-Hall.

Darby, Michael R., and Karni, Eli, 1973, "Free Competition and the Optimal Amount of Fraud," *Journal of Law and Economics*, 16: 67–88.

Dawes, Harry, 1934, "Labour Mobility in the Steel Industry," *The Economic Journal*, 44: 84–94.

Debreu, G., 1959, *Theory of Value*. New York: Wiley.

Demsetz, H., 1967, "Toward a Theory of Property Rights," *American Economic Review*, 57: 347–359.

Demsetz, Harold, 1982, *Economic, Legal, and Political Dimensions of Competition*. New York: North Holland.

Demsetz, Harold, 1983, "The Structure of Ownership and the Theory of the Firm," *Journal of Law and Economics*, 26: 375–90.

Demsetz, Harold, and Lehn, Kenneth, 1985, "The Structure of Corporate Ownership: Causes and Consequences," *Journal of Political Economy*, 93: 1155–77.

Dickens, William T., Katz, Lawrence F., Lang, Kevin, and Summers, Lawrence H., 1989, "Employee Crime and the Monitoring Puzzle," *Journal of Labor Economics*, 7: 331–347.

Dietrich, Michael, 1994, *Transaction Cost Economics and Beyond*. New York: Routledge.

Dobb, Maurice, 1925, *Capitalist Enterprise and Social Progress*. London: George Routledge and Sons, Ltd.

Dobb, Maurice, 1928, *Russian Economic Development*. New York: F. P. Dutton and Co.

Doeringer, P., and Piore, M., 1971, *International Labor Markets and Manpower Analysis*. Lexington, Mass.: D. C. Heath and Co.

Dong, Xiao-Yuan, 1991, "Production and Monitoring Incentives in China's Collective Farming: Theory and Evidence," Ph.D. dissertation, University of Alberta.

Dong, Xiao-Yuan, and Dow, Gregory, 1993, "Monitoring Costs in Chinese Agricultural Teams," *Journal of Political Economy*, 101: 539–53.

Dunlop, J., 1957, "The Task of Contemporary Wage Theory," in G. W. Taylor and F. C. Pierson, eds., *New Concepts in Wage Determination*. New York: McGraw-Hill.

Dunlop, J., 1958, *Industrial Relations Systems*. New York: Holt.

Durbin, E. F. M., 1936, "Economic Calculus in a Planned Economy," *Economic Journal*, 46: 676–90.

REFERENCES

Easterbrook, Frank, and Fischel, Daniel, 1983, "Voting in Corporate Law," *Journal of Law and Economics*, 26: 305.

Eaton, B. Curtis, and White, William, 1962, "Agent Compensation and the Limits of Bonding," *Economic Inquiry*, 20: 330–343.

Edwards, Richard, 1979, *Contested Terrain: The Transformation of the Workplace in the Twentieth Century*. New York: Basic Books.

Elster, John, 1979, *Ulysses and the Sirens*. Cambridge: Cambridge University Press.

Eswaran, Mukesh, and Kotwal, Ashok, 1989, "Why are Capitalists the Bosses?" *Economic Journal*, 99: 162–76.

Etzioni, A. W., 1971, *Modern Organizations*. Englewood Cliffs, N.J.: Prentice-Hall.

Fama, E. F., 1970a, "Efficient Capital Markets: A Review of Theory and Empirical Work," *The Journal of Finance*, 25: 383–417.

Fama, E. F., 1970b, "Multiperiod Consumption–Investment Decisions," *American Economic Review*, 60: 163–174.

Fama, E. F., 1972, "Ordinal and Measurable Utility," in M. C. Jensen, ed., *Studies in the Theory of Capital Markets*. New York: Praeger.

Fama, Eugene, 1978, "The Effects of a Firm's Investment and Financing Decisions on the Welfare of its Security Holders," *American Economic Review*, 68: 272–84.

Fama, Eugene, 1980, "Agency Problems and the Theory of the Firm," *Journal of Political Economy*, 88: 288.

Fama, Eugene F., and Jensen, Michael C., 1983a, "Agency Problems and Residual Claims," *Journal of Law and Economic*, 26: 327–49.

Fama, Eugene F., and Jensen, Michael C., 1983b, "Separation of Ownership and Control," *Journal of Law and Economics*, 26: 301–26.

Fama, Eugene F., and Jensen, Michael C., 1985, "Organizational Forms and Investment Decisions," *Journal of Financial Economics*, 14: 101–19.

Fama, Eugene F., and Miller, Merton H., 1972, *The Theory of Finance*. New York: Holt, Rinehart, and Winston.

Farrell, Joseph, and Shapiro, Carl, 1989, "Optimal Contracts with Lock-in," *American Economic Review*, 7979: 51–68.

Feldman, J., and Kanter, H., 1965, "Organizational Decision-Making," in J. March, ed., *Handbook of Organizations*. Chicago: Rand McNally.

Feldman, Martha S., and March, James G., 1981, "Information in Organizations as Signal and Symbol," *Administrative Science Quarterly*, 26: 171–86.

Feller, David E., 1973, "A General Theory of the Collective Bargaining Agreement," *California Labor Review*, 3: 663–856.

Ferguson, Adam, 1767, *An Essay on the History of Civil Society*. Edinburgh.

Festinger, L., 1954, "A Theory of Social Comparison Processes," *Human Relations*, 7: 117–40; reprinted in Herbert H. Hyman and Eleanor Singer, eds., *Readings in Reference Group Therapy*. New York: The Free Press, 1968.

FitzRoy, Felix R., and Kraft, Kornelius, 1986, "Profitability and Profit-Sharing," *Journal of Industrial Economics*, 35: 113–30.

Freeman, Richard, 1976, "Individual Mobility and Union Voice in the Labor Market," *American Economic Review*, 66: 361–68.

References

Freeman, R. L., and Medoff, J. L., 1979, "The Two Faces of Unionism," *The Public Interest,* 57: 69–93.

Friedman, James, 1971, "A Non-Cooperative Equilibrium for Supergames," *Review of Economic Studies,* 38: 1–12.

Friedman, M., 1970, "The Social Responsibility of Business Is to Increase Its Profits," *New York Times Magazine,* September 13, 32ff.

Fudenberg, D., Holmstrom, B., and Milgrom, P., forthcoming, "Short-Term Contracts and Long-Term Agency Relationships," *Journal of Economic Theory.*

Fudenberg, Drew, and Maskin, Eric, 1986, "The Folk Theorem in Repeated Games with Discounting or with Incomplete Information," *Econometrica,* 54: 533–54.

Fudenberg, Drew, and Tirole, Jean, 1991, *Game Theory.* Cambridge: MIT Press.

Furubotn, E. G., and Pejovich, S., 1972, "Property Rights and Economic Theory: A Survey of Recent Literature," *Journal of Economic Literature,* 10: 1137–62.

Galbraith, John Kenneth, 1967, *The New Industrial State.* Boston: Houghton Mifflin.

Garnier, Germain, 1815, *Abrege elementaire des principes de l'Economie Politique.* Paris.

Gintis, Herbert, and Ishikawa, Tsuneo, 1987, "Wages, Work Discipline, and Unemployment," *Journal of Japanese and International Economies,* 1: 195–228.

Goldberg, Victor P., 1976, "Regulation and Administered Contracts," *Bell Journal of Economics,* 7: 426–48.

Goldberg, V. P., 1977, "Competitive Bidding and the Production of Precontract Information," *Bell Journal of Economics,* 8: 250–61.

Goldberg, V. P., 1979, "Protecting the Right to Be Served by Regulated Utilities," *Research in Law and Economics,* 1: 145–56.

Goldberg, Victor, 1980a, "Bridges Over Contested Terrain: Exploring the Radical Account of the Employment Relationship," *Journal of Economic Behavior and Organization,* 1: 249–74.

Goldberg, V. P., 1980b, "The Law and Economics of Vertical Restrictions: A Relational Perspective," *Texas Law Review,* 58: 91–129.

Goldberg, Victor, 1980c, "Relational Exchange: Economics and Complex Contracts," *American Behavioral Scientist,* 23, no. 3: 337–52.

Goldberg, Victor, and Erickson, John R., 1987, "Quantity and Price Adjustment in Long-Term Contracts: A Case Study of Petroleum Coke," *Journal of Law and Economics,* 30: 369–98.

Grabowski, H., and Mueller, D., 1975, "Life Cycle Effects on Corporate Returns on Retentions," *Review of Economics and Statistics,* 57: 400–9.

Greenwald, Bruce, and Stiglitz, Joseph, 1986, "Externalities in Economies with Imperfect Information and Incomplete Markets," *Quarterly Journal of Economics,* 101: 229–64.

Grossman, Sanford J., and Hart, Oliver D., 1980, "Takeover Bids, the Free Rider Problem, and the Theory of the Corporation," *Bell Journal of Economics,* 11: 42–64.

Grossman, Sanford J., and Hart, Oliver D., 1984, "The Costs and Benefits of Ownership: A Theory of Vertical Integration," unpublished manuscript, March.

377

Grossman, Sanford J., and Hart, Oliver D., 1986, "The Costs and Benefits of Owner-ship: A Theory of Vertical and Lateral Integration," *Journal of Political Economy*, 94: 691–719.

Grossman, S. J., and Stiglitz, J. E., 1976, "Information and Competitive Price Sys-tems," *American Economic Review*, 66: 246–53.

Gouldner, A. W., 1954, *Patterns of Industrial Bureaucracy*. Glencoe, Ill.: Free Press.

Gustafson, W. Eric, 1959, *Periodicals and Books,* in Max Hall, ed., *Case Studies in Metropolitan Manufacturing*. Cambridge: Harvard University Press.

Hall, R. E., 1975, "The Rigidity of Wages and the Persistence of Unemployment," *Brookings Papers on Economic Activity*, 3: 301–49.

Hansmann, Henry, 1984, "The Viability of Worker Ownership: An Economic Perspec-tive on the Political Structure of the Firm," in M. Aoki, B. Gustafsson, and O. Williamson, eds., *The Firm as a Nexus of Treaties*. London: Sage Publications.

Hansmann, Henry, 1988, "Ownership of the Firm," *Journal of Law, Economics, and Organization*, 4: 267–304.

Harrison, B., 1972, *Education, Training, and the Urban Ghetto*. Baltimore: Johns Hopkins University Press.

Hart, Oliver, 1989, "An Economist's Perspective on the Theory of the Firm," *Colum-bia Law Review*, 89: 1757–74.

Hart, Oliver, and Holmstrom, Bengt, 1987, "The Theory of Contracts," in Truman F. Bewley, ed., *Advances in Economic Theory – Fifth World Congress*. Cambridge: Cambridge University Press.

Hart, O., and Moore, J., 1988, "Property Rights and the Nature of the Firm," Massa-chusetts Institute of Technology, Dept. of Economics Working Paper No. 495.

Hart, Oliver D., and Moore, John, 1990, "Property Rights and the Nature of the Firm," *Journal of Political Economy*, 98: 1119–58.

Hayek, F. A., 1933, "The Trend of Economic Thinking," *Economica*, 13: 121–37.

Hayek, F. A., 1945, "The Use of Knowledge in Society," *The American Economic Review*, 35: 519–30.

Hayek, Friedrich, 1972, *Individualism and Economic Order*. Chicago: Henry Regnery Company.

Healy, Paul M., Palepu, Krishna G., and Ruback, Richard S., 1992, "Does Corporate Performance Improve After Mergers?" *Journal of Financial Economics*, 31: 135–75.

Heckerman, D. G., 1975, "Motivating Managers to Make Investment Decisions," *Journal of Financial Economics*, 2: 273–92.

Henderson, Huburt D., 1922, *Supply and Demand*. New York: Harcourt, Brace, and Co.

Henry, Robert S., 1942, *This Fascinating Railroad Business*. New York: Bobbs-Merrill.

Hirschman, A. O., 1970, *Exit, Voice, and Loyalty*. Cambridge: Harvard University Press.

Hodgeskin, Thomas, 1827, *Popular Political Economy*. London.

References

Holderness, Clifford, Kroszner, Randall, and Sheehan, Dennis, 1995, "Changes in Corporate Stock Ownership since the Great Depression," working paper, University of Chicago, Graduate School of Business.

Holmstrom, Bengt, 1982a, "Managerial Incentives – A Dynamic Perspective," in *Essays in Economics and Management in Honor of Lars Wahlbeck*. Helsinki: Swedish School of Economics.

Holmstrom, Bengt, 1982b, "Moral Hazard in Teams," *Bell Journal of Economics*, 13: 324–40.

Holmstrom, Bengt, and Milgrom, Paul, 1987, "Aggregation and Linearity in the Provision of Intertemporal Incentives," *Econometrica*, 55: 303–28.

Holmstrom, Bengt, and Milgrom, Paul, 1990, "Regulating Trade Among Agents," *Journal of Institutional and Theoretical Economics*, 146: 85–105.

Holmstrom, Bengt, and Milgrom, Paul, 1991a, "Measurement Cost and Organization Theory," working paper, Stanford University.

Holmstrom, B., and Milgrom, P., 1991b, "Multitask Principal–Agent Analyses: Incentive Contracts, Asset Ownership, and Job Design," *Journal of Law, Economics, and Organization*, 7: 24–52.

Holmstrom, Bengt and Ricart i Costa, Joan, 1986, "Managerial Incentives and Capital Management," *Quarterly Journal of Economics*, 101: 835–60.

Holmstrom, Bengt, and Tirole, Jean, 1989, "The Theory of the Firm," in R. Schmalensee and R. Willig, eds., *The Handbook of Industrial Organization*. Amsterdam: North Holland.

Homans, G. C., 1953, "Status Among Clerical Workers," *Human Organization*, 12: 5–10; reprinted in G. C. Homans, *Sentiments and Activities*. New York: Free Press of Glencoe, 1962.

Hubbard, R. Glenn, and Weiner, Robert J., 1986, "Regulation and Long-Term Contracting in U.S. Natural Gas Markets," *Journal of Industrial Economics*, 35: 71–79.

Hyman, H. H., 1942, "The Psychology of Status," *Archives of Psychology*, 269; reprinted in part in Herbert H. Hyman and Eleanor Singer, eds., *Readings in Reference Group Theory*. New York: The Free Press, 1968.

Itoh, Hideshi, 1989, "Coalitions, Incentives and Risk Sharing," mimeograph, Kyoto University, Japan.

Itoh, Hideshi, 1991, "Incentives to Help in Multi-Agent Situations," *Econometrica*, 59: 611–37.

Jarrell, Gregg A., Brickley, James, and Netter, Jeffrey M., 1988, "The Market for Corporate Control: The Empirical Evidence Since 1980," *Journal of Economic Perspectives*, 2: 49–68.

Jensen, Michael C., 1972, "Capital Markets: Theory and Evidence," *Bell Journal of Economics*, 3: 357–98.

Jensen, M. C., 1978, "Some Anomalous Evidence Regarding Market Efficiency," *Journal of Financial Economics*, 6: 95–101.

Jensen, Michael, 1983, "Organization Theory and Methodology," *Accounting Review*, 58: 319–39.

Jensen, M. C., and Meckling, W. H. 1976a, "Can the Corporation Survive," Center for Research in Government Policy and Business Working Paper No. PPS 76–4. Rochester, New York: University of Rochester.

Jensen, Michael C., and Meckling, William H., 1976b, "Theory of the Firm: Managerial Behavior, Agency Costs and Ownership Structure," *Journal of Financial Economics,* 3: 305–60.

Jensen, M. C., and Meckling, W. H., 1977, "On the Labor-Managed Firm and the Co-determination Movement," unpublished manuscript.

Jensen, M. C., and Meckling, W. H., 1979, "Rights and Production Functions: An Application to Labor-Managed Firms and Co-determination," *Journal of Business,* 52: 469–506.

Jensen, Michael C., and Warner, Jerold B., 1988, "The Distribution of Power Among Corporate Managers, Shareholders, and Directors," *Journal of Financial Economics,* 20: 3–24.

Johnson, Harry G., 1963, "The 'Higher Criticism' of the Modern Corporation," *Columbia Law Review,* 63: 399–432.

Jones, Eliot, 1927, *The Trust Problem.* New York: Macmillan.

Joskow, Paul L., 1977, "Commercial Impossibility, the Uranium Market, and the Westinghouse Case," *Journal of Legal Studies,* 6: 119–76.

Joskow, Paul L., 1985, "Vertical Integration and Long-Term Contracts: the Case of Coal-Burning Electric Generating Plants," *Journal of Law, Economics, and Organization,* 1: 33–80.

Joskow, Paul L., 1987, "Contract Duration and Relationship-Specific Investments: Empirical Evidence," *Journal of Law, Economics, and Organization,* 4: 95–117.

Joskow, Paul L., 1988b, "Price Adjustment in Long-Term Contracts: The Case of Coal," *Journal of Law and Economics,* 31: 47–83.

Kaldor, Nicholas, 1934, "A Classificatory Note of the Determinateness of Equilibrium," *The Review of Economic Studies,* 1: 122–36.

Kaldor, Nicholas, 1934, "The Equilibrium of the Firm," *Economic Journal,* 44: 60–76.

Kandel, Eugene, and Lazear, Edward, 1992, "Peer Pressure and Partnerships," *Journal of Political Economy,* 100: 801–17.

Kanter, Rosabeth Moss, 1987, "The Attack on Pay," *Harvard Business Review,* 65: 60–67.

Kaplan, Steven N., 1989, "The Effects of Management Buyouts on Operating Performance and Value," *Journal of Financial Economics,* 24: 581–618.

Kenney, R. W., and Klein, B., 1983, "The Economics of Block Booking," *Journal of Law and Economics,* 26: 497–540.

Kerr, C., 1954, "The Balkanization of Labor Markets," in E. Wight Bakke, et al., *Labor Mobility and Economic Opportunity.* Cambridge: Technology Press of MIT.

Kessler, Friedrich, and Stern, Richard H., 1959, "Competition, Contract, and Vertical Integration," *Yale Law Journal,* 69: 1–129.

Khalil, Elias L., 1994, "Can Transaction-Cost, Competence-Bundle, and Process

References

Theories of the Firms Sustain the Market/Firm Dichotomy Thesis?" working paper, Ohio State University, Mansfield Campus.

Kihlstrom, Richard, and Laffont, Jean-Jacques, 1979, "A General Equilibrium Entrepreneurial Theory of Firm Formation Based on Risk Aversion," *Journal of Political Economy,* 87: 719–47.

Kohlstrom, Richard, and Matthews, Steven, 1990, "Managerial Incentives in an Entrepreneurial Stock Market Model," *Journal of Financial Intermediation,* 1: 57–79.

Kirzner, I., 1973, *Competition and Entrepreneurship.* Chicago: University of Chicago Press.

Klein, Benjamin, 1974, "The Competitive Supply of Money," *Journal of Money, Credit and Banking,* 6: 423–53.

Klein, Benjamin, 1983, "Contracting Costs and Residual Claims: The Separation of Ownership and Control," *Journal of Law and Economics,* 26: 367–74.

Klein, Benjamin, 1988, "Vertical Integration as Organized Ownership: The Fisher Body–General Motors Relationship Revisited," *Journal of Law, Economics, and Organization,* 4: 199–213.

Klein, Benjamin, Crawford, Robert G., and Alchian, Armen, 1978, "Vertical Integration, Appropriable Rents and the Competitive Contracting Process," *Journal of Law and Economics,* 21: 297–326.

Klein, Benjamin, and Leffler, Keith, 1979, "The Role of Market Forces in Assuring Contractual Performance," *Journal of Political Economy,* 89: 615–41.

Klein, Benjamin, and McLaughlin, Andrew, 1978, "Resale Price Maintenance, Exclusive Territories, and Franchise Termination: The Coors Case," unpublished manuscript.

Klein, Peter G., and Shelanski, Howard, A., 1994, "Empirical Research in Transaction Cost Economics: A Survey and Assessment," Business and Public Policy Working Paper BPP-60, Haas School of Business, University of California, Berkeley.

Klein, W. A., 1976, "Legal and Economic Perspectives on the Firm," unpublished manuscript, University of California, Los Angeles.

Knight, Frank, 1921, *Risk, Uncertainty and Profit.* London: The London School of Economics and Political Science.

Knight, Frank, 1933, *Risk, Uncertainty and Profit,* preface to the re-issue. London: London School of Economics Series of Reprints, No. 16.

Knight, Frank H., 1965, *Risk, Uncertainty and Profit.* New York: Harper and Row.

Kreps, David M., 1990, "Corporate Culture and Economic Theory," in James E. Alt and Kenneth A. Shepsle, eds., *Perspectives on Positive Political Economy.* Cambridge: Cambridge University Press.

Kroszner, Randall, and Rajan, Raghuram, 1995, "Organization Structure and Credibility: Evidence from Commercial Bank Securities Activities before the Glass–Steagall Act," National Bureau of Economic Research working paper.

Krueger, Alan, 1991, "Ownership, Agency, and Wages: An Examination of Franchising in the Fast Food Industry," *Quarterly Journal of Economics,* 106: 75–101.

Kruse, Douglas, L., 1988, "Essays on Profit-sharing and Unemployment," Ph.D. dissertation, Harvard University.

Laffont, Jean-Jacques, and Tirole, Jean, 1989, "Provision of Quality and Power of Incentive Schemes in Regulated Industries," in W. Barnett, B. Cornet, C. d'Aspremont, J. Gabsewicz, and A. Mas-Colell, eds., *Equilibrium Theory and Applications*. Cambridge: Cambridge University Press.

Lazear, Edward, 1989, "Pay Equality and Industrial Politics," *Journal of Political Economy*, 97: 561–80.

Lazear, Edward, and Rosen, Sherwin, 1981, "Rank-Order Tournaments as Optimum Labor Contracts," *Journal of Political Economy*, 89: 841–64.

Leff, Nathaniel H., 1978, "Industrial Organization and Entrepreneurship in the Developing Countries: The Economic Groups," *Economic Development and Cultural Change*, 26: 661–76.

Leffler, Keith B., and Rucker, Randal, 1991, "Transaction Costs and the Efficient Organization of Production: A Study of Timber-Harvesting Contracts," *Journal of Political Economy*, 99: 1060–87.

Leibenstein, Harvey, 1963, *Economic Backwardness and Economic Growth*. New York: John Wiley and Sons.

Leibenstein, H., 1966, "Allocative Efficiency vs. X-Efficiency," *American Economic Review*, 56: 392–415.

Leibenstein, H., 1976, *Beyond Economic Man: A New Foundation for Microeconomics*. Cambridge: Harvard University Press.

Leibenstein, Harvey, 1980, "X-Efficiency, Intrafirm Behavior and Growth," in Shlomo Maital and Noah M. Meltz, eds., *Lagging Productivity Growth*. Cambridge, Mass.: Balinger.

Leibenstein, Harvey, 1982, "The Prisoners' Dilemma in the Invisible Hand: An Analysis of Intrafirm Productivity," *American Economic Review*, 72: 92–97.

Leiberstein, S. H., 1979, *Who Owns What is In Your Head*. New York: Hawthorn Publishers.

Lewis, D., 1969, *Convention: A Philosophical Study*. Cambridge: Harvard University Press.

Levine, David I., and Tyson, Laura D'Andrea, 1990, "Participation, Productivity, and the Firm's Environment," in Alan S. Binder, ed., *Paying for Productivity*. Washington, D.C.: The Brookings Institution.

Lerner, Abba, 1972, "The Economics and Politics of Consumer Sovereignty," *American Economic Review*, 62: 259.

Livernash, E., 1957, "The Internal Wage Structure," in G. W. Taylor and F. C. Pierson, eds., *New Concepts in Wage Determination*. New York: McGraw-Hill.

Llewellyn, Karl N., 1931, "What Price Contract? An Essay in Perspective," *Yale Law Journal*, 40: 704–51.

Lowry, S. Todd, 1976, "Bargain and Contract Theory in Law and Economics," *Journal of Economic Issues*, 10: 1–19.

Macaulay, Stewart, 1963, "Non-Contractual Relations in Business: A Preliminary Study," *American Sociological Review*, 28: 55–70.

References

MacDonald, Glenn, 1984, "New Directions in the Economic Theory of Agency," *Canadian Journal of Economics*, 17: 415–40.

Macgregor, David H., 1906, *Industrial Combination*. London: George Bell and Sons.

Machlup, Fritz, 1961, *International Trade and the National Income Multiplier*. New York: A. M. Kelley.

Machlup, F., 1967, "Theories of the Firm: Marginalist, Behavioral, Managerial," *American Economic Review*, 57: 1–33.

Machlup, Fritz, and Taber, Martha, 1960, "Bilateral Monopoly, Successive Monopoly, and Vertical Integration," *Economica*, 27: 101–19.

MacLeod, W. Bentley, 1988, "Equity, Efficiency, and Incentives in Cooperative Teams," in Derek Jones and Jan Svejar, eds., *Advances in the Economic Analysis of Participatory and Labor-Managed Firms*, Vol. 3. Greenwich, CT: JAI Press.

MacNeil, I. R., 1974, "The Many Futures of Contracts," *Southern California Law Review*, 47: 691–816.

MacNeil, I. R., 1978, "Contracts: Adjustments of Long-Term Economic Relations under Classical, Neoclassical, and Relational Contract Law," *Northwestern University Law Review*, 72: 854–906.

Malcomson, James, 1984, "Work Incentives, Hierarchy, and Internal Labor Markets," *Journal of Political Economy*, 92: 486–507.

Malmgren, H., 1961, "Information, Expectations, and the Theory of the Firm," *Quarterly Journal of Economics*, 75: 399–421.

Manne, Henry G., 1962, "The 'Higher Criticism' of the Modern Corporation," *Columbia Law Review*, 62: 399–421.

Manne, Henry, 1965, "Mergers and the Market for Corporate Control," *Journal of Political Economy*, 73: 110–20.

Manne, Henry G., 1967, "Our Two Corporate Systems: Laws and Economics," *Virginia Law Review*, 53: 259–85.

March, J. G., and Simon, H. A., 1958, *Organizations*. New York: Wiley.

Marglin, Stephen, 1974, "What Do Bosses Do? The Origins and Functions of Hierarchy in Capitalist Production," *Review of Radical Political Economics*, 6: 60–112.

Marris, R., 1964, *The Economic Theory of Managerial Capitalism*. Glencoe, Ill.: The Free Press.

Marx, Karl, 1967, *Capital: A Critique of Political Economy, Volume I. The Process of Capitalist Production*. Edited by Frederick Engels. Translated from the Third German Edition by Samuel Moore and Edward Aveling. New York: International Publishers.

Masten, Scott E. and Crocker, Keith J., 1985, "Efficient Adaptation in Long-Term Contracts: Take-or-Pay Provisions for Natural Gas," *American Economic Review*, 75: 1083–93.

"The Master Spinners' and Manufacturers' Defence Fund Report of the Committee," 1854.

Mauss, M., 1954, *The Gift: Forms and Functions of Exchange in Archaic Societies*, London: Cohen and West.

Mayo, E., 1949, *The Social Problems of an Industrial Civilization*. London: Routledge and Kegan Paul.

McAfee, R. Preston, and McMillan, John, 1991, "Organizational Diseconomies of Scale," mimeograph, University of California, San Diego.

McManus, J. C., 1975, "The Costs of Alternative Economic Organizations," *Canadian Journal of Economics*, 8: 334–50.

McNulty, Paul, 1984, "On the Nature and Theory of Economic Organization: The Role of the Firm Reconsidered," *History of Political Economy*, 16: 233–53.

Meade, J., 1971, *The Controlled Economy*, London: G. Allen and Unwin.

Meade, James, 1972, "The Theory of Labor-Managed Firms and of Profit-Sharing," *Economic Journal*, 82: 401–428.

Meckling, W. H., 1976, "Values and the Choice Model of the Individual in the Social Sciences", *Zeitschrift fur Volkswirtschaft und Statistik*, 112: 545–60.

Meij, J., 1963, *Internal Wage Structure*. Amsterdam: North-Holland Publishing Co.

Merton, R. K., 1957, *Social Theory and Social Structure*, revised and enlarged edition. Glencoe, Ill.: The Free Press.

Milgrom, Paul, 1988, "Employment Contracts, Influence Activities and Efficient Organization Design," *Journal of Political Economy*, 96: 42–60.

Milgrom, P., and Roberts, J., 1986, "Relying on the Information of Interested Parties," *Rand Journal of Economics*, 17: 18–32.

Milgrom, Paul, and Roberts, John, 1988a, "An Economic Approach to Influence Activities and Organizational Responses," *American Journal of Sociology*, 94: S154–79.

Milgrom, Paul, and Roberts, John, 1988b, "Economic Theories of the Firm: Past, Present, and Future," *Canadian Journal of Economics*, 21: 444.

Milgrom, Paul A., and Roberts, John, 1990, "Bargaining Costs, Influence Costs, and the Organization of Economic Activity," in James E. Alt and Kenneth A. Shepsle, eds., *Perspectives on Positive Political Economy*. Cambridge: Cambridge University Press.

Milgrom, Paul, and Roberts, John, 1992, *Economics, Organization, and Management*. Englewood Cliffs, N.J.: Prentice-Hall.

Minahan, John, 1988, "Managerial Incentive Schemes and the Divisional Structure of Firms," mimeograph, University of Massachusetts.

Mitchell, Daniel J. B., and Kimbell, Larry J., 1982, "Labor Market Contracts and Inflation," in Martin Neil Baily, ed., *Workers, Jobs, and Inflation*. Washington D.C.: The Brookings Institution.

Monsen, R. J., and Downs, A., 1965, "A Theory of Large Managerial Firms," *Journal of Political Economy*, 73: 221–36.

Monteverde, K. M., and Teece, D. J., 1982a, "Appropriable Rents and Quasi Vertical Integration," *Journal of Law and Economics*, 25: 321–28.

Monteverde, K. M., and Teece, D. J., 1982b, "Supplier Switching Costs and Vertical Integration," *Bell Journal of Economics*, 13: 206–13.

Montias, J. Michael, 1970, "The Price Mechanism in Socialist Countries – Discussion," *American Economic Review*, 60: 321–3.

Montias, John M., 1976, *The Structure of Economic Systems*. New Haven: Yale University Press.

Morris, Charles, 1980, *The Cost of Good Intentions*. New York: W. W. Norton.

References

Mossin, J., 1973, *Theory of Financial Markets*. Englewood Cliffs, N.J.: Prentice-Hall.

Mueller, D. C., 1972, "A Life Cycle Theory of the Firm," *Journal of Industrial Economics*, 20: 199–219.

Mulherin, J. Harold, 1986, "Complexity in Long-Term Contracts: An Analysis of Natural Gas Contractual Provisions," *Journal of Law, Economics and Organization*, 2: 105–17.

Myers, S. C., 1968, "Procedures for Capital Budgeting under Uncertainty," *Industrial Management Review*, 9: 1–19.

Nader, Ralph, 1976, *Taming the Giant Corporation*. New York: Norton.

Nalbantian, Haig R., 1987a, "Incentive Compensation in Perspective," in Haig R. Nalbantian, ed., *Incentives, Cooperation, and Risk Sharing: Economic and Psychological Perspectives on Employment Contacts*. Totowa, N.J.: Rowman and Littlefield.

Nalbantion, Haig R., ed., 1987b, *Incentives, Cooperation, and risk Sharing: Economic and Psychological Perspectives on Employment Contracts*. Totowa, N.J.: Rowman and Littlefield.

Nelson, Richard R., and Winter, Sidney, G., 1980, "Firm and Industry Response to Changed Market Conditions: An Evolutionary Approach," *Economic Inquiry*, 18: 179–202.

Nelson, Richard R., and Winter, Sidney G., 1982a, *An Evolutionary Theory of Economic Change*. Cambridge, Mass.: Belknap Press of Harvard University Press.

Nelson, Richard R., and Winter, Sidney, 1982b, *Toward an Economic Theory of Evolutionary Capabilities*. Ann Arbor: University of Michigan, Institute of Public Policy Studies, discussion paper no. 44.

Neuberger, Egon, and James, Estelle, 1973, "The Yugoslav Self-Managed Enterprise: A Systemic Approach," pp. 245–84 in Morris Bornstein, ed., *Plan and Market: Economic Reform in Eastern Europe*. New Haven: Yale University Press.

Nilsson, Eric, 1989, "International Trade and the Social Relations of Production," Ph.D. dissertation, University of Massachusetts.

North, Douglas, 1981, *Structure and Change in Economic History*. New York: Norton.

Nove, Alec, 1958, "The Problem of Success Indicators in Soviet Industry," *Economica*, 25: 1–13.

O'Dell, Carla, and McAdams, Jerry, 1987, *People, Performance, and Pay*. Austin, Texas: American Productivity Center.

Okun, A., 1975, "Inflation: Its Mechanics and Welfare Costs," *Brookings Papers on Economic Activity*, 2: 366–73.

Ortiz, Fernando, 1963, *Contraputo del Tabaco y el Azucar*. Barcelona: Editorial Ariel.

Ortuno-Ortin, Ignacio, Roemer, John E., and Silvestre, Joaquim, 1993, "Investment Planning and Market Socialism," in S. Bowles, H. Gintis, and B. Gustafsson, eds. *The Microfoundations of Political Economy: Problems of Participation, Democracy, and Efficiency*. Cambridge: Cambridge University Press.

Pagano, Ugo, 1985, *Work and Welfare in Economic Theory*. Oxford: Basil Blackwell.

Panzar, John, and Willig, R., 1975, "Economics of Scale and Economics of Scope in Multi-Output Production," unpublished working paper, Bell Laboratories, Murray Hill, N.J..

REFERENCES

Pearlstine, N., 1970, "Auto Pact Tension Eases; Strike Chances Viewed as Tied to Chrysler, GM Parleys," *Wall Street Journal,* 176 No. 48 (Sept. 4).

Pejovich, S., 1969, "The Firm, Monetary Policy and Property Rights in a Planned Economy," *Western Economic Journal,* 42: 277–81.

Penrose, E., 1958, *The Theory of the Growth of the Firm.* New York: Wiley.

Penrose, Edith T., 1959, *Theory of the Growth of The Firm.* Oxford: Blackwell.

Perrow, Charles, 1983, *Normal Accidents: Living with High-Risk Technologies.* New York: Basic Books.

Phelps, E. S., et al., 1970, *The Microeconomic Foundations of Employment and Inflation Theory.* New York: Norton.

Piore, M., 1973, "Fragments of a 'Sociological' Theory of Wages," *The American Economic Review,* 63: 377–84.

Plant, Arnold, 1932, "Trends in Business Administration," *Economica,* 12: 45–62.

Polanyi, Michael, 1958, *Personal Knowledge: Towards a Post-Critical Philosophy.* Chicago: University of Chicago Press.

Preston, L. E., 1975, "Corporation and Society: The Search for a Paradigm," *Journal of Economic Literature,* 13: 434–53.

Publishers' Association v. Newspaper and Mail Delivery Union, 114 N.Y.S. 2d 401 (1952).

Putterman, Louis, 1984, "On Some Recent Explanations of Why Capital Hires Labor," *Economic Inquiry,* 22: 171–87.

Putterman, Louis, 1986, "The Economic Nature of the Firm: Overview," pp. 1–29 in L. Putterman, ed., *The Economic Nature of the Firm: A Reader.* New York: Cambridge University Press.

Putterman, Louis, 1988, "The Firm as Association Versus the Firm as Commodity: Efficiency, Rights, and Ownership," *Economics and Philosophy,* 4: 243–66.

Putterman, Louis, 1990, *Division of Labor and Welfare: An Introduction to Economic Systems.* Oxford: Oxford University Press.

Putterman, Louis, 1993a, "Ownership and the Nature of the Firm," *Journal of Comparative Economics,* 17: 243–63.

Putterman, Louis, 1993b, "Exit, Voice, and Portfolio Choice: Agency and Public Ownership," *Economics and Politics* 5: 205–18.

Putterman, Louis, 1993c, "Incentive Problems Favoring Noncentralized Investment Fund Ownership," pp. 156–68 in P. Bardhan and J. E. Roemer, eds., *Market Socialism: The Current Debate.* New York: Oxford University Press.

Putterman, Louis, 1995, "Markets, Hierarchies, and Information: On a Paradox in the Economics of Organization," *Journal of Economic Behavior and Organization,* 26: 373–90.

Putterman, Louis, and Rueschemeyer, Dietrich, eds., 1992, *States and Markets in Development: Synergy or Rivalry?* Boulder, Colo.: Lynne Rienner.

Putterman, Louis, and Skillman, Gilbert, 1992, "The Role of Exist in the Theory of Cooperative Teams," *Journal of Comparative Economics,* 16: 596–618.

Radner, R., 1970, "Problems in the Theory of Markets under Uncertainty," *The American Economic Review,* 60: 454–60.

Radner, Roy, 1986, "The Internal Economy of Large Firms," *Economic Journal,* 96: 1–22.

References

Raimon, R., 1953, "The Indeterminateness of Wages of Semiskilled Workers," *Industrial and Labor Relations Review*, 6: 180–94.

Richardson, G. B., 1961, *Information and Investment: A Study in the Working of the Competitive Economy.* London: Oxford University Press.

Richardson, G. B., 1972, "The Organization of Industry," *Economic Journal*, 82: 883–96.

Richardson, G. B., 1990, *Information and Investment: A Study in the Working of the Competitive Economy, with a New Foreward by David Teece.* Oxford: Oxford University Press.

Riordan, Michael, 1990, "Vertical Integration and the Strategic Management of the Enterprise," in M. Aoki, B. Gustafsson, and O. Williamson, eds., *The Firm as a Nexus of Treaties.* London: Sage Publications.

Robertson, D. H., 1930, *Control of Industry.* London: Nisbet and Co.

Robbins, L., 1932, *An Essay on the Nature and Significance of Economic Science.* New York: Macmillan.

Robinson, E. A. G., 1934, "The Problem of Management and the Size of the Firm," *The Economic Journal*, 44: 242–57.

Robinson, Joan, 1932, *Economics is a Serious Subject, the Apologia of an Economist to the Mathematician, the Scientist and the Plain Man.* Cambridge: W. Heffer and Sons.

Roemer, John, 1994, *A Future for Socialism*, Cambridge: Harvard University Press.

Ross, A., 1958, "Do We Have a New Industrial Feudalism?" *The American Economic Review*, 62: 134–9.

Ross, S. A., 1973, "The Economic Theory of Agency: The Principal's Problem," *American Economic Review*, 62: 134–9.

Ross, S. A., 1974, "The Economic Theory of Agency and the Principle of Similarity," in Michael Balch, Daniel McFadden, and Shih-yen Wu, eds., *Essays on Economic Behavior under Uncertainty.* Amsterdam: North-Holland.

Ryan, Alan, 1987, "Property," in John Eatwell, Murray Milgate, and Peter Newman, eds., *The New Pelgrave: Dictionary of Economics.* New York: Stockton Press.

Samuelson, Paul, 1957, "Wages and Interest: A Modern Dissection of Marxian Economics," *American Economic Review*, 47: 884–912.

Schall, L. D., 1972, "Asset Valuation, Firm Investment, and Firm Diversification," *Journal of Business*, 45: 11–28.

Schelling, T., 1971, "On the Ecology of Micromotives," *The Public Interest*, 25: 61–98.

Schmidt, Peter and Strauss, Robert P., 1976, "The Effect of Unions on Earnings and Earnings on Unions: A Mixed Logit Approach," *International Economic Review*, 17: 204–12.

Schotter, Andrew, 1981, *Economic Theory of Social Institutions.* Cambridge: Cambridge University Press.

Schumpeter, Joseph A., 1950, *Capitalism, Socialism, and Democracy.* New York: Harper and Brothers.

Selznick, Philip, 1948, "Foundations of the Theory of Organization," *American Sociological Review*, 13: 25–35.

REFERENCES

Selznick, Philip, 1949, *TVA and the Grass Roots; A Study in the Sociology of Formal Organization*. Berkeley: University of California Press.

Shapiro, Carl and Stiglitz, Joseph, 1984, "Equilibrium Unemployment as a Worker Discipline Device," *American Economic Review*, 74: 433–44.

Shove, G. F., 1933, "The Imperfection of the Market: A Further Note," *The Economic Journal*, 43: 113–24.

Shubik, M., 1970, "A Curmudgeon's Guide to Microeconomics," *Journal of Economic Literature*, 8: 405–34.

Silver, M., and Auster, R., 1969, "Entrepreneurship, Profit and Limits on Firm Size," *Journal of Business*, 42: 277–81.

Simon, Herbert, 1951, "A Formal Theory of the Employment Relationship," *Econometrica*, 19: 293–305. Reprinted in *Models of Man*. New York: Wiley, 1957.

Simon, H. A., 1955, "A Behavioral Model of Rational Choice," *Quarterly Journal of Economics*, 69: 99–118.

Simon, H. A., 1957, *Models of Man*. New York: Wiley.

Simon, H., 1959, "Theories of Decision Making in Economics and Behavioral Science," *American Economic Review*, 49: 253–83.

Simon, Herbert, 1991, "Organizations and Markets," *Journal of Economic Perspectives* 5: 25–44.

Smith, A., 1937, *The Wealth of Nations*, Cannan edition. New York: Modern Library. Originally published 1776.

Solow, R. H., 1980, "On Theories of Unemployment," *American Economic Review*, 70: 1–10.

Sombart, Werner, 1930, "Capitalism," *Encyclopedia of Social Sciences*, 3: 200.

Sonnenschein, Hugo, 1987, "Oligopoly and Game Theory," John Eatwell, Murray Milgate, Peter Newman, eds., in *The New Palgrave: A Dictionary of Economics*. London: Macmillan.

Stackelberg, H. von, 1934, *Marktform und Gleichgewicht*. Vienna: Springer-Verlag.

Stigler, George, and Friedland, Claire, 1983, "The Literature of Economics: The Case of Berle and Means," *Journal of Law and Economics*, 26: 237–68.

Stiglitz, Joseph E., 1981, "The Allocation Role of the Stock Market: Pareto-Optimality and Competition," *Journal of Finance*, 36: 235–51.

Stinchcombe, Arthur L., 1983, "Contracts as Hierarchical Documents," unpublished manuscript, Stanford Graduate School of Business.

Stoft, S., 1980, "Cheat-Threat Theory," thesis prospectus, University of California.

Summers, C., 1969, "Collective Agreements and the Law of Contracts," *Yale Law Journal*, 78: 527–75.

Teece, David J., 1976, *Vertical Integration and Vertical Divestiture in the U.S. Petroleum Industry*. Stanford, Calif.: Stanford University.

Teece, David J., 1977, "Technology Transfer by Multinational Firms: The Resource Cost of Transferring Technological Knowhow," *Economic Journal*, 87: 242–61.

Teece, David J., 1980, "Economics of Scope and the Scope of Enterprise," *Journal of Economic Behavior and Organization*, 1: 223–47.

Teece, David J., 1982, "Towards an Economic Theory of the Multiproduct Firm," *Journal of Economic Behavior and Organization*, 3: 39–63.

References

Thompson, E. A., 1970, "Nonpecuniary Rewards and the Aggregate Production Function," *Review of Economics and Statistics,* 52: 395–404.

Thurow, L., 1971, "Measuring the Economic Benefits of Education," report, the Carnegie Commission on Higher Education.

Tirole, Jean, 1986, "Hierarchies and Bureaucracies: On the Role of Collusion in Organizations," *Journal of Law, Economics, and Organization,* 2: 181–214.

Titmus, R. M., 1971, *The Gift Relationship: From Human Blood to Social Policy.* New York: Random House.

Trivers, R. L., 1971, "The Evolution of Reciprocal Altruism," *Quarterly Review of Biology,* 46: 35–57.

Ullman-Margalit, Edna, 1978, *The Emergence of Norms.* New York: Oxford University Press.

Ure, Andrew, 1835, *The Philosophy of Manufactures or an Exposition of the Scientific, Moral, and Commercial Economy of the Factory System of Great Britain.* 2nd edition, London.

Urquhart, David, 1843, *Familiar Words as Affecting England and the English.* London.

Usher, Abbott P., 1921, *Introduction to the Industrial History of England.* London: G. C. Harrap and Co., Ltd.

Wachtel, H., and Betsy, C., 1972, "Employment at Low Wages," *Review of Economics and Statistics,* 54: 121–29.

Wachter, M. L., and Williamson, O. E., 1978, "Obligational Markets and the Mechanics of Inflation," *Bell Journal of Economics,* 9: 549–71.

Wakefield, E. G., 1849, *A View of the Art of Colonisation.* London.

Watts, Ross L., and Zimmerman, Jerod, 1978, "Auditors and the Determination of Accounting Standards, an Analysis of the Lack of Independence," Working Paper GPB 7806, University of Rochester, Graduate School of Management.

Weitzman, Martin L., 1980, "Efficient Incentive Contracts," *Quarterly Journal of Economics,* 94: 719–30.

Weitzman, Martin L., 1984, *The Share Economy: Conquering Stagflation.* Cambridge: Harvard University Press.

Weitzman, Martin L., 1986, *The Case for Profit Sharing.* London: Employment Institute.

Weitzman, Martin L., and Kruse, Douglas, 1990, "Profit Sharing and Productivity," in Alan S. Blinder, ed., *Paying for Productivity: A Look at the Evidence.* Washington D.C.: The Brookings Institution.

White, Horace, J., Jr., 1936, "Monopolistic and Perfect Competition," *American Economic Review,* 26: 645.

Williamson, O. E., 1964a, "The Economics of Antitrust: Transaction Cost Considerations," *University of Pennsylvania Law Review,* 122: 1439–96.

Williamson, O. E., 1964b, *The Economics of Discretionary Behavior: Managerial Objectives in a Theory of the Firm.* Englewood Cliffs, N.J.: Prentice-Hall.

Williamson, Oliver E., 1967a, "The Economics of Defense Contracting: Incentives and Performance," in *Issues in Defense Economics.* New York: National Bureau of Economic Research.

REFERENCES

Williamson, Oliver E., 1967b, "Hierarchical Control and Optimum Firm Size," *Journal of Political Economy,* 75: 123–38.

Williamson, O. E., 1970, *Corporate Control and Business Behavior.* Englewood Cliffs, N.J.: Prentice-Hall.

Williamson, O. E., 1971, "The Vertical Integration of Production: Market Failure Considerations," *American Economic Review,* 61: 112–23.

Williamson, O. E., 1975, *Markets and Hierarchies: Analysis and Anti-Trust Implications.* New York: The Free Press.

Williamson, Oliver, 1979, "Transaction-Cost Economics: The Governance of Contractual Relations," *Journal of Law and Economics,* 22: 233–61.

Williamson, Oliver E., 1980, "The Organization of Work: A Comparative Institutional Assessment," *Journal of Economic Behavior and Organization,* 1: 5–38.

Williamson, Oliver E., 1985, *The Economic Institutions of Capitalism: Firms, Markets, and Relational Contracting.* New York: The Free Press.

Williamson, Oliver, 1988, "The Logic of Economic Organizations," *Journal of Law, Economics, and Organization,* 4: 65.

Williamson, Oliver, 1994, "Evaluating Coase," *Journal of Economic Perspectives,* 8: 201–4.

Williamson, Oliver E., and Teece, D. J., 1982, "European Economic and Political Integration: The Markets and Hierarchies Approach," in Pierre Salmon, ed., *New Approaches to European Integration,* forthcoming.

Williamson, Oliver, Wachter, Michael, and Harris, Jeffery, 1975, "Understanding the Employment Relation," *Bell Journal of Economics,* 6: 250–78.

Williamson, Oliver E., and Winter, Sidney G., eds., 1991, *The Nature of the Firm: Origins, Evolution, and Development.* New York: Oxford University Press.

Willig, Robert, 1979, "Multiproduct Technology and Market Structure," *American Economic Review,* 69: 346–51.

Wilson, R., 1968, "On the Theory of Syndicates," *Econometrica,* 36: 119–32.

Wilson, R., 1969, *La Decision: Aggregation et Dynamique des Orders de Preference, Extrait.* Paris: Editions du Centre National de la Recherche Scientifique.

Winter, Sydney G., 1982, "An Essay on the Theory of Production," in S. H. Hymans, ed., *Economics and the World around It.* Ann Arbor, Mich.: The University of Michigan Press.

Winter, Sydney G., 1991, "On Coase, Competence, and the Corporation," in Oliver Williamson and Sidney Winters, eds., *The Nature of the Firm: Origins, Evolution, and Development.* New York: Oxford University Press.

Wolfson, Mark A., 1983, "Empirical Evidence of Incentive Problems and Their Mitigation in Oil and Gas Tax Shelter Programs," unpublished manuscript, Stanford University.

World Bank, 1991, *World Development Report 1991.* New York: Oxford University Press.

Yunker, James A., 1992, *Socialism Revised and Modernized: The Case for Pragmatic Market Socialism.* New York: Praeger.